Brenda Engel

D1452372

ACCOUNTING ETHICS

... AND THE NEAR COLLAPSE OF THE WORLD'S FINANCIAL SYSTEM

ACCOUNTING

ETHICS

... AND THE NEAR COLLAPSE
OF THE WORLD'S FINANCIAL SYSTEM

By

MICHAEL PAKALUK, Ph.D.

MARK CHEFFERS, C.P.A., A.B.V.

ALLEN DAVID PRESS ~ SUTTON, MASSACHUSETTS
2011

Published in the United States by
Allen David Press
9 Main Street, Suite 2F
Sutton, MA 01590

ISBN 978-0-9765280-3-6

Printed in the United States of America

To

John Henry Pakaluk

and

Allen David Cheffers

Contents

Preface

"This accountancy is a noble profession, and most of those who engage in it are good men. Indeed good preponderates everywhere—overwhelmingly in accountancy. After all the argument and disputation, after all the theory and doctrine, after all the study and analysis, the conclusion of the whole matter is this, that a professional man does not live unto himself alone, and what he does carries an influence far and wide. Every unworthy deed is a power for evil. Every good deed helps the world."

— A.P. Richardson, 1931, *The Ethics of a Profession*

IT WAS A FINE SUMMER'S MORNING in Sydney, Australia. Mark Cheffers, a young CFO at a newly-formed mining company, paused for a moment from stacks of papers awaiting his attention and looked out the window to survey the stunning scene of the Harbor Bridge and famed Opera House across the bay. He truly was sitting on top of the world. Only three years ago he had moved from the United States to Sydney with his young bride. They had spent their first years of marriage working in different offices for KPMG in the U.S., and then, inspired by a desire to work overseas, had accepted positions at PricewaterhouseCoopers in Sydney. Mark had risen quickly up the ranks and, when just 27 years old, had been invited to become the acting CFO of a newly formed publicly-traded mining company. During his first year he had spent extraordinary amounts of time building accounting systems from scratch, integrating foreign operations, evaluating acquisitions, and preparing filings associated with hundreds of millions in secondary share offerings. But his successes made all of that effort more than worthwhile. He could only imagine what would be the next step in his career. Poised as he was to become one of the youngest CFOs of a company of that size in the world, his prospects seemed bright, and he had big dreams. Senior Vice President at Exxon in a few years? CFO for Mobil? The sky was the limit.

At just that moment, interrupting this brief reverie, the firm's Director of Finance knocked on his door and entered. "Mark, mate," he said, "We're facing a bit of a problem; we have a cash call on one of our overseas projects, and we've tied up most of our cash and collateral on a significant acquisition. It shouldn't be a real problem, as our cash deficiency really ought to last for at most one week." Mark had anticipated the cash call and obviously had known about this particular acquisition, but he had not realized that the Director of Finance had tied up so much cash and collateral. The Director continued, "I need you to approach XYZ Bank for a short term loan." "Are we offering collateral?" Mark asked. "If they want collateral you will have to offer them some of the same collateral that is tied up in our acquisition deal." Mark clarified, "Are you telling me that I might have to double-pledge our security for this loan?" "It's a small point," stated the Director. "This cash flow issue is very short term. It won't have to happen again, and we absolutely have to make this cash call. Besides, there is no risk," he said with an upbeat tone in his voice.

Mark sat there, stunned. His reaction to the Director's suggestion was simple, immediate and instinctual: "*No.*" And after another brief moment, "You will have my resignation by the end of the day."

As he said this, he thought back to the high standards of the culture he had experienced at PricewaterhouseCoopers and KPMG, where even the slightest suggestion of that sort of thing would not have been tolerated. That is the way he had always been taught to approach things. Acting in any other way was simply not an option for him. The moment he saw that management was prepared to commit fraud, it was obvious to him that he could not continue to work there. So Mark composed that letter of resignation. He gave them three weeks' notice to find someone to replace him, and went home and informed his wife, "We're returning to the States." As for obtaining the loan—the company's chief accountant down the hall agreed to do the deed.

Mark and his wife returned to the United States and now, jobless, lived first with their in-laws and then in a modest apartment in one of the less appealing neighborhoods of Worcester, Massachusetts. From a glamorous apartment which overlooked Sydney harbor on one side and the Pacific ocean on the other, to a dreary rented floor of a triple-decker in a seedy part of Worcester, all in the name of —integrity! Well, he had his integrity.

Yet there was also something else. It did not take long for the maxim "honesty is the best policy" to be verified. Within a month after Mark resigned, there was a sudden and unanticipated collapse in the global gold market. The mining company found itself facing calls on its loans. It was placed in receivership. Federal investigations ensued. As the company's acting CFO, Mark would have been the first person held responsible if he had cooperated with that "little," "low risk" fraud. His career and life would have been ruined.—That is how much had actually hung in the balance when he made that quick, instinctual decision to do the right (and very inconvenient) thing. It turned out that Mark's act of integrity saved him and his family from complete economic and personal ruin.

Moving to Worcester proved to be a good choice in another way. It seemed a good time to get that M.B.A. that he had long thought about. So Mark applied to and was accepted at Harvard Business School. After gaining his degree, he began a new career as a forensic accountant, participating in numerous successful, high-profile investigations and prosecutions.

In the course of this work he happened by chance upon accounting irregularities at both AIG and Enron well before these scandals became public. The story about Enron bears repeating and the story about AIG is discussed at length in our first few chapters.

One day in mid-2001, Jonathan Weil, a reporter from the *Wall Street Journal*, called Mark and asked him for a favor. Could he look at various financial statements and other materials that the reporter had acquired about Enron and give his opinion as to whether anything unusual was evident? Jonathan had called Mark for his professional collaboration before, but this would be a larger task, involving the review of numerous documents. Mark took a day off to look over the materials. ("When Jon calls and asks you for a favor like that, you do it," Mark later explained, "Jon is a great investigator.")

Afterwards Mark called the reporter and rather embarrassingly told him: "I can't figure out what's going on here. And that's saying something. These disclosures are almost impossible to penetrate. I can, however, tell you one thing: no good reason exists for some of these entities mentioned in their proxy report not to be consolidated in the financials." This was months before Enron's announcement in October 2001 of a major restatement. After the restatement but prior to Enron's ensuing bankruptcy, Mark, who by this point had become a recognized expert on accounting malpractice matters, corresponded again with Jon Weil. "What do you think of the restatement?" Jon asked. Again, after reviewing the restatement in detail, Mark responded that this was not good news at all—that, in his opinion there was another big shoe to drop. Enron had not come completely clean with its restatement. In particular, they were obfuscating their involvement with Special Purpose Entities (SPEs). Three weeks later, led in part by the *Journal*'s tenacious pursuit of the truth, Enron filed for bankruptcy protection. And then all hell broke loose, as billions of losses were incurred by investors.

Following on Enron's bankruptcy, Mark began fielding calls not just from the *Journal* but also from reporters around the world. Needless to say, his conversations with reporters would eventually turn to the liability exposure facing Andersen, then one of the Big Five accounting firms.

And as regards Andersen's exposure? After Enron's declaration of bankruptcy, Mark was one of the first commentators to stake out the claim that Andersen's exposure simply dwarfed anything that the profession had seen before—that it would make the $110 million dollar settlement in the Waste Management scandal appear miniscule. A story from the December 8, 2001 *Chicago Tribune* is indicative of coverage at that early time in the scandal. Andersen was downplaying everything. The story told how Andersen officials were refusing to comment on the specifics of the Enron case, saying that the problem rested with "an antiquated model for corporate financial reporting." An Andersen spokesman was quoted as saying, "When things go wrong, sometimes it's the people. But very often it's the system, and the issues that system is struggling with," adding, "We have been on record for some time that the reporting model needs to be modernized." Most other commentators referenced in the article took a comparable view. Mark was almost alone when he was quoted as saying, presciently, that "This could be a watershed case" and that Andersen had "an extraordinary exposure," because they had actually helped design the off-balance sheet entities that were hiding Enron's debt. The *Tribune* story quoted Cheffers as saying that "the potential size of claims against Andersen could be greater, because it was at least partly aware of the nature of many Enron transactions under scrutiny ... That could overcome rules designed to limit shareholder actions against auditors."

Needless to say, the *Tribune* story and Mark's forecast did not go over well in Chicago, the home of Andersen's world headquarters. The reporter who wrote the story later told Mark that he took much heat for Mark's remarks and was reassigned to some other beat—that is, until Andersen's collapse. Actually, the *Tribune* reporter had toned down Mark's concern about Andersen's liability exposure. The precise words that Mark had used in speaking to him were: "I believe that you could take all of the liability exposures faced by every accounting firm in their collective histories, and add them all up, and they would not amount to the exposure facing Andersen at this time."

From the beginning of his career as an auditor and forensic accountant, Mark approached accounting malpractice and fraud from two points of view. As a participant in prosecutions, he would take on the viewpoint of the public and the aggrieved individual investor. He passionately wanted to see that there was fair compensation for the negligence and unprofessionalism that unfortunately can sometimes occur among accountants. But as a CPA himself, he had always had a deeply-felt zeal for the honor and integrity of the profession, confirmed by his own experiences. As Mark has relayed to me on a number of occasions, "I did not consider myself to be as virtuous as I should be. But I wanted to live up to the expectations that had been set for me by several of the audit firm mentors I had worked for and admired over the years. The example that these professionals set was very important to me." Both of these attitudes went hand-in-hand. His dismay at accounting failure was a function of his passion for the standards that the profession itself pledges to uphold.

It was this twofold passion and concern that became the source of a book, when Mark approached me in late 2004 and suggested that we collaborate. Mark had co-authored an earlier text on accounting malpractice.[1] But he was largely unfamiliar with philosophy and theories of ethics, some main areas of expertise for me. Would I be interested in combining forces and jointly writing a book with him on accounting ethics?

I leapt at the chance, for several reasons. First, I had long admired Mark's expertise and tenacity as an auditor and forensic accountant. I wanted to learn more about the field firsthand. Second, I was fascinated with the application of ethical principles to the world of business, because so much can be at stake there. In the world of academic philosophy and classical scholarship, where I was principally engaged, if someone makes a foolish mistake, this might perhaps be pointed out in a review or critical notice, which would be the worst thing that would follow from it. But in business a mistake or act of folly can cost large sums of money. Hence, sound ideas are tested and verified quickly, directly, and in practice—which appealed to me very much. Third, I was interested in what might be called "The Fundamental Problem of Accounting Ethics," which involves how we use rules to

---

[1] Cheffers, M.L., C.M. Renda, and J.R. Bourassa: 2001, *Challenges for the Next Decade: A Primer on Accounting Malpractice and Its Prevention* (AccountingMalpractice.com, Manchaug, MA).

guide our practices and the limitations of rules. This problem had been considered at some length by philosophers as diverse as Aristotle and Wittgenstein. The field of accounting seemed an interesting field in which to examine it, because drawing up rules is something that accountants do very well; it seems part of the mindset of an accountant. In the efforts of accountants, then, one may see as clearly as anywhere else the limits of rules: if a rule *could* accomplish something, accountants would have been able to construct a rule to accomplish it, and, contrariwise, any defect in rules devised by clever accountants will likely imply a defect in rules *tout court*.

Fourth, and finally, to collaborate with Mark on a book on accounting ethics seemed a way simply to achieve something good. Philosophers perhaps more than other academics are beset by a concern that their thought and writing actually lead to something fruitful and helpful to others. That is why, I am convinced, many philosophers in mid-career abandon serious philosophy and turn instead to political activism (although admittedly philosophy is difficult enough, and many quit simply because they find other things easier). If through writing a book with Mark on accounting ethics I could lend some clarity and contribute to the ethical idealism of what is undeniably an extremely important profession in modern society, then, I figured, I would be doing something genuinely good.

Thus, our first textbook, *Understanding Accounting Ethics*, was born. It was an unusual collaboration: a seasoned auditor and forensic accountant joining forces with an expert in ethics and classical philosophy. The book was well received and welcomed by practitioners for bringing needed light to the ethical nature of the profession.

But that was 2005. Since that time we have seen major convictions and sentencings in the Enron and WorldCom scandals. Other scandals have come to light, especially in relation to the financial crisis, especially scandals involving AIG and an apparent scandal involving Lehman Brothers. The effects—and shortcomings—of Sarbanes-Oxley have become clearer. Moreover, through the helpful, positive feedback of instructors who used the previous, second edition of *Understanding Accounting Ethics*, and through our own experiences in teaching from the book, especially in CPE courses for practitioners, we noted many additional ways in which it could be improved. Hence we are bringing out now a new and substantially revised treatise. When we started, we intended to produce a third edition. But as 11 out of its 15 chapters are completely new, we are renaming it simply *Accounting Ethics*, to signal its substantial, original content.

It would be appropriate here to say something about the structure of this book and how it differs from the second edition of *Understanding Accounting Ethics*. In *Accounting Ethics* we continue, as before, developing the subject in harmony with the principles for education in accounting ethics recommended by the major study of the subject sponsored by the International Federation of Accountants (IFAC).[2] We agree with the conclusion of that study, that accounting education may usefully be understood as involving four steps: (1) gaining *knowledge*; (2) acquiring *perceptiveness*; (3) exercising *judgment*; (4) planning for continued *growth in professionalism*. These dimensions underlie the book's treatment of the subject. However, in the current edition they do not, as before, provide its framework, which is dictated instead by pedagogical considerations most appropriate to our theme.

At the beginning of the entire text we place a brief Introduction, meant to orient the student and explain through a vivid example the basic approach which we adopt here—which will likely be unfamiliar to students—and the book's most important themes. Then, in Chapters 1 through 3, we immediately launch into a case study: the many accounting scandals involving AIG. The reasons for beginning with a case study are threefold. First, although theory is more fundamental than practice, we have found that accounting students and practitioners want to see from the beginning, reasonably enough, the significance of accounting ethics as illustrated in actual experiences. The case study is for them both an entryway into the subject and a hook. Second, the AIG scandal exhibits very clearly the great importance of accounting ethics, insofar as it can be shown, as we do in these chapters, that a failure in accounting ethics was one of the most important causes of the current financial crisis. This theme is so important that we mention it in the subtitle of the book. Third, it happens that one of the authors of this book had direct, personal experience of the AIG case; hence, the case in this context imports all of the compelling interest of a first-person narrative. It represents an intertwining of our personal viewpoint, as authors and instructors, with one of the most important examples of accounting irregularities in history.

After the significance of accounting ethics has been clearly illustrated through such an important case, we are then in a position to give the necessary theoretical and conceptual background to the subject. We first give the necessary conceptual

---

[2] IFAC: 2006, *Approaches to the Development and Maintenance of Professional Values, Ethics and Attitudes in Accounting Education Programs* August, 192 Pp. (Available at: http://www.ifac.org/Members/DownLoads/Information_Paper_Final.pdf.)

background to the theory of the virtues (Chapter 4) and then introduce all of the important principles, and draw all the necessary distinctions, for careful thought about personal responsibility (Chapter 5). After examining the crucial relationship between rules and principles (Chapter 6), we look at the several influential, but misguided, alternative approaches to ethics (Chapter 7). These four chapters give the necessary theory for the book and serve as its foundation.

The theoretical chapters cover the themes of "The Virtues" and "Personal Responsibility," but they do not yet cover the third important theme in the book, "Professionalism." That theme is so important that we deal with it in a separate section and devote three chapters to it. We look at how the profession of accountancy originally understood itself (Chapter 8), and then we look at the pressures and forces which have tended to push accountancy away from its original self-understanding as a profession and more in the direction of its regarding itself as no more than a business (Chapter 9). Finally, we set a basis for the analyses which come later in the text by looking more carefully at the direct evolution of the current Code (Chapter 10).

The last third of the book is devoted to case studies and questions of practice. We give substantial attention to high-profile cases, which have garnered much media attention and are to varying degrees part of popular consciousness (Enron, Chapter 11; WorldCom, Chapter 12; Lehman Brothers, Chapter 13). In these high-profile scandals and (in the case of Lehman) apparent scandals, all of the significant aspects of accounting ethics can be seen, as it were, "writ large." Consider the following analogy. Suppose you wanted someone to become alert and sensitive to the distinctive marks of a particular period in art, say, the Italian Renaissance. You would not show such a person a tiny miniature sketch, or a precious watercolor. No, you would begin with the greatest and most remarkable examples of art from the period, such as Michelangelo's *David* or Raphael's *School of Athens*. Likewise, one of the best ways to teach the requisite "sensitivity" to ethics is through the use of remarkable and dramatic cases of ethical malfeasance in accounting.

Yet most practitioners will deal with more mundane problems and dilemmas, and so we also consider ten cases drawn from everyday practice (Chapter 14). Since these cases are all derived from actual forensic accounting practice, they admit of two sorts of answer. One sort of answer is the ideal answer, the solution that might seem best working from the basic ethical principles of the discipline. But then there is the "actual answer," that is, how things actually played out in the courts and in the public domain. To look at cases that have this second "answer" is especially useful to a student, for a variety of reasons: the student sees in a vivid way that "ideas have consequences;" he can observe the connection that typically holds between idealism and long-term advantage; and he can study the relationship between poor ethical decisions and exposure to risk in the daily practice of an accountant.

Finally, Chapter 15 considers how a student (or practitioner) may continue to grow in ethics and as a professional. Clearly, a concern with ethical and professional practice cannot stop with a single ethics course. Aiming to be good at anything is not a matter of studying something for a few hours and passing an exam. This holds for a sport such as golf, performance on a musical instrument, a profession itself, and also the ethical aspect of a profession. Thus, any adequate treatment of accounting ethics must include a thorough and realistic discussion of practical steps that should be taken, over time, to foster growth in ethics and professionalism. Such growth can be fostered either by an individual, with a view to his own actions solely, or by a firm, with a view to the culture and organization of the firm as a whole, and the effects that these have on practitioners in the firm. We discuss both of these tasks in Chapter 15. Given that this book is, after all, something of a philosophical text as well, we preface this very practical discussion with a consideration of the very old question of whether virtue can be taught. That is, first we ask, "Can virtue be taught?"; we answer that question affirmatively; and then, given that it can, we explain how.

Readers of *Understanding Accounting Ethics* will understand that our examination of accounting ethics has been distinctive for taking a so-called "virtue-based" approach. We believe that, given the shortcomings in any system of accounting or professional rules, the most helpful way to view the subject is with regard to the "virtues" of an accountant, which need to be grasped in relation to the "distinctive role" that an accountant is meant to occupy in a modern market economy. That is, we deal with accounting ethics in complete continuity with ancient discussions of "function" (*ergon*) and "excellence" (*aretê*), which stretch back to Socrates, Plato, and Aristotle. One benefit of this approach is that we can actually give an explanation for why codes of professional conduct for accountants emphasize the ideals and principles that they do—competence, objectivity, independence, integrity, due diligence, and confidentiality. Another benefit of taking this approach is that we can develop analogies between a profession such as accounting, and Plato's notion of a skill (*technê*) as a form of service to another, hence highlighting the "altruistic" aspect of the profession. Our approach also ties in nicely with recent calls from accounting ethicists, such as Steven Mintz, to foster a culture of "heroes of accounting," and with the recognized importance of stories and examples for the teaching of virtues.

In this edition, as in the second edition of *Understanding Accounting Ethics*, we continue to give paramount emphasis to the theme of *truth*. We maintain that the distinctive role of an accountant is to foster the conditions of trust within a modern market economy. But someone can foster trust only by being *trustworthy*, and someone is trustworthy only if he is consistently and reliably *truthful* in what he discovers and reports. Hence one of the most fundamental descriptions of an accountant is that he is a "seeker of truth" as regards the financial condition of an enterprise.

We have not aimed to reproduce in this book the texts of the codes of professional conduct of the major accounting professional bodies, since these are readily available on the internet in their most recent, updated forms, together with the latest authoritative rulings and interpretations. We are presuming here that any comprehensive course in accounting ethics will include the appropriate study of relevant codes, laws, and regulations. Our aim here is to provide the foundations for such a study.

We should again like to acknowledge the helpful assistance of Ryan Shea, whose research and preparation of supplementary materials has proved invaluable.

Michael Pakaluk
Naples, Florida
March 2011

A Very Brief Introduction to Accounting Ethics

"To be willing to exercise his judgment objectively and dispassionately, the accountant must be a man of high character, prepared to recognize and observe high ethical obligations even to his own immediate disadvantage. To be able to do so he must be free from any relation to the subject matter or to the parties in interest which might cloud his judgment or impair his loyalty to the investors to whom his paramount duty is owed."—George Oliver May

ALL OF THE BASIC PRINCIPLES OF ACCOUNTING ETHICS are apparent in any situation in which someone needs to make a judgment under pressure, since an accountant is basically a judge in financial matters, whose judgment becomes especially important when large sums of money are on the line. An accountant makes a judgment about the significance of a transaction, or the results of operations and financial position of a business enterprise. So the basic principles of accounting ethics may be illustrated in an example of a judge making a judgment under pressure.

Suppose for instance that you are a referee in a sport. This is a good example for our purposes, since a referee is also a kind of judge. We might choose any kind of referee in any sport, but to make the example concrete, let us pick a line official in soccer, the man who looks for offside plays. Suppose you are such a line official. It is a tied championship game, and, in the final seconds, the home team sends the ball up to its striker, who makes an amazing shot and scores a goal. But the striker was offside by just a hair. It is a close call; nonetheless, in your best judgment, as far as you could tell, he was offside. So you call an offside, which nullifies the goal, and the home team goes on to lose in overtime. Making that call was difficult to do: but you have to stick to your guns and stand up for what is right, even though it means taking back a goal and potentially earning the bad will of the home team and the home crowd.

Now, what contributes to helping you make the right call in the circumstances, and what could militate against your making the right call? What enabled you to make that call? What put you in a position to do so? What tends to go against your making that (right) call? What could swerve you away from it? It is possible to tally up the main factors on each side.

Good factors. Factors helping you to make a good call:

1. *Competence and skill.* You are a competent referee. You have a good training, and, importantly, you have confidence in your training. You have the expertise, the skill, of making close calls correctly, which you have acquired from a lot of practice. You do not need to "rethink" making a correct call on each occasion. You tend to have confidence that your call is the correct call, even for close plays.

2. *Clear vision of the facts.* You had a clear view of the play. You took care to put yourself in the right position to see the play. You have an unobstructed view. Your eyes are working well. You were not distracted, and you paid attention.

3. *Professionalism.* You regard yourself as a professional, and you are proud of that fact. You wear a uniform, which signals to others that you are a professional. You understand that you have a special job, "to call them as I see them." You are aware that you are going to be supported in your calls by your fellow professionals, your fellow referees. You also understand that the integrity of your profession hinges on your "calling them as you see them." If you make an incorrect call, or, worse, carry on irresponsibly, everyone in your profession is harmed.

Bad factors. Factors which would militate against a good call:

1. *Attachments.* You will get something that you really want if you make the wrong call. Perhaps you have a friend on the home team. Or maybe during the course of the game you have come to take a liking to the home team. Perhaps you placed a bet on the home team. There are many possible attachments like that. The point is that an attachment is something pulling you in a direction which may or may not coincide with the correct call.

2. *Fears.* You will avoid something that you fear if you make the wrong call. Someone threatened to harm you if the home team loses. Or someone threatened to harm your family if the home team loses. Or maybe you are concerned that the

crowd will be very upset with you if you call the play offside. There are potentially many such fears. The point is that a fear is something "pushing" you away in a direction which may or may not coincide with the correct call. Just as an attachment may alter your judgment by "pulling" you toward something, by attraction, so a fear may alter your judgment by "pushing you" away from something, by aversion.

3. *Corruption*. The league is corrupt. Or most of your fellow referees are corrupt. "Everyone is doing it." "Nobody will care." "That's the way things are done here." Corruption undermines integrity. It can make you not care whether you "get it right or not." You will be less willing to make a sacrifice because you think your single, noble action will not make any difference.

4. *Cynicism*. You are cynical about the job of a referee anyway. You think that sometimes plays are so close that there is no right or wrong call. You see the job of a referee as making the game exciting and to "even out" the bad calls of other referees. It is a long time since you were idealistic about your profession. You believe you are only in it for the paycheck.

Now, if we next consider what it means to strengthen the good factors and weaken the bad factors in the example we have been considering, we can draw three important lessons from all this. These lessons serve as the main themes of this book on accounting ethics.

FIRST LESSON: *Character matters, and training matters.* Strengthening the good factors and weakening the bad factors is to a large extent a matter of insuring that the person who is the referee has certain necessary personal traits (which classically were referred to as "virtues"). Sometimes we sum up the kind of referee we would want by saying he would be an "ethical" referee, but this concept can be analyzed, and, to be more precise, we want the referee to be someone who is:

- Knowledgeable and well trained—so that he has the ability to make a close call correctly.
- Self-confident—that is, he needs to be good at making close calls but also he needs to know that he is good at it.
- Diligent—so that he gets into position to make the call and has access to all the relevant facts.
- Dedicated—he really wants to make the right call; he is almost fanatical about "getting it right."

- Professional—he recognizes that he belongs to a group or class of other professionals bound to a certain standard of conduct; he prides himself on being part of this group.
- Not greedy—he does not place bets on games, or try to make a profit from a game, other than by doing his job well and earning the modest sum he gets as a referee.
- Impartial and fair-minded—for instance, he would remove himself as a referee if he had a friend on one of the teams.
- Fearless, courageous—it is not easy and maybe even impossible to divert him from making the right call by threats; if he feels threatened, he "gets his back up" and becomes even more stubborn.
- Not corruptible—he does not let the bad example of others influence him.
- Idealistic—he believes in the honor of his profession, maybe even he naively believes in truth, and he thinks that it matters to be truthful.

SECOND LESSON: *Character is different from intelligence.* Strengthening the good factors and weakening the bad factors has very little to do with book learning or skill in rational thought. It is not a matter of logic, cleverness, or IQ. We do not acquire those traits listed above through taking courses, or by logical thinking, but rather by doing the right thing over time and through a dedication to self-improvement. Becoming the sort of person who makes a good judgment under pressure means developing character traits—for example, acquiring a simplicity and austerity which can keep you clear of greed, or acquiring the courage which can enable you to handle situations which cause anxiety and stress. It does not mean learning a method of thought, or engaging in some process of "values clarification." It does not mean learning a set of rules and regulations. Nonetheless, the right sort of study is necessary—such as the instruction offered in this book, to set someone off in the right direction and encourage him in that path.

THIRD LESSON: *Individuals need to take responsibility.* Although, in matters such as we have been considering, regulation by authorities has an important role to play, in the end everything hinges on personal responsibility. The officials of the soccer league should of course crack down on any corruption. Of course, corrupt referees should be identified and punished. Naturally, there should be laws which prohibit a referee from placing bets on a game. All of these assertions are true, without doubt. But, at the same time, no regulation is ever sufficient for keeping things on the right track. It is always possible to "game the system," whatever rules and laws are in place. Moreover, laws deter only when someone can get caught. Yet it is necessary that a referee make the right call even if no one will know if he has deliberately made a bad call. As someone once wisely said, "You have a virtue if you do the right thing even when no one is looking." Thus, inevitably, making the right judgment under pressure hinges on particular persons carrying out their responsibilities well.

This brief example of a line official in soccer shows all of the same factors that are important in accounting ethics, and the three lessons just sketched correspond to the three main themes of this book. An accountant, as was said, is a kind of "referee" in financial matters, since an accountant basically plays the role of a judge. Accordingly, the three main themes of this book are:

1. *Accounting ethics is about accountants who are ethical.* Character matters. Hence, accounting ethics should focus on the "virtues" of a good professional and the sort of character that a good professional should have. What are the specific traits of character which an accountant should acquire? What kind of person do we want to insure that a professional accountant becomes? Note that we are not saying, merely, that an ethical accountant is an ethical person who happens to become an accountant—although that is true enough. Being a good person in general, and being an ethical accountant, will indeed tend to go together. For example, someone who was caught shoplifting in high school, or who plagiarized on term papers in college, unless he has changed his ways, will enter professional life with continuing deficiencies in honesty and integrity that will likely spill over into his accounting practice. Similarly, in the other direction, an accountant who as a professional engages in fraud will probably go astray in his personal life as well. But what we mean, beyond this, is that *professionalism itself* in accounting is largely a matter of a practitioner's having acquired certain traits of character specific to the profession, such as professional integrity, simplicity, love of the truth, and fearlessness.

2. *Good character cannot be acquired by study and thinking alone.* The study of "methods of ethics," "ethical theories," "values clarification," and even rules and regulations, is of secondary importance in accounting ethics. The field of accounting ethics should be directed at such questions as (asked by a student of accountancy) "How do I insure that I become the sort of person that a professional accountant needs to be?" and (asked by a manager or partner) "How do I foster a culture in a firm which encourages the members to be and to become the sort of persons that professional accountants need to be?"

3. *Rules are not enough.* Regulation, although important, is of limited use in accounting ethics, because personal responsibility, individual discretion, and professional judgment are central and unavoidable. Rules can always be gamed. Regulations tend to be framed to prevent the last abuse, not the next one. Rules need to be interpreted. Rules cannot cover all possible facts and circumstances. Simply having rules does not make anyone follow those rules. Thus, personal responsibility is unavoidable.

What follows is a textbook in accounting ethics which takes these three themes seriously. Our main goal is to make clear what the ideals of the profession are, and to inspire a student of accountancy to strive to become the sort of person who will be an exemplary professional. We do so by a combination of approaches:

Case studies both large and small. We look at high-profile accounting scandals (AIG, Enron, WorldCom, and putatively Lehman Brothers) as well as ethical dilemmas taken from ordinary accounting practice. Case studies are analogous to actual experience. Through the study of a case with all its facts and circumstances, a student may begin to acquire the kind of insight that is ultimately solidified through lived experience. Also, case studies are immensely helpful for illustrating general principles through the lens of particular facts and circumstances.

Historical studies. We get clear about the nature of accountancy as a profession by looking at the development of that profession over time. History is important because part of the task of a student of accountancy today is to recover the original meaning of the accounting profession, which, it seems, has been obscured by some modern trends that tend to assimilate accountancy to a business rather than a profession.

Ethical reflection. We present the student with the basic theory of the virtues, and of ethical action, as developed by classical philosophers such as Socrates, Plato, and Aristotle. Since accounting ethics is a special branch of ethics in general, it must be situated within a sound ethical theory.

PART I

WHY ACCOUNTING ETHICS MATTERS

Accounting Ethics and the Financial Crisis

1

"Obviously no one can claim to be a member of a profession, or expect to succeed in one, unless he is prepared, when necessary, to subordinate his own interest to that of his client.... The high-minded accountant who undertakes to practice in this field assumes high ethical obligations, and it is the assumption of such obligations that makes what might otherwise be a business, a profession. Of all the group of professions which are closely allied with business, there is none in which the practitioner is under a greater ethical obligation to persons who are not his immediate clients; and it is for this reason I believe accounting ought, and can be made, to take an outstanding position in this group."—George Oliver May

WHAT ROLE DID FAILURES OF ACCOUNTING ETHICS PLAY in the Great Financial Crisis of 2007-8? Probably the most commonly cited causes of the crisis are:

➤ an unregulated "shadow banking" system;
➤ weakened underwriting standards for loans;
➤ a bubble in the housing market, encouraged by a Fed policy of low interest rates and taxpayer guarantees for Fannie Mae and Freddie Mac;
➤ unreliable ratings from the credit ratings agencies;
➤ the introduction of greater risk into the financial system through CDOs (collateralized debt obligations).

Failures of accounting ethics are usually not included on anyone's list. And yet they should be. According to Federal Reserve Chairman, Ben Bernanke, the single event which most threatened the world's financial system was the impending bankruptcy of American International Group (AIG) on September 16, 2008, and yet that bankruptcy was caused by failures of accounting ethics.

Unethical Accounting a "But For" Cause of the Financial Crisis

After months of major financial centers' taking billions in capital impairments related directly and indirectly to a failing housing market, and following closely upon the lightening quick collapse of Lehman Brothers, Bernanke was faced with a shocking revelation. AIG was grappling with more than $100 billion in collateral calls and derivative losses which overnight could wipe out the capital adequacy of numerous large financial institutions, both in the US and abroad. Emergency meetings were held by nearly every regulatory body and affected financial institution. The boomerang effect of AIG's failure to deliver on its promises could cause the collapse of the entire financial system of the world. But how did AIG get to that place? Put simply, by a culture of unethical accounting and financial reporting.

Unethical accounting was a "but for" cause (as lawyers say) of AIG's woes: "but for" the effects and implications of a culture that routinely promoted unethical accounting and financial reporting, AIG would have been a trouble-free company in 2008. Hence, "but for" unethical accounting, AIG would not have gotten to the place where it could have caused potential damage on a scale unheard of in business history. "But for" unethical accounting, there would have been no need of a massive, taxpayer-funded AIG bailout.

In this chapter and the next, we explain why this was so. We tell the troubling yet fascinating story of AIG's use of unethical accounting from the late 1980s onward. The story implies an important lesson about accounting ethics. Sometimes accounting ethics is thought of as a kind of "luxury" or "add on." People suppose that accountants "really" need to learn and take to heart the technicalities of accounting standards, whereas attention to ethics is something "extra." Or they presume that *legal* risk and *legal* exposure—"compliance" with laws and regulations—are the only important normative considerations for accounting, or for business generally. However, although both technical competence and a concern with compliance are certainly important, on their own they are by no means sufficient. Ethical accounting is necessary also; it is not at all a "luxury."

Indeed, as the AIG story shows, the world's economy has evolved to such a point that the health, viability, and stability of that economy now depends upon the revival of a stubbornly ethical accounting practice.

The lesson of our story is, in a way, a natural extension of a similar lesson which might have been drawn from reflection on the bankruptcies of Enron and WorldCom, which are discussed in later chapters of this book. These were the high-profile accounting scandals of an earlier crisis. After the collapse of Enron and WorldCom, it became clear that the integrity of the entire financial reporting system, and thus of the equity markets, could be vitiated by failures in accounting ethics. After all, how could the financial statements of any company be trusted, if a highly-rated and widely-admired company such as Enron could hide 40 billion dollars of debt off its balance sheet? Many of the issues which led to the Enron and WorldCom collapse were addressed by the Sarbanes-Oxley Act of 2002. However, regulation never fully solves ethical problems. No rule or law can make unethical practice impossible. As mentioned, a new regulation is typically a matter of "fighting the previous war." Only ethical behavior can prevent the *next* scandal. That remains true today, as it was before the crisis, and as it was before Enron and WorldCom.

The Scope of the AIG Scandal

To get a sense of the increased dangers, it is fruitful to compare the difference in scale of the problems in AIG, as compared with those earlier scandals. In the accompanying chart, we give the difference in "cost" in billions of dollars of the bankruptcies of Enron and WorldCom, and what would have been the bankruptcy of AIG if not for a taxpayer bailout. The main cost of the Enron and WorldCom scandals was the evaporation of shareholder value, when the market capitalization of those companies went from many billions of dollars to essentially zero. The cost of AIG has been not only a similar loss of shareholder value, but also the cost to taxpayers of the bailout, which so far has amounted to $183 billion. The bankruptcies of Enron and WorldCom were the largest ever seen to that point and were regarded as breathtakingly large in their time, and yet they have been dwarfed by AIG's cost.

But what was it that made a taxpayer bailout of AIG seem a necessity? What was the proximate cause of AIG's near bankruptcy?

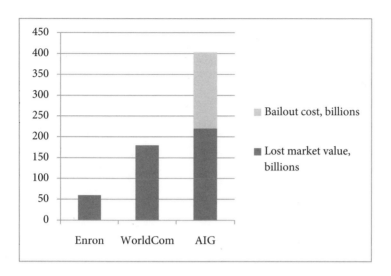

Weapons of Financial Mass Destruction

AIG's threat to the world's economy was the result of its involvement in an exotic derivative called a Credit Default Swaps ("CDS"). A CDS is a financial derivative which in many cases functions much like an insurance policy. Recall that a financial derivative may be defined as a contract which is settled in relationship to some "underlying" financial event. For a CDS, the underlying event is a so-called "credit event," that is, some kind of failure of a debtor to meet a debt obligation, such as a default on a loan or a bankruptcy. The *buyer* of a CDS makes regular payments to the *seller*, in exchange for which the seller agrees to pay the buyer the value of a loan in the case of default on repayment.

In the case in which the buyer of the CDS is the creditor of that loan, then the CDS functions as insurance. For example, after the Valdez oil spill, Exxon borrowed $5 billion from J.P. Morgan to pay for damages related to the spill. To manage its balance sheet and minimize its needed reserves, J.P. Morgan then entered into a contract with the European Bank for Reconstruction and Development (EBRD), according to which Morgan would make regular payments to EBRD, in exchange for which EBRD agreed to pay Morgan $5 billion in case Exxon went bankrupt. This contract is said to be the forerunner of the modern CDS. As is clear, the contract was essentially an insurance contract.

However, it is not necessary that the buyer of a CDS be the actual creditor of the loan which is the "underlying" financial reality. For instance, if Smith believes that his neighbor, Jones, is likely to default on his mortgage payments, it would theoretically be possible for Smith to buy a CDS, where the seller of that derivative would pay Smith the entire remaining amount owed on Jones' mortgage, in case Jones were to default. A CDS like this, where the buyer has no interest in the underlying debt obligation, is sometimes called a "naked" CDS. (In contrast, a CDS in which the buyer is the creditor is a "covered" CDS.) A naked CDS can play an important role in a market, by signaling the market's estimation of risk associated with some debt instrument. At the same time, a naked CDS is similar to buying fire insurance on one's neighbor's house and can create perverse incentives.

Until the time of the financial crisis, CDSs, whether "covered" or "naked," were completely unregulated. Even though a CDS often functions like insurance, the seller of a CDS was not, in the past, subject to the regulations which insurers face, overseen by the National Association of Insurance Commissioners (NAIC), such as requirements to hold reserves which are adequate to cover anticipated losses. AIG was subject to NAIC regulation for all of its traditional insurance lines of business, but it carved out its CDSs as a non-insurance product, and, just to be sure they would escape regulatory notice, placed them in a trading office in one of its London subsidiaries.

All things considered, should a "covered" CDS be treated as a type of derivative, or should it be treated as insurance? In 2000 the question was posed to the Superintendent of Insurance for NY, who decided then that CDSs were not insurance. But recently, in testimony before the Financial Crisis Inquiry Commission (FCIC), a subsequent Commissioner, Eric Dinallo, stated that he thought that this was a mistake, and that NY would begin regulating non-naked, or "covered" CDSs as insurance.

Be that as it may, since CDSs were treated as derivatives, as opposed to insurance, they were made exempt from regulation by the Commodities Futures Modernization Act of 2000. Furthermore, there were no reporting requirements for CDSs—no need, for instance, to report them to a central registry or clearinghouse—so that the extent of CDSs and how they affected various players in the world's economy could not be known with clarity. That is why Warren Buffett famously described them as "financial weapons of mass destruction."

Much of the damage which CDSs posed to the world's economy was the result simply of uncertainty over how extensive these contracts were, and over the extent to which the various counterparties of these contracts were interconnected. "We forgot that the biggest competitive advantage of the U.S. financial system has always been that we offer safety, security, and transparency. If we destroy that perception, the long-term cost to our society is incalculable," remarked Dinallo in his testimony to the FCIC.

It is quite possible that the partial similarity between CDSs and insurance encouraged AIG's extensive involvement in CDSs. In any case, the Financial Products division of AIG (AIG-FP) sold CDSs which, by the time of the pending financial crisis, put the company on the hook, potentially (or "notionally") for $450 billion. The "underlying" financial realities to which these CDSs were related were typically CDOs, which in many cases were securitized by subprime residential mortgage backed securities (RMBSs).

The Link between Unethical Accounting and AIG's Woes

Contrary to what one might initially suppose, AIG was not threatened with bankruptcy from any need to pay up on these CDSs, as a result of triggering "credit events" in the subprime market. When AIG sold CDSs for a CDO, the stipulated triggering credit event was always a default at the so-called "super senior" tranche level of the CDO, which almost never occurred:

> A CDO consists of a "tower" of loans with the uppermost level, known as the "super senior" level, having the first right to the entire tower's cash flow in the event of defaults and consequent losses upon an agreed-upon level. [AIG]'s approach to the management of its risk was to structure the credit default swaps so that they would only be triggered if the underlying losses were severe enough to rise to the highest levels in the tower, a risk that [AIG] determined to be exceedingly unlikely even under severe economic scenarios.[3]

Rather, what threatened AIG was the need to post collateral for CDSs. The details are somewhat technical but worth going over. Each CDS which AIG-FP sold included a document called a Credit Support Annex (CSA), which clarified some of the terms of the CDS, including the conditions under which AIG would be required to post collateral. The CSA made the posting of collateral contingent on such things as the credit rating of the CDO; the fair value of the CDO relative to its

---

[3] Testimony of Robert E. Lewis, Chief Risk Officer of AIG, before the Financial Crisis Inquiry Commission [FCIC], June 30, 2010.

value at the time of sale of the CDS; and, most importantly, AIG's own credit rating. In particular, the CSAs stipulated that no requirements for posting collateral would be triggered so long as AIG maintained a credit rating of AA or above. That is why AIG's death spiral began in May 2008, since at that time its credit rating was lowered from AA to AA-. After that point, AIG's need to post collateral led to further downgrades in its credit rating, leading to more collateral calls, and further downgrades, and so on. On September 16, 2008, AIG was on the verge of going bankrupt from being unable to meet its collateral calls.

By why was AIG's credit rating downgraded? After all, when it wrote all of those CDSs, it was one of the few major companies with a pristine AAA credit rating.

AIG's slide from a rating of AAA to a rating of AA—putting it right on the brink of needing to post collateral for its CDSs—was the direct result of its corrupt accounting culture. This is stated by Rodney Clark, the Standard & Poors (S&P) executive overseeing the credit rating of AIG, in his testimony to the Congressional Oversight Panel (May 26, 2010):

> S&P downgraded AIG on March 30, 2005, when it lowered AIG's rating from 'AAA' to 'AA+.' Our opinion of AIG had changed in large part due to the company's involvement in a number of questionable financial transactions, and reflected our revised assessment of AIG's management, internal controls, corporate governance and culture. ... In June 2005, we again lowered our rating on AIG — this time to 'AA' — reflecting our revised credit assessment based on significant accounting adjustments that had just been announced by the company. Despite strong overall earnings, we believed that AIG's adjusted financial statements indicated greater volatility and lower profitability than had been previously reported.

Finally, AIG's downgrade from AA to AA- in the eyes of the credit rating agencies, which put AIG over the brink and triggered those collateral calls, was the result of a finding of a "material weakness" in its internal controls.

Reflections on AIG's Demise

AIG began to write CDSs on the assumption of a AAA credit rating, and it continued to write them, and did not unwind them, after it lost that rating. The Congressional Oversight Panel in its report on "The AIG Rescue" commented:

Former AIG CEO Hank Greenberg has asserted publicly and in a conversation with Panel staff that the company should have exited the multi-sector CDO sector after AIG lost its AAA rating in March 2005, arguing that the economics and risks of this business changed with the ratings downgrade, since counterparties could contractually demand more collateral if the value of the CDOs began to deteriorate.

But, as we shall see in more detail below, Greenberg was forced out as CEO of AIG because of accounting improprieties. It is plausible that Greenberg would have made the decision to limit AIG's exposure in CDSs if he had stayed on as CEO. And how ironic would that have been! The man who led AIG to its first downgrade because of accounting related financial improprieties, which led to a massive restatement of earnings and years of material weakness assertions, may have been the only person knowledgeable enough of the risks of CDSs to have helped AIG avoid the collateral call risks!

One should note in passing that AIG-FP's use of AIG's AAA rating to write $450 billion in CDSs was already something of a bait-and-switch, since AIG-FP would not have been so highly rated if it were a stand-alone financial services company. AIG received that rating largely on account of the healthy reserves of its insurance subsidiaries. And yet, because of protective insurance regulation, these reserves could not be and were not available to support the derivatives sold by AIG-FP. So, when the time came to post collateral for the depreciating CDSs, AIG was prohibited by its insurance regulators from endangering its insurance collateral to pay out to the buyers of CDSs. In short, AIG's huge insurance portfolio remained relatively safe, but the publicly traded parent company became effectively bankrupt.

So, in sum, there were both *direct* and *indirect* links between unethical accounting at AIG and its arriving at the brink of bankruptcy—requiring a taxpayer "rescue" to the extent of $180 billion, to prevent its collapse and the potential collapse of all of its counterparties. The *indirect* link was this: after the discovery of unethical accounting practices at AIG (resulting one year in a more than $ 4 billion restatement implicating nearly every major accounting area), Hank Greenberg was forced to resign as CEO, and Howard Smith, regarded as AIG's insurance accounting savant, was forced to resign as CFO. Because of the complexity of AIG, apparently no one could properly mind the shop after Greenberg and Smith resigned, or notice the excessive risk which AIG assumed by continuing to write CDSs after it lost its sterling credit rating. The *direct* link was that unethical accounting practices led directly to AIG's rating downgrades. These downgrades made AIG vulnerable to collateral calls, which it could not meet and which, indeed, it never really anticipated meeting.

It is also worth observing that, after the departure of Greenberg and Smith, auditors and investigators began digging deeply into what could be described as the most complex, vast and opaque establishment of corporate entities, investments and affiliate interrelationships ever created by a corporation. As will be discussed later, the culture of fear of reprisals, financial rewards for silence, and financial reporting manipulations, was so rife that it literally took four years for AIG to gain its first clean Sarbanes-Oxley Section 404 (Internal Controls) opinion. Unfortunately and ironically, this focus on cleaning up all of the accounting and financial reporting problems may have allowed AIG-FP to go on relatively unfettered. There were too many fires to put out.

Conclusion

AIG was bailed out because regulators such as Treasury Secretary Hank Paulson, Federal Reserve Chairman Ben Bernanke, and New York Fed President Timothy Geithner, feared that AIG's bankruptcy—following closely on the heels of the Lehman Bros' collapse—would risk worldwide financial collapse. An example of the reasoning which weighed heavily on Geithner and others may be found in a New York Federal Reserve Bank memo, "Systemic Risk of AIG Bankruptcy," of September 16, 2008, which concluded that "Bankruptcy of AIG CP [commercial paper] has significant contagion potential... In contrast to Lehman, failure would be more global..." The memo proposed a scenario in which "AIG would fail to perform on annuities and stable value wraps; the latter drives asset sales and breaking-of-the buck for money funds."

But big things begin small. Thus in the following two chapters we tell the two-decade long story of how AIG was brought to the brink of bankruptcy by a festering of unethical accounting practices. Our narrative will make it clear how failures in accounting ethics did not simply threaten to vitiate the financial markets (as happened earlier with Enron and WorldCom) but also nearly precipitated the collapse of the entire world's financial system.

Recommended additional reading:

The Financial Crisis Inquiry Report: Final Report of the National Commission on the Causes of the Financial and Economic Crisis in the United States, (January, 2011), especially Part III and Chapter 19, "September 2008: The Bailout of AIG."

The Strange Tale of Coral Re

2

"If you want to be a rich man, and if you think you can be one, you should not enter any of the professions. There is no honest way to get rich in any of them. There are lawful ways, but not ways that you and I would call honest." –Marquis G. Eaton

OUR STORY ABOUT THE ORIGINS OF A CULTURE of financial manipulations and arrogance at AIG, which almost brought crashing down the entire financial system of the world, begins where the personal anecdote about Mark Cheffers, recounted in the Introduction, leaves off. As we said, it is a story where the ordinary personal experience of one of the authors of this text becomes intertwined with accounting issues which were to have global significance.

After leaving Giant Resources, Ltd., the Australian enterprise where he was serving as acting CFO, in early January of 1988, Mark moved back with his wife and two young children to his wife's home town of Worcester, Massachusetts. Looking for a way to move his career forward, he found that it was not too late to apply to MBA programs. He was admitted to Harvard Business School in the spring, and decided to attend there, but he needed to find temporary work for the six months before school began.

There was a CPA firm out of Baltimore which had contracted to assist the Delaware Insurance Department with its regulatory insurance examinations around the country. Mark interviewed for the position and was hired on the spot. As a former Price Waterhouse manager, auditor, and public company CFO, he was something of a rare find for them. The job was perfect for Mark because the first assignment, an examination of a relatively risk averse life insurance company based in Worcester, would last just about six months.

To Mark it seemed like a step down from his high-flying position at Giant Resources. His first assignment was quite mundane. Yet honest, ordinary work is always noble. "There I was," he reflects, "back to being a junior auditor, ticking and tying financial transactions."

Mark liked the job well enough to continue with it part time while studying in the Harvard MBA program. His second assignment turned out to be much more interesting and somewhat controversial. He was given the task of assisting with the regulatory examination of First State Insurance Company. In particular, he was to examine the reinsurance recoverable accounting related to First State, a subsidiary of the Hartford Insurance Group (now Hartford Financial Group), an examination that went on for about a year. The job involved working closely with a regulator named Ralph Nakash, a crusty but dynamic insurance examiner, who had had a fair amount of industry experience, including having worked for the American International Group (AIG). They made a good team, as Mark liked Ralph's fairly aggressive investigative style and profited from his leadership and experience.

The First State job turned out to be a serious examination, because First State had many issues related to collection of reinsurance associated with its surplus lines business. A "surplus line" is a range of non-traditional lines of insurance which generally cannot be purchased from an insurance company in the insured's state. Surplus lines might include such things as professional liability protection, unusual property coverage or even nuclear pools, matters for which it is hard to find insurance for at all, let alone being able to price the risks appropriately.

As for reinsurance recoverable, one may think of it as akin to accounts receivable. A direct insurer insures excess risk with a reinsurer. Typically the direct insurer expects to recover covered losses from the reinsurer if losses or claims arise. But if a reinsurer cannot pay his portion of a claim, then the direct insurer is faced with a choice of either a complete write-off or a commutation agreement. (In a commutation agreement the reinsurer pays only partially for a loss.) Accounting for uncollectible reinsurance requires determining how much of any loss covered by reinsurance will actually be recoverable. As with accounts receivable, a reserve needs to be established to cover any deficits associated with projected claims on reinsurers which arise from commutations or write-offs

First State had been selling a large book of business related to surplus lines (the third largest in the country), and it was experiencing substantial problems with collection from reinsurers around the globe. First of all, First State was working on a lot of commutations. In addition, the accounting support for the reinsurance claims at First State was very poor—it was confused and not supported by a whole lot of reliable documentation. Then too, both surplus lines and reinsurance businesses had a cowboy aspect to them back then. "From my background," Mark reflected, "I was expecting to see certain minimum evidentiary items associated with reinsurance claims associated with surplus lines which I wasn't seeing."

As a result, Ralph Nakash required First State to take a substantial write-down. In a statutory insurance examination, a write down takes place by assigning a "'non admit" status to certain assets. (An insurance receivable is generally booked as an asset, although it appears as a contra account to loss and claims reserves on the liability side of the balance sheet.) In total, Ralph and Mark's examination led to Hartford Group's taking a hefty $594 million dollar write-down, which required Hartford's then parent company, ITT, to invest an additional $680 million in Hartford, to fund loss reserves. "The Hartford was not very happy," Mark reflected, "but I think that they were glad ultimately that we caused them to deal with their surplus lines problems." As for Mark, he gained valuable experience which came in handy for his next assignment.

A Genie in a Bottle

Mark's third assignment involved the Lexington Insurance Company, a subsidiary of AIG. Ralph Nakash was not on that assignment, perhaps because he had previously worked for AIG. "I always suspected," Mark said, "that he was not put on that assignment because he had caused such a ruckus at the Hartford. The state regulatory regime was not overly interested at that time in finding major problems with their insureds." AIG struck Mark as being so complex and non-transparent that it was essentially not auditable. To illustrate this point to his friends, Mark would take out the Lexington Yellow Book, which had a big chart of AIG's subsidiaries and how they were all supposed to fit together. (The Yellow Book collects and discloses all of the statutory reporting requirements associated with each US insurance company.) "You don't know what 'complex' means until you've seen a chart like AIG's corporate structure," Mark would say. (See the following chart.) The Yellow Book for Lexington also gave a list of all the companies with which Lexington had a reinsurance agreement, in a section called "Schedule F." By looking at the Schedule one could also appreciate how many reinsurance arrangements there are. Schedule F for Lexington was 20 pages long.

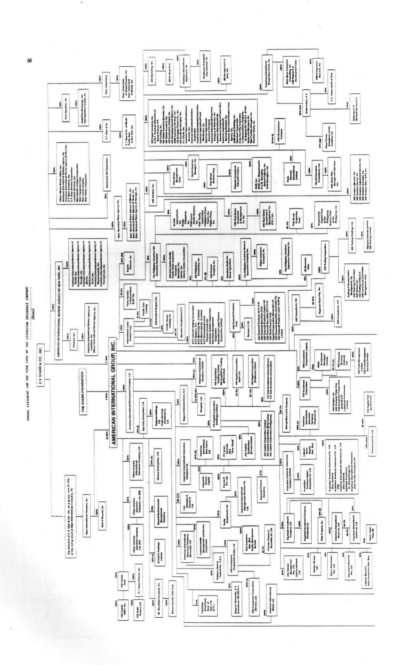

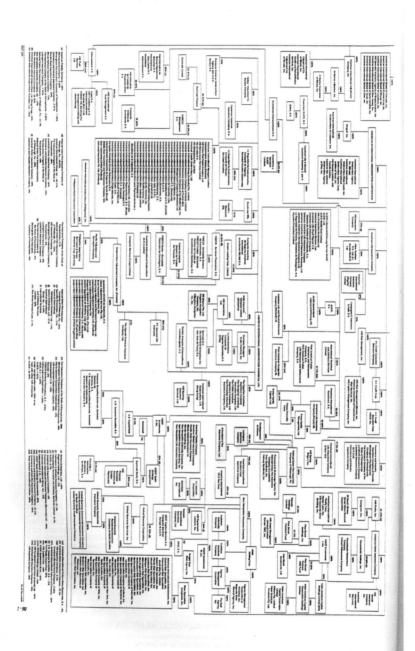

The surplus lines business had gone bad in the mid- to late 80s, resulting in loss ratios that were causing huge losses for insurance companies. This was especially bad luck for Lexington, because, if First State was the third largest insurer in that market in the country, Lexington was the largest. In fact it was three or four times larger than First State. Mark expected to see problems in Lexington similar to those he had encountered at First State, but greatly magnified. "I was not particularly looking forward to this engagement because I was anticipating a lot of problems," he says.

Two points should be emphasized here about the effect of unrecoverable reinsurance on the direct insurer. The first point involves the extent of potential loss. If the direct insurer incurs large losses on its underlying insurance business, it can lose exceptional amounts of money if its reinsurers cannot pay, because it suffers a double loss: it becomes responsible for all the losses that the reinsurer was supposed to cover, but it also suffers from the loss of the premium moneys which it paid to that reinsurance company. Note that this is not like a loss on an investment, such as when an equity investment loses its value from a company's bankruptcy. Reinsurance involves a kind of leverage: it enables the direct insurer to leverage its capital in order to write more business. So the full effect of this leveraging is felt when the reinsurance claim is deemed not collectable. It not only adversely affects the capital of the direct insurer on a dollar-for-dollar basis, but also forces the insurer to write less business, because its capital has been reduced. This can result in a downward spiral of lower capital and less premium writings. (Think of ITT having to invest $680 million in the Hartford.) In short, the financial impact of having to write down an unrecoverable reinsurance receivable can be dramatic.

The second important point about reinsurance involves the time lag in which a loss becomes "manifest" (as it is called). For accounting purposes, when a loss potential (or contingency) becomes known (or knowable) the insurer is required to set aside loss reserves for ultimate payment of those losses—even if the exact losses are not known at the time. This is required even when those losses may take years to develop into claims. (Think about a hurricane where the loss is reasonably estimable after a couple of days, but the actual claims may take years to come in and require payment.) Both generally accepted accounting principles (GAAP) and statutory accounting rules require that those losses be recorded immediately, so that those funds then available to pay claims can be reserved. This is done both for the benefit of the insured, who has incurred a loss, and for the company, so that they can know how much capital they have available to write business. With respect to the role of reinsurers, they also have to set up reserves on these losses, but the amount of cash or security they might have to pay or present at the time of loss accrual is dependent on the particular reinsurance contracts. In most circumstances, some security is required from the reinsurer. If the reinsurer cannot post that security, then discussions might begin immediately concerning the issues at hand.

As mentioned, in the mid-80s there were big losses on surplus lines: direct insurers in general were looking at write offs and commutations, and they were trying to defer repaying losses as long as possible. An insurer would be in a better position to deal with unrecoverable reinsurance receivables if its reserve for that purpose was relatively large. Thus, when Mark began to look at Lexington's reinsurance book and its recoverable numbers, the first thing he asked about was the reserve for unrecoverable insurance receivable. What did he find? "I found that there was virtually none to speak of!" Mark recollects, "You have to understand how odd that was. It was strange beyond belief that when the business in surplus lines was so bad, a responsible company had apparently made no provision whatsoever for adverse results. My discovery of this very odd state of affairs started me off on a couple of months' odyssey, to figure out what was going on."

Eventually, after a fair bit of persistence on Mark's part, one of the reinsurance managers told Mark that the reinsurance recoverable "problem" was being taken care of by a reinsurance agreement with a third party, which insured against uncollectible reinsurance recoverables. Mark's eyebrows went up at that. The name of the entity was "Coral Reinsurance Ltd," a Barbados domiciled insurance company. In reply Mark said, "You mean that there exists in this world a party that will pay you when one of your reinsurers decides that it can't pay you?" Mark asked. "Yes," was the response. Mark said, "And where do I get a bottle with a genie like that in it?"

The concept of insurance against uncollectible reinsurance recoverables seemed so ridiculous to Mark that he started asking several more questions, such as: Where were the financials of Coral Re? Could he be shown the reinsurance contracts? Who controls Coral Re? What kind of due diligence was done on this company, not only by Lexington but also by AIG?—because, as it turned out, Coral Re was insuring collectability of reinsurance for *every* AIG subsidiary, not just Lexington.

Looking under a Rock

Mark had difficulty making headway. At one point he asked the chief financial person at Lexington for the due diligence on Coral Re. The initial response was, "We don't have any." Mark comments, "It got to be a bit of a joke. You have to consider my background. A number of my clients at Price Waterhouse in Sydney were investment banks, equity funds, and savings banks. I had the assignment of auditing their financial derivative contracts and internal controls, and I was considered one of the firm's experts on such matters. From my perspective this wasn't even a close call. It couldn't be taken seriously, even as more and more senior people repeated the same line. It just didn't make any sense."

Next Mark asked for the financial statements for Coral Re, and he was told by the CFO of Lexington that they did not have them. Mark replied, "The answer you just gave me is so absurd, that I can't take it seriously even in the remotest sort of way. You mean to say you are sending hundreds of millions of dollars to a company in Barbados, without any knowledge of what they are doing, in the hopes that maybe they will send you back millions or even billions of dollars?" A couple of days later the Lexington CFO did manage to find the financial statements for Coral Re after all.

"They kept insulting my intelligence in this way. More than that, they insulted the intelligence of my friend, Joe Maiato, a tenacious and bright CPA who was the Senior Insurance Examiner with Delaware. We thought about investigating Coral Re by flying down to Barbados, but that ultimately proved unnecessary. Joe and I decided just to call Barbados Information in Barbados to get a phone number for Coral Re, and Joe just called the number given to us by Information. But when we called, what do you suppose the person answering the phone said? She said, 'American International Group'!"

It would be an understatement to say that that provided a clue as to who really controlled Coral Re. One of the documents Mark had acquired from Lexington about Coral Re gave the name of an officer of that company, so Joe referred to this person and asked the phone receptionist if he could speak with this him. The receptionist explained that that person was as a senior VP at AIG, who lived in Chicago, and that she was a part-time receptionist who was the only Coral Re employee in that Barbados office!

"So we had an absurd contract in our hands," Mark explained, "involving an absurd entity, with no practical independence, and which, furthermore, was a billion dollar company with one part time employee. That information started yet a further odyssey. Joe and I got additional senior people in Delaware involved, and other regulators from New York State and Pennsylvania, and we also got the National Association of Insurance Commissioners (NAIC) involved." The task of coordinating everyone's investigations and reaching a joint conclusion took several years.

At one point during this process, Mark said to Joe, "There must be a private placement memorandum for Coral Re. If we want to get the whole picture, a self-contained 'confession' so to speak for this deal, we need to get a hold of that." AIG was of no help, since it was not exactly cooperating with Joe and Mark's efforts. However, Mark noticed in one of the contracts in his possession that, very oddly, the Arkansas Development Finance Authority (ADFA) was listed as an investor in Coral Re. "Oh...," I realized, "since they're a government entity, I can get it from them." So Mark started calling ADFA and worked his way up the ladder, all the way up to the president of ADFA, Bob Nash, who brushed his inquiry aside. (See the reprint of the memo below.)

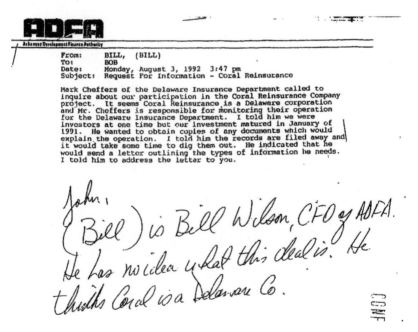

In response to Mark's questions, Nash said that the investment had "run its course," and that ADFA was now out of it. That really puzzled Mark. "Investments don't 'run their course'!" he said. (A couple of hours after talking with Nash, Mark received out of the blue a phone call, clearly intended to intimidate, from a partner in a high-powered Chicago law firm, who wanted to convey to Mark that he had no business looking into ADFA's relation to Coral.)

Mark figured that he was not going to get any help from Bob Nash. (Nash's involvement with ADFA would end shortly thereafter anyway, when he was appointed undersecretary of agriculture by his longtime friend, Bill Clinton). Even so, Mark's colleague Joe initiated a conversation with a reporter in Arkansas, who submitted a Freedom of Information Act (FOIA) request to ADFA, asking for the Private Placement Memorandum. "Eventually we did get our hands on it," Mark explained. "And that is where the fun began," he added.

No Risk Investment, No Risk Insurance

The Private Placement Memorandum laid out the terms of the initial investment, making it clearer than anything that Coral Re was not a real company but merely the form of a company, set up to hide billions of potential losses incurred by AIG. (A copy of the Executive Summary of the Private Placement Memorandum is included at the end of this chapter.) The Memorandum made it clear that a new entity was being established, Coral Re, which was to be owned by ten individuals and one quasi-government entity, the ADFA. The ADFA was to be the owner of last resort according to the Memorandum, as each of the individual owners was given a put option that required the ADFA to purchase their ownership interests, if for some reason the owners deemed it prudent to exit the "investment." The owners were each lent approximately $5 million from the Sanwa bank of Chicago, which they then used to purchase their equity interests in Coral Re. Coral Re, in turn, purchased Certificates of Deposit in Sanwa Bank for an amount equaling the amount lent by them to the equity holders. In short, it was a "round trip of cash," and no money effectively left the bank.

The private placement memorandum offered these stealth equity holders a healthy guaranteed return on their investment, with no risk, since the loans were both non-recourse and supported by the aforementioned put options. According to the Memorandum, the investors were guaranteed an annual profit, deriving from a so-called "2% risk premium" on their pooled initial "investment" of $60 million. Sanwa would be paid fees and commissions equaling 50% of this "risk premium" during the first year, and 25% in subsequent years; also, each year the cost of the loan would be deducted (37.5 basis points, or about $15,000). Hence the investors, for their phony initial "investment" of $5 million, would each receive about $25,000 the first year and roughly $45,000 every year thereafter, with absolutely no risk.

Sanwa, the organizing bank, for its part received special fees for the deal, as did the ADFA, as the investor of last resort. But what did AIG get for all of its efforts? AIG got to have Coral Re agree to guarantee the collectability of all of its failing reinsurance recoverable claims. The arrangement enabled AIG to claim that billions of dollars in uncollectible accounts receivable were all collectible, thanks to an amazing entity, Coral Re, which had come along just in time to guarantee the collection of all these uncollectible receivables!

To be sure, it was necessary that Coral Re be presented, in the legal documents, as a legitimate non-related third party, since obviously if it bore no risk it could not count as a genuine insurer and would have to be consolidated into AIG. Moreover, Coral Re had to receive funds from someone or other, so that it could follow through on its guarantees to pay AIG for its bad debts. What would be the source of Coral Re's funds? Perhaps you have anticipated the answer already. As can be seen from the Private Placement Memorandum, the payer of those guarantees was going to be AIG itself. Essentially, Coral Re was set up to allow AIG not to accrue losses on its uncollectible receivables related to reinsurance agreements until the losses had been realized in cash, and even then not until up to a year later.

When Mark and Joe shared the Private Placement Memorandum with the various state regulators concurred, they all reached the same judgment. Here is a representative quotation from the analysis provided by a senior executive at NAIC:

> ... the overall arrangement [is] one by means of which AIG has attempted to circumvent statutory accounting procedures and disclosure requirements regarding reinsurance commutations and uncollectible reinsurance recoverables. ... it becomes, in my view, impossible to maintain that Coral bears or was ever intended to bear any exposure to an underwriting loss, which means that there is simply no basis for arguing that anything other than deposit accounting should be applied to the entire transaction...
>
> If reinsurance credit for the Coral arrangement were therefore to be disallowed, it would seem that the first order of business would be to require the companies involved to write off all previously ceded reinsurance acknowledged to be unrecoverable, with restatement of liabilities and surplus, and to make proper disclosure in the notes to the financial statement of such amounts and of the impact of commutations

of previously ceded reinsurance. It would then presumably be appropriate to account for the Coral transaction as a deposit with no reduction of liabilities on the cedents' books.

There would seem to be no question that this elaborate exercise has resulted in a substantial misrepresentation of the operating results and financial condition of the companies involved.

Such is the "how" involving the strange company called Coral Re, but what is the "why"? That is, what goals did AIG ultimately achieve through these improprieties?

As mentioned, in certain surplus lines, the losses being incurred at the time were horrendous, with loss ratios far exceeding expectations. Other insurers in the same lines of business besides AIG had been incurring huge losses and exiting the business. (The Hartford, for instance, as we have seen, did the right thing—and ended up being penalized for it.) Consequently, premium prices in these markets were climbing in some cases by factors of five. These circumstances offered AIG a chance to make extraordinary amounts of profits. Insurance is an exception to the general rule that a business only gets into more trouble and just digs deeper by hiding its losses. In the insurance business, if an insurer can stay in a marketplace while others are bailing, it can grow to dominate a market, while enjoying extraordinary profits because of the high premiums. That is just what AIG did. From the very high premiums it could demand in the surplus lines market, AIG acquired reserves for writing even more insurance, and in this way it attained domination in that market. AIG's unethical and highly dubious effort involving Coral Re was successful beyond belief. The Coral Re scam paved the way for AIG to grow in the following decade into the world's largest insurance company.

Lessons of Coral Re

Coral Re may be viewed as the "Mother" of all Special Purpose Entities (SPEs) and Off Balance Sheet (OBS) irregularities. It was created long before Enron perfected that accounting manipulation. Lexington and other AIG's subsidiaries survived the deterioration of business in the surplus lines market through having AIG create an OBS entity, shift all of those potential reinsurance collectible losses to this putative third-party entity, and only record a loss internally when the amount was paid— because one does not need to book the loss. (When the time came for paying the loss, AIG would tell Coral Re, and at that time there would be a round trip of cash between AIG and Coral Re.)

A key aspect of Coral Re's existence was that it had to be perceived as independent of AIG, since otherwise consolidation principles would eliminate any of the loss deferral benefits. Hence, despite the fact that AIG originated, managed and controlled every aspect of Coral Re's business, AIG was successful in hiding this entity from auditor or regulatory notice for more than seven years. By the time that regulators finished their investigation and reached a common conclusion, in 1995, AIG had profited tremendously from the entity's existence. By then it cost AIG nothing to agree with regulators' demands to wind down its activities with Coral Re, as AIG's CEO, Hank Greenberg, and its CFO, Howard Smith, agreed to do.

Coral Re was established in 1987. Cheffers discovered it in the early 1990s. The state regulators and NAIC were on board and had completed their investigations by 1995. But what was done to punish AIG or keep it from engaging in similar improprieties in the future? In the end, not very much. AIG was given a warning and told not to do it again, a warning which the company ignored, as it later went on to create three other offshore entities, to take on certain of Coral's business (see next chapter). The lesson AIG apparently "learned" from their Coral Re experience was to figure out how to do it again without being caught. No significant action was taken by the regulatory authorities against Greenberg or Smith. In short, in retrospect it seems that a gross accounting irregularity was successful and no one was really the wiser for it. Only when the later irregularities grew much more serious was significant attention paid to the problem.

Why were no serious penalties assessed for AIG? There are four main reasons. First, it is not clear who could have penalized AIG. There was no national insurance regulator *per se*, and it was difficult to get individual states to work together sufficiently on the Coral Re case. Second, AIG played hardball, and any regulators or politicians who insisted on enforcement would have had to pay huge personal costs and face serious difficulties. For example, AIG put pressure on the state insurance regulators by influencing state representatives through campaign contributions. AIG even went so far as to hire a private investigator to look into the private lives of some state regulators. At the same time, enforcement action could have looked unnecessary, because by the mid-'90s AIG was a very healthy and highly successful company, so that Coral Re looked like water long under the bridge. Third, Greenberg, held effective ownership control of AIG, through executive positions which he held in two entities, which together controlled up to

17% of AIGs shares. This made it even more difficult to consider his removal, which is probably the step that would have needed to be taken to remedy the problem. Fourth and finally, Coral Re was a political hot potato because of ADFA's involvement and possible links to the Clinton Administration. No one wanted to touch it—especially given swirling rumors, on the one hand, about ADFA being used for money laundering, and, on the other hand, about possible connections between AIG, ADFA and US intelligence agencies. (Not that it would have been impossible to find out the truth: someone who was wondering why in the world ADFA was involved in this—with the put options, payments, and everything else—would simply have had to follow the money.)

Nearly every accounting principle was violated with the creation, operation and consummation of Coral Re. After Coral Re it would be reasonable to wonder whether any of AIG's financials could have been believed under Greenberg and Smith. What should have happened—and what typically would happen in such a case—was for both Greenberg and Smith to be decisively removed from their positions, in the mid-nineties, after the documented revelations associated with Coral Re. If such a step had been taken, then AIG, at that point perhaps a healthy insurance company, would have been given a chance to recover its balance and right itself. However, because that sort of a decisive step was not taken, very soon afterwards even more serious problems developed and broke out, as will be described in the next chapter.

Recommended additional reading:

Any introduction to reinsurance, such as MunichRe, *Reinsurance*, available at http://www.munichreamerica.com/publications/underwriting/pub_underwriting_r einsurance_basic_guide.shtml.

I. EXECUTIVE SUMMARY

Investors ("Investors") are being solicited to jointly establish Coral Reinsurance Company Ltd. ("Coral" or the "Company"), incorporated in Barbados. The Company is designed to reinsure certain risks from several of the U.S. subsidiary insurance companies of American International Group, Inc. ("AIG"). AIG's interest in creating the Company is to create a reinsurance facility which will permit its U.S. companies to write more U.S. premiums. For a U.S.-domiciled company, a high level of surplus is required to support insurance premiums in accordance with U.S. statutory requirements. The statutory requirements in Barbados are less restrictive.

The proposed transaction involves incorporating a Barbados-based reinsurance company to be capitalized with $60 million of equity provided by the Investors. Private individual Investors will have the opportunity to finance their investment with a non-recourse loan to be provided by The Sanwa Bank, Limited, acting through its Chicago Branch ("Sanwa"). The loan to any individual Investor will be secured by a pledge to Sanwa of the Investor's Common Stock and dividends of the Company, and Sanwa's recourse would be limited to such Common Stock and dividends. (See "Financing by Sanwa Bank")

The reinsurance premiums of the Company would be generated by reinsurance premiums ceded by a group of AIG subsidiaries. It is anticipated that such annual reinsurance premiums would be approximately $480 million. However, the Company may, depending on circumstances, reinsure more or less. In any case, the annual reinsurance premium will not exceed $600 million. Under the reinsurance treaties, the maximum loss of the Company in respect of a given year would be $950 million although the amount actually payable by the Company would be further limited by the "stop-loss" arrangement described below. Pending payment of losses, the

- 1 -

Company would invest the AIG premiums (less the risk premium and the stop-loss premiums as described below) in interest-bearing securities (the "Reinsurance Fund"). The Company's obligations under the reinsurance treaties would be supported by a letter of credit issued by a commercial bank and the Reinsurance Fund would be pledged to secure the Company's obligations to such bank in respect of the letter of credit.

The $60 million equity investment made by the Investors will be held and invested separately in five year Certificates of Deposit with Sanwa (the "Sanwa CD's"). The interest rate on the Sanwa CD's will reset every three months at a return equal to the London Interbank Bid Rate for 90-day United States deposits. In addition to investment income earned on the $60 million equity contribution, the Investors will, for the first three underwriting years, earn an additional 2% risk premium annually on their equity investment ($1.2 million). Thereafter, Investors will continue to earn a 2% risk premium, except in the event that premium volume is less than $360 million. In such case, Investors will have their risk premium reduced from 2% to 1.5%, regardless of the ultimate amount of annual premiums written by the Company. Any individual Investor who chooses to finance his purchase with a non-recourse loan provided by Sanwa will incur various fees and commissions related to such loan. These fees and commissions will equal approximately one half of the risk premium in the first underwriting year and one quarter of the risk premium in subsequent underwriting years.

In order to insulate the Company from reinsurance risk in excess of the amount available from the $480 million of premiums paid annually under the reinsurance agreement, the Company would execute a "stop-loss" agreement with a third party insurance company (subject to approval by the Board of Directors) to cover any such excess losses. For the purpose of determining such excess, the $480 million of premiums paid annually would be increased by investment income in the Reinsurance Fund and any recoveries of previously paid losses, and decreased by the risk premium, premiums ceded under the stop-loss agreement, investement losses in the Reinsurance Fund (if any), and return premiums paid. In the event that no "stop-loss" agreement is available that is acceptable to the Board of Directors in respect of any future year, the Board of Directors would not establish reinsurance treaties in respect of such year and, in addition, holders of a majority of the shares of Common Stock of the Company may elect to exercise their exit option with respect to existing treaties. The Board of Directors must unanimously approve any new reinsurance treaties entered into by the Company.

The Company will pay dividends on a quarterly basis, as directed by the Board of Directors. Each year, it is anticipated that 100% of the investment income earned on the $60 million equity capital plus the proceeds from the risk premium will be distributed to shareholders. Further, the Investors will have "exit provisions" starting January 1, 1989 which would allow the termination of the Company's liability, upon a vote of the holders of a majority of the shares of Common Stock, sixty months after the inception of each underwriting year. After December 31, 1991 or upon the exercise of the exit option, all shareholders will have the right to redeem the outstanding shares of its Common Stock for book value. Pursuant to an Agreement Among Shareholders (the "Shareholder Agreement"), one holder will refrain from exercising its redemption right and will maintain a $6 million investment of Common Stock in the Company and remain as the sole shareholder of the Company for up to an additional forty-eight months, until termination of the Company's liability.

The Company will bear all expenses related to both its creation and ongoing operation. Administrative services will be provided by American International

Management Company (Barbados) Ltd. ("AIMC"), an AIG subsidiary. Both the Investors and AIG will have the opportunity to review the financial and operating results of the Company on an annual basis.

A Culture
of Accounting
Corruption

3

> "How much of this sort of stuff do they do?" Mr. Houldsworth asks in the
> call. "I mean, how much cooking goes on in there? I mean, I know they've got a bit
> of a slight reputation for it."
> "Um, they're fairly aggressive," Mr. Garand replies. "They'll do whatever they
> need to make their numbers look right."
>
> ("Ghost of Coral Re Returns in Gen Re Fraud Trial," *Business Insurance*, Feb. 18,
> 2008.)

A GENERAL CULTURE OF ACCOUNTING CORRUPTION AT AIG was uncovered by
investigators in 2004. The corruption could be traced back to Coral Re, and it led to
a major restatement in 2005. As we saw, this restatement in turn led to AIG's credit
downgrade and its exposure to risks in the CDS market. In this chapter, we tell the
story of how AIG's improprieties were discovered on a broader scale. We explain
how they took place and what AIG's motives were, and what followed from them.

A key player in this story is Eliot Spitzer, then Attorney General (AG) of the
State of New York and later Governor. Some background about Spitzer is helpful.
After Spitzer attended Harvard Law School, his early career as a lawyer took an
unusual path, since he alternated between practicing law at some of New York
City's most prestigious corporate law firms, and working in the Manhattan District
Attorney's office, investigating crime. There he developed a reputation as a tough
and savvy prosecutor of organized crime. The combination of an insider's
knowledge of corporate shenanigans, and a prosecutor's zeal in stamping out

corruption, which Spitzer gained from these different types of experiences, would mark his public personality and shape his career path.

Spitzer apparently formulated political aspirations early on, probably having his eyes on the Governorship and beyond. After being elected as AG in 1998, Spitzer became famous, and notorious, for using the AG's office to prosecute Wall Street corruption. His main weapon was a then obscure New York State Blue Sky law from 1921 called the Martin Act, which, under later court interpretations, gave the AG tremendous power to prosecute financial improprieties. (A "Blue Sky" law is a state law which regulates securities, as opposed to a Federal law, such as the Securities Acts of 1933 and 1934.) The ramifications of the Martin Act had been overlooked for decades. However, a young lawyer who interviewed for a job in Spitzer's office, named Eric Dinallo (later, as mentioned above, Superintendant of Insurance for NY and subsequently a candidate for AG), drew Spitzer's attention to the extensive powers which the Martin Act gave to the AG for fighting corporate corruption. For example, under the Martin Act, the AG can subpoena documents and depose witnesses, who have no right to counsel and no protection from self-incrimination. Moreover, there is no need for the AG to show actual fraud or actual harm in order to convict: a mere intent to defraud is enough. Finally, all documents uncovered by the AG in his investigation become available afterwards to trial lawyers for use in civil suits. Spitzer controversially used the Martin Act to prosecute Wall Street firms falling under its jurisdiction but which traditionally had been policed only by Federal authorities.

AIG and Bid Rigging

AIG entered Spitzer's radar screen at first indirectly, through Spitzer's 2004 investigation of a bid rigging scam at a major insurance broker, Marsh & McLennan. According to Spitzer's suit against Marsh, the scam worked as follows. Suppose a client's insurance policy with carrier X was coming up for renewal. (In that case, carrier X is referred to as the "incumbent" insurance carrier.) Marsh, from its knowledge of the client, would specify a price for the renewal of that policy which it thought the client would be satisfied with. Marsh would then ask carrier X whether it would be willing to renew the policy at that price. If so, then Marsh would ask X to submit what it called an "A" bid at that price, which would be a phony bid that was guaranteed to win. Marsh would then call around to other companies and ask them to submit "B" bids at a higher price. These were phony bids which were designed not to be competitive. (There was also another category of non-competitive bids, for various miscellaneous situations, referred to as "C" bids.)

Why would these other companies go along with Marsh and submit non-competitive bids? Because if they did not, then, when they happened to be the incumbent insurer, Marsh would exclude them from being able to make a guaranteed "A" level bid. Also, Marsh would not steer any new clients their way. If a company wanted to profit from the game when its turn arrived, it had to be willing to play the game when it was someone else's turn.

Spitzer's suit named not only Marsh but also several insurance carriers that participated in the scam, including AIG. According to the complaint:

> The "A, B, C" quote system was strictly enforced by Marsh through William Gilman, Executive Director of Marketing at Marsh Global Broking and a Managing Director. Gilman refused to allow AIG to put in competitive quotes in B Quote situations, and, on more than one occasion, warned that AIG would lose its entire book of business with Marsh if it did not provide B Quotes. Gilman likewise advised AIG of the benefits of the system. As he put it: Marsh "protected AIG's ass" when it was the incumbent carrier, and it expected AIG to help Marsh "protect" other incumbents by providing B Quotes (*NY v. Marsh & McLennan*).

But AIG was furthermore related to the case through family connections. The CEO of AIG, Hank Greenberg, had two sons involved in the scam. Jeff Greenberg was the CEO of Marsh, and Evan Greenberg was the CEO of another insurance carrier named in the suit as participating in the scam (ACE Ltd.).

Marsh settled a civil suit related to the matter in February 2005 for $850 million, and subsequently it paid out hundreds of millions of dollars to settle related shareholder lawsuits.

AIG and Brightpoint

There were reasons enough for Spitzer to entertain suspicions about AIG even apart from its participation in the Marsh bid-rigging scam, as the company in late 2004 had recently settled two different SEC complaints for selling fraudulent financial products, one of them involving Brightpoint, a telecommunications company, and another involving PNC Financial Group.

The settlement was widely viewed as evidence of further, yet undiscovered improper business practices in AIG. For instance, a report in a *New York Times* business section column at the time carried the headline, "Experts Say the A.I.G. Case is Tip of the Iceberg." The column described the potential for abuse and fraud in the "finite insurance" and "alternative risk transfer" business of AIG. "They do repeatable-type products," a senior insurance industry executive was quoted in the article as saying about AIG, "There are more PNC's and Brightpoints out there." ("Finite insurance" is a non-traditional, typically short-term contract for some clearly specified and limited risk, which may include retrospective as well as prospective features, and where the premiums are typically far in excess of expected loss. Abuse and fraud are possible when the contract involves no real transfer of risk and masks some other kind of transaction. In that case, such transactions have the "form" of insurance but in "substance" are something else.)

The irregularity involving Brightpoint was a transaction putatively involving such "finite insurance" but which really amounted to income smoothing. Income smoothing is unethical and is typically illegal, as it conveys to investors a misleading impression of the financial position and results of operations of a company.

In October of 1998, Brightpoint announced that it would recognize a one-time charge, in the range of $13 to $18 million, arising from losses sustained by one of its U.K. divisions doing business in cell phones. However, later the company realized that it had far underestimated the losses, which were going to be more in the neighborhood of $29 million. Fearing a strong negative reaction from shareholders and punishment in the market—and unable to recover insurance from its loss insurers—Brightpoint turned to assistance from the "Loss Mitigation Unit" of one of AIG's subsidiaries (National Union Fire Insurance Co.). Brightpoint entered into a putative "finite insurance" contract with this AIG subsidiary, according to which it would pay three premiums of $5 million each ($15 million total), in exchange for being able to record an insurance receivable of $11.9 million in 1998. Brightpoint's plan was to net this receivable against its U.K. division's earnings, thereby bringing the net loss into the previously announced range. The SEC complaint describes the impropriety in the contract as follows:

> the "retroactive coverage" should not have been accounted for as insurance. It was merely a "round-trip" of cash — a mechanism for Brightpoint to deposit money with AIG, in the form of monthly "premiums," which AIG was then to refund to Brightpoint as purported "insurance claim payments." In drafting the Policy, Delaney and Harcharik [the Corporate Controller and Director of Risk Management at

Brightpoint, respectively] took pains to ensure that the "retroactive coverage" raised no "red flags" for the Auditors: They created a blended fidelity coverage and retroactive policy that was designed to look like traditional, non-retroactive indemnity insurance, and they gave the policy an effective date of August 1998.

Which accounting principle was most relevant here? As the SEC complaint states, according to GAAP, a recovery cannot be booked as an "insurance" recovery unless there is transference of risk:

> A recovery is not an "insurance" recovery for accounting purposes unless the insurance policy transfers some risk from the insured to the insurer. If a policy does not involve risk transfer, GAAP treats it as a financing arrangement, with all premiums to be accounted for as deposits.

Because a proper accounting of the transaction would have been contrary to their purposes, Brightpoint executives had to engage in duplicity to make what was essentially a deposit look like an insurance recovery. Along these lines the SEC complaint observes:

> In constructing the Policy, Brightpoint faced two accounting obstacles: First, the policy had to look like insurance. If it looked like a deposit, Brightpoint would not be able to net anticipated recoveries against the loss. Second, the policy could not look like retroactive insurance, i.e., insurance designed to cover a loss already quantified and known, because Brightpoint might then be required to expense the full $15 million "premium" immediately. Under GAAP, the insured is obligated to recognize the full premium expense associated with a retroactive policy at the time it recognizes the benefits of the policy.

Note that the two "obstacles" that confronted AIG in the Brightpoint transaction were similar to ones it faced as regards Coral Re. Recall that, first, AIG's reinsurance agreement with Coral Re similarly had the appearance of being an insurance policy when there was no real transference of risk. Second, the agreement contained a carefully contrived prospective element, which masked the retrospective character of the substance of the arrangement. The observations of the Pennsylvania state insurance examiner, in his confidential analysis of the policy terms for Coral Re, can be transferred over without difference to the Brightpoint policy terms:

This is an ingenious agreement obviously designed to enable the company to avoid having to follow applicable statutory accounting procedures and disclose on its annual statement unrecoverable reinsurance balances and losses sustained on reinsurance commutations ...While much of the language in the agreement is fairly standard verbiage, the nature of the transaction makes it, in my view, impossible to construct a rationale for treating it as a reinsurance transaction.

AIG and PNC Financial Services

The next improper transaction of AIG which came to light, involving PNC Financial Services, was also similar to Coral Re, insofar as it involved creating an entity which appeared to be independent and was not consolidated, but which actually was not independent and should have been consolidated.

In the scheme which AIG sold to PNC, AIG created a Special Purpose Entity (SPE) which would be putatively independent of PNC, because the entity would be in part initially funded by AIG. PNC then transferred badly performing investments to this SPE, thereby removing them from its balance sheet.

The scheme was referred to as "C-GAITS" ("Contributed Guaranteed Alternative Investment Trust Security") or, alternatively, as "PAGIC" transactions. It was the brainchild of a unit of AIG called AIG Financial Products (AIG-FP), which would later become notorious (as we have seen) as the unit which sold CDSs and which exposed AIG to the risk of bankruptcy. AIG tried to sell this "product" to various companies; however, only PNC ended up purchasing it, for fees totaling $40 million. PNC used PAGIC transactions to remove from its balance sheet $762 million of loan and venture capital assets for the last three quarters of 2001. After that point, the Federal Reserve discovered the scheme, determined that it was improper, and directed PNC to consolidate the SPE.

The transactions were irregular because the SPEs did not meet the minimal GAAP standards for non-consolidation; moreover, AIG did not have a true ownership stake in the entity. The SEC complaint against AIG explains the first GAAP issue in this way:

> At all relevant times, GAAP provided that for non-consolidation to be appropriate, the majority owner of the SPE had to be an independent third party who made a substantive capital investment in the SPE, had control of the SPE, and had substantive risks and rewards of ownership of the assets of the SPE. Conversely, non-consolidation was not appropriate

when the majority owner of the SPE made only a nominal capital investment, the activities of the SPE were virtually all on the sponsor's or transferor's behalf, and the substantive risks and rewards of the assets or the debt of the SPE rested directly or indirectly with the sponsor or transferor. Three percent was the minimally acceptable amount under GAAP to indicate a substantive capital investment sufficient for non-consolidation, though a greater investment could be necessary depending on the facts and circumstances. GAAP further provided that fees paid to the owner of the SPE for structuring the transaction were treated as a return of the owner's initial capital investment.

The PAGIC SPEs nominally met the GAAP third-party investment requirement for non-consolidation, because AIG agreed to contribute cash to the SPE equivalent to 3% given the value of the investments contributed by PNC. However, in substance, AIG's investment fell below that mark, for two reasons involving AIG's remuneration for the deal. First, the terms of the PAGIC transactions stipulated that AIG would receive a substantial fee from PNC upon the structuring of the transaction, and these fees (in contrast to continuing management fees) should have been treated under GAAP as in effect a return to AIG of part of its initial investment. Second, the terms of the PAGIC transaction stipulated that AIG would issue a zero-coupon note to PNC which, on maturity, would pay an amount equal to AIG's initial investment. This was to guarantee that AIG would eventually receive at least the return of its original investment. But through payments on the note, again, AIG's interest in the SPE would fall below minimal GAAP requirements.

Moreover, the PAGIC deal was structured in such a way that AIG assumed no substantive risks and enjoyed no substantive rewards relative to the SPE. It assumed no risks because the fees it received were greater than the cash it contributed, and also it happened that the terms of the SPE stipulated that AIG would receive a set dividend regardless of the performance of the investments that PNC contributed. It enjoyed no rewards, because PNC had the right to liquidate the SPE at any time, thereby capturing for itself, if it wished, any improvement in value of the investments it had transferred to the entity.

The SEC in its complaint charged (in standard language for a civil suit) that AIG was "reckless in not knowing" that the PAGIC SPE did not satisfy GAAP requirements for non-consolidation. Yet AIG seems to have been sufficiently cognizant of the impropriety of the arrangement, as evidenced in how AIG handled the matter of the "SAS 50" letter which they used in marketing the PAGIC transactions.

Some background about SAS 50 letters is in order. Often it is helpful for a company to obtain accounting advice about some definite transaction, or to seek a "second opinion" about the accounting treatment of a transaction, particularly in cases of a dispute with the external auditor. To deal with these and similar situations, the Auditing Standards Board (ASB) of the AICPA in 1986 issued its Statement of Auditing Standards 50, "Reports on the Application of Accounting Principles," which standardized the process by which a company could seek to consult with an accountant (a so-called "reporting accountant") other than its external auditors (also known as its "continuing accountant").

The intent of SAS 50 was that the reporting accountant of a SAS 50 letter would become familiar with all the facts and circumstances of a definite transaction, and furthermore consult with the continuing accountant, before finally issuing his own report. However, SAS 50 letters came to be abused and employed by companies as part of their sales pitches for structured financial products. An SAS 50 letter as used for marketing purposes would discuss a "hypothetical transaction" and offer a judgment about the accounting treatment of that transaction as hypothetically described and at a general level. The danger was that any eventual, actual transactions could very well have different facts and circumstances—perhaps facts and circumstances which differed only slightly, but where those differences would amount to a substantial difference in the nature of the transaction. Moreover, for such a hypothetical transaction, the reporting accountant would typically rely solely on management's description of that transaction: indeed, precisely because the transaction was hypothetical, there could be no possibility of the reporting accountant consulting with a continuing accountant. (Because of these abuses, the SEC's chief accountant insisted in 2002 that the AICPA amend SAS 50 to rule out letters giving judgment on hypothetical transactions—for which see SAS 97.)

As it turns out, AIG sought an SAS 50 letter from a partner in the national office of one of the major accounting firms, as to whether the SPE would be non-consolidated in a hypothetical PAGIC transaction. The partner eventually penned a letter opining that such an SPE need not be consolidated. However, he had concerns about the zero coupon note, and he informed AIG of his concerns. In the hypothetical transaction which AIG asked him to comment upon, AIG would be the issuer of the zero coupon note. But the partner was concerned that, in that case, the payments that AIG would receive for the note could be construed as a return to

AIG of part of its original investment in the SPE, and thus AIG's interest in the SPE would fall below the 3% minimum then required by GAAP. (It should be interjected that this transaction was being evaluated in a pre-Enron and post SFAS 125/140 world, where off-balance sheet accounting was all the rage. The potential for accounting manipulation and misrepresentation in OBS entities was soon to explode onto the world scene in a very negative way. On this, see Chapters 11-13 below.) Because of his concerns, the partner crafted the letter in reference to a hypothetical transaction described merely as one in which the counter-party would be issued "a zero coupon note maturing in 30 years"—that is, he deliberately left out the detail that the note would be issued by AIG, and he explained to AIG his reasons for leaving this out, namely, that if this detail were specified more exactly, then the entity would need to be consolidated. However, AIG subsequently used this letter, *without the noted concern*, and also without drawing attention to the partner's concerns, in order to sell PAGIC transactions to PNC. (In the actual PAGIC transactions, AIG ended up indeed being the issuer of the zero coupon note.)

Second Opinions and Accounting Ethics

The whole issue of the SAS 50 letter for the PAGIC transactions raises important questions of accounting ethics, which are worth mentioning here even though they are secondary to our consideration of AIG's improprieties. For example:

1. The partner who wrote the SAS 50 letter which AIG used for marketing purposes, as it turns out, was the same expert who helped AIG originally design the PAGIC transactions. Should he have written a letter purporting to give an objective judgment as regards the accounting treatment of a transaction which he had himself helped design? In doing so, did he review his own work? Or does the concept of reviewing one's own work not apply if a transaction is merely hypothetical?

2. This partner was concerned that if AIG issued the note, then the SPE would not satisfy GAAP requirements for non-consolidation. Clearly he would have recognized the purpose of the transaction and, specifically, he was aware that, if the SPE needed to be consolidated, then the transaction would have had no value to any potential client of AIG. Suppose he also had reason to suspect that AIG would *not* be selling the transaction unless they were the issuer of the note. Was it enough, then, that in his SAS 50 letter he merely deleted reference to AIG as the issuer, or

was he bound to go farther than this and state specifically that, in the transaction described, AIG positively could not be the issuer?

3. As part of its due diligence in entering into the PAGIC transactions, PNC sought advice from its external auditor as to whether the transactions satisfied GAAP requirements for non-consolidation by PNC. At the time, PNC's auditor happened to be the same accounting firm as the one where the author of the SAS 50 letter was a partner. Because of all the technical issues involved, the firm's engagement team referred the matter to the relevant expert in its national office, who was the very same partner who had helped design the transaction and issued the SAS 50 letter in the first place! The partner did not recuse himself from giving an opinion. Quite the contrary: in the written opinion of the transaction which he sent back to the engagement team, the partner quoted liberally from the SAS 50 letter he had written for AIG! We may therefore ask: Should the partner have recused himself from reviewing the transaction? Even supposing that his initial advice was legitimate under then binding accounting standards, would not these subsequent activities cross an ethical line?

4. Also, how much of the blame does this partner deserve as an advisor to and judge of the transaction, and how much of the blame needs to be apportioned out to the many CPAs who were involved in this transaction, both at AIG and PNC, and who were all simply trying to achieve some misleading result, which they recognized as misleading?

As regards point 3 above, it should be noted that the SEC served the accounting firm with a "cease and desist" order for violations of auditor independence, observing that:

> The National Office partner provided advice on the structure, prepared four SAS 50 letters that AIG used in marketing the product, participated in conference calls with potential purchasers of the product and, on at least one occasion, accompanied an AIG marketing team to assist in AIG's marketing of the C-GAITS product to a potential customer. The National Office partner charged AIG for his services. As a result of the activities of the National Office partner, [the Firm] was invested both financially and reputationally in the success of the C-GAITS [PAGIC] product and therefore had a conflict of interest when it evaluated the accounting for that product for its audit client PNC.

The SEC imposed upon the firm the sanction of disgorgement fees with interest, totaling $1.6 million. Moreover, in a secondary class action lawsuit, shareholders sued the firm for the decline in value of PNC shares as a result of the poor advice given to PNC about the PAGIC transactions, and in 2007 the firm settled this suit for $9 million.

So the firm paid a high price for the ethical lapses of one of its partners, a circumstance which has become one of the most challenging aspects of operating a major accounting firm. These firms retain thousands of the best and brightest accounting, tax, and consulting minds in the world, and they expect high levels of innovation and productivity. That a few might go overboard almost seems expected. That many more than a few of them do not, might well be the surprise.

The PNC and Brightpoint deals proved costly for AIG as well. On November 30, 2004, AIG entered into a "deferred prosecution agreement" with the Department of Justice, whereby it agreed to pay $80 million in penalties, $40 million in disgorgement of fees received through the PNC transactions, and $6 million in interest, for a total of $126 million. At the same time AIG agreed, in the words of the settlement document, "to implement a series of reforms addressing the integrity of client and third-party transactions," as well as agreeing to a retrospective review, to be conducted by an independent consultant chosen jointly by the Justice Department, the SEC and AIG.

AIG's Restatement and Gen Re

As mentioned, also in the wake of the Brightpoint and PNC settlements, AG Spitzer's office began to use the powers of the Martin Act to investigate the "finite insurance" and "alternative risk transfer" business generally, with special attention to AIG. Spitzer reasoned, quite accurately, that AIG was simply marketing to other companies, often under the guise of "insurance," various accounting-driven schemes which it had already been using internally. We have seen how this was true already as regards Coral Re. Coral Re was an unconsolidated SPE which should have been consolidated given that it was under AIG's control. Compare the PNC transactions to Coral Re in this regard. Moreover, Coral Re had the appearance of an insurance contract but in reality represented a "round trip of cash" from AIG to itself. Compare the Brightpoint transactions to Coral Re in this regard.

On Valentine's Day 2005, as part of his broad investigation, Spitzer served AIG with subpoenas under the Martin Act, which understandably provoked a crisis in AIG's Board. Immediately the Board authorized a wide-ranging internal investigation of its accounting practices, to be overseen by external counsel and its external auditors. Within a month, as the investigation began to uncover the wide scope of internal accounting malfeasance at the company, Hank Greenberg was forced to resign as CEO, and Howard Smith was fired in part on the grounds of failing to cooperate with the investigation.

AIG's internal investigation eventually led to its announcing a restatement in a much delayed annual report for 2004. The restatement covered its financials for the previous five years, including, most spectacularly, a lowering of net income by $1.3 billion (11%) for 2004 and by $3.9 billion (10%) for all five years. The restatement continued for 22 pages and identified improper accounting in several main areas, such as loss reserves and net investment income, detailing such matters as the conversion of underwriting losses to capital losses and unsupported "top level" adjustments. In addition, the restatement refers to extensive violations of GAAP in accounting for derivatives; deferred taxes; foreign currency translation; deferred acquisition costs; deferred compensation; and commutations, among other areas.

Perhaps the most significant category was that which was covered first in the restatement, "Risk Transfer." As explained in the restatement:

> To recognize the cash flows under an insurance contract as premium and losses, GAAP requires the transfer of risk. If risk transfer requirements are not met, an insurance contract is accounted for as a deposit, resulting in the recognition of cash flows under the contract as deposit assets or liabilities and not as revenues or expense. AIG has concluded, based upon its internal review, that there was insufficient risk transfer to qualify for insurance accounting for certain transactions where AIG subsidiaries either wrote direct insurance or assumed or ceded reinsurance. These transactions are now recorded using deposit accounting. The changes resulting from the change to deposit accounting affect both the consolidated balance sheet and statement of income.

The restatement (as previously alluded to) identified in particular three off-shore entities, similar to Coral Re, which had assumed no real risk: Union Excess and Capco, two Barbados-domiciled companies which ostensibly provided reinsurance, and Richmond, a Bermuda-based reinsurance holding company. This revelation was shocking given that, as mentioned, as a result of the Coral Re investigation, AIG had signed an agreement in 1995 with the various state insurance examiners that it would not in the future enter into agreements similar to that which it had with Coral Re.

But the most egregious example of a sham insurance contract involving no real risk transfer was AIG's transaction with General Reinsurance ("Gen Re"). The restatement described the transaction with deadpan conciseness:

> In December 2000 and March 2001, an AIG subsidiary entered into an assumed reinsurance transaction with a subsidiary of General Re Corporation (Gen Re) involving two tranches of $250 million each. In connection with each tranche, consolidated net premiums written and consolidated incurred policy losses and benefits increased by $250 million in the fourth quarter of 2000 (with respect to the first tranche) and the first quarter of 2001 (with respect to the second tranche). The first tranche of the transaction was commuted in November 2004, reducing premiums and reserves for losses and loss expenses by approximately $250 million in the fourth quarter 2004. AIG has concluded that the transaction was done to accomplish a desired accounting result and did not entail sufficient qualifying risk transfer. As a result, AIG has determined that the transaction should not have been recorded as insurance.

Fuller details of the story may be gleaned from the various SEC complaints relating to the transaction and from related legal documents. The Gen Re transaction was apparently conceived by Hank Greenberg following an earnings release of October 26, 2000, in which AIG announced a $59 million decline in loss reserves. That announcement was viewed critically by stock analysts, several of whom downgraded AIG's stock. Moreover, the market punished AIG with a 6% drop in share price the day of the release. In response and almost immediately, Greenberg called John Ferguson, the CEO of Gen Re, and suggested a deal, which Gen Re was happy to accommodate, since AIG was one of their most important clients. The deal was a sham reinsurance transaction designed to give a false appearance of increased loss reserves at AIG. The terms of the deal were that Gen Re would pay "premiums" to AIG of $250 million each over two successive quarters, in exchange for which AIG would nominally provide $600 million of reinsurance coverage for Gen Re. AIG would then apply these anticipated "premiums" to its loss reserves.

The transaction was improper in many respects. First, as a reinsurance policy, AIG was now strangely playing the role of reinsurer in relation to Gen Re, the reverse of their usual business relationship. Second, AIG assumed no real risk: indeed, as recorded phone conversations show, AIG and Gen Re executives picked the number $600 million arbitrarily—so that the putative "coverage" would be a higher figure than the "premiums"—but AIG would never be at risk for that amount. A recorded conversation between two Gen Re executives shows they were aware of what was wanted by AIG in the deal:

> Monrad: So let's assume they take the deposit liability. I will tell you any way we structure it yes it's got to look more like deposit because they are not really looking to take risks! Well I think if we spend a lot of time trying to figure out how to transfer 500m of risk, we won't get this deal done in the time they want.
>
> Houldsworth: Yeah, I mean as you say, if there's enough pressure on their end, they'll find ways to cook the books won't they?! [Monrad laughs] It's no problem there, it's up to them! We won't help them to do that too much. We'll do nothing illegal![4]

In fact Gen Re accounted for the transaction on their end as a deposit, rather than insurance, and they informed AIG that they would be adopting this "asymmetrical" treatment of the transaction.

Third, the premiums were irregular. Gen Re never paid a penny to AIG. It conveyed only a $10 million "advance" on its $250 million premiums. However, even this advance was a sham, since the $10 million came from AIG and was provided to Gen Re through an elaborate side transaction (which also provided Gen Re with its $5 million fee for agreeing to the deal). In substance, AIG was paying itself for a transaction, the sole purpose of which was to claim $500 million of phantom loss reserves, thus shoring up its share price. As the Gen Re CFO stated in an e-mail: "Given that we will not transfer any losses under this deal it will be necessary for [AIG] ·to repay any fee [(i.e., premium paid by Gen Re)] plus the margin they give us for entering this deal."

The result of the transaction was that AIG reported increased loss reserves. Its Q4 2000 earnings release stated that "AIG had a very good quarter and year. ... We added $106 million to AIG's general insurance net loss and loss adjustment reserves for the quarter." Analysts reacted well, making observations such as that "We think this quarter was a good example of AIG doing what it does best: growing fast and making the numbers" and "AIG put to rest a minor controversy from last quarter by adding $106 million to reserves." But as the restatement later revealed, AIG actually suffered a decline of $144 million in loss reserves during the period, and the ostensible increase was arrived at solely by adding the phony $250 million

---

[4] See *SEC vs. John Houldsworth and Richard Napier*, June 10, 2005.

premium from the Gen Re deal. Similarly, in Q1 of 2001 AIG reported a phony $63 million increase in loss reserves, masking what was in reality a $187 million decrease.

Recap: From Coral Re to Financial Crisis

One of the ironies of the Gen Re deal is that, in the midst of it, Gen Re executives invoked Coral Re as a paradigm of how AIG was prepared to do whatever was necessary to "make the numbers." The $500 million notionally pledged by Gen Re to AIG even included, at the perverse inspiration of Gen Re executives, reserves that Gen Re had acquired from Coral Re:

> The idea of adding Coral Re to the loss portfolio originated with Hans-Peter Gerhardt, a former Cologne Re executive in Cologne, Germany. In a recorded Nov. 14, 2000, phone conversation, Mr. Gerhardt and Mr. Houldsworth discuss contracts that could be transferred to AIG: "What about ceding the Coral reserves back to them?" Mr. Gerhardt asks. "Oh, you're a bad boy," Mr. Houldsworth answers. "We could. Yeah, we could." The next day, Mr. Houldsworth sent an e-mail to Gen Re's then-chief financial officer, Elizabeth A. Monrad, attaching a list of portfolio contracts that included Coral Re, which accounted for $254 million of the portfolio's $500 million in reserves. "We're giving them their own losses back, effectively, there. So we thought that was quite sweet," Mr. Houldsworth said later that day in a recorded call to Ms. Monrad and Richard Napier, a former Gen Re senior VP. [5]

As mentioned, AIG's internal control deficiencies and restatement led directly and indirectly to AIG's near collapse. A taxpayer-funded bailout was required to avert a possible associated collapse of the world's financial system. The executives who succeeded Greenberg and Smith were incapable of getting a grasp on AIG, given its complexity. As also mentioned earlier, it is not implausible that Greenberg would have seen the dangers of AIG's exposure through CDSs linked to the housing market. At least, had he stayed on, he would have noticed that the business of writing CDSs had changed significantly for AIG once the company lost its AAA credit rating.

We can characterize AIG's corrupt accounting culture in this general way:

---

[5] "Ghost of Coral Re Returns in Gen Re Fraud Trial," *Business Insurance*, Feb. 18, 2008.

(i) *Form over substance.* AIG was prepared to use transactions having only the *form* of insurance, not the *substance*, in order to achieve, as necessary, accounting-driven results.

(ii) *Unethical bootstrapping.* AIG employed "ends justifies the means" reasoning to justify accounting improprieties, and especially a form of reasoning which one might call "bootstrapping" –that is, AIG relied on the fact that its improprieties in retrospect would look harmless, once those improprieties had achieved their intended result. An example would be how it stabilized its business and achieved market dominance through Coral Re.

(iii) *Unethical Golden Rule behavior.* AIG related to other companies, in transactions it was prepared to purchase and sell, as it habitually related to itself and as it dealt with its own financial reporting internally.

All three of these characteristics were evident in the Coral Re, and in the high-profile scams that AIG engaged in subsequently (Brightpoint, PNC, Gen Re). Furthermore these characteristics provide the nexus for AIGs transition to massive CDS exposure.

Who's to Blame?

How should blame be apportioned for AIG's demise?

The New York State Attorney General. Some observers have wanted to put the blame on Spitzer, as seen for example in these assertions from a *Wall Street Journal* editorial of August 10, 2009:

> AIG shareholders appear to have been hurt far more by the company's 2005 Spitzer-driven earnings restatement than by Mr. Greenberg's alleged failures as the "control person" in charge when AIG booked improper items. And we haven't even gotten to the loss of AIG's AAA credit-rating that followed his Spitzer-dictated ouster, the new management's decision to go all-in on the U.S. housing market, or the failed regulation of AIG conducted by the Spitzer-appointed New York Insurance Superintendent Eric Dinallo.

Remarkably, the *Journal*'s editors here blame AIG's woes on a restatement, that is, on truthful accounting! In doing so they are obviously blaming the messenger rather than the message. AIG's difficulty was certainly not its restatement, but the culture of arrogant and corrupt accounting which made such an extensive restatement necessary—and which would have cost the jobs of any CEO and CFO in similar circumstances.

Insurance Regulators. It seems that it had to be the case that gross deficiencies existed in the regulatory examinations of AIG in total, and of its insurance subsidiaries in general. Insurance regulators were present in AIG subsidiaries throughout the years in question to a far greater extent than the external auditors. Even so, regulators could say in their defense that their regulatory authority derives from state insurance laws, many of which are inadequate to allow full regulation of an international company. Also, given the complexity of AIG, how could any regulator have been responsible for examining all of its activities?

The external auditor. What about the responsibility of the external auditor? One might plead both on behalf of and against. On their behalf one could plead in extenuation that Howard Smith no doubt controlled the information available to the external auditors and regulators (which he knew well how to do, from actual experience), insuring that they would not discover accounting improprieties. Smith, after all, knew insurance industry auditing from the auditor's point of view: he was regarded as the leading insurance expert at Coopers and Lybrand ("C&L"), before he left C&L in 1984 to become first VP and Comptroller and later CFO at AIG. Furthermore, in view of his tremendous prestige, the force of his personality, and his reputation for integrity, no one would have dared to contradict him or say anything which implicitly imputed wrongdoing to him.

On the other hand, one might plead against C&L in the first place, that they should have recognized that their independence as regards AIG was potentially compromised, once Smith left to work for AIG. After that point could they guarantee an independent and impartial audit? If not, then would they be bound by the ethics of the profession to walk away from a major client? And yet audit firms have always believed that the movement of their own personnel to clients can only improve ethical levels and financial reporting standards in those companies, because such personnel previously had been formed by the high ethical standards of these firms. It probably would not have occurred to C&L that they could not rely on Smith for honesty in financial reporting at AIG.

Nonetheless, one may wonder how an auditor can insure a thorough and impartial audit given the CFO's control over their access to information. How can an auditor insure such an audit given the perceived prestige and knowledge of the CFO? Is it possible to find members of an engagement team that are capable of going head-to-head against a CFO such as Smith? How can an auditor insure such an audit if there are past ties between the CFO and the audit firm?

Sarbanes-Oxley attempted to address only the last issue, in Section 206, entitled "Conflicts of Interest":

> It shall be unlawful for a registered public accounting firm to perform for an issuer any audit service required by this title, if a chief executive officer, controller, chief financial officer, chief accounting officer, or any person serving in an equivalent position for the issuer, was employed by that registered independent public accounting firm and participated in any capacity in the audit of that issuer during the 1-year period preceding the date of the initiation of the audit.

And yet does this requirement really address the question? It assumes that it would not be a good thing for an auditor to move to a client, because that could promote opportunities for corruption. However, if those opportunities are real, the provision is inadequate, because a one-year cooling off period would clearly not remove the effects of a past association. Moreover, the force of the law could be eluded simply by switching audit firms for the one year period, and then proceeding as before. (Sarbanes-Oxley also requires audit partner rotation every five years. But such rotation can potentially weaken the partners in relation to a prestigious and knowledgeable CFO.) So one might wonder in the end whether a law such as Sarbox 206 can substitute for the auditor's own judgment as to whether it is in a position to provide a quality audit.

Too often the external auditor is accorded all the blame when circumstances of financial reporting improprieties arise, yet, other than one partner in the PNC deal, no audit firm personnel have been implicated, or identified as having been involved in any way, in the origination, advising, or administration of financial improprieties that took place at AIG. In other words, unlike Arthur Andersen (AA), which, as we shall see below, was actually involved with Enron in an advisory role, giving direction as to how to create financial improprieties, AIG's auditors were not. Thus any critique of the external auditor would have to be focused on actual auditing deficiencies. Yet, while it seems that auditing deficiencies must have existed, the facts and circumstances here point primarily to widespread lack of ethical behavior and professionalism among the internal CPAs throughout the AIG organization, to whom we next turn.

Internal accountants and the accounting profession in general. Given the nearly 20 years of evident accounting manipulations at AIG, one needs to consider the responsibility of the hundreds of CPAs who worked for AIG. Each one of these persons, as part of his or her profession, had committed to uphold the highest levels of integrity with respect to presenting economic activity to investors and other third parties. Given that this is so, why were there no whistleblowers—not a single one? Why are there no stories of CPAs who resigned from a lucrative job at AIG because they refused to go along with some existing or suggested unethical practice? Clearly, if accounting ethics and professionalism are to regain their original luster, attention should be focused on improving or creating vehicles for CPAs to enforce proper accounting within these large organizations. One example of this kind of thing, although flawed, would be the incentives for whistleblowers under Dodd-Frank.

Some commentators, after too quickly and too easily placing all the blame on the external auditor, look for radical or even revolutionary change. Justice William O. Douglas once wrote, in a preface to a book by a seasoned critic of the accounting profession (Abraham Briloff), that:

> The author demands an understandably high price of the attesting accountant, who is preparing himself to fulfill this essential role. He expects him to undergo a "ritualistic purging" and to forego the rewards that may be derived from the rendering of management services and the other "peripheral services" that he describes.
>
> The burdens that Mr. Briloff puts upon the profession are substantial, but, as he readily admits, our economic society is in urgent need of this service. If the accounting profession does not respond effectively to the challenges presented, there may be little alternative but to have possibly a new profession fill the breach.

Justice Douglas' speculations about a "new profession" seem as unrealistic as speculations about systems of government other than democracy, about which Winston Churchill famously said: "Many forms of Government have been tried and will be tried in this world of sin and woe. No one pretends that democracy is perfect or all-wise. Indeed, it has been said that democracy is the worst form of government except all those other forms that have been tried from time to time." Some serious issues exist in the current auditing system, but it is certainly better than the alternatives.

The better path would be to strive for a revitalization and renewal of the accounting profession generally. In order to do so, first we need to consider what exactly a profession is, how it differs from a business, and what it meant originally to say that accounting in its foundation was a profession rather than a business. But before taking up that worthy task, in the next few chapters we present and explore some fundamental, background ideas in ethics.

Concluding Thought: On Character, Accounting Ethics, and Some Challenges

After a Continuing Professional Education (CPE) class in which we discussed the accounting woes of AIG, a CPA in the class offered the following remarkable story.

When he first began practicing, he said, he worked in the Manhattan office of then C&L. Because there were over 500 CPAs in the office, he was told that he had to specialize, and he was assigned to insurance company auditing. C&L had just acquired a large firm which specialized in insurance, and they wanted to build up this specialty.

His first engagement was the audit of a small insurance company on Long Island. He filled the trunk of his car with the company's work papers and spent the weekend in his NY apartment pouring over them. What he found in the papers, he said, was simply a repetition of numbers and unrelated conclusions supported by no analysis. When he carried out a proper analysis on his own, he determined that the company was essentially bankrupt and that his firm really needed to issue an "adverse" opinion.

When he reported his conclusions to the audit manager, the manager, after appearing to do some quick calculations on his own, said he did not know what he was talking about and removed him from the audit. This CPA then complained to the partner, explaining his conclusion and reasoning. The partner took the complaint seriously and referred the matter to the actuarial department. The firm's actuaries did a careful re-analysis, which coincided almost exactly with our CPA's judgment. When the partner learned about this, he reinstated the CPA, filed a report to the state insurance examiner, and insisted that an "adverse" opinion be issued.

The CPA telling the story said that for the rest of his career he looked back to this partner's intervention as a model of integrity and high principle.

The name of that partner? Howard I. Smith, the future CFO of AIG.

This story is an example of the sorts of actions and interventions that won Smith a reputation for integrity at C&L. The story is highly relevant, as well as fascinating, because it tends to answer one question about C&L's auditing of AIG. Arguably the most important decision an auditor makes concerns the integrity and competence of management. Howard Smith's move to AIG would have been perceived by other professionals in the firm as a huge reduction in the possibility of irregularities at AIG, because of Smith's impeccable reputation. It has long been one of the most difficult challenges for auditing firms to observe objectively the actions of a former colleague, when that colleague had been known as one of that firm's leaders in the areas of competence and integrity.

Recommended additional reading:

The People of the State of New York v. Marsh & McLennan Companies, Inc., et al., Index No. 04-403342

Securities and Exchange Commission v. Brightpoint, Inc., American International Group, Inc., Phillip Bounsall, John Delaney and Timothy Harcharik (S.D.N.Y. Civ. 03 CV 7045 (HB)

Securities and Exchange Commission v. American International Group, Inc., Civil Action No. 1:04CV02070 (GK)(D.D.C. filed November 30, 2004)

AIG 10-K filing for 2004

Securities and Exchange Commission v. General Re Corporation, Civil Action No. 10 Civ 458 (S.D.N.Y.)

Securities and Exchange Commission v. Ronald Ferguson, Elizabeth Monrad, Robert Graham, Christopher Garand, and Christan Milton, Case No. 06 Civ 0778 (S.D.N.Y.)

PART II

ETHICS FOR ACCOUNTANTS

The Virtues

4

"The function of the public accountant in the community is to help promote the confidence necessary for the smooth running of our business economy; confidence between borrower and lender, between debtor and creditor, between management and stockholders, and between the buyer and seller of securities."
–Samuel Broad

In this chapter we change gears significantly. In the preceding chapters, we looked in much detail at particular scandals associated with AIG and the culture of accounting corruption within that company. We did so to put before you, the reader, a very clear example of a failure in accounting ethics. But also the example shows the importance of accounting ethics. Given the complexity and interdependence of the modern financial system, and the shortcomings inherent in any scheme of regulation, accounting ethics has become so important that arguably the soundness of the world's financial system depends upon it.

Of course, the example raises the question, *What is accounting ethics?*, which in turn raises the question, *What is ethics?* We need to understand ethics generally, and get clear about its central concepts, before we can get clear about accounting ethics. Professional ethics of any kind depends upon ethics in general. This dependence of the specialized upon the general and more fundamental used to be widely acknowledged and understood. This dependence was an important reason why it was held that all students should receive a good generalist education. At the founding of the profession, it was thought for these reasons that students of accounting, like those preparing for any other profession, need a good generalist education. So in this chapter we will supply some of the background which would likely have been supplied by a good generalist education and which is necessary for understanding the more applied material presented later in this book.

Introduction: Four Aspects of Ethics

Ethics involves the evaluation of actions. Suppose someone does something: he acts. We can analyze this action into four aspects or stages:

past influences→character→the nature of the act itself→effects of the act

A full understanding of his act will obviously need to take into account all four of these aspects or stages. Furthermore, if the agent's act is to be reasonable and "right," all four of these aspects have to be in some way correct, and the act needs to be related to them correctly.

Various systems of ethics have developed from a kind of reductionism which makes only one of these aspects paramount and tries to explain the significance of the other three in terms of it. For example, utilitarianism is the view that only the effects of an action are relevant for evaluating it. For utilitarianism, the act itself, the agent's character, and past occurrences or traditions bearing upon the act are irrelevant except insofar as they make a difference for the action's effects. On this view, for instance, an accountant would justifiably commit fraud if doing so led to the best consequences. Other theories which are legalistic in character ("Kantianism" would be an example, also what is called "deontology") hold that only the intrinsic character of the action is relevant to evaluating it: consequences do not matter, and neither do traditions or the agent's character. On this view one should always follow what one regards as the correct rule, whatever the consequences. Still other theories make the agent's character paramount: these are called "virtue" theories or "virtue-based" theories. The fourth alternative, the view that only traditions and past influences matter in the evaluation of an action, is a possible view, but it is rarely defended by ethicists, perhaps because on this view ethicists would have little chance of being the important authorities on ethics!

We aim to avoid any sort of reductionism in this book. We believe that, in accounting ethics as in ethics in general, all four of these aspects potentially enter into the evaluation of an action. However, we do put a good deal of emphasis on a practitioner's character, for reasons explained in the Introduction above. We also regard this emphasis as a corrective to an unfortunate tendency in professional ethics for accountants in recent years. The founders of the profession of accountancy never failed to draw attention to the importance of a practitioner's character. In a word, they believed in the priority of persons over rules and regulations. Yet in recent years this aspect of accounting ethics has received little or no attention.

Our particular emphasis on character corresponds to a similar development in philosophy over the past decades, where, on account of the writings of Elizabeth Anscombe, particularly her essay, "Modern Moral Philosophy," and Alasdair MacIntyre's important book, *After Virtue*, there has been a resurgence of interest across disciplines in the classical theory of the virtues.

Key Concepts

The main concepts involving character and virtue are contained in the following thesis, which may be called "The Fundamental Thesis concerning the Virtues":

> A good thing (or person) of a certain kind is that which has the virtues needed in order to carry out its distinctive work.

The thesis links the terms "good" and "virtue" to the more fundamental notion of "distinctive work," so let us look at each of these.

Distinctive work. The distinctive work of a kind of thing may be defined as follows:

> The distinctive work (of a kind of thing): the good which that kind of thing alone can achieve, or which it can achieve better than anything else.

Plato was the first philosopher to identify and define the notion of "distinctive work," in book I of the famous dialogue, the *Republic*. The Greek term for "distinctive work" is *ergon*, which also provides the root for the unit of work in modern physics, the "erg." *Ergon* is also the basis for our word, "ergonomics," which means the study of making human effort or work more efficient. *Ergon* is sometimes translated as "function," "role," "job," "task," or "characteristic work." Only kinds of things have an *ergon*; an individual has an *ergon* through being a member of a kind. The reason is that an *ergon* is a niche or slot into which something fits, and any individual which can fit into that niche is, to that extent, equivalent with any other.

As an example, consider a tool chest which contains a Phillips-tip screwdriver and a hammer. The hammer cannot be used to screw in Phillips-head screws. Only the screwdriver can do that: that is its *ergon* or "distinctive work." The distinctive work of a Phillips-tip screwdriver is to screw in Phillips-head screws. Similarly, although someone might use any heavy tool to bang in a nail—if the handle of a screwdriver is heavy, it can do the job—still, the hammer does that job better than anything else. The *ergon* or "distinctive work" of a hammer is to hammer in nails. Again, if you open a drawer in a kitchen and see a whisk and a spatula, you see immediately that the whisk is for whipping, and the spatula for getting under something and flipping it over. You could not possibly whip cream with a spatula or flip eggs with a whisk. Each implement has its own *ergon* or "distinctive work," which each alone can do or can do far better than anything else.

Living things as well as inanimate tools may have a distinctive work, for instance, as playing a role in a larger system. The distinctive work of plants, within the various ecosystems of the earth, is to produce oxygen through photosynthesis. Likewise, human beings obviously have various types of acquired "distinctive work," which depend upon their being trained for or appointed to a particular role or job: for example, the distinctive work of a musician is to play music; that of a carpenter is to make things out of wood.

Virtue. Virtue may be defined as follows:

> The virtue of a kind of thing is an enduring trait which places it in good condition
> and enables it to carry out its distinctive work well.

The word "virtue" represents what the classical philosophers meant by the Greek term *aretê* and the Latin term *virtus*. Classically, a virtue is a strength or excellence. A virtue strengthens, improves, and perfects that which has it. This meaning is evident in the Latin term, which comes from the word for "man," *vir*. In Latin, a virtue is literally the same as "manliness." (Compare the English word, *virility*.)

Nowadays we often think of virtues negatively, as keeping people from doing things which people who lack virtue would do. But classically virtues were thought of positively, as enabling someone to achieve things which others without the virtues could not do. Courage would be a clear example: only someone who has courage will want to climb mountains or pursue whitewater rafting. Again, nowadays, if we use the word "virtue" at all, we tend to use it only in moral contexts (although this is not entirely true—think of the phrase, "in virtue of"), but classically the word for virtue would be applied to any excellence or strength of anything. An excellence of an inanimate object or an animal would be called a virtue.

Virtues are relative to the distinctive work of a person, animal, or thing. The distinctive work of a knife is to cut. What counts as a virtue for a knife is relative to this distinctive work. A virtue of a knife would be a trait that placed it in good condition and enabled it to cut well. Sharpness, then, is a virtue in a knife. Again, the distinctive work of a hammer is to hammer nails. What counts as a virtue in a knife is relative to this distinctive work. A hammer, then, needs to have a good handle, a flat striking surface, and weighty head. These are all "virtues" in a hammer because they are traits the possession of which enables a hammer to carry out its distinctive work well. What counts as a virtue relative to one kind of distinctive work might be irrelevant or a hindrance to something with some other distinctive work. Sharpness is a virtue in a knife, but if a screwdriver had a sharp blade, it would be dangerous, as you might cut yourself with it, and furthermore the tip would not be sturdy and would probably chip or crack. Again, thick fingers and calloused hands might be virtues for the hands of a carpenter but a hindrance for a violinist.

Any virtue has an opposite, namely, a vice. A vice puts something in bad condition and keeps it from carrying out its distinctive work well. On this definition, dullness is a "vice" in a knife. A slippery handle would be a "vice" in a hammer. Persistent distractedness would be a "vice" in a musician, who needs to pay attention and keep time.

Good. When something has all of the virtues it needs to achieve its distinctive work well, and it has no "vitiating" vices, then we call it "good." Since goodness is a sort of perfection, a thing really needs to have all of the relevant virtues to be accounted as good. A single vice can nullify and disqualify it from being good. Indeed, its other virtues can become "dangerous" if joined to a vice. (Consider the old maxim: "The corruption of the best is the worst.") A hammer with a solid, heavy head but slippery handle is more dangerous than a light-weight hammer with an insubstantial striking head.

Note that on this classical way of defining goodness, goodness is not something subjective. Goodness is also not a matter of feelings or preferences. In cases in which there is a fact of the matter as to what the distinctive work of something is, then there is a fact of the matter as to what traits that thing should have in order to do that work well, and then there is a fact of the matter as to whether a thing of that kind meets those criteria and truly is good in its kind. (Often only an expert can say what the distinctive work of a thing is: consider how the mechanic at an auto repair shop can tell you exactly what the job is of an unusual looking tool, but a non mechanic would not have a clue.)

This completes our introduction and definition of the fundamental terms, "distinctive work," "virtue," and "good." (It is useful for the student to memorize those definitions and be able to give additional, pertinent examples of each, which clarify those definitions.)

Application to Human Life

Classical philosophers were most interested in the application of these concepts to human life as a whole, in order to determine what happiness is for us. That is not our main concern, of course; our main concern here is obviously with clarifying accounting ethics. Nonetheless, there is an important relationship between the classical account of human happiness and accounting ethics. Also, by looking briefly at that account, we will get better acquainted with the key concepts just introduced.

If the aforementioned concepts are to be applied to human life, the first question to consider is whether a human being has a distinctive task. We tend to find this suggestion problematic, but in the classical world it was regarded as obvious that human beings were set apart from the rest of the world by having intelligence, and so their "job" in life was to use that intelligence well. Think of it as like natural talents. In a family, one child may have an evident musical talent, another an athletic talent, and so on. We can "spot" this talent early on, and then we conclude that the child would do well by developing and grooming that talent. Similarly, classical philosophers looked at the "family" of living things on the face of the earth and thought that they could "spot" that human beings had a definite talent for reasoning which the other animals lacked—after all, only the human beings were writing philosophy books and even wondering about this sort of thing anyway!

Furthermore, classical thinkers viewed the world as an admirably balanced and ordered system: that is why they called it a "cosmos," which means literally "lovely arrangement." So it seemed natural to them that no species would even exist in such a system unless it had a role to play. Think of this in the way you might take the case off of a computer and see some kind of unit or gadget inside: you would be certain that it had a purpose, even if you did not know what that purpose was, because you believe that the computer is a highly ordered arrangement.

We defined a distinctive task as that which that thing alone can do, or which it can do better than anything else, and it certainly looks to be the case that "acting rationally" is something that only human beings can do.

If action for us were only a matter of thinking—suppose we were disembodied minds, and the only thing we could do was to think—then the only virtues for us would be the "intellectual virtues," that is, those commonly recognized traits which help us to discover the truth about the world and to plan effectively. These traits would include such things as: broad knowledge; persistence in problem-solving;

flexibility; methodical work; critical exactness; insight; resourcefulness; and effective expression. However, we are not disembodied minds. Usually we need to act while experiencing motives and desires which we seem to share with non-rational animals—such as hunger and thirst, sexual desire, weariness, fear and rage. Furthermore, we are affected by other motives which, even if the other animals do not have them, these motives at least seem to be either non-rational or prone to becoming irrational, such as desires for security, desires to dominate over others, desires for possessions, and desires to be paid attention to and get recognized.

We cannot do well at acting rationally (our distinctive work) while being affected by those sorts of desires and drives, unless we have acquired traits which enable us to rationalize and control them. For example, someone without courage will simply panic through fear and run away when faced with serious danger, which typically is highly unreasonable. In contrast, someone with the virtue of courage will act coolly and do "what needs to be done," even if he sees the danger and experiences strong emotions of fear. Courage is a trait which makes our fears rational and enables us to control them.

Suppose someone acquired all of the virtues necessary for doing well at acting rationally, in all the different contexts of human life, and he had no vices. Then, by the definition given above of "good," he or she would be a good human being.

Classical philosophers, especially Aristotle, then used this realization to explain what happiness was for a human being. Their approach to happiness was quite different from our own. We tend to use the word "happiness" to mean a good mood or feeling, as in "I'm feeling happy today." But Aristotle argued that happiness was a type of activity and an achievement, rather than a feeling. (Something akin to this view survives today when we say things such as "Happiness is playing golf": we are identifying happiness with an activity, not a mere feeling.)

Among classical philosophers such as Aristotle, happiness was a term indicating success: to have lived a happy life was the same as having been a success at human life. What could count as success at living a human life? Surely, carrying out well the distinctive work of a human being. But that is to do well at acting reasonably, and, as we have seen, the virtues are necessary for that. Thus, for classical philosophers such as Aristotle, happiness would be a matter of acquiring the human virtues, and becoming good, and then putting them into practice over the course of one's life. Happiness for them was neither more nor less than that: a life well lived, in which the distinctive "talents" of a human being were exemplified and consistently expressed in one's actions.

On this classical account, happiness is a difficult accomplishment. Happiness requires as much dedication and attention as success in a sport or at playing a musical instrument. It requires many years of training, followed by years of successful practice. But just as important as what happiness is, is what it is not. Happiness is not something that happens to us, but something we do and achieve, and so it cannot be identified with pleasures and comforts. Happiness is not a matter of wealth, since wealth is a means to an end, not an end. Happiness is not a matter of power and influence, since what matters is whether these are used well, which is a matter of virtue. Happiness is not a matter of honors and distinction, because these are worthless unless they are tendered for the right things and on the right reasons, but only virtuous achievement is ultimately deserving of honor.

These last observations point to the harmony between this classical approach and accounting ethics. Obviously, someone who took happiness to consist in piling up wealth would prefer wealth over virtuous action, whenever there was a conflict between the two. In contrast, someone who regarded happiness simply as the practice of virtuous action would regard exemplary professionalism in accounting as actually constitutive of his ultimate good.

The Cardinal Virtues

Two important ideas that can serve to consolidate one's grasp of this classical theory of the virtues are the doctrine of the Cardinal Virtues, and the doctrine of the Mean. We shall discuss these two ideas in this section and the next.

The phrase "cardinal virtues" comes from the Latin word for "hinge," *cardo*. The term is used on the grounds that there are four human virtues which are so important that all other virtues hinge on them. Each cardinal virtue is like a tree trunk from which other, lesser virtues spring. Plato was the first philosopher to give a list of four main virtues, which are these:

> courage (or fortitude, bravery, valor)
> moderation (or temperance, self-mastery)
> justice (or fairness, equal dealing, lawfulness)
> prudence (or practical wisdom)

Although Plato's list quickly became standard, the label itself, "cardinal virtues" was not coined until the 5th century A.D. by Ambrose of Milan. Furthermore, Plato simply gave the list, but it was left to later thinkers to explain why these virtues are "hinge" virtues.

The cardinal virtues were later explained to be cardinal because each represented the way in which an important center of human psychological life was rendered able to "do well in acting reasonably." On this view, courage (fortitude, bravery, valor) is specifically the virtue of the "fight or flight" center of the human soul. It concerns those motives that arise when we are faced by a challenge or threat. We have a mixed response to frightening things. Fear makes us want to run away. But sometimes we become emboldened and want to eliminate the threat through an attack. Courage is the virtue that enables us to do the right thing when we are dealing with fears and the impulse to attack. Courage is primarily concerned with threats to our bodily integrity: valor in war is the greatest example of courage. Yet we also face challenges to courage that come from intangibles. For example, an accountant who risks losing his job when he does not go along with a fraudulent accounting treatment definitely has to have courage.

Moderation (temperance, self-mastery) is the virtue that enables us to deal with desires that surround the fundamentally animal impulses for food, drink, and sex. Often these are a craving for comfort, which is sometimes associated with a desire for emotional comfort in particular: as when someone consumes a half-gallon of ice cream out of loneliness or sadness. Sometimes they are desires to avoid discomfort or inconvenience. What we call "luxuries" often play to this aspect of ours which wants complete comfort and does not like to put up with any discomfort. Moderation is important for any endeavor and in every walk of life, because a person who lacks moderation will lack self-discipline and is vulnerable to being drawn off his path. Tiger Woods has provided an unfortunate example of how a lack of moderation can threaten to undermine and destroy the career of even the most dedicated professional. Accountants have had their careers ruined in similar ways. Lack of moderation implies a diminution in our self-control and therefore our freedom, the extreme example of which is an addiction.

Justice (fairness, equal dealing, lawfulness) is a virtue involving that center of our psychology where we formulate and embrace ideals. When someone in his relations with others formulates and embraces the correct ideal of equality, and does so habitually, as a kind of second nature, and with a solid persistence, then he may be said to have the virtue of justice. The persistent embrace of the ideal is said to be a matter of what he "wills." Justice pertains to a person's will, in the same way that moderation pertains to his animal appetites, and courage to his "fight or flight" responses. The relevant equality is typically what is called "proportional" rather than "arithmetic" equality. Proportional equality is when amounts are awarded in relation to inputs ("merit"), so that although the amounts are absolutely considered different, in relation to the inputs they are equal. For example, if one person puts in 60% of a business operation and another puts in 40%, then justice would dictate that the profits be split in the same proportion. Such an allotment would be an "equal" allotment, even though one person will get half as much again as the other. Usually a strictly equal allotment will be a sign of injustice rather than justice, because it hardly ever happens that inputs ("merit") are the same. Justice is related to lawfulness, because the law also will typically assign benefits and burdens in proportion to merit. It is obvious that people find it difficult to "will" what is just, when that result comes into conflict with their own interests. Very few people are happy to accept being personally disadvantaged for the sake of an ideal of equality, and yet someone who had the virtue of justice would do so without hesitation and as a matter of course. A great example of justice is the story of how the young Abraham Lincoln, when he was working as a shop clerk, walked miles out of his way to return the money to a customer who had accidentally overpaid for some merchandise in the shop.

Finally, prudence is an intellectual virtue by which we see what goods and principles (or "values") are important in human life, and how they should be ranked. Prudence also recognizes when those goods and principles are at stake in any decision we have to make. It succeeds in honoring them correctly, and then it formulates a decision about what is to be done, giving as it were a "command" which our emotions and desires will come to conform to, so long as we have the other cardinal virtues. One may draw a distinction between enduring, occasional, and particular judgments of prudence. Enduring judgments are those that are true whatever the circumstances, such as "honesty is the best policy" or "never steal." Occasional judgments are rules of thumb which come into play in selected circumstances only and are the kinds of judgments that are encapsulated in proverbs and rules of thumb, such as "penny wise and pound foolish" or "make hay while the sun shines." Particular judgments are decisions about what should be done here and now. We learn prudence largely by being mentored and through imitation, which is why histories and good biographies of eminent men and women are highly valuable for acquiring prudence.

So the cardinal virtues are courage, moderation, justice, and prudence.

The Mean

As was said, we are not disembodied minds, and typically we need to act in circumstances in which our initially non-rational, and sometime animal-like, desires and motives come into play. That is why, we said, it is not enough to have the virtues pertaining to the intelligence alone (such as accuracy and being methodical), but we also need virtues that "give rational shape" to those desires and motives, as courage and moderation do. Thus a distinction has traditionally been drawn between virtues of thinking, or "intellectual virtues," and virtues of character, or "moral virtues."

When we are in circumstances in which a moral virtue such as courage or moderation would come into play, there is a way in which one should ideally act in those circumstances. For example, an accountant asked to do something fraudulent but threatened with the loss of his job should ideally refuse to do so and stand firm. But people's emotions can get the best of them and tip them in one direction or another. Emotions frequently tip us in one direction by altering our perceptions of a situation. For example, someone who is walking past a cemetery on a very dark night, and is feeling a great deal of fear, will misperceive harmless sights and sounds as frightening threats. At other times emotions cause us to rationalize a course of action which our better self knows is not correct. Or sometimes emotions even cause us to act "irrationally" altogether, as when someone, as we say, "flies off the handle," or "flies into a rage," or "panics and runs."

There are usually two ways of getting tipped away from the right way of acting through our desires and emotions. One way takes us too far, and another way makes us fall short—although typically one such way is the more common mistake and the one we need to struggle against the most. For example, most of us in general fear things more than we should. We overestimate a danger and see "specters in the dark" when there are not any. Anxiety is a great example of this: anxiety, which is so widespread, is exactly a matter of having too much fear, since anxiety is fear when we do not even recognize or know the source. But although fearing things too much is the more common error, sometimes we go astray in the opposite direction. People can be complacent about troubles that threaten them. They can become "apathetic."

Or consider, as another example, the desires with which moderation is concerned: desires for food, drink, sex, and comfort. Most people go too far in enjoying these things and want them too much. We are just as much prone to overeating as we are prone to feeling anxious. Very few of us eat no more than we should at a meal. But here too it is possible to want these things too little. Someone who in the prime of life had no libido would be like that. Likewise, people who are sad or grieving sometimes care less for the pleasures of food than they reasonably should.

Aristotle noticed that because a desire can vary in degree, it can make us go astray in two different ways, either by being inappropriately strong, or by being inappropriately weak, and that therefore there are two ways of going astray for every moral virtue. These ways tend to be opposed to each other. For example, the person whose zest for the pleasures of the table is depressed will tend to act in ways that are contrary to the person whose appetite is over-stimulated. Likewise, the person whose fear is exaggerated will tend to act in ways that are contrary to the person who is apathetic and complacent. If someone gets hardened in one of these ways of going astray, so that it becomes habitual for him to act in ways corresponding to his excessive or deficient motivation, then he will have a "vice." A vice is a bad trait corresponding to a virtue which is a good trait. Thus, Aristotle pointed out, there are two vices for each virtue. One vice, the vice of excess, is such that those who have it will habitually go too far in their motivation. Another vice, the vice of defect, is such that those who have it will habitually not go far enough. As these two vices are opposed, the virtue occupies a kind of intermediate position between them. This is Aristotle's famous doctrine of virtue as a "mean."

On this view, to act virtuously is a matter of hitting that right and appropriate intermediate place between two extremes. To say that one should do what is intermediate, in this sense, is the same as to say "nothing in excess," because a deficiency can always be described as an excess of restraint or caution: for example, the person who has the depressed zest for the pleasures of the table may be described as going to excess in abstaining.

It is hard to find and achieve the mean, because our emotions affect our perceptions. Someone who tends to fear things too much will actually perceive them as being more fearful than they are, so his fear will seem to him to be perfectly appropriate. He will not be aware that his fear is excessive. Also, we often use our desires to estimate the appropriateness of our actions. For example, most people eat until they are no longer hungry. That is, they use their hunger for food as a guide to how much food they should eat. Hence, if their desire for food is too strong, they will eat too much. That is why when people begin to diet, and start eating no more than they should, they usually have to endure days or weeks of feeling hungry, until their desire eventually adjusts to their new regimen. To go on a diet implies "calorie counting," that is, using an objective standard to determine how much one should eat, rather than relying on one's subjective feelings of hunger. So a variety of techniques are necessary in dealing with our desires and achieving the mean. We have to know our bad tendencies and correct for them. We have to rely on the example of good people similar to us. We have to use objective standards as much as possible.

For these and other reasons, Aristotle and the great classical philosophers taught that the moral virtues depend upon the virtue of prudence (or "practical wisdom"). Prudence enables us to make such estimations well. At the same time, prudence depends upon the moral virtues, because if someone develops a vice, he loses his sense of what things are truly important in life. The virtues of courage, moderation, and justice depend upon prudence for a refinement of their target, and, in turn, prudence relies on those virtues for its soundness and accuracy of estimation. We may call this relationship "the mutual dependence of prudence and the moral virtues."

Acquiring the Virtues

We distinguished between intellectual and moral virtues: these different types of virtues are acquired in different ways. Prudence is acquired first by obedience, that is, by obeying legitimate, prudent authority, especially one's parents. It is unfashionable to emphasize obedience today, and yet obedience is crucially important. By participating in authority as being subject to it, a person grows to appreciate the virtues that should be shown in authority when someone is actually wielding authority. Only someone who has been a good follower can become a good leader. A second way of acquiring prudence, as we said, is by studying examples of good prudential judgment. Since good prudential judgment is manifested in particular facts and circumstances, the study of histories and biographies proves to be particularly helpful for the acquisition of prudence. Third, as a person approaches maturity, his prudence needs to be matured and refined through direct instruction, adapted to the matter at hand, as this book aims to do in its limited way.

Note that there is an analogy between prudence and good judgment in any endeavor. Consider sports. An athlete's first way of acquiring good judgment is by "obedience" to a coach. A second way is the study of how top athletes respond in particular challenges or contests. A third way is by particular study adapted to the athlete's particular sport. Prudence is good judgment.

Prudence issues in judgments, which, as we said, are either "enduring," "occasional," or "particular." Enduring judgments are based on, or consist in, what are sometimes called "first principles of practical reason." All reasoning has to begin from starting points. This is true of practical reasoning as well as scientific or mathematical reasoning. Just as mathematical reasoning has its axioms, so practical reasoning has its first principles. The Golden Rule is an example of a basic principle of practical reasoning: "Do unto others as you would have them do unto you." We "see" the truth of such principles and find it almost impossible to deny them in practice. Another such principle is "do not steal": Augustine pointed out that even the thief who has devoted his life to stealing will object if someone tries to take something from him without his consent, showing that, despite his lifestyle, he never really succeeds in rejecting that fundamental principle. Obviously these "first principles of practical reasoning" do not need to be taught, and cannot be—after all, they are first principles. Yet they can be reinforced. If we could prove them, then they would not be first principles. Yet we can, however, arrive at an understanding that there must at least be some first principles of that sort. A particularly good argument for that conclusion is found in *The Abolition of Man* by C.S. Lewis. But the application of basic principles to particular cases can be taught, as is seen in the "case method."

Note that the case method, although valuable, is limited. The case method is valuable for getting clear about the application of correct, general principles. It can also help us become clear about what general principles we already implicitly hold. But it cannot tell us which general principles are correct.

The word "conscience" is another way of describing the virtue of prudence. Conscience comprises both (1) our implicit acceptance of those niggling "first principles of practical reason" and (2) any judgments that we reach about the application of these principles to particular cases. What is called "conscience" is not an autonomous or infallible source of ethical discernment. Someone's conscience can be either sound or unsound. Someone's conscience may be either well-informed or badly formed. Anyone who lacks the virtue of prudence is guaranteed to have a badly formed conscience. It is true that a person must always follow the dictates of his conscience—if they truly are the holdings of his conscience, and not simply a strong emotion or subconscious irrational preference. A person must always follow his conscience, because he has no higher internal guide than that. To act against one's conscience is always wrong. And yet, for all that, a person is not blameless simply because he follows his conscience. His conscience may be badly formed, and he may be responsible for that. As the moralists have said: "An erring conscience must be followed, but an erring conscience does not excuse." Following one's conscience is a necessary but not sufficient condition of acting blamelessly.

In contrast to intellectual virtues such as knowledge and prudence, moral virtues such as courage, moderation, and justice, are not acquired by instruction but by putting them into practice. In this respect they are similar to any practical skill or ability, say, playing the trumpet. When someone learns to play the trumpet, he begins with easy things and progresses to more difficult things. He has to listen to what his teacher says and follow that, because it takes a long while for him to develop an "ear" for it himself. Each and every time he picks up his instrument he needs to try to make a good sound, because otherwise he will only become more entrenched in his bad habits. He will find practicing unpleasant for many years and begin to enjoy it only once he becomes skillful. His skill is elicited and increased by finding the right groups to join, where he can find both support and competition. It is not possible to become really good at the trumpet without progressing to ever more skilled ensembles.

Each of the same principles applies to the development of the moral virtues, which we will illustrate with a list:

1. It is necessary to begin with small and easy challenges, for example, being brave when confronted by a dog, and then progress to difficult challenges, such as being brave when confronted by enemy gunfire.

2. At the beginning, the development of moral virtue is a matter of following what a good authority tells you, such as a parent, teacher, or coach.

3. Each and every time you face a circumstance in which a moral virtue comes into play, you need to the best of your ability to do the right thing— that is one reason why it is important to "examine one's conscience" at the end of each day. You need to identify and confirm whether you have acted to the best of your ability.

4. Acting virtuously will often be irksome as one is growing up, until one attains a mature grasp of the virtue. After that, virtuous action will actually often be pleasant, while acting contrary to that virtue will seem noxious and repulsive.

5. Finding the right friends is essential for acquiring virtue. As we mature, acting virtuously becomes less a matter of following rules set down by authorities and more a matter of doing what everyone else finds natural to do in one's peer group. Good friends support and inspire one another to act better than each would have acted apart from that group. Having even one friend who supports us can make the difference between doing the right thing and failing to do it.

The Virtues of an Accountant—Inductively Considered

Recall the Fundamental Thesis about the Virtues, namely, "A good thing (or person) of a certain kind is that which has the virtues needed in order to carry out its distinctive work." We formulated this thesis at first as regards inanimate objects, because tools such as knives and hammers are made to have a distinctive work. They provide very clear examples of the thesis. But, as we saw, the thesis applies analogously to persons.

The acquired, distinctive work of a person is the role that that person plays, as a member of some group which makes a distinctive contribution to society. The distinctive work of a physician is to heal and alleviate physical pain. The distinctive work of a policeman is to enforce public order. The distinctive work of a plumber is to install and maintain plumbing in buildings.

What is the distinctive work of a member of the accounting profession? Accountants engage in all kinds of tasks, such as helping with tax returns; financial advising; assistance in the management of a company; and so on. Which of these is accountancy's distinctive work? We will discuss this question more fully below, when we discuss accounting as a profession. But it is possible to answer the question adequately now by appeal to the definition of "distinctive work." Recall that definition: the distinctive work of a thing is what that alone can do, or can do better than anything else. Tax returns can be done equally well, or better, by commercial tax preparers. Financial planning may be done equally well, or better, by trained financial planners. Financial management may be carried out equally well, or better, by savvy CFOs who are not CPAs. The one task which seems to belong to the accounting professional alone is "attest" work in the broadest sense and original sense of that term,[6] where an accountant formulates and verifies an accurate representation of the results of operations and financial position of a company, as found in the financial statements of that company. An accountant is something like a financial truth-teller, where part of the job of telling the truth is grasping well the financial reality which is being represented and finding the best terms for representing it.

Thus, we can speak of the "virtues" of an accountant relative to this distinctive work. Recall the definition of a virtue, as a trait which puts something in a good

---

[6] The original meaning of "attest," as a common dictionary definition has it, is to "authenticate, affirm to be true, genuine, or correct, as in an official capacity."

condition and enables it to achieve its distinctive work well. Thus, we may define the virtues of an accountant as follows:

> The virtues of an accountant *qua* accountant are those traits, which are so ingrained that they have the aspect of second nature to the practitioner, which make an accountant a good professional and enable him or her to carry out attest or truth-telling work well (in the broadest and original sense of that term).

We say "*qua* accountant" in the above definition, because we are primarily interested in the virtues that pertain to an accountant in his or her acquired role as an accounting professional engaged in attest or truth-telling work, not the virtues which pertain to him or her simply as being a human being, which are the same for an accountant as for everyone else. Of course an accountant should have all of those human virtues as well. As we said in the Very Brief Introduction above, someone who lacked moderation would be vulnerable to getting drawn off the path of dedicated professionalism. Again, someone who lacked basic justice and did things like steal could hardly be a good worker, never mind a good professional. Similarly, anyone who was imprudent would constantly be making foolish decisions about his life (resulting in a dysfunctional family life, wrecked friendships, or finances in ruins) which would minimally prove a big distraction to his professional life.

So how can we identify the specific virtues needed by an accounting professional to carry out attest or truth-telling work well? One way to do so is to approach the question "inductively," by looking at the list of traits which is offered by authorities in accounting who have cared about such things. As mentioned, in recent years not much attention has been given to this question of the character of accountants. Hence, one would need to go back to the founders of modern accountancy to find such statements. When one does so, one finds that, again and again, the same traits get mentioned:

> integrity
> pride
> tenacity in seeking the truth
> tenacity in stating the truth
> stubbornness
> simplicity

The list is evident in sample affirmations taken from the founders of modern accounting, such as those which follow (where the pertinent words and phrases are placed in bold):

"Questions and cross-questionings, of owners, of stockholders, of directors, of presidents, are often to be answered as supplementary to the report; the answer must be intelligent, ready, and never resentful. These gentlemen desire truth and nothing else; **it belongs to the spirit of professional Accountancy to seek out and reveal to them the truth.**"— Charles Waldo Haskins[7]

"[T]he ideal conception of its true mission by the profession itself—a conception from within and not dependent upon extraneous exigencies— places Accountancy far outside the pale of all ordinary callings, and sets it upon a platform of its own as a learned profession, self-impelled to culture, to moral enlargement, and to scientific attainment; it lays a basis of confidence for every business enterprise that in professional Accountancy there is **a self-centered soul of economic truth.**"—Charles Waldo Haskins[8]

"1. The written records, the accounts of business transactions, in a vast number of cases were imperfectly, inaccurately or fraudulently stated. And many still are. Consequently **the public accountant's first duty was to *fight figures.***

2. It is astounding how many relevant figures may be omitted from records of business transactions, how many debits find their way to the credit side of ledgers, and how many debits are entirely omitted—so that **public accountants must *find facts.***

3. The third compelling reason for the employment of public accountants, and much the most important, is his duty, after fighting the figures and finding the facts, **to assemble the figures and the facts and to *tell the***

---

[7] Haskins, C.W.: 1904, *Business Education and Accountancy* (Harper & Brothers Publishers, New York and London), pp. 163-4.

[8] Ibid., p. 165.

truth **about them, with clarity, conciseness and intelligence** so that he who runs may read."—Robert H. Montgomery[9]

"Eternal vigilance is the price of accounting as well as of liberty. And so I see very little change from year to year in the more important attributes of the public accountant. For more than 48 of the 50 years under review I have intimately known the leaders of the profession in this country and in England and Scotland. Then, they were **fearless seekers for the truth**. Fifty years ago, poor as they were, no power on earth could have swerved them from their search. Nearly fifty years later, as I look into the faces of my brothers in our profession from far and near, from the ends of the earth, I see in these new faces **the same proud determination, the same courage, the same stubbornness**, the same men I saw nearly fifty years ago. And to those who are not here I extend a grateful prayer. I don't want to have anything to do with supermen. I want men in the profession with **simple minds and indomitable courage to seek and tell the truth**."—Robert H. Montgomery[10]

The Virtues of an Accountant—Deductively Considered

The other approach is to figure out, or deduce, the virtues of an accountant from what we know about the virtues beforehand. There are two ways of doing so. The first is to consider the distinctive work of an accountant and reason about what traits would be needed in someone, for him or her to carry out that distinctive work well. We said that the accountant's distinctive work is attesting (in the broadest and original sense). But to attest is to formulate and declare the truth, and in order to formulate and declare the truth, one must first find it (tenacity in seeking and stating the truth). In this work of finding and declaring the truth, one will need to be able to resist threats and attempts to intimidate (stubbornness, courage) and not be vulnerable to manipulation because of one's own financial attachments or desire for money (simplicity). A big aid in doing so will be a recognition of one's own status as a professional (pride) and a commitment to abiding by the standards of

---

[9] Montgomery, R.H.: 1937, "Report of the President: What Have We Done, and How?" (American Institute of Accountants, Year 1937), p. 316.

[10] Ibid., p. 317.

one's profession (integrity). So the same list may be arrived at in this way, deductively, as became apparent inductively.

The other way of figuring out the virtues deductively is to use the cardinal virtues as a pattern. We said that the cardinal virtues are the main traits that someone will need to succeed at his "distinctive work" as a human being. But all human work is a kind of specification of our distinctive work as human beings. Each position in society, each role we can assume, involves our taking our distinctively human talents and good traits, and applying them to some specialized task. For example, if each human being needs to be prudent in order to succeed at living a distinctively human life well, people in different roles will need different kinds of prudence: there is a kind of prudence which is needed in leading a household well; another necessary for leading a business well; another necessary for governing a town, state, or the Federal government well; and so on. Again, everyone needs courage in order to stand firm in the midst of threats, but courage will take different forms in different walks of life: the courage needed in a firefighter is one thing, and that of a physician is something else, and so on.

Continuing along these lines, we reason that the virtues of an accountant will be specifications of the cardinal virtues—good traits which are analogous to the cardinal virtues and which match the specific requirements and difficulties of the work of an accountant. Proceeding in this way, we arrive at almost the same list:

Justice. The accountant's tenacity in finding and declaring the truth is the analogue of the cardinal virtue of justice. Justice is a fair distribution, in which what is allotted corresponds to that which merits it. (Justice involves "rendering to each his due.") Similarly, a true statement in an accountant's accounting is like a just distribution. It involves "calling a spade a spade." For example, in auditing work the financials of some companies *deserve* an unqualified opinion, others do not. In internal accounting, this transaction *deserves* this kind of accounting treatment, and that transaction does not. Uncovering and declaring the truth for an accountant requires exactly the same tenacity of will that is needed in other domains for insuring that justice is done. Again, as we said in the Very Brief Introduction, an accountant, like a judge, needs to insure that his judgment remains impartial. The virtue of justice implies a habit of impartial judgment.

Prudence. An accountant needs to put things in the right order and pursue them correctly, as regards an accountant's distinctive work. For example, as we shall see, an accountant needs habitually to make principles prior to rules; he needs to place substance above form. An accountant needs to plan his work well. Again, he needs to apply accounting principles correctly to particular facts and circumstances, making use of good professional judgment. All of these constitute the analogue, for an accountant, of the virtue of prudence. (Note that this trait is not directly emphasized in the quotations above from founders of accounting, probably on the grounds that it was understood by them to be included under professionalism and professional training.)

Courage. In attest work, an accountant will often face threats and intimidations, especially the potential loss of a client or the potential loss of a job. As we said in the Very Brief Introduction, stubbornness and courage are needed in such situations, so as not to be deterred from carrying out one's professional work well.

Moderation. This is the cardinal virtue that least directly enters into the work of an accountant. Still, it plays a role, as can be seen in the emphasis on "simplicity" in the quotations above. Moderation plays two important roles in an accountant's life and work. First, any accountant who is excessively devoted to luxuries will be at risk of having his judgment swayed by considerations of his own financial advantage. Second, and more mundanely, often the effort of seeking and uncovering the truth requires considerable inconvenience and perseverance— working long hours, going the extra mile. But someone will be less willing to do if he is especially devoted to his own comfort.

A Word on Magnanimity

It may be noted that the deductive consideration based on the cardinal virtues did not arrive at any virtue corresponding to what the founders of accounting refer to as "pride." To explain "pride," we need to supplement our list of virtues and look briefly at the virtue which was highly regarded by classical writers and referred to as "magnanimity."

"Magnanimity" means "greatness of spirit" (from Latin *magna*, "great," and *anima*, "spirit" or "soul"). It refers to someone who knows his worth or value, and who acts in such a way as to preserve that worth. Magnanimity so understood leads us to excel, and it helps us to triumph against adversity. For that reason, classical authors such as Cicero tended to regard magnanimity as a special form of courage. Aristotle gave it a special place and called it the "crown" of the virtues, because magnanimity presupposes and amplifies all of the other virtues.

Although "magnanimity" may seem a pretentious word, what it refers to is common and valuable. We see magnanimity among athletes all the time: consider an athlete who knows his abilities, and who, as a result, competes with an attitude of self-confidence. Magnanimity is self-reflexive: it is excellence aware of itself. When Babe Ruth, according to the story, pointed to a spot in the bleachers and hit the next pitch there for a home run, he was showing magnanimity. We also see magnanimity among soldiers and leaders. When MacArthur famously said upon leaving the Philippines, "I will return," he was expressing magnanimity. Lincoln's Second Inaugural Address is commonly praised for its magnanimity: "with malice toward none, with charity for all." Magnanimity was shown by Lincoln in showing restraint even though as victors the Union had attained complete control over the Confederate states.

Magnanimity is sometimes called "proper pride." It has a distinctive manifestation for any member of a profession. In a later chapter we discuss at length what it means to be a professional and belong to a profession. Here it is enough to say simply that a professional, in a public and visible way, makes claims about his or her own expertise, and professes adherence to high ideals. These are both rightly sources of "pride." An accountant should "take pride" in his or her status as a professional. To do so implies an even greater desire to excel and to "show" one's skill and professionalism.

So what the founders of modern accountancy referred to as "pride" is really the analogue for an accountant of the highly important virtue of magnanimity.

Illustrative Legal Case

Throughout this text we examine important legal cases that have a bearing on accounting ethics. We do so not simply because the cases are fascinating, but also because they illuminate the interrelationship between ethics, professional practice, and law.

United States v. Arthur Young, 465 U.S. 805 (1984) concerns whether the auditing firm Arthur Young was required to hand over to the IRS the tax accrual working papers that it had used in estimating contingent tax liability for Amerada Hess Corporation ("Amerada"). In conducting a routine audit of Amerada, the IRS discovered what it regarded as a questionable payment from a "special disbursement account," after which it began a criminal investigation against Amerada. The IRS issued a summons to Young, to turn over the working papers, and Amerada instructed Young not to do so. A district court ruled the papers "relevant" to the IRS investigation, pursuant to the relevant law empowering such investigations, and therefore it required Young to surrender the papers. An appeals court agreed with the finding of relevance, but found that the working papers fell under an initial, so-called "worker product immunity," protecting the working papers and other instruments of an accountant's professional work. This immunity was postulated by the court on analogy with a similar immunity for attorneys recognized by *Hickman v. Taylor*, 329 U.S. 495 (1947). The appeals court determined that the IRS, although it had shown relevance, had not shown sufficient cause to overcome this immunity. The Supreme Court agreed with the lower courts as regards relevance but denied that the working papers of accountants were protected by any "worker product" immunity.

In denying this sort of immunity, the Supreme Court had to determine, negatively, that the accountant-client relationship was not analogous to the attorney-client relationship, and, positively, that the accountant plays a role that would make that sort of immunity inappropriate. Thus the case is of great importance as setting down in law a characterization of what we have called the "function" of an accountant. The crucial passage from Hickman is the following:

> Historically, a lawyer is an officer of the court and is bound to work for the advancement of justice while faithfully protecting the rightful interests of his clients. In performing his various duties, however, it is essential that a lawyer work with a certain degree of privacy, free from unnecessary intrusion by opposing parties and their counsel. Proper preparation of a client's case demands that he assemble information, sift what he considers to be the relevant from the irrelevant facts, prepare his legal theories and plan his strategy without undue and needless interference. That is the historical and the necessary way in which lawyers act within the framework of our system of jurisprudence to promote justice and to protect their client's interests.

Note that Hickman fashions the immunity on the presumption that a lawyer is acting in a certain confidence "protecting the rightful interests of his clients" and in order "to protect [the] client's interests." That is, that an attorney essentially has a fiduciary relationship to the client. This is the very point that the Supreme Court denies as regards accountants:

> The Hickman work-product doctrine was founded upon the private attorney's role as the client's confidential adviser and advocate, a loyal representative whose duty it is to present the client's case in the most favorable possible light. An independent certified public accountant performs a different role. By certifying the public reports that collectively depict a corporation's financial status, the independent auditor assumes a

public responsibility transcending any employment relationship with the client. The independent public accountant performing this special function owes ultimate allegiance to the corporation's creditors and stockholders, as well as to the investing public. This "public watchdog" function demands that the accountant maintain total independence from the client at all times and requires complete fidelity to the public trust. To insulate from disclosure a certified public accountant's interpretations of the client's financial statements would be to ignore the significance of the accountant's role as a disinterested analyst charged with public obligations.

We cannot accept the view that the integrity of the securities markets will suffer absent some protection for accountants' tax accrual work-papers. The Court of Appeals apparently feared that, were the IRS to have access to tax accrual work-papers, a corporation might be tempted to withhold from its auditor certain information relevant and material to a proper evaluation of its financial statements. But the independent certified public accountant cannot be content with the corporation's representations that its tax accrual reserves are adequate; the auditor is ethically and professionally obligated to ascertain for himself as far as possible whether the corporation's contingent tax liabilities have been accurately stated. If the auditor were convinced that the scope of the examination had been limited by management's reluctance to disclose matters relating to the tax accrual reserves, the auditor would be unable to issue an unqualified opinion as to the accuracy of the corporation's financial statements. Instead, the auditor would be required to issue a qualified opinion, an adverse opinion, or a disclaimer of opinion, thereby notifying the investing public of possible potential problems inherent in the corporation's financial reports. Responsible corporate management would not risk a qualified evaluation of a corporate taxpayer's financial posture to afford cover for questionable positions reflected in a prior tax return. Thus, the independent auditor's obligation to serve the public interest assures that the integrity of the securities markets will be preserved, without the need for a work-product immunity for accountants' tax accrual work-papers.

Note that the court first gives an argument based on the nature of accounting, and then argues from the consequences of the doctrine. The court's phrase, "a public responsibility transcending any employment relationship with the client," refers to what we have identified as the attitude of professionalism for accountants. The claim that "The independent public accountant performing this special function owes ultimate allegiance to the corporation's creditors and stockholders, as well as to the investing public" corresponds to what we have identified the accountant's altruism. What the court refers to as the "public watchdog" function is exactly what we have referred to as the function of an accountant as providing the indispensable conditions of trust for the sound operation of the marketplace. This "function" or "distinctive task," as we shall see in the next chapter, is the basis from which one can deduce the distinctive virtues of an accountant. Note finally that the court's opinion that the denial of any "worker product immunity" for an accountant's working paper would best contribute to full disclosure by companies is based on the presumption that accountants adhere to their "ethical and professional" obligation "to ascertain for [themselves] as far as possible whether the corporation's contingent tax liabilities have been accurately stated," which corresponds to "due diligence."

Recommended additional reading:

Aristotle, *Nicomachean Ethics*, books I and II

Michael Pakaluk, *Aristotle's Nicomachean Ethics: An Introduction*, chapters 1-3

United States v. Arthur Young, 465 U.S. 805 (1984).

Responsibility for Actions

5

"Since that which is done under compulsion or by reason of ignorance is involuntary, the voluntary would seem to be that of which the moving principle is in the agent himself, he being aware of the particular circumstances of the action."—Aristotle

PROFESSIONAL ETHICS, LIKE ETHICS IN GENERAL, involves the evaluation of action. In the last chapter, we identified the four main aspects that enter into someone's doing an action (tradition, virtue, the character of the act itself, and the effects of the act), and we focused on the highly important role played by the virtues. In this chapter, we discuss the evaluation of action itself, and, in particular, what makes someone responsible for an action, what removes responsibility, and what reduces or diminishes responsibility. The material in this chapter is essential for evaluating one's own actions as a professional on the correct basis; for evaluating the actions of colleagues, when it is necessary to do so; and for evaluating the actions of those under one's authority in a professional context.

A "Human Action" versus an "Action of a Man"

Some actions reveal the sort of persons we are, and say more about us, than others. Suppose that an executive is giving a PowerPoint presentation on his company's earnings at a conference for analysts, and, while he is explaining one of the slides, he holds his hand up to his chin and strokes his goatee. He is doing two things: he is explaining the slide, and he is stroking his goatee. But the former action tells us a lot more about him than the latter, as it expresses his goals, plans, and thoughts. Suppose that the same executive, as he continues his presentation, now stops stroking and begins unthinkingly to clean out his ear wax while he speaks. This action—cleaning out his ear wax—tells us something about him. We would blame him for doing so, since to do that in public and while giving a presentation is "bad manners" and, as we say, "makes a bad impression." But still, it remains true that what he is saying about his goals and plans for the company tells us even more about him.

This example illustrates a distinction which traditionally has been referred to a as the difference between a "human action" (in Latin, *actus humanus*) and the "action of a man" (*actus humani*). A human action is one in which distinctively human abilities come into play, like setting goals, deliberating, establishing priorities, and making decisions. In contrast, a mere "action of a man" is an action which happens to be done by a man but could basically have been done by other animals, which do not have rational abilities. Cleaning out earwax, for example, is an act of self-grooming, the way a dog might groom itself by licking its feet. Stroking one's beard is not unlike the way a dog may rub against a piece of furniture because that feels good. We would hold someone responsible for both of these actions, as both actions tell us something about the speaker. What do we know about someone who cleans out earwax in public? He was not raised well; he lacks self-awareness; and he does not have good friends (who would have long ago pointed out to him that that sort of thing gives a poor impression). But note that we make such judgments based more on what the act *signals* than what the act *expresses*. These acts signal that something is lacking in such a person. But they express very little. When it comes to the act itself, to what he is actually doing, and what that reveals, then precisely *how* he picks out his earwax tells us little or nothing about him. Chances are, he does not clean out his earwax in any distinctive way.

In sum, we are responsible for all acts that we do, for "acts of a man" as well as for our "human acts." But the human acts are more central, as they express something and do not merely signal, as is illustrated by the diagram below. The diagram raises the questions: What makes an act non-voluntary? When is it the case that something that we do is nonetheless not even a mere "act of a man"? If we are less responsible for an "act of a man," and if that sort of act reveals less about us, when are we not responsible at all for something that we do? When does something that we do tell someone nothing at all about us? In short, what distinguishes the non-voluntary from the voluntary: what makes an action fall outside both circles?

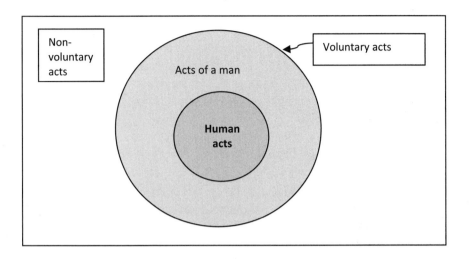

Non-voluntary actions

The short answer is that *force* and *ignorance* render an action non-voluntary. By "force" we mean that something comes from outside the person and makes him move or makes his limbs move. Suppose you are standing relaxed next to a friend at a party, and, before you can notice it, someone comes up from behind you, grabs your arm, and swings it into the side of that friend. At first your friend, seeing your arm hit him, thinks that you punched him, and perhaps he gets upset. But then, when he finds out that it was a kind of practical joke, and that someone came up from behind you and moved your arm, he completely ceases to blame you (except insofar as he judges that you might have resisted but did not), and instead he turns his attention to the person who moved your arm and perhaps gets angry at him. Your friend recognizes that "you didn't do that" and that you are not responsible. Your body moved, but it was not your action. Your striking your friend was non-voluntary. Or suppose you are driving your car and someone recklessly swerves into you, causing you to bang into a parked car. You are not responsible for hitting that car but rather the person who swerved into you.

Force, as we have explained it, needs to be distinguished from *necessitation* and *coercion*, neither of which render an action completely non-voluntary. Necessitation is where we are led by circumstances to do something we do not want to do because the alternative is even worse. For example, you are the captain of a trading ship, and a storm rises up, which is so severe that if you do not throw your cargo overboard to lighten the ship, the ship will sink. The storm *necessitates* that you take actions that you deeply dislike. Or you are a doctor, and your patient develops gangrene in a limb, which *necessitates* that you amputate the limb in what doctors call a "life over limb" decision. The gangrene makes it necessary that you cut off a limb. Coercion is similar to necessitation, except that a person is behind it all and deliberately makes our circumstances such that we end up doing something we deeply dislike. For example, when someone is robbed at knife point, he is *coerced* to hand over his money. He does not want to do so, but the alternative would be even worse. He makes a "life over money" decision.

A sign that necessitation and coercion do not render an action non-voluntary, is that we are praised and blamed, and held responsible, for our necessitated or coerced actions. The captain who throws the cargo overboard will either be praised for making a difficult but prudent decision, or blamed (if he acted precipitously) for destroying all of that cargo when it was not really necessary to do so. A doctor who makes the right decision to amputate is praised, but if he undertook such a drastic operation without good grounds, he would be harshly blamed. Someone who refused to hand over his wallet when he was mugged would likely be blamed. We might criticize him for caring more about his money than his life. We would especially blame him if his unwillingness to part with his money put others at risk.

Sometimes accountants are exposed to explicit or implicit coercion. For example, a CFO may subtly let an accountant know that he expects a certain unjustifiable result, and that if the accountant does not provide that result, then the accountant's job is at risk. Or again a company may threaten to take its business elsewhere if the external auditor does not agree with a certain improper accounting treatment. In such cases, the accountant would, and should, be blamed for giving in to the coercion. As we shall see later, an accountant as a professional is bound to adhere to his or her best professional judgment, even at potentially great personal cost.

Ignorance may also render an action non-voluntary. Not any ignorance does so, but only *non-culpable ignorance of particulars*. To understand this, first one needs to understand ignorance of particulars and then non-culpable ignorance.

Ignorance of particulars is to be contrasted with ignorance of generalities, such as laws, rules, regulations, principles, and priorities. As is often said, "ignorance of the law is no excuse." Imagine a thief who claimed that he was not responsible for stealing what he knew to be someone else's property, on the grounds that he "did not know that stealing was wrong." That would be absurd. He very well ought to know that stealing is wrong: certainly, he knows that it is wrong when someone tries to steal from him. In a similar vein, an accountant who gave an inappropriate accounting treatment for a transaction could not excuse himself by saying that he was ignorant of the relevant standard. If he did not know the relevant standard, he should either have first learned it or not accepted the engagement.

Ignorance of particulars is ignorance of the facts and circumstances of a case which are relevant to a correct decision. But ignorance of particulars excuses and renders an action non-voluntary only if the agent is not culpable for his ignorance. "Culpable" here means that he is both (1) responsible for his ignorance and (2) blameworthy. To say that he is responsible for his ignorance is to say that *he would have known what he should have known, if he had tried to find out*. To say that he is blameworthy is to say that, if he had any doubts, he should have tried to find out. Suppose for example that a father of small children pulls his car out of the driveway without checking behind the car and runs over one of his children. That would be a tragedy, yet commonsense and the law would hold the father responsible, because he might have looked first, and he should have looked first. The father could not reasonably excuse himself by saying "I did not know that a child was behind the car," since he would have known that a child was there had he looked (he was responsible for his ignorance) and he should have looked (he is rightly blamed for not looking). His ignorance, then, is culpable. Or, again, if some boys decide to throw rocks over a wall for fun without checking whether anyone is on the other side, and they hit someone, it is not a good excuse for them to say that they did not know anyone was there. They could have looked, and they should have.

In accounting, the concept of culpable ignorance of particulars is contained in the concept of what is called "due care" (or "due diligence"). Due care means taking the steps one should take to learn everything that one should know before making a decision, including the relevant facts and circumstances of the case. If an accountant fails to take these steps, then it is no excuse to say "I did not know," because the accountant should have known. An accountant who is ignorant of relevant facts and circumstances because he failed to exercise due care is culpably ignorant.

It is important to emphasize, here as well as in all other discussions of human actions, that we can act by both "commission" and "omission." Commission is when we do something that we might not have done. Omission is when we fail to do something which we might have done. An executive giving a PowerPoint presentation can be blamed both for what he says (commission) and for what he should have but failed to say (omission). The father who fails to check behind his car can be blamed both for what he does, backing up the car without having checked first (commission), and for what he failed to do, namely, check first behind his car (omission). There may even be mere "actions of a man" which are omissions. Suppose someone in the audience of the PowerPoint presentation has just had a full meal and, in the dark conference room, drifts off in a kind of pleasant fog, not paying attention. He is responsible for not paying attention (an omission), but drifting off after a meal is a mere "action of a man" rather than a "human action." (In contrast, there are "human actions" which constitute going to sleep, such as getting ready for bed in the evening by flossing, brushing one's teeth, and changing into one's pajamas.)

Mitigation

Mitigation is when someone is responsible for his action, but his responsibility is reduced. There are various types of mitigation; we shall briefly mention three cases.

(1) *Mitigation by emotions which overstrain human control.* This is when we do something that we would not want to do ordinarily, and which is against what we would decide to do if we were cool, calm, and collected, but which we were led to do by emotions which are understandable in the circumstances. The classic case would be a man who unexpectedly comes upon his wife committing adultery and in an act of rage kills her and her lover. In a calm moment, he would agree that it is wrong to kill; also, that he should seek reconciliation and forgiveness, if possible, rather than kill his own wife. But he is carried away by emotions. His killing is a "crime of passion." We regard his responsibility as diminished because it is understandable that he felt such strong emotions; it is difficult to act reasonably given that one is feeling such strong emotions; and persons besides himself were responsible for the circumstances which led him to feel those strong emotions.

(2) *Mitigation by psychological conditions.* Many people have psychological conditions which can just about compel them to act in certain ways (commission) or just about block them from acting in certain ways (omission). (We say "just about" in order not to prejudge the case, because many experts hold that there is nearly always some element of freedom, and that the agent in nearly all cases is at least in some very limited sense able to act otherwise.) For example, some people who suffer a psychological trauma in childhood will experience an overpowering psychological reaction throughout their lives when they encounter something associated with that trauma—a person who was sexually abused as a child by someone wearing a certain cologne, for the rest of his life may have overpowering

anxiety attacks whenever he smells that cologne. The anxiety attacks might keep him from functioning at his job or carrying on a conversation (both of these are failures of "omission"), but his responsibility for his dysfunctional behavior would be considerably, if not completely, mitigated. Similarly someone who went on a sudden, enormous spending spree when in the manic phase of a yet undiagnosed manic-depressive illness would not be held fully responsible for his fiscal foolhardiness. As may be seen, mitigation by psychological condition is usually something for experts to determine.

(3) *Mitigation by external dislocation.* By "external dislocation" we mean something similar to what was earlier described as "force," that is, something comes from the outside, in a way you were not responsible for, which alters your perceptions of a situation and makes you less responsible for your decisions. An extreme example would be kidnapping. Or again, many times in warfare an invading army has taken women and children captive and turned them into slaves. These women and children can come to "like" or "prefer" their life among the enemy, but they cannot be held very much responsible, because these preferences were formed as a result of the violent intervention of kidnapping. Less extreme examples would be entrapment and inducement. Suppose a law-abiding citizen is approached by undercover police officers who use all kinds of attractive persuasions to "sell" him on the idea of cooperating with a fraud. Eventually the citizen goes along with them. Since he never would have thought of engaging in fraud if he had not been approached by the undercover officers, his responsibility is lessened on the grounds of entrapment.

How do considerations of mitigation apply to accounting ethics? They apply in the sense that they provide a contrast, because typically unethical behavior by an accountant cannot be mitigated. An accountant cannot claim mitigation of the first type, on the grounds that extreme emotions were aroused, because an accountant as an impartial and objective judge should not have any extreme emotions about the transactions or companies he is expected to form an opinion about. Neither can an accountant claim mitigation by psychological condition, because, as a professional, an accountant should be aware of any psychological conditions that could affect his professional performance and remove himself from engagements or circumstances in which his judgment might be impaired. Finally, an accountant cannot claim mitigation through external dislocation, because he is supposed to have a reliable and objective judgment which is the same whatever his circumstances. For example, we shall see in the case study of the WorldCom scandal that many internal accountants cooperated with management in perpetrating fraud at WorldCom. It would not be an excuse for them that, because they were so involved in the day-to-day affairs of the company, "things looked different from within the company from the way they might look to an outside observer." They could not reasonably claim that working for WorldCom was a kind of dislocation which made them judge financial matters differently. First of all, they freely decided to work at WorldCom. But, secondly and more importantly, as professional accountants they are supposed to remain objective and adhere to the highest professional standards, whether they are within a company or outside it.

Nature, Habits, Actions, and Feelings

At this point, it is helpful to consider what we have been saying about actions in relation to what we said in the previous chapter about the virtues, because in general someone's human actions are the expression of his character.

Nature and second nature. Human beings need to develop over time. They do not come out of the womb ready to live their lives, as some animals do. Rather, they need to be instructed, to be taught, to be introduced into customs and culture, and to learn the ideas and attitudes of a society. Let us call "human nature" what someone is like when his is born. Mere human nature is incomplete. It needs to be added to and built up by education and good upbringing. Those habits, attitudes, customs and traits that someone acquires through education and upbringing can be referred to as his "second nature." A person's second nature comes to guide his behavior as much as his mere human nature does, maybe even more so.

Habits. A habit is part of our "second nature." A habit may be defined as a disposition to act in a certain way, which makes it easy and pleasant to act in that way. Habits may be good or bad. The disposition that makes it easy and pleasant to bite one's nails is a bad habit. The disposition that makes it easy and pleasant to stay in bed too late is a bad habit. In contrast, the disposition that makes it easy and pleasant to brush one's teeth at night, even when one is tired, is a good habit. A habit is bad if it is a disposition to do something that is bad for ourselves or for someone else. A habit is good if it is a disposition to something that is good for ourselves or for someone else. We typically acquire habits by repeatedly doing the actions that those habits are of. For example, a person acquires the habit of brushing his teeth in the evening by repeatedly choosing to brush his teeth in the evening.

Character. Every virtue is a good habit, but not every good habit is a virtue (it would be an abuse of language to say that the habit of brushing one's teeth at night is a virtue). Similarly, every vice is a bad habit, but not every bad habit is a vice (although someone might metaphorically refer to nail-biting as a "vice"). There are broadly three main reasons for wanting to do something: it is *admirable*; it is *useful*; it is *pleasant*. Habits reveal and consolidate our ranking of these things. For example, someone who brushes his teeth in the evening reveals his preference for health (something admirable and useful) over the comfort of going to bed right away (something pleasant). His preference is consolidated and preserved by that good habit. Habits which reveal and consolidate a correct ranking of these things in important matters are virtues; those which reveal and consolidate an incorrect ranking of these things in important matters are vices. Virtues and vices in that sense reveal someone's "heart."

Actions express character. Because we have a "second nature" as well as a "nature," by the time someone is an adult, just about everything that he does comes from his character. In reality, there is no such thing as a "random act of kindness." Someone who tried to do what he fancied was a "random act of kindness" would not be acting at random, but out of kindness. (When we put the matter that way, then it becomes clear that "consistent" acts of kindness would much better than "random," that is, *rare* acts of kindness.)

Feelings or emotions. We present now some basic but important points about feelings in contrast to habits and character. (1) A feeling is an emotion. An emotion is a reaction to something good or bad which we perceive or imagine, which has an aspect of bodily disturbance and heightened stimulation. For example, I perceive what I take to be someone's slighting me, and I feel anger in response: anger is a desire for revenge (to "get back" at someone and punish him) in response to seemingly being unjustly treated by someone else in a way that seems a slight. (2) Emotions are typically transient, since they last only as long as we continue to perceive or imagine what aroused them in the first place. For example, I remain angry at someone only so long as I continue to perceive and think about his slight—which is called "nursing" one's anger. (3) Emotions can be justified or unjustified. Emotions are unjustified when they are based on a mistaken perception or something wrongly imagined. For instance, I can get angry at an imagined slight. In that case my anger is "groundless" or "unjustified." (4) Emotions are therefore open to rational assessment. We are not passive victims of our emotions. We can reason with and reason ourselves out of our emotions. (5) Emotions are not more "honest" or "real" than any other aspect of our psychology, such as thoughts or opinions. (6) Emotions should not substitute for judgment or subvert judgment, as when someone reaches a well-grounded judgment but then goes back on it because of emotion such as fear or sympathy.

An important distinction is that between an emotion which proceeds from and in some sense is caused by a prior judgment, and an emotion which leads to and causes a judgment. The former is called a "consequent" emotion, and the latter is called an "antecedent" emotion. For example, when I judge correctly that someone has treated me unjustly, and then I feel anger, I experience a consequent emotion. The emotion results from that well grounded judgment. In contrast, when I am angry about something or other, and this anger causes me to imagine that someone's harmless remark was meant as an insult, then my emotion played the role of an antecedent emotion. Antecedent emotions typically lead to irrational judgments which we later may attempt to "rationalize." Emotions should typically follow reasons, not reasons emotions.

Admittedly, it sometimes happens that an emotion is implicitly based on good reasons, which, however, are not yet explicitly recognized by the person feeling the emotion—as for example when someone really admires someone, but he does not yet understand why. In such cases, emotions can be highly instructive, and they have their own implicit "logic." They can incorporate what we call "intuitions."

Emotions and habits. Emotions, as reactions involving bodily agitation, are not entirely under our control; we can perhaps best shape and control them by putting them in relation to habits, including habitual judgments, so that the way we feel an emotion corresponds to some habitual way of acting or thinking. Many therapists recommend that if someone wants to feel a certain way about something, then he should *act* as though he feels that way, and then eventually his feelings will come along and follow his actions, corresponding to them. For example, a man comes to a therapist and complains that he does not love his wife any more. What he really means is that he does not feel emotions of love toward his wife, or that he feels them less strongly than he used to feel them. The therapist proposes, as the remedy, that the man should simply start acting consistently as though he does love his wife. So the man starts saying affectionate things and doing thoughtful acts, like buying flowers. He develops habits of thinking romantic thoughts and doing thoughtful things for his wife. These thoughts and actions tend to elicit emotions of love. When the actions become habitual, then the emotion comes to be felt habitually as well. There can be a lag, but typically the emotions will eventually follow.

"Good intentions." We said that willing, deliberating, planning, and deciding entered into what we called distinctively "human actions." Strictly speaking, "intention" belongs in that class. The word "intention" is used in two main senses.

(1) Sometimes it means something we would like to do in the future, as in "I intend to go on a diet soon." In this sense, an intention is a wish, which may or may not be effective. It may or may not lead to any concrete or intelligent action. (2) Sometimes it means something we are actually willing and pursuing at the moment, as in "It is my deliberate intention to marry this woman." In this sense, an intention is something we will and which is effective. These two senses are easy to confuse. When people say "the road to hell is paved with good intentions," they are using the word in the first sense. They mean that people who merely wish to achieve something good in an ineffective way are not getting any closer to heaven but maybe the opposite. On the other hand, when they excuse someone by saying that "his intentions were good," they could very well be meaning the word in either the first or the second sense. If they mean it in the first sense, they are saying that he should be excused because his actions (which perhaps were not intelligent and were ill-considered) had consequences other than those he wished for. If they mean it in the second sense, they are saying that he should be excused because, despite his best efforts, things turned out otherwise. So "intention" is an ambiguous word which should be scrutinized carefully.

Kinds of Actions

Actions come in kinds. Every action that we do belongs to a "kind" and can be evaluated as a member of that kind. We never carry out purely unique, singular, or unrepeatable actions—despite, once again, what the bumper sticker tells us, about doing "random acts" of kindness. Every action that seems unique actually admits of a more general characterization, placing it in a class of similar actions.

Each action belongs to both a "physical" kind and an ethical or "moral" kind. Its physical kind is the sort of action that it is, when it is considered simply as objects that move in space and time. The action as described by a physicist or engineer is its physical kind: a description of the size, movement, and forces of objects. In contrast, its moral kind is the sort of action that it is, when it is considered in relation to the purposes and preferences of the persons involved. Suppose a surgeon makes an incision in a patient. The physical kind would be the action as described physically: "a sharp blade inserted so-and-so many millimeters into the skin and moved along such-and-such a path for a length of so-and-so many centimeters." Textbooks on surgery will give a precise description of the kind incision to use for each kind of operation. When they do so they are characterizing the "physical kind" of the action. Obviously each action admits of descriptions at increasing levels of generality (a 10 centimeter incision; an incision; a cutting with a sharp object). The lowest-level and most precise description will be similar to the one just given. But in contrast the moral kind of the incision would be that it is "a medical act of surgery." As a medical act, it has as its goal the healing and health of the patient, and it is accomplished with medical training.

Actions which are very similar as regards their physical kind may be very different as regards their moral kind. An action of cutting the flesh with a sharp knife may be either a medical act of healing, or a vindictive act of assault and murder. The same doctor who is making an incision to repair the damaged heart might have made exactly the same incision if he were corrupt and were aiming to remove a healthy heart from a still living patient to sell it on the black market for cash.

Actions fall into moral kinds which are either *good, bad,* or *indifferent,* as kinds of actions. That is to say, actions are either all good, simply as members of that kind; all bad, simply as members of that kind; or good or bad depending on the circumstances. For example, an action which falls under the kind, "helping a friend who is lost" (this is a kind of action, which is a moral kind) is always good. Every instance of that kind of action is good. In contrast, an action which falls under the kind, "murder" (that is, the deliberate killing of a non-aggressor) is always bad. Each instance of that kind of action is bad. On the other hand, an action that falls under the kind, "picking up a stick" (which is a kind of action too, a moral kind) is neither good nor bad, simply as a member of that kind. It is an "indifferent" kind of action. One cannot read off from the mere description, "picking up a stick," that the action will be good or bad. However, in any particular circumstance, picking up a stick will amount to either a good or a bad action. Suppose someone, in order to lead astray, picks up a stick on a trail which he knows was left there by one member of a hiking party to point the way to his mates: this would be a bad action. But suppose someone picks up a random stick by the side of the trail to give to his injured friend for use as a walking stick: this would be a good action.

In accounting, any action which is an action of giving a fair representation of a transaction, or of the financial condition or results of operations of a company (all "moral" kinds of actions), is always good, simply as being a member of one of those kinds. Fraud, in contrast, is a "moral" kind of action which is always bad, simply as being a member of that kind. (Note that when we say that fraud is a "moral" kind of action, we are of course using the word "moral" as contrasting with "physical," not as contrasting with "immoral.")

The moral kind of an action is *objective*. What we mean by this is that (i) there is fact of the matter as to what kind of action an agent did; also, (ii) the agent may be wrong about what he did; his own assessment is not determinative; and the mere fact that an agent thinks he did an action of a certain kind does not imply that the action really was that kind of action. As an example from ordinary life, consider someone who intends to pay a compliment to someone but in fact ends up unwittingly insulting him, as for instance if a man tells a woman, "You look pretty thin for someone who is in her third trimester," when in reality he has forgotten the due date, and the fact that she has already given birth, and that her excess girth is due not to the baby but to the fact that she has not lost her "baby weight." He wanted to compliment her, but he insulted her. What did the man objectively do? Did he do what he intended, or what he accomplished? He did what he accomplished: he insulted her, although he meant to compliment her. The kind of action we do is something objective, which is not fixed by our "intentions."

In accounting, a practitioner may wish and "intend" to use the right accounting treatment for a transaction, but if he is ignorant of something, makes a mistake, or judges incorrectly, then his accounting will be incorrect, no matter what he wanted to do or supposed he was doing. It is vital to professional ethics that a professional recognize that the assessment of actions is objective. Indeed, the very notion of "generally accepted accounting principles" presupposes that that is so.

Aspects of Actions

There are two important aspects of an action to take into account besides its "kind," namely, its "circumstances" and its "ends."

Circumstances. Any particular action, although a member of a "kind" and falling in a general class, nonetheless takes place in detailed circumstances, which constitute the action's concreteness. The concrete, particular details of an action are its "circumstances." The "kind" in which the action belongs is, as it were, the skeleton of the action, the circumstances are its flesh and clothing. Or the "kind" is like a mould, and the circumstances are the stuff and matter that fill that mould.

Consider our example of the executive giving an earnings report to a room of analysts. The (moral) "kind" of this action would be "giving an earnings report presentation." But the circumstances would include such things as: the time at which the presentation is given; the place where it is given; the persons in attendance; the media used for the presentation; and the style of the presentation.

The circumstances are, roughly, those things which could have been different in the planning of this one particular presentation. One and the same presentation might have been scheduled on a different date and time, or been held in a different room, or might have used handouts instead of PowerPoint, or had a slightly different list of invitees, and so on. Obviously, it would have been the same presentation, and the same kind of action, if it had been moved to the adjoining room.

Usually the circumstances of an action are not relevant to our assessment of that action. We would form roughly the same judgment about the accuracy, quality and success of the executive's presentation, regardless of the room in which he gave the presentation, and regardless of whether some particular analyst was invited or not. But sometimes the circumstances are relevant, and, when they are relevant, then they must be stated explicitly in any reference to the action, or else an account of that action will be misleading. For example, for a company to loan money to an individual is not a big deal. But if that individual is one of the executives of the company, then there is a big difference. That circumstance would usually need to be disclosed, as implying a so-called "related party" transaction. In ordinary life, it is bad for one person to strike another. But suppose the person whom he strikes is his own father—then the action is much worse, from a so-called "aggravating circumstance." Sometimes the circumstances make a bad action out of an action which would otherwise be good: it is good for a physician to treat a patient but bad for a physician to treat a patient when the patient happens to be himself. Sometimes the circumstances make an action better or worse than one would judge, considering it simply as a member of that kind. It is good for someone to repay a debt (eventually) but even better to repay a debt promptly (which is a circumstance of the action).

Ends of an action. An "end" is the same as a "goal," "point," or "purpose." The end is what we ultimately hope to achieve or gain. Generally our actions are for ends which have a hierarchical structure, terminating in something fundamental. For example, you are reading this sentence, in order to understand this paragraph, in order to understand this chapter, in order to understand accounting ethics, in order (if we put the best spin on it) to become an excellent practitioner. In such a hierarchical structure, a goal nearer to the action is said to be a "more proximate" goal, and one that is more distant from the action is said to be a "more remote" goal. In the above example, the most remote goal which was stated, of the action of reading the sentence, was the goal of being an excellent practitioner; the most proximate goal was to understand the paragraph.

Our actions typically fall within ordered hierarchies such as that which was just given. But our actions admit of an abbreviated description, whereby we pick out only two goals, one which is immediately achieved in the action, and one which the action is for. In such cases we say that the former is "the" proximate goal, and the latter is "the" remote goal. The basic rule of thumb to apply here is that *both the proximate and the remote goal of an action need to be good for the action to be good.* If the proximate goal is bad, the action is bad: it does not matter if the remote goal is good. (As we say, "The end does not justify the means," and "Do not do evil that good may come.") If the remote goal is bad, the action is bad: it does not matter if the proximate goal is good. (Good in the service of bad is bad.) The principle that both the proximate and the remote goals need to be good is an instance of the more general principle governing the moral life, that *for an action to be good, everything about it needs to be good.* In contrast, for an action to be bad, it suffices if it is bad in one respect only. There is an asymmetry between good and bad. Goodness requires that everything be good. Badness occurs if only one important thing is bad.

Examples from ordinary life would be as follows.

(i) Good proximate goal and good remote goal; action is good: someone earns money to give to a worthy charity.

(ii) Good proximate goal and bad remote goal; action is bad: someone earns money to give to a terrorist organization.

(iii) Bad proximate goal and good remote goal; action is bad: someone steals money to give to a worthy charity.

An example from accounting practice would be as follows.

(i) Good proximate goal and good remote goal; action is good: an accountant gives a correct valuation of a company to assist the principals in finding a fair sales price in the purchase and sale of that company.

(ii) Good proximate goal and bad remote goal; action is bad: a practitioner, with complete accuracy, gives a fair accounting of the condition and results of operation of a company (good proximate goal—a truthful accounting) for a report which he has good reason to believe will be used misleadingly in claims about future performance, to entice investors (bad remote goal).

(iii) Bad proximate goal and good remote goal; action is bad: an accountant offers a correct valuation of a company to be used by the owner, who is his friend, in obtaining a fair sales price (the proximate goal here is "bad" because it involves at least the appearance of an impairment of the practitioner's independence).

Cooperation and Complicity

Many actions are not done by an individual on his own but by him together with others. In such cases, there may be questions as to how much responsibility for their joint action is shared between them. Sometimes too, people make use of what we would be doing anyway in order to advance their bad plans and purposes. Finally, sometimes we happen to benefit from the bad things which others are doing or have done. In these kinds of cases one needs to bring into play the concepts of *cooperation* and *complicity*.

In order to get clear about these concepts, we first need to distinguish between "formal" and "material" association. Formal association is when two or more persons are members of the same group; they share the purposes of that group; and they have the training or background necessary to be competent members of that group. Because of this similarity between them, they are equals as belonging to that group. Their association is "formal" because of their shared purposes and background, which is usually expressed in an explicit agreement or contract. Formal association may be captured using the notion of "distinctive work": in a formal association, there is a significant sense in which the persons who associate have the same distinctive work, as members of that association. Material association, in contrast, is when one person assists another, but not by being part of the same group. Their association is referred to as "material" because one person provides the "material conditions" or preconditions for the other person to do his or her work. They are not equals, and they do not share in the same distinctive work.

This description has been rather abstract, so let us make it concrete by means of an example. Have you ever arrived at an orchestra concert early and noticed the men who set up the stage for the musicians? They put chairs and stands in their proper position, move the piano and harp as needed, and make sure that the lighting is correct. When they are done with their work, these men leave the stage, and then the musicians come on stage, to go through their warm-up prior to the concert. In this example, the instrumentalists associate with one another through a *formal* association. The stage helpers associate with the instrumentalists through a *material* association. The instrumentalists belong to the same profession; they all participate in the orchestra; they sign contracts to be part of the orchestra.

They are equals insofar as they are all members of the orchestra, and each has the same distinctive work: each is a classical musician. In contrast, the stage helpers belong to a different profession; they are not part of the orchestra; they sign a different kind of contract. They are not the "equals" of the instrumentalists, and they have a different distinctive work.

These last two points are highly important. The stage helpers are not equals, because the stage helpers assist the instrumentalists, not the instrumentalists the stage helpers. The work of the stage helpers is for the sake of the work of the instrumentalists, not the other way around. Also they do not have the same distinctive work, because the work of the stage helpers is generic in comparison. The stage helpers are employed by the concert hall to set up the stage no matter what kind of show or music is being played—rock, jazz, folk, ballet, and so on. They provide generally useful labor for any sort of show, no matter what kind of show. One may see from this example that material assistance is said to be "proximate" or "remote" depending upon how directly adapted the assistance is. The electric company providing electricity to the concert hall is giving remote material assistance. The stage helpers in contrast are giving fairly proximate assistance.

We can now distinguish formal from material cooperation. One person *formally cooperates* with another when they are members of the same formal association or they associate as if they were. One person *materially cooperates* with another when they have only a material association between them. In formal cooperation two persons are together doing the same thing. In material cooperation, one person is doing one thing, and the other is doing something else, and the one thing provides the preconditions for some other person's doing that other thing.

The rule of thumb for judging cooperation is this: we should simply refuse to cooperate formally with someone who is doing something wrong, and we should try to avoid material cooperation. As regards material cooperation, *remote material cooperation is generally acceptable, whereas proximate material cooperation should be avoided unless the ramifications for not assisting are grave* (that is, unless we are justifiably "necessitated"). The rule seems complex, but a simple example will clarify.

Consider the following employees in a company: the CFO, an internal accountant, the CFO's personal assistant, and an IT person who provides general IT services for the company. Suppose the CFO is committing fraud and enlists the assistance of the internal accountant; moreover, the CFO's personal assistant and the IT person know about the fraud: because of their access in their work to privileged information, they surmise that a fraud is being committed by the CFO. The CFO's personal assistant provides actual clerical help for documents that, as he is aware, the CFO is using to commit the fraud. The IT person is similarly aware that the CFO makes use of his work of keeping the computers running in order to carry out the fraud.

Given what we have said, can these people cooperate with the CFO or not? Are they in effect forced to resign their jobs? The internal accountant cannot cooperate: this would be formal cooperation in wrongdoing, which is never permissible. The CFO's personal assistant is providing proximate material cooperation: he should change jobs, unless there were some catastrophic cost to himself or to his family in doing so. The IT person is providing only remote material assistance and does not need to try to find another job. (For the purposes of this example, we refrain from discussing any duties to report or whistle-blowing obligations that these various employees might have.)

Complicity is different from cooperation and implies benefitting *after the fact* from ill gotten gain. Suppose the trustees of a large charitable foundation discover after the death of their founding benefactor that that benefactor had made his billions through a variety of scams and frauds. The truth about his ill gotten gain came to light too late for the law to do anything about it, as the statute of limitations has been exceeded. Moreover, the persons he defrauded are now either dead or impossible to identify. Would the trustees be complicit in the benefactor's misdeeds by continuing to administer the trust? Or suppose a wealthy benefactor wishes to donate money to a university and get "naming rights" for the university's library, when it is well known that he acquired his money dishonestly. Should the university accept the gift, on the grounds that nothing can undo the past, and that, if they accept the money, then at least it will be used for a good purpose? Or should the university decline the gift?

These are the kinds of questions raised by the notion of complicity. The basic rule for avoiding complicity is: first of all, never act unjustly; and, given that you are not acting unjustly, never act in such a way that you either come to depend on someone else's wrongdoing, give an incentive for that wrongdoing, or are led to take pleasure in that wrongdoing.

Consider the following example in illustration. Suppose a "Body Worlds" type artists needs human cadavers to inject with chemicals that "plasticize" and reveal the structure of various systems of the human body. He gets his cadavers from a sinister government. Eventually he learns that this government rounds up political prisoners and executes them with a bullet to the head, and then sells their cadavers to him. This explains why the corpses have been in such good physical condition. The rule above would dictate that he stop buying cadavers from this government. First, it would be an injustice to "reward" with a payment the people who murdered the person whose body you are buying. Second, the fact that your "Body Worlds" type business implies a demand for fresh cadavers creates an incentive for this sinister government to execute more political prisoners. Third, your own desires are likely to become distorted, because, if you ever were short of cadavers, you might begin to want the government to do you the favor of executing more political prisoners.

Cases of complicity arise also in accounting ethics. Suppose an internal accountant discovers a material accounting error from the past from which his company has profited immensely. In justice—because of his commitment to his profession—he should aim to correct the error, if possible, and inform the external auditor. Failure to act would seem to imply complicity with the error.

Lesser of Two Evils and Double Effect

You are the driver of a runaway trolley car whose brakes have unaccountably failed and which is careening down a hillside track. Up ahead there are five men working on the track. The trolley will certainly hit them and probably kill them. But you have the option of switching the trolley onto a side track, where only one workman is working. Should you do so?

Someone might argue that if you switch to the other track, then by your actions you bring about the death of the one man and are responsible for that, whereas if you leave the trolley as it is, then you are not responsible for anyone's death, even though the trolley strikes and kills five men, because you were not responsible for the brakes' failure. However, this is incorrect reasoning. If you do nothing, you will be responsible for an act of omission, namely, the act of omitting to switch to the side track when you saw that you could and were able to do so.

The right thing to do in the circumstances is to switch the trolley over to the track where it strikes only one person. If you do so, you will be acting in accordance with a valuable rule known as "lesser of two evils." This means that when someone has a choice between two courses of action, both of which are unfortunate and undesirable, he is bound to choose the least unfortunate and least undesirable alternative. We see people following the "lesser of two evils" principle all the time. For example, when a jet test pilot realizes that his plane is going to crash, he tries to steer it away from a crowded, inhabited area, if possible, and toward an uninhabited area. The plane is going to crash either way, but, given that it is, he chooses to do the least possible damage. Another example would be United Airlines Flight 93 during the 9/11 attacks: the passengers rushed the cockpit and overpowered the terrorists at a time when they knew that the airplane was flying over rural countryside, before the plane reached the Washington D.C. metropolitan area. They acted in a way that they knew was likely to result in the crash of the plane, but they were choosing the lesser of two evils.

When someone chooses the lesser of two evils, he does not choose to do anything evil on its own; rather, what he is choosing to do is a compound action, "this instead of that." The trolley driver, when he switches the train to the other track so that it strikes the single man, is not choosing "to kill this one man" but rather he is choosing "to kill one man instead of five." It is only because we wrongly view the action in isolation that we imagine his choice is wrong. Similarly, the passengers on Flight 93 were not trying "to crash the plane" but "to crash the plane in the country instead of in the city."

The principle of the lesser to two evils sometimes enters into accounting decisions. Suppose that there are unusual facts and circumstances which render neither of two possible accounting treatments exactly right; in that case a practitioner should use the least unacceptable treatment.

Another important principle of choice is called the principle of "double effect." Double effect applies when each of the following four conditions holds:

(i)   you do an action which has two upshots ("effects"), one good and one bad;

(ii)   the action itself is an instance of a kind of action that is either good or indifferent;

(iii)   there is a reasonable proportion between the good and the bad upshots ("effects"), such that it makes sense to achieve the good upshot "at the price" of the bad upshot;

(iv)   you do not in any way enjoy or secretly take satisfaction in the bad upshot ("effect").

When those conditions hold, the agent can claim that he is not responsible for the bad upshot ("effect"). He can foresee perhaps that his action will have that bad upshot, but he can reasonably say that it is an unintended side-effect of his action and not something that he himself is either doing or is responsible for.

The classic illustration of double effect is killing in self-defense. Suppose you use proportional force to fend off an attacker. It just so happens that the attacker is attacking you so violently that you need to use force which is lethal to him in order to stop him. Then all four conditions hold. Condition (i): The action you are engaging in has two upshots: you save your own life (good upshot), but you need to take his (bad upshot). Condition (ii): An action of proportional self-defense is good. Condition (iii): It makes sense for a person to prefer his own life over another's, if he cannot preserve both. Condition (iv): The defender ought to lament the fact—regard it as a highly unfortunate tragedy—that he had to use lethal force to preserve his own life. Thus the defender can say that it was an unfortunate side-effect of defending himself that the attacker lost his life.

Other classic examples of double effect include: when a doctor gives pain-killing medicine to someone who is in pain from a mortal illness, when that medicine has the side-effect of to a small degree shortening the patient's life (this side effect is bad, but it makes sense for him to gain freedom from suffering "at the price of" some minor shortening of his life); when in war there is a "collateral damage" to civilians from attacks on military facilities, assuming, again, that there is a reasonable proportion between the value of the military target and the civilian deaths which are incurred as an unfortunate side-effect. (Note that the former case is different from euthanasia, and the latter is different from a direct attack on non-combatants. Euthanasia and direct attacks on non-civilians are never justified.)

Double effect comes into play in accounting ethics not infrequently, as when a practitioner's doing the right thing implies bad effects for a company. Suppose, to revert to our standard case, that an internal accountant refuses to go along with a CFO's request to give a dubious or fraudulent accounting treatment, in circumstances where the correct accounting treatment could very well prove harmful to the interests of the company. Suppose the CFO gets angry and charges that the accountant through his stubborn insistence on a different accounting is harming the company and guilty of insubordination. The accountant should stand firm, relying on the principle of double effect: he can foresee that his decision to abide by the correct accounting treatment may have the unfortunate upshot that the company's interests will be harmed; however, he is not responsible for that, because he is only doing his job—indeed, he has no choice as a professional but to give the correct accounting treatment—and the harm to the company comes as a foreseeable but unintended side-effect of his professional actions.

Conscience

The term "conscience" has two main meanings. First, it can mean those basic principles of morality that we habitually accept and may call to mind when we contemplate doing something opposed to these principles, just as someone who is contemplating stealing something may call to mind the principle "Do not steal; stealing is wrong!" Conscience in this sense is likened to a voice of good counsel, like a "good angel" sitting on one's shoulder. (Classically, conscience in this sense is referred to as "synderesis.") Second, it can mean the *application* of those principles of morality to a particular question of action, in given circumstances, in light of principles such as those we have discussed in this chapter. Conscience in this second sense is one's best and considered judgment about what one should do in a particular case. (Classically, conscience in this sense is called *conscientia*.)

Conscience is therefore not an emotion. It is different from a deeply felt feeling. Conscience is different from considerations of our own self-interest, ease, or comfort.

People can have a more clear or a less clear conscience. The more we act in accordance with what our conscience says, the clearer conscience becomes in us; the more we disregard our conscience, the less clear it becomes. Conscience should be instructed and informed. As discussed last chapter in our account of prudence, we need to "form" our conscience. We do so by studying reliable authorities on religion and morality, by studying sound books of philosophy, and by seeking out the advice of prudent persons. Conscience can be right or wrong. Someone's conscience is right when it says that he should do or refrain from something, when objectively he should do or refrain from it. Someone's conscience is wrong when it tells him he should do something, but objectively he should not do it, or when it tells him he should refrain from something, but objectively he should do it.

The philosopher Karl Jaspers tells the story that after the end of World War II he was in a hospital and spoke with an injured German youth who had been a guard in a concentration camp. The youth was deeply upset about something, and Jaspers probed him to find out what it could be. It turns out that once when the youth was guarding a line of Jewish prisoners, waiting to enter the gas chambers and meet their deaths, he noticed that a little Jewish boy was sneaking away to make his escape. The youth did nothing about this; he pretended he had not noticed and let the Jewish boy escape. But this failure of duty was now gnawing away at him. He could find no peace because he let the boy get away. This story provides a very clear case of a badly-formed conscience. The conscience of the

German guard told him not to let the prisoner escape, but clearly it was not wrong to let the prisoner escape. The guard's conscience was badly formed and wrong. He had an erring conscience.

As mentioned in the previous chapter, a person should always follow his conscience, even when it is wrong. "An erring conscience should always be followed." The reason is that conscience is the highest guide in us. If we do not follow conscience, we are preferring the ways staked out by something lower in us. However, at the same time, "an erring conscience does not excuse." The mere fact that someone followed his conscience does not make his action right—because his conscience might be badly formed. Doing what one's conscience says is necessary for acting rightly but not sufficient. Consider once again the case of the concentration camp guard. He should have followed his conscience—he had no alternative, since he had no better guide than his conscience. Yet if he had followed his conscience, rounded up the boy, and sent the boy into the gas chambers, he could not claimed that he had acted well, on the grounds that he had followed his conscience. He would still have been complicit in the murder of the boy and of the other prisoners he was sending to the gas chambers.

People do great wrong by erecting some other standard of what they "ought" to do besides what their conscience is telling them. This happens in accounting practice as well. Typically accountants who are complicit in fraud know in their conscience that they are not doing the right thing. But they put up some other standard to guide their behavior—they are "only doing what everyone else is doing," or they figure that "that how things are done here," or they are "providing exceptional client service," and so on.

A Relevant Legal Case

Feit v. Leasco 332 F. Supp. 544 (E.D.N.Y. 1971), brings in interesting considerations of the "common good." It also follows up on the case considered in the previous chapter, as it bears upon the nature of the market economy as regards which accountants are meant to serve as "public watchdogs."

Feit was one among many shareholders of Reliance Insurance Company ("Reliance") who was persuaded to accept a tender offer of shares of Leasco in a successful takeover. Leasco wished to gain control over Reliance because through research it had discovered that Reliance possessed over $100 million of "surplus surplus," that is to say, of capital over and above what might reasonably be thought to be needed to cover even an extraordinary rise in insurance claims. This "surplus

surplus" was the reason for the takeover. It was apparently known to a few analysts but not known by Reliance shareholders. Leasco failed to disclose its existence, or its plans for use of the surplus after the takeover. Its management was found guilty of violating the Securities Acts for concealing or omitting material facts and was ordered to pay recovery money damages.

The case raised issues of disclosure and materiality, because it was alleged that Leasco had not disclosed material facts. The case is relevant for accounting ethics as helping to define the role of auditing and accounting in financial markets. Accountants are the ordinary agents and certifiers of the disclosures of publicly traded companies.

The court proposed a general conception of the marketplace as a manner of association in which "insiders" and "outsiders" buy and sell on a level playing field:

> The prospective purchaser of a new issue of securities is entitled to know what the deal is all about. Given an honest and open statement, adequately warning of the possibilities of error and miscalculation and not designed for puffing, the outsider and the insider are placed on more equal grounds for arms-length dealing. Such equalization of bargaining power through sharing of knowledge in the securities market is a basic national policy underlying the federal securities laws.

The primary purpose of those laws is "to place potential securities purchasers on a parity with their vendors to the extent practicable." This claim then serves as the basis of the court's rejection of the defendants' claim that the disclosure of the surplus surplus was not material, on the grounds that Leasco's offer to exchange was so attractive, that it would have been accepted by Reliance shareholders even if they knew about that surplus surplus. What is important for materiality, the court maintains, is not that a reasonable investor would have decided otherwise, had he known of the fact, but rather that the fact is the sort of thing that a reasonable investor would have wanted to know about and to be able to take into account, in making his decision—even if he would have decided in the same way. Materiality thus needs to be determined relative to this ideal of a market as displaying "parity." In no way can the investor be *manipulated* or *forced* to act; and the investor can be manipulated even if he ends up carrying out the very same purchase or sale that he would have carried out if he had decided fully on his own:

> The solicited Reliance shareholders who received the prospectus in question "ought reasonably to [have been] informed" of an estimate of surplus surplus "before purchasing" the Leasco package. 17 C.F.R. §

230.405(l). It was a fact which these investors needed to "make an intelligent, informed decision whether or not to buy the security." *Escott v. BarChris Construction Corp.*, 283 F. Supp. 643, 681 (S.D.N.Y. 1968). It was a matter which had "an important bearing upon the nature or condition * * * or * * * business" of Reliance tending to deter acceptance of the exchange offer (id.) and "which in reasonable and objective contemplation might [have affected] the value of [Reliance's] stock." *Kohler v. Kohler*, 319 F.2d 634, 642 (7th Cir. 1963). See *Chasins v. Smith, Barney & Co.*, 438 F.2d 1167, 1171 (2d Cir. 1971); *SEC v. Texas Gulf Sulphur*, 401 F.2d 833, 849 (2d Cir. 1968), cert. denied sub nom. *Coates v. SEC* and *Kline v. SEC*, 394 U.S. 976, 89 S. Ct. 1454, 22 L. Ed. 2d 756 (1969); *List v. Fashion Park*, 340 F.2d 457, 462 (2d Cir.), cert. denied sub nom. *List v. Lerner*, 382 U.S. 811, 86 S. Ct. 23, 15 L. Ed. 2d 60, rehearing denied, 382 U.S. 933, 86 S. Ct. 305, 15 L. Ed. 2d 344 (1965). It was a fact to which "a reasonable man would attach importance in determining" whether to accept the Leasco exchange offer. *List v. Fashion Park*, supra at 462.

Given this general conception of the marketplace as involving parity and fairness, disclosure becomes important for two reasons. First, it protects the investor, a major aim of the Securities Acts of 1933 and 1934:

The ultimate goal of the Securities Act is, of course, investor protection. Effective disclosure is merely a means. The entire legislative scheme can be frustrated by technical compliance with the requirements of the Securities and Exchange Commission's Form S-1 for preparation of registration statements in the absence of any real intent to communicate. It is for this reason that the SEC, through its rule making power, has consistently required "clearly understandable" prospectuses.

Much less important for the court is the effect that a requirement to disclose has upon business practice:

The second—and for our purposes less important—goal of the full disclosure policy is deterrence. This consideration arose from excesses of the 1920's and the havoc subsequently wreaked on investors. The drafters accepted as an article of faith and common sense that if management must bare all on pain of civil and criminal liability its dirty intra-corporate linen will be cleaned before the registration statement is filed.

Concomitantly, such disclosure has the prophylactic effect of promoting general business integrity.

In conclusion, *Feit v. Leasco* offers a striking explication of the good judgment that would be required in an accountant, to have a good sense of the requirements of disclosure and materiality. A prospectus discloses properly, only if it promotes the aims of the securities laws, and something it includes or omits can be judged to be material, only in relation to an abstract ideal of the fair positioning and equitability of the investor, vis-à-vis the management of a company and other "insiders."

Recommended additional reading:

Aristotle, *Nicomachean Ethics*, III.1-5

Feit v. Leasco

Michael Pakaluk, *Aristotle's Nicomachean Ethics: An Introduction*, chapter 4

Principles versus Rules

6

"If you should put down all the rules in the world you would have cases to which the rules would not apply. You have to use your experience ... and that is the reason why we are here as professional accountants—because we have to gain experience, judgment, and tact in dealing with accounts, and taking the best of the many different ways of determining matters. ... You cannot lay down definite principles, but you can lay down broad principles that will cover most cases. When you come to interpret the principles, you will have to take the case in point and do the best that you can with it upon a conservative basis."

—Arthur L. Dickinson

It is perhaps inevitable that people who have acquired expert training of one kind or other will understand ethics, by analogy, as similar to what they are expert in. Thus, physicists might wish to understand ethics as "forces" operative among persons. Psychologists will tend to view ethics as a matter of emotions and feelings. Sociologists can see ethics as a matter of establishing and maintaining relationships of power and control. Evolutionary biologists might look at ethics as a mechanism of adaptation.

Along the same lines, a tendency of accounting experts today is to regard professional ethics as a matter of mastering rules. Expertise in accounting, or at least public accounting, is to a large extent regarded as a matter of mastering a set of formally promulgated accounting rules , and mastering the exceptions to those rules, and the exceptions to the exceptions, and being familiar with formally endorsed interpretations (all of which would constitute GAAP). Thus, similarly, accounting ethics can easily be regarded as a matter of mastering formally promulgated "ethics" rules—and rules about those rules, and rules about the rules about those rules, and so on.

Such seems to be the conception of professional ethics underlying the activities of a leading authority, the Professional Ethics Executive Committee (PEEC) of the American Institute of Certified Public Accountants (AICPA). The Committee meets on a quarterly basis to discuss and promulgate new rules and interpretations involving the AICPA Code of Professional Conduct ("Code"). To get a good sense of this approach, the reader of this book might consult the agendas and minutes of its meetings, which are published online. To pick an example at random, at the May 2010 open meeting, the PEEC among other things considered the definition of "immediate family member" and how such persons might affect a practitioner's independence. Among many different rules, it was proposed, for instance, that "An immediate family member's participation in certain share-based compensation arrangements or nonqualified deferred compensation plans would not impair independence if the covered member is not on the attest engagement team or in a position to influence the attest engagement team when certain prescribed safeguards are applied to reduce the financial self-interest threat to an acceptable level." Also, a continuing project of organizing such rules was discussed ("codification"); and the harmony (or "convergence") of the PEEC's body of rules with those of a comparable European rule-making committee was considered. Thus, the PEEC's deliberations were concerned with the articulation, codification, and convergence of rules.

Whether professional ethics for an accountant is best approached as a complex system of rules resembling an articulated legal code is a question that will be taken up below, in the chapters on professionalism in accounting (chapters 8-10). In this chapter, however, we wish to consider in a more general way the place of rules in accounting practice—the way in which rules should be used in ethical accounting practice. This requires that the proper place of rules be appreciated, including the relationship of rules to underlying "principles" (or "objectives"). Briefly, it is important to see that, although rules are undeniably necessary, they are by no means sufficient for ethical practice. In short, "rules are not enough."

What a Rule Is

A rule is a law; thus, in order to understand rules, it is necessary to understand laws. A law is (i) a generalization, which is rational, about how cases are to be treated, (ii) set down to promote the common good of some association, (iii) by some person or persons who have authority over that common good, and (iv) which is promulgated. Let us consider each of these elements in turn.

A generalization, which is rational, about how cases are to be treated. A law has the general form, "whenever such-and-such is the case, then so-and-so must do (or must refrain from, or may do, or may refrain from) such-and-such," together with a stipulation of the penalty for non-compliance. Thus, a law is a generalization which specifies the similar treatment that should be given to similar cases. There should be a reason for what we do: we act for reasons. But if there is a reason why we should act in a certain way, given certain circumstances, then that reason holds equally well when we are confronted again with the same circumstances. Thus, the fact that we should act for a reason, and be "rational," together with the fact that we encounter similar cases on different occasions, implies that our actions should follow laws.

In accounting, likewise, a rule is a generalization which specifies the similar accounting treatment that should be given to similar cases. Accounting theory provides the reason why a case (for example, a transaction, or a company's financial position) should be accounted for in one way rather than another. Because the theory is constant, that same reason applies to all similar cases. Thus it is possible to formulate a rule for those cases.

Set down to promote the common good of some association. When an individual sets down a rule for himself ("When the clock says 6 a.m., you must wake up"), we call this a resolution, a plan, or a schedule. Only a rule which pertains to some association is a law. Because a law deals with more than one person, it aims to coordinate the actions of many persons. By the "common good of an association" we mean the purpose for which that association was formed and the reason why it exists. For example, the common good (or purpose) of an athletic association, such as a football league, is to provide frequent opportunities for competitive play. The common good (or purpose) of a book club is to provide an incentive for its members to read interesting books. Similarly every association has a purpose which is its common good.

The common good of the accounting profession is the reason why accountants organized themselves into a profession in the first place. We shall discuss this matter in depth in later chapters on professionalism in accounting (chapters 8-10 below). But, briefly, as we said above, the common good or purpose of the accounting profession is to report the truth about a financial enterprise in a trustworthy way. In a word, the purpose of accountancy as a profession is "truth and trust." Accounting rules are meant to give authoritative guidance, based on the best accounting theory, as to the most truthful accounting treatment of particular cases. These rules coordinate the actions of all members of the profession, bringing about a desirable uniformity of result and judgment.

Set down by some person or persons who have authority over that common good. Since a law is a rule which is meant to coordinate the actions of many persons in an association in such a way as to promote the purpose of that association, there would be chaos if each person attempted to set down such rules, or if different groups within the association did so. It is necessary for there to be only one body of law governing an association. Thus, a law must be set down by some person or persons who have been designated to take care of the common good (purpose) of that association, the so-called "government" or "officers" of the association.

In accounting, rules originally became authoritative through an informal process whereby they were sifted and tested through practice and critical deliberation. That is, a kind of consensus was reached over time, in the way that scholars or scientists come to recognize the best accepted theory or interpretation. The phrase "generally accepted accounting principles" originally referred to precisely that sort of consensus. More recently, the profession has recognized certain "standard setting" bodies as authoritative. Currently the Financial Accounting Standards Board (FASB) is the chief such authority for public accounting.

Promulgated. Since a law is meant to be followed by the many members of an association, and since it coordinates their actions, it must be made public and be grasped by them and followed. An implicit custom is not yet a law. Many people who are merely happening to do the same thing on similar reasons is not yet a law. In accounting, likewise, rules set down by authoritative bodies are published and made available to accounting professionals, who correspondingly have a duty to become familiar with and practice in accordance with these rules.

Rules Are Necessary But Not Sufficient

Rules are necessary for a variety of reasons, some of which we have seen already. As we said, rules are necessary for rationality and consistency, because to be rational we need to treat similar cases similarly, and rules help to insure that. Again, rules are necessary for the coordination of the actions of many.

But furthermore rules enable us to capture and preserve the insights of those experts who have the best judgment; they enable many people to profit from those insights. On this point, compare how Americans view the "Founding Fathers" such as Washington, Jefferson, and Madison who crafted the United States Constitution. The U.S. Constitution has long been admired as an ingenious expression of "statecraft." The Founders had an extraordinary insight into politics. The fundamental law which is the Constitution captures and carries forward their insights to the benefit of future generations. Likewise, in accounting, rules promulgated by FASB, or by executive committees of the AICPA, are meant to make available to all practitioners the judgments of leading experts who are most knowledgeable of the relevant difficulties and implications in deciding perplexing cases.

Finally, because a law is necessarily "promulgated," that is, it must be explicitly articulated and made public, it becomes open to critical examination and discussion, which can lead in turn to better laws. Until we articulate a rule, we cannot improve it. In the same vein, authoritative bodies in accounting offer "exposure drafts" of proposed rules and welcome "comment letters" from experts. Even after they are promulgated, rules are subject to constant examination and criticism, all of which should lead to improvements in practice.

However, although rules are necessary and helpful in their place, they are not sufficient, because they are incomplete. There are two basic reasons for their incompleteness: (i) entirely new sorts of cases may arise, which were not contemplated before, and which will require the formulation of new rules; (ii) cases which have already been considered may occur in the context of facts and circumstances which were not foreseen, but which will imply that the case needs to be treated differently. The first reason derives mainly from our inability to see the future; the second derives additionally from the apparently limitless varieties of particular circumstances which may arise, and which cannot all be taken into account in advance. Indeed, because a rule needs to have a certain simplicity, in order to be understandable and capable of being followed, one would not want a rule to take into account all possible variations in cases, even if these could all be recognized in advance.

As an example of the first kind of completeness, consider the following classic case. Suppose the prince of a medieval walled city, which is at war with a neighboring city, sets down the rule that "The city gate is not to be opened by any civilian except with my express permission." One day the prince leads a band of all of his soldiers in an attack on that neighboring city. They meet strong resistance and are repulsed. They flee back in haste and, on as they are returning, the prince is killed. As the band approaches the city gates, they start yelling to the people inside to open the gates and let them in. However, the prince had set down the law that *no civilian is allowed to open the city gates without his express permission*, and the prince is now dead. Should the townspeople open the gates? Obviously they should, because the prince had not contemplated this particular case when he set down the law. (Note that even if he had, there would have been some *other* sort of case which he would not have foreseen.) In accounting, rules often suffer from this sort of incompleteness relative to advances in technology and relative to an increasing complexity of business transactions. Information systems raise questions about internal control that never arose in the days of paper slips and receipts. Credit default swaps and collateralized debt obligations raise accounting questions that could not have been imagined before these instruments were developed.

A simple example of the second sort of incompleteness would be the following. You are driving a car on a highway and you are coming to the toll booth. The law says that you must stop and pay the toll. You know that if you fail to stop, lights and alarms will go off, and you might be chased by a police car and given a ticket. However, as you are reaching the toll booth, you look in your rear view mirror and see the car behind you approaching at a very high speed. You see that the driver of that car is not paying attention and seems to be texting or somehow fiddling around with a cell phone. So, instead of stopping, you speed through the toll booth to avoid a rear-end collision. Here a common case ("car approaching a tool booth") is indeed subject to law ("car must stop and pay the toll"), but the case reasonably needs to be dealt with differently because of the unusual facts and circumstances which alter the significance of the case.

The Incompleteness of Rules

The fundamental incompleteness of rules (or laws) has been recognized since classical times. In light of this incompleteness, Aristotle said that anyone who wanted to be a good member of an association needed to have two virtues: he needed the virtue of justice, so that he had a firm disposition to know the law and follow the law, but he also needed the virtue of "equity" (which in Greek is called *epieikeia*), so that he could recognize when the law as stated was incomplete, and he would be able to do the right thing in those unusual circumstances. The justice expressed solely by the law needs to be adapted and corrected, Aristotle said. Cicero likewise famously asserted that "strict justice is strict injustice." He meant that someone who aimed to follow the law slavishly, without regard to the purpose or point of the law, would end up doing monstrously bad things. The example above of the medieval city shows clearly that this is so: if the townspeople in the circumstances followed the strict letter of the law, they would do something seriously wrong. In accounting we see similarly that someone who slavishly follows accounting rules and is solely "rule based" can easily go astray and may even become complicit in fraud.

What should one do when one comes upon a case with respect to which the relevant law is incomplete? To what standard should one appeal? On what basis should one decide? As the two examples above show, there are two grounds on which one may reach a reasonable judgment.

The first is the "intention of the lawgiver." That is, one considers what the lawgiver was attempting to achieve through the law. Then, one does what in the circumstances will achieve that purpose. In the example of the medieval city, the prince's purpose in setting down that law about the city gates was the safety of the city. Obviously, if the city's army is butchered outside the city gates, the city will not be safe. So to follow the prince's command in the circumstances would imply the frustration or negation of the prince's purposes. That is why in the imagined case it would be right for the townspeople to open the city gates.

The second standard to which one may appeal is some broad rule or standard—some principle perhaps of "common sense"—which applies generally in the interpretation of the law. In American law, for instance, it is possible to appeal to a principle known as "necessity," which is roughly the principle that the law may be broken when it is necessary to do so to avoid some greater harm, such as the loss of life or limb. In the example of the tool booth, the driver who passes right through without paying the toll could appeal to this "necessity."

It is tempting to find an analogue for each of these in accounting. For example, sometimes a distinction is drawn in accounting between the "objective" of an accounting standard and the "principles" underlying a standard. So we might try to define terms exactly and say that a consideration of the first sort ("what is the *purpose* of this rule?") should be referred to as an appeal to the "objective" of the accounting standard which includes that rule, and that a consideration of the second sort ("what general *principles govern the interpretation* of this rule?") should be referred to as an appeal to accounting "principles." However, in practice, people are not that precise and will use the term "principle" indifferently to refer to any consideration in some domain which is more basic than a rule and which, if followed, would lead to a "true and fair" presentation when the strict following of the rule would not.

Rules in the Service of Principles

A simple example will illustrate how *objectives* might be distinguished from *principles* and *rules*. Suppose you receive in the mail from a friend a houseplant which comes with the instructions: "Give plenty of sunshine and sufficient water (although do not overwater); and feed regularly with plant food." You are the parent in the household and give instructions to your children for taking care of it. To do so, you need to make the instructions concrete. So you set down rules. "Move the plant to the living room in the afternoon, where it can get sun. Give it half a cup of water each morning. Each week on Saturday morning, mix a teaspoon of plant food in with the water." Some observations about the example:

(i)   A healthy plant is something good. It is presupposed by the instructions that you as the owner want to have and to enjoy this good of a healthy plant.

(ii) The instructions have a purpose: their point is to insure the realization of that good of a healthy plant. The instructions are general rules of thumb that need to be followed if the plant is to remain healthy, grow, and flourish. They are what you need to do in order to achieve that good. The instructions are constants. Because they are directly related to the objective, they state ways in which the plant should be treated which are always true. But note that instructions cannot be implemented as they stand. They are too general. It is not that instructions are like the rules, only more general, in the way that "Water the plant some time each day" is more general than "Water the plant each morning," which in turn is more general than "Water the plant at 8 am every morning." Rather, *the instructions lack the specificity needed to be acted on at all.*

(iii) The commands you give your children are a way of connecting the instructions to actual actions that persons can do. The instructions so to speak need to be *operationalized*. You need to be able to check that they have been fulfilled and carried out. The commands are not constant: as situations change, the commands might change. For example, you may determine that half a cup is too much water and reduce that to a third of a cup. Or if the morning routine is so rushed that the children are forgetting to water the plant, you might change the time of day for watering to the evening, before they go to bed. Likewise, when the seasons change, and the sun is in a different location, you might tell them to move the plant to a different room, or to let it stay where it is.

(iv) You presuppose as the parent that your children will use some modicum of intelligence in interpreting your commands. If they sleep late and do not finish breakfast until 12:01pm, when it is the afternoon instead of the morning, you would still expect them to water the plant that day. If the half cup measure is missing, you would expect them to estimate that amount using common sense.

(v) There are ways of treating the plant which should always be avoided, and it is presupposed that no one would do this. It is not necessary to give instructions about this. For instance, the plant should not be left out in the snow, or put in a hot shower, or washed in the dishwasher. You should never cut it at the stalk, or pour bleach on it. There are myriad ways in which the plant could be mistreated, but the instructions presume (because after all you purchased the plant) that you will not mistreat it in obvious ways.

(vi) But if there are predictable ways in which children might, through ignorance or inadvertence, damage the plant, then you might make instructions about these in particular. For example, you might tell them to carry it always with two hands, so that they do not lose their grip and drop it, which they risk doing.

The example provides a nice analogy for accounting. In this example, the objective is a healthy plant: likewise, in accounting, the objective in general is always a true and fair representation (of a transaction, or the results of operations or financial position of a company), although the objective of a particular standard will be the true and fair representation of a particular sort of transaction, etc. For instance, an accounting standard dealing with business combinations would have as its objective the true and fair representation of when a combination has occurred and the ramifications of the combination.

The instructions for dealing with the plant would correspond to what in accounting are referred to as the principles. Principles are ways of proceeding which are directly related to the objective but which are not yet operational or actionable. They flow from the objective and are necessary for the attainment of the objective; thus they are constants. Because they lack concreteness, they are not "rules at a higher level of generality." It would be a mistake to characterize them as more general rules.

The commands given to the children are analogues of accounting rules. The commands are concrete specifications which are in the service of the instructions.

Similarly, accounting rules are typically operationalized and specified in detail, but they are in the service of the accounting principles which further the accounting objective. Rules can and should change, when circumstances change.

Again, just as it is presupposed that the parents' commands will be interpreted by the children with a modicum of intelligence, so it supposed that accounting rules will be interpreted with intelligence and professional judgment. In particular, it is presupposed that they will never be used—or, more precisely, abused!—in order to "trump" the principle or principles which they meant to serve.

Finally, just as it is presupposed in the example, but it hardly needs to be stated, that there are certain ways of dealing with the plant which should always be avoided without exception, since they will harm or destroy the plant, so in accounting anything which attacks the objective of accounting (a true and fair presentation, together with trustworthiness) is presumed to be excluded, especially fraud. It is always presupposed in accounting that an accountant will do nothing misleading or fraudulent, and yet no accounting standard begins or ends with a directive such as "Commit no fraud."

Virtues as Safeguarding Principles

We discussed in chapter 4 the virtues of an accountant. Do these virtues play any role in keeping objectives, principles, and rules in their proper place? Does an accountant need to have the virtues in order to be able consistently to treat rules as in the service of principles and as never trumping principles? Yes, the virtues of an accountant do play such a role, and obviously so.

We distinguished between human virtues and the specific virtues of an accountant. The former make someone a good human being, the latter make someone a good accounting professional. Both sorts of virtues play this role.

The human virtues play this role because they constantly require and call forth something analogous in nearly all domains of life, so that an accountant who is a also a good human being, when he keeps rules in their proper place as in the service of principles, will simply be carrying out in the domain of accounting what he does as a matter of course elsewhere. Each virtue works through a subtle interplay with what has been referred to as "prudence" or "practical wisdom." The virtue pursues an ideal (a matter of the "heart," of "commitment" and "idealism"), and prudence determines and states the best concrete realization of this ideal, in the circumstances. For instance, someone who has the virtue of moderation (self-mastery) is devoted to the ideal of only eating those things that are consistent with general good health and propriety, and not in excessive amounts. But prudence determines what this amounts to in particular circumstances. Sometimes moderation may require eating very little (as when someone for health reasons needs to lose weight), but in other circumstances moderation may require eating heartily (as when you are invited over by a friend to share in some great event he is celebrating, and friendliness and good cheer imply that you share with him in eating all kinds of special foods and treats). These are superficially opposite courses of action, but they are both dictated by prudence, and both represent the ideal of moderation, which is the "rationalization" of the otherwise animalistic appetite for food, so that the way we deal with food expresses our rationality.

All of the human "moral" virtues work in the same way. They involve the use of practical intelligence to specify "rules," as it were, which concretize the ideals that the virtue is committed to.

We said that the virtues specific to accounting included dedication to the truth; courage (and stubbornness); simplicity; and professionalism. The crucial virtue here for keeping rules in the service of principles is dedication to the truth, because when rules inappropriately trump principles the truth is obscured or effectively denied. Courage is helpful too, because frequently when an accountant ought not let rules trump principles, he is placed in a position where he must contradict management or even a fellow practitioner, which, when this is justified, requires courage. Simplicity is valuable too, because it requires a "simple" insight to recognize that rules are trumping principles, as will be abundantly clear in the Enron case study below in chapter 11. Finally, professionalism plays a role, insofar as recognizing when rules are trumping principles requires professional judgment, and a practitioner will be more prepared to place confidence in this judgment, the greater his sense of professionalism and the more "proper pride" (or magnanimity) he takes in being a professional.

So what is approvingly referred to as "principles-based" accounting, as opposed to mere "rules-based" accounting, is not something that can be achieved merely by pointing out the problems in the latter, or by promoting some conceptual view or framework, or some document or study, in which the perils of "rules-based" accounting are demonstrated and the merits of "principles-based" accounting are argued for. This would be to suppose that "principles-based" accounting is only a matter of achieving the right point of view, as if only an intellectual virtue were at stake. Rather, principles-based accounting is a kind of approach that implies a certain kind of character in an accountant.

The Insufficiency of Rules: An Example

One may illustrate that rules are not sufficient for the good practice of accounting by a consideration of the following simple but representative fact pattern as regards possible conflicts of interest.

Suppose that Alison, Bill, and Cathy are members of Accurate Accounting, LLP, and are engaged to audit Classic Car Company of New England.

- Alison has a relative who has at various times invested in Classic Car Company.
- Bill has a relative who is an employee of Classic Car Company.
- For part of her work on the engagement, Cathy uses the services of a consulting company, which employs a relative of an employee of Classic Car Company.

We ask: Would the independence of Alison, Bill, or Cathy be considered impaired? What would we need to know in order to decide this? Will an appeal to the relevant rules suffice to decide these matters?

Suppose a practitioner consults what seems to be the relevant rule, for instance, one of the formulations provided by the AICPA in its Code of Professional Conduct of the standard of Independence. (The AICPA supplements these rules with interpretations which aim to identify the usual sorts of conflict of interest for practitioners and render decisions about them.) Applying such a rule to the present case, we might determine something like the following. As regards Alison, her independence would be regarded as impaired if four conditions were satisfied:

(i) If the investment of Alison's relative were material to the relative; and

(ii) If the relative had invested during the time of the engagement or when Accurate Accounting expressed its opinion; and

(iii) If Alison knew of the relative's investment; and

(iv) If the relative were Alison's spouse or dependent.

If all of these conditions were satisfied, then, on the usually accepted rule, Alison's independence would be considered impaired.

As regards Bill, his independence would be regarded as impaired if two conditions were jointly satisfied:

(i) If the relative had a position at Classic Car that was audit sensitive; and

(ii) If the relative were Bill's spouse or dependent.

As regards Cathy, her independence would be regarded as impaired (indirectly so, on the grounds that the consulting firm on which she depended would not be regarded as independent) if three conditions were satisfied:

(i) If Cathy had relied upon the consulting company for a significant part of the engagement; and
(ii) If the relative of the employee of the consulting company, who works for Classic Car, were a spouse or dependent; and
(iii) If that relative who works for Classic Car had significant influence in that company or were involved in audit-sensitive work in that company.

These considerations, although admittedly complex, are familiar to someone who has studied the rules for independence and are perhaps not especially difficult. They are something like the standard conditions that need to be taken into account in order to make decisions in these sorts of cases about independence.

However, we are not so much interested in the rules, and in these conditions, as much as in a fact about this appeal to rules, which is obvious once noted, but which is not unimportant for all that. The important fact is that this appeal to rules, which we had hoped would decide the matter for us, is not sufficient on its own to decide our difficulty. This is perhaps a surprising fact, given the complexity of these rules, and the detail to which these particular concerns about conflict of interest have been worked out. Our point is this: if rules are insufficient to decide a commonplace and relatively simple case like this, then we can be assured that they are insufficient generally.

Our appeal to rules is insufficient on its own for a variety of identifiable reasons. It is useful to articulate these reasons and briefly examine them individually:

1. Rules typically state only necessary, not sufficient conditions: as was said, they are usually open-ended and cannot take into account all possible cases.
2. Rules make use of terms that require interpretation. We cannot indefinitely clarify rules with further rules: at some point we must rely upon good judgment in interpreting the rules.
3. We must appeal to idealizations in order to interpret the rules: rules are useless if used by someone who lacks a good sense of these idealizations.
4. Even to care about interpreting the rules correctly, we need to place our getting them right over considerations of self-interest, convenience, comfort, and inclination. Rules are useless except for someone with the correct motivation.

5. Rules on their own are unmanageable: we can practically speaking make sense of them, remember them, and use them as guides for action, only in relation to the principles they are meant to embody.

6. We cannot be said actually to follow a rule, unless we can recognize when our actions are in conformity with that rule; yet our successfully recognizing this is itself not contained in the rule, and it must presuppose some other disposition.

Let us consider each of these points in turn. Taken together, they serve to illustrate that rules are for principles, not principles for rules, and that rules are not enough.

1. Rules can state only necessary, not sufficient conditions: they are essentially open-ended and cannot take into account all possible cases.

By a "necessary condition" we mean a "that without which not." It is a "requirement," or a *sine qua non*. We call such a condition "necessary" because, if it is not satisfied, then that which requires it cannot exist. To get clear about this, consider the following claim:

(S1) A good source of electricity is a necessary condition for a washing machine to wash clothes.

That is: without a good source of electricity, the machine will not work. Electricity, then, is a "necessary condition" of washing one's clothes in a washing machine: the machine requires electricity. In contrast, a sufficient condition is something that suffices to bring a thing into existence or realize it. Once we bring about a sufficient condition for a thing, then immediately we bring about that thing as well. A sufficient condition implies or guarantees the existence of that of which it is a condition. Consider, for example, this claim:

(S2) A good source of electricity is not a sufficient condition for a washing machine to wash clothes.

This is true since, after all, the machine might be broken, or you might lack water or detergent, in which case it will not be enough simply to have a good source of electricity.

Rules about conflicts of interest, such as the AICPA interpretations cited above, typically give only necessary conditions for an accountant's independence, not sufficient conditions. They give *requirements* of independence; they state what *must be the case*, if a practitioner is to be independent; they identify some of the things (usually the most salient or most common things) that cannot be lacking in an independent practitioner. But such rules do not provide sufficient conditions.

No matter how complicated or detailed the rule, it remains a possibility that a practitioner satisfies all the stated rules, but still lacks independence—because (say) there exists a conflict of interest, which arises out of circumstances not envisaged by or articulated in the rules. This is an extremely important point. It follows from it that the following is a fallacy:

(S3) I followed all the relevant rules, therefore I acted properly.

The rules, as we noted, do not express sufficient conditions of proper conduct; thus, to follow the rules is not itself a guarantee of propriety.

It is instructive that rules and codes will typically add a reminder such as the following:

(S4) "It is impossible to enumerate all circumstances in which a member's independence might appear impaired to a third party. For instance, a member's relationship with a cohabitant may be equivalent to that of a spouse."

We might amend the rule to take this into account and add that additional relationship, of course, but that will by no means remediate the basic incompleteness of the rule.

2. Rules make use of terms that require interpretation. We cannot indefinitely clarify rules with further rules: at some point we must rely upon good judgment in interpreting the rules.

Look again at the statements above of the relevant rules. The rules make use of the terms such as "material," "significant," "substantial," "audit-sensitive," and so on, which themselves require intelligent interpretation.

For instance, Bill's independence is affected if his spouse's position at Classic Car is "audit-sensitive." Is there some rule that clarifies what an "audit-sensitive" position is? A code might provide a rule to help us interpret its rule, such as the following:

(S5) "In general, someone's activities would be considered audit-sensitive if such activities were normally an element of or subject to significant internal accounting controls."

But note that this further rule contains an important qualification: it holds only "in general" (or "for the most part"). That is, it is not meant to rule out other cases, where an employee's activities are not "normally an element of or subject to significant internal accounting controls" yet are audit-sensitive nonetheless. (It is not difficult to contrive such cases.) Furthermore, this rule as well contains terms that require interpretation: it refers to activities that "normally" are an element of internal accounting controls, where these controls are furthermore "significant." But what counts as being "normally" an element? What counts as a "significant" control? If we tried to define these terms with further rules, we would find that terms requiring interpretation would crop up once again, in our rules for understanding rules about rules.

It will not help to try to enumerate cases, because such an enumeration could not possibly be exhaustive. For instance, a code might and will add something like the following:

> (S6) "For example, the following positions would normally be considered audit-sensitive: cashier; internal auditor; accounting supervisor; purchasing agent; or inventory warehouse supervisor. The list is not meant to be exhaustive."

The list is illustrative only: as it states, it is not exhaustive (note that it uses "or," not "and," to link the items together). The practitioner must therefore grasp the sort of thing that is meant by the items on the list and be prepared to recognize, as similar, an indefinite number of cases which, however, are not enumerated.

Because rules are in this way incomplete, we therefore reach the following extremely important conclusion: It is in principle impossible to capture in rules everything that is contained in an ethical principle or ideal. It follows, therefore, that a good practitioner must always use good judgment in arriving at a sound interpretation of accounting rules.

3. We must appeal to idealizations in order to interpret rules: rules are useless if employed by someone who lacks a good sense of these idealizations.

Very frequently, in order to interpret those open-ended terms contained in a rule, we need to appeal to what an ideally "reasonable person" or "impartial observer" would judge to be the case.

For instance, in (S4) above it was stated that various relationships besides being a spouse or dependent can affect the independence or perceived independence of a practitioner. Suppose for instance that Bill has a cousin who works at Classic Car. Ordinarily, the relationship of cousin might be considered sufficiently remote as not to affect independence. But suppose that, in this case, Bill and his cousin grew up together and regard themselves as "best friends" and akin to brothers. Suppose that in many other contexts Bill and his cousin have collaborated on business enterprises and initiatives. Should Bill's relationship to his cousin, then, be taken to affect his independence? How should Bill decide? The relevant rule on its own gives no answer: the relevant rule mentions only spouses and dependents.

What we need to do, in that case, is to appeal to a kind of idealization of the rule, as interpreted by an ideal interpreter. The idealized rule would be something like this:

> (S6) Independence is affected if a practitioner has a relationship to an employee which is close enough that it might tend to influence or sway his or her judgment.

But whether that idealized rule is satisfied is something that we might wish to judge by imagining how a reasonable observer, with knowledge of the relevant facts, and with a good grasp of human nature and how people typically act, would look upon the situation. What we would need to consider is: Would such an observer conclude that Bill's judgment was in danger of being swayed, or that someone looking on might be confident that Bill's judgment had not been swayed? Thus, the AICPA code adds a remark like the following:

> (S7) In addition, in situations involving assessment of the association of any relative or dependent person with a client, members must consider whether the strength of personal and business relationships between the member and the relative or dependent person, in conjunction with the specified association with the client, would lead a reasonable person aware of all the facts, who took into consideration normal strength of character and normal behavior under such circumstances, to conclude that the situation poses an unacceptable threat to the member's objectivity and appearance of independence.

But how do we decide what a "reasonable person aware of all the facts" would decide? In many cases a practitioner can seek the advice of an experienced and detached colleague. But even in that case he or she would have to rely on his or her own sense of whether that colleague had given sensible advice after all. Thus, the interpretation of any rule requires, not only an appeal to how a reasonable person would judge or view things, but also some actual person's reasonability.

There is no escaping the conclusion, then, that to interpret rules correctly requires that we ourselves have good sense; experience; familiarity; and reasonability about those matters with which the rules deal.

4. Even to care about interpreting the rules correctly, we need to place our getting them right over considerations of self-interest, convenience, comfort, and inclination. Rules are useless except for someone with the correct motivation.

So far we have been looking at various ways in which, from the nature of the case, "rules are not enough." A rule only roughly circumscribes an area in which correct conduct is found; it cannot exactly point out correct conduct. No rule can cover in advance all possible cases in human action: a rule must remain open-ended. A rule must be interpreted, and we need to use good sense in interpreting it. But an even more basic insufficiency of a rule is—obviously—that people need to be committed to following the rule, and this commitment itself cannot come from the rule. Why? Well, how might we construct a rule that tried to be the source of concern for itself? Suppose that we added to a rule an imperative enjoining commitment, "And you must be committed to following this rule!" For instance:

> (S8) A member should refuse an engagement with an enterprise if his or her spouse does audit-sensitive work for the enterprise—and a member must be committed to following this rule!

Clearly, the clause enjoining commitment is itself part of the rule; hence it has force only if someone is already committed to following the rule. It adds no additional force on its own. Furthermore, to follow the rule seems less important than the good of independence, which the rule is meant to safeguard. Thus, what the first part of the rule enjoins (avoiding something that compromises independence) is more important than what the second part of the rule enjoins (simply following the rule). So anyone who lacked commitment to the first part of the rule, which concerns the more important goal, could hardly acquire that sort of commitment on account of the second part of the rule, which concerns a lesser goal.

Neither would it help to add a separate rule enjoining commitment to all of the rules. Suppose that at the end of the AICPA Code of Professional Conduct one were to add a rule that stated:

> (S9) Members are to follow all of the rules in this Code.

Then we would have the same problem as before: since (S9) is a part of the Code, it can add no force to the Code; and in any case what the rules of the Code enjoin is more important than what (S9) enjoins.

No doubt it is with a view to this difficulty that the AICPA Code at the start appeals, not to a rule, but to the free and voluntary commitment of practitioners to abide by the standards and principles of accounting. In fact the very first lines of the Code are as follows:

(S10) Membership in the American Institute of Certified Public Accountants is voluntary. By accepting membership, a certified public accountant assumes an obligation of self-discipline above and beyond the requirements of laws and regulations.

Note the words: "beyond the requirements of laws and regulations."

5. Rules on their own are unmanageable: practically speaking, we can make sense of them, remember them, and use them as guides for action, only if we understand them in relation to the principles they are meant to embody.

The cases of Alison, Bob, and Cathy sketched above are different from one another. Alison has a close relative who invests in a client company; Bob has a similar relative who is an employee; Cathy employs an agent who has a relative in the company, whose activities would be related in a special way to an audit Cathy might perform. How do we collect these and other similar instances together, as variations on a similar theme? Of course, we take them all to be illustrations of how "independence" might be diminished.

And yet this ability to collect particular particulars and treat them as instances of the same thing is important. We unify cases relative to a rule, and we in turn unify rules relative to principles or ideals which the rules are meant to safeguard. If we lacked a grasp of the relevant principles and ideals, each rule would stand on its own, in isolation. It would be "meaningless"—something to follow simply as a kind of game or challenge.

6. We cannot be said actually to follow a rule, unless we can recognize when our actions are in conformity with that rule; yet our successfully recognizing this is itself not contained in the rule, and it must presuppose some other disposition.

Here is an instance of what we mean, from science. Suppose a student is doing a science experiment and wants to follow the rule, "Heat the mixture until it reaches 50 degrees Centigrade." He therefore begins to heat the mixture; then he places a Centigrade thermometer in the mixture; and finally he removes the heat from the mixture when the thermometer reads 50 degrees.

The student would be unable to follow the rule without a thermometer. He needs some way of checking that his behavior conforms to the rule. But, more than this, he has to have some assurance that the thermometer is accurate. Perhaps he has purchased it from a reputable company. Or perhaps to verify the thermometer's accuracy he performs a test, such as placing it in boiling water at sea level, to make sure that in those circumstances it reads 100 degrees, as it should.

Suppose that when he places the thermometer in boiling water, to check its accuracy, he finds that it reads 95 degrees. It would be likely, then, that the thermometer was in error; yet the student could not immediately be confident of that. He would need to investigate more, taking steps to see if he cannot remove the ostensible error. Perhaps the thermometer was inaccurate, or perhaps the water was impure, or something else interfered with its reading.

The student's reliance on the thermometer, and his being disposed to investigate if he had reason to think that it was erroneous—all of this is presupposed in his using the thermometer to check whether the mixture has indeed reached 50 degrees Centigrade. That is to say, to use some measurement or criterion to verify that one has followed a rule, is to presuppose that one has taken reasonable and sufficient precautions to insure that one is correct in thinking that one's behavior thus conforms to the rule. It must be reasonable for a rule-follower to rely on those instruments and measures for self-checking, on which he or she does rely.

A similar condition holds for accountants. In any task of accountancy or auditing, this condition, as we have said, is commonly accepted and is called "diligence," "reasonable diligence," "due diligence," or "due care."

Here are some examples from the AICPA book of professional standards, where this condition is referred to:

> (S11) In conducting a review, "…if the accountant becomes aware that information coming to his attention is incorrect, incomplete, or otherwise unsatisfactory, he should perform the additional procedures he deems necessary to achieve limited assurance that there are no material modifications that should be made to the financial statements in order for the statements to be in conformity with generally accepted accounting principles" (AR §100.30).

Of course the demands of reasonable diligence increase with the nature of a practitioner's services and in proportion to the degree of assurance claimed (compilation, review, audit). This is in part what is meant by due diligence: diligence in proportion to the significance of the claim and the risk of error.

Proportionate diligence is everywhere presupposed by the AICPA Code of Professional Conduct. Consider for instance Cathy in our example. When she makes use of the services of a consulting agency, she should do so on the condition that this does not affect her independence. Her independence might be affected, if there were some close relationship between a member of that consulting agency and a member of the client company. To what extent, then, is she responsible for checking to be sure that there is not such a relationship? She should use the discretion and diligence that is required given the task at hand and the circumstances:

> (S12) The member should make a reasonable inquiry to determine whether such relationships exist, and if they do, careful consideration should be given to whether the financial interests in question would lead a reasonable observer to conclude that the specified relationships pose an unacceptable threat to the member's independence.

Rules in the Service of Principles: An Example

Let us consider the relationship between rules and principles from another angle. As we have seen, rules do not exist on their own: rules are used by, and are meant to guide, a reasonable interpreter. But that means that the relationship between rules and principles is not fixed: it is something that we are free to alter, based on how we look upon rules. Basically, we are faced with a choice: as was said, we can either regard rules as expressing and safeguarding principles— "rules in the service of principles"—or take rules as sufficient and fully determinative of any relevant principles— "rules as trumping principles."

A common example in accounting illustrates the point, that is, whether for purposes of accounting a lease should be treated as an operating lease or a capital lease. As introductory accounting books will explain, leases fall along a scale: at one end of which is a pure rental arrangement, where some property is used for a short term in exchange for what amounts to rent; at the other end of which is a mortgage type arrangement, where ownership is effectively transferred from lessor to lessee, and the lease payments are in substance the same as payments on outstanding debt. Although there are close calls and difficult cases, there is typically a fact of the matter as to whether the lessee assumes the benefits and burdens of ownership, and thus the lease is of the latter type.

Now how would one deal with this issue of the proper treatment of a lease if taking the approach of "rules in the service of principles"? First, one would articulate the relevant principles and take these to be ultimately authoritative. For instance:

> *Principle 1*: The accounting treatment of a transaction should fairly represent that transaction. (The principle of transparency.)
>
> *Principle 2*: When the burdens and benefits of ownership are assumed by the lessee, then, although the transaction has the form of a lease, in substance it is equivalent to a mortgage arrangement. (The principle of "substance over form.")

Next, one might articulate rules which would serve as "rules of thumb" for identifying when the condition mentioned in Principle 2 obtains, that is, when in fact what has the form of a lease is in substance the purchase of property with 100% financing. SFAS 13 articulates four such rules, which we may summarize as follows (omitting some technicalities and qualifications):

> *Rule 1*. If ownership is transferred at the end of the lease, then the lease should be treated as a capital lease.
>
> *Rule 2*. If the lessee has an option to buy the property at a bargain price (below market value), thus effectively guaranteeing purchase, then the lease should be treated as a capital lease.
>
> *Rule 3*. If the length of the lease is for at least 75% of the total useful life of the property, then the lease should be treated as a capital lease.
>
> *Rule 4*. If the lease payments equal at least 90% of the value of the property, then the lease should be treated as a capital lease.

We would be taking the approach of "rules in the service of principles" if we were to state clearly that the principles are paramount and authoritative in the interpretation of the rules. Thus: if following the rules were to result in an accounting treatment that represented as an operating lease a transaction in which, in fact, ownership is transferred, then the rules would have to give way to the principles. In actual practice, of course, what happens is that there is some latitude in how one estimates fair value and income stream, so that it can often happen that either an operating lease or a capital lease treatment could be reasonably defended, depending upon how one fixes the parameters. So the rules alone would give no determinate answer, and the practitioner would need to decide upon that accounting treatment that both accords with the rules and preserves the principles.

On the other hand, a practitioner would be taking the approach of "rules trumping principles" if the only question that he or she considered was whether the numbers could reasonably be manipulated to justify whatever accounting treatment was desired. (And in some cases an operating lease treatment may be more advantageous for a company's financial report than a capital lease treatment.) In that case, the practitioner would be approaching the accounting issue as if "rules were enough"—when they clearly are not.

It is noteworthy that even relatively authoritative presentations of accounting principles can blur the distinction between rules as serving and rules as trumping principles. For instance, *Miller's Comprehensive GAAP Guide* begins its discussion of the accounting treatment of leases well enough:

> Some lease agreements are such that an asset and a related liability should be reported on the balance sheet of an enterprise. The distinction is one of substance over form (basic principle) when the transaction actually transfers substantially all the benefits and risks inherent in the ownership of the property.

When the *Guide* cites the maxim of "substance over form," this is equivalent to saying that principles are prior to rules. So far so good. But then the *Guide* continues:

> Established in GAAP are criteria to determine whether a lease transaction is in substance a transfer of the incidents of ownership. If, at its inception, a lease meets one or more of the following four criteria, the lease should be classified as a transfer of ownership... [The four rules from SFAS 13 are then given.]

But here the *Guide* lapses inadvertently into language that suggests that rules trump principles. Rules or criteria in fact do not "determine" (as the *Guide* puts it) whether a lease transaction is in substance a transfer of ownership. They do not determine this in the sense that they are not exhaustive (they are necessary but not sufficient conditions), and they may be indeterminate in their application and require good judgment: as we have seen, a transaction can frequently either satisfy one of the criteria or not do so, depending upon defensible judgments as to value and income. Thus to say, as the *Miller Guide* does, that these criteria "determine" whether ownership is transferred is to invite and even encourage the view that the rules are enough and that the relevant principles can be put aside.

A Relevant Legal Case

We have argued that ethics is indispensable for accounting practice. Because of this, a practitioner who does not aim to act ethically, will not even succeed in acting legally. Some legal cases are cautionary examples of this truth.

A case that illustrates nicely that "rules are not enough" is *U.S. v. Simon*, 425 F.2d 796 (2nd Cir. 1969). Simon was a senior partner with Lybrand, Ross Bros. & Montgomery, who was convicted, along with fellow members of Lybrand, under the Securities Exchange Act of 1934, of drawing up and certifying a false and misleading financial statement, when auditing Continental Vending Machine Corporation ("Continental"). Continental's president was one Harold Roth, who had a 25% stake in both Continental and an affiliate company, Valley Commercial Corporation ("Valley"), and who essentially controlled both companies. Valley's business was ostensibly to provide financing for vending machine companies, including Continental. Eventually it became a money-laundering instrument for Roth. Roth would raid money from Continental in order to fund his speculations in the stock market. He did this by having Continental transfer money to Valley, in transactions that had no legitimate business purpose, and then personally "borrowing" the money from Valley.

At first, these transfers of money from Continental to Valley (called by Roth the "Valley Receivable") were small in comparison with the legitimate loans that Valley, in conjunction with various banks, extended to Continental (the "Valley payable"). Moreover, Roth's investments did well enough, so that he was able to return the money to Valley, and transfer it back to Continental, by year's end. But when Roth's investments went south, and he became desperate and in need of larger sums, his raids on Continental became progressively larger, and his ability to return the money became more problematic, as the following table indicates:

Year	Advances	Repayments	Receivable
1958	$3,356,239	$2,583,172	$0
1959	4,586,000	3,510,451	384,402
1960	2,511,000	2,670,500	397,996
1961	2,390,674	1,520,000	848,006
1962	4,708,000	1,986,500	3,543,335

By September of 1962, Roth informed Simon that Valley would fall short of repayment by the $3.5 million indicated on the table above. Roth's lawyer and Simon then contrived to secure approximately that amount with collateral provided by Roth. To indicate this, Simon composed the following footnote, which was included in the 1962 financial report which Simon drew up and certified:

> "2. The amount receivable from Valley Commercial Corp. (an affiliated company of which Mr. Harold Roth is an officer, director and stockholder) bears interest at 12% a year. Such amount, less the balance of the notes payable to that company, is secured by the assignment to the Company of Valley's equity in certain marketable securities. As of February 15, 1963, the amount of such equity at current market quotations exceeded the net amount receivable."

But there were various deficiencies in this footnote: it treated the "Valley Receivable" as though it could be offset by the "Valley Payable" (which it could not, because the latter was a legitimate loan owed to Valley along with several banks); it failed to indicate that Valley was simply unable to repay; and it failed to indicate why Valley was unable to repay. Furthermore, the collateral which Roth had offered consisted largely of shares from Continental itself (!), which clearly could have value only if Continental's financial condition was secure, which was precisely what was in doubt. Finally, the value of such collateral as Roth had offered had plummeted after the end of 1962, before the publication of the report, and this was known to Simon.

In its prosecution of the case, government attorneys and experts offered their own version of how footnote 2 should have been written, if it were not to be deceptive:

> "2. The amount receivable from Valley Commercial Corp. (an affiliated company of which Mr. Harold Roth is an officer, director and stockholder), which bears interest at 12% a year, was uncollectible at September 30, 1962, since Valley had loaned approximately the same amount to Mr. Roth who was unable to pay. Since that date Mr. Roth and others have pledged as security for the repayment of his obligation to Valley and its obligation to Continental (now $3,900,000, against which Continental's liability to Valley cannot be offset) securities which, as of February 15, 1963, had a market value of $2,978,000. Approximately 80% of such securities are stock and convertible debentures of the Company."

What is of interest for our purposes, is that Simon's attorneys were able to find many expert witnesses—experienced accountants—who testified that Simon's footnote 2 was entirely in accord with GAAP and GAAS! As the Court observes:

> The defendants called eight expert independent accountants, an impressive array of leaders of the profession. They testified generally that, except for the error with respect to netting, the treatment of the Valley receivable in Note 2 was in no way inconsistent with generally accepted accounting principles or generally accepted auditing standards, since it made all the informative disclosures reasonably necessary for fair presentation of the financial position of Continental as of the close of the 1962 fiscal year. Specifically, they testified that neither generally accepted accounting principles nor generally accepted auditing standards required disclosure of the make-up of the collateral or of the increase of the receivable after the closing date of the balance sheet, although three of the eight stated that in light of hindsight they would have preferred that the make-up of the collateral be disclosed. The witnesses likewise testified that disclosure of the Roth borrowings from Valley was not required, and seven of the eight were of the opinion that such disclosure would be inappropriate. The principal reason given for this last view was that the balance sheet was concerned solely with presenting the financial position of the company under audit; since the Valley receivable was adequately secured in the opinion of the auditors and was broken out and shown separately as a loan to an affiliate with the nature of the affiliation disclosed, this was all that the auditors were required to do. To go further and reveal what Valley had done with the money would be to put into the balance sheet things that did not properly belong there; moreover, it would create a precedent which would imply that it was the duty of an auditor to investigate each loan to an affiliate to determine whether the money had found its way into the pockets of an officer of the company under audit, an investigation that would ordinarily be unduly wasteful of time and money.

This expert testimony was rejected by the jury, which, as mentioned, found Simon and his associates guilty. The appeals court sustained the verdict, observing:

> We join defendants' counsel in assuming that the mere fact that a company has made advances to an affiliate does not ordinarily impose a duty on an accountant to investigate what the affiliate has done with them

or even to disclose that the affiliate has made a loan to a common officer if this has come to his attention. But it simply cannot be true that an accountant is under no duty to disclose what he knows when he has reason to believe that, to a material extent, a corporation is being operated not to carry out its business in the interest of all the stockholders but for the private benefit of its president. For a court to say that all this is immaterial as a matter of law if only such loans are thought to be collectible would be to say that independent accountants have no responsibility to reveal known dishonesty by a high corporate officer. If certification does not at least imply that the corporation has not been looted by insiders so far as the accountants know, or, if it has been, that the diversion has been made good beyond peradventure (or adequately reserved against) and effective steps taken to prevent a recurrence, it would mean nothing, and the reliance placed on it by the public would be a snare and a delusion. Generally accepted accounting principles instruct an accountant what to do in the usual case where he has no reason to doubt that the affairs of the corporation are being honestly conducted. Once he has reason to believe that this basic assumption is false, an entirely different situation confronts him.

Note the court's claim that what "ordinarily" holds—that is, what gets defined by rules—is not sufficient to determine what counts as correct in this particular case. Rather, the court refers to the role of an accountant in fostering public trust and the "reliance" placed by the investor or creditor on an audit report.

There are two ways to interpret the court's decision. One is to say that Simon failed in fact to follow GAAP and GAAS, because accepted accounting rules require that material facts be disclosed, and the nature of Continental's advances to Valley was certainly material. But the court takes a different approach. It concedes the claim of the defendants that their report and certification were in conformity with all definite rules comprised by GAAP and GAAS under a defensible interpretation of those rules, but it maintains that these rules require judgment in their application, and that the ideals of disclosure and transparency, essential to an accountant's role, must be decisive, when merely following rules would yield a misleading result.

That is to say: rules are not enough. And, for the jury which decided Simon's guilt, this was basic common sense.

Recommended additional reading:

Office of the Chief Accountant, Securities and Exchange Commission, *Study Pursuant to Section 108(d) of the Sarbanes-Oxley Act of 2002 on the Adoption by the United States Financial Reporting System of a Principles-Based Accounting System* http://www.sec.gov/news/studies/principlesbasedstand.htm

United States v. Ebbers, 458 F.3d 110 (2d Cir. 2006), cert. denied, 127 S.Ct. 1483 (2007)

United States v. Simon

In re Global Crossing, Ltd. Sec. Litig., 322 F. Supp.2d 319, 339 (S.D.N.Y. 2004)

Alternative Approaches

7

WE HAVE BEEN ADVOCATING A VIRTUE-BASED APPROACH to accounting ethics, as filled out by a certain understanding of the role of principles and rules, and as supplemented by a proper concept of professionalism (which we will say more about in chapters 8-10 below). We believe that this approach is already implicit in accounting professionalism. That is, our approach simply articulates and systematizes the concept of accounting professionalism which is already implicitly presupposed by excellent practitioners.

In this chapter, we critically examine various alternative approaches. Our examination will serve to confirm the correctness of the approach taken here, by contrast. But this examination is additionally important because many of the views examined here have been very influential—not only in philosophy but also at the level of popular thought—and yet they are incompatible with accounting professionalism, in the sense that no practitioner could consistently both embrace those views and maintain high standards of accounting professionalism.

The alternative approaches that we shall examine include *relativism, situation ethics, conventionalism, scientism, emotivism, utilitarianism, Kantianism, Nietzscheanism,* and the *"threat-safeguard"* approach. We shall examine each of these in turn. But first a word is necessary about the fact of pluralism in ethics.

Pluralism in Ethics

Pluralism means the existence of different and incompatible beliefs about something. Every area of life is beset by pluralism. In courts of law, people often have different opinions about what evidence should be omitted and how that evidence should be weighed. In politics, people have different views about the basic direction a country should be going in. Even those who share the same basic view may differ about the best means for achieving the same end. In science, people can favor different theories and differ about whether claimed experimental evidence supports a theory or not. In mathematics, even when something is proved, people differ over the interest or importance of a theorem. In accounting, practitioners can differ in general matters, for example, about how widely fair-value accounting should be employed, or in particular, for example, about what accounting treatment is best for a certain transaction.

The near omnipresence of pluralism in human life shows that ethics is not a special case. Indeed, given the diversity-in-sameness of the human race—that, although we have the same nature, we have very different experiences and attitudes—one would be surprised if we did not show both unanimity in some matters, and pluralism in others, in each of the different areas of human life. Pluralism is typically exaggerated, because it is easier to notice the times when people disagree, overlooking the many more occasions when people are so much in agreement that no "issue" even arises.

In ethics, we may speak of pluralism as regards *particular decisions*, or as regards the proper *criteria* for making decisions, or even as regards *ways of life*. For example, someone is trying to decide whether to change jobs and asks the advice of his friends. One friend is in favor of the job switch, the other not—which is a disagreement over a particular decision. As they discuss things further, it becomes clear that the one friend takes considerations of compensation to be paramount, while the other regards possibilities for future advancement as paramount—which is a difference in the criteria they favor for making the decision. Finally, perhaps it becomes clear after even further discussion that the one friend favors a settled and secure life and the other an adventurous and risky life—which would be a difference in their attitudes about ways of life.

One of the most interesting sources of pluralism in ethics comes from the spirit of reform. Human culture and institutions seem to need periodic reform. When a reformer arises, he introduces pluralism of each of the three sorts we mentioned. He advocates new ways of doing things, and new criteria for evaluation, and these usually go along with a new way of life. For example, Martin Luther King Jr. advocated integration (a different way of doing things), he said that people should be judged "by the content of their character rather than the color of their skin" (a different criterion of evaluation), and he favored a society marked by peaceable humanism and personalism (a different approach to life).

Pluralism has always existed in ethics. A good example of pluralism in the assessment of a particular circumstance, from very ancient times, is the *Book of Job*. Job suffers all kinds of disasters, and some of his friends conclude from this that he should repent, because he must have sinned. But Job insists that he did not sin and claims that he is being tested. Again, in Greek philosophy, while Socrates was teaching that virtue was the most important good in human life, there arose various instructors in public speaking and legal advocacy, the so-called "sophists," who regarded political power instead as the paramount good. This was pluralism as regards which criteria to apply. In ancient Rome, the philosophical schools of Stoicism, Epicureanism, and Scepticism each advocated a different way of life and competed with one another for disciples. This was pluralism over ways of life.

Pluralism in Academic Ethics

Beginning in the late 19th century, academic philosophy investigated and developed a new kind of pluralism in ethics, a pluralism of so-called "theories" or "methods" of ethics. Many textbooks in professional ethics adopt this sort of pluralism. We do not, and in this section we explain why. (Readers who are not interested in the reasons why we do not take such an approach should skip this section and go on to the next.) The seminal book for this approach was Henry Sidgwick's *Methods of Ethics*.

This was not a pluralism of ways of life, but a pluralism of academic theories, not a pluralism of ethical outlooks, but a pluralism of theories *about* ethics— theories which attempted to *explain* the basis of moral reasoning. In his book, Sidgwick looked at the two theories which he regarded as most consistent with the scientific psychology of his day—utilitarianism (which we shall consider below) and egoism (which is the view that each person should promote only his own interests). He compared these theories with the conventional morality of his time (which he called "common sense morality"). After a very elaborate argument, he concluded that (i) conventional morality was implicitly utilitarian, yet also (ii) there was no satisfactory way of deciding, in any particular case, whether utilitarianism or egoism should provide the basis for one's decision. Sidgwick regarded human practical rationality as fundamentally divided between the two incompatible outlooks of utilitarianism and egoism. According to Sidgwick, in fact, all of us are inextricably caught up in a kind of ethical schizophrenia. Whether in any particular situation someone should act selflessly (as utilitarianism, he thought, would dictate) or selfishly (as egoism would dictate) was arbitrary and up for grabs.

This was a strange and most unsatisfactory conclusion. But because of the detail and seeming rigor of Sidgwick's arguments, his book proved enormously influential. His "methods of ethics" approach set the agenda which has been followed by the typical introductory course in ethics in universities today.

In such a course, a student is typically introduced to four putative "methods of ethics": (i) Aristotle's ethics, which appeals to happiness and relies on notions of virtue; (ii) Kant's ethics, which appeals to duty and relies on the so-called "categorical imperative"; (iii) Mill's ethics, which appeals to feelings of well-being and relies on the utilitarian principle of "the greatest good for the greatest number"; and (iv) Nietzsche's ethics of self-aggrandizement. After being introduced to these four "methods," the student is then shown how these different "methods" often lead to different and incompatible judgments when applied to difficult moral conundrums.

We regard the "methods of ethics" approach as pedagogically and philosophically unsound. That is why, unlike many texts in professional ethics, we have not followed the outlines of typical university ethics courses in this book. The main reason that "methods of ethics" approach is pedagogically unsound—and which makes it particularly ill-suited to a textbook in professional ethics—is that it tends to inculcate relativism. Relativism is the view that there is no absolute truth— that what *seems* true to each person *is* true. Students who take an introductory ethics course which adopts the "methods of ethics" approach are not in a good position to evaluate the soundness of Aristotle in comparison with Kant, Mill, and Nietzsche. They should no more be expected to do this, than they should be expected to evaluate the soundness of competing versions of string theory in physics. Faced with conflicting and seemingly irresoluble differences in approach and argument, students are tempted to give up and conclude that there is no correct theory, or that all of them are in their own way correct. It is exceedingly difficult for a beginning student to remain convinced that there is a truth in a certain domain, while at the same time holding that he has not yet been capable of finding it.

Even worse than this, when students come to see how the different "methods" may be used to justify different and incompatible decisions, they can become cynical and conclude that the "methods" are no more than elaborate rationalizations, to be hauled in after the fact to justify whichever conclusion one antecedently favors. Such a cynical conclusion would be especially disastrous for an aspiring accountant to reach. Professionalism and ethics in accounting require that a practitioner reject a "results-based" approach to accounting, where accounting treatments are adjusted to arrive at the result one wants (on this see chapter 12 below, on WorldCom). A student who adopted a results-based approach to accounting ethics would probably be more likely to take a results-based approach to accounting.

The "methods of ethics" approach, besides being pedagogically unsuitable, is also philosophically unsound, because ethical reasoning is not in fact a matter of identifying and choosing among alternative "theories" of ethics. In order to carry out such a project well, we obviously would need to have some reason for even engaging in this project of identifying the various theories, and some basis for choosing among them. But only some ethical viewpoint which was *prior* to those theories could provide such grounds. We do not and cannot have the detachment needed for that sort of abstract evaluation. And if we ever could detach ourselves from our own humanity, and view our own ethical reasoning from a merely theoretical point of view, we could never then succeed in returning back to a practical orientation of action and practice.

Finally, it is a mistake to present the four purported "methods" of ethics as though they were on a par. The Aristotelian virtue-based approach advocated here can incorporate and account for the best aspects of the others, whereas they cannot similarly incorporate and account for the Aristotelian approach. There is a fundamental asymmetry among them—which serves as further testimony to the soundness of the Aristotelian approach.

Relativism

As mentioned, when people exaggerate the extent of pluralism in ethics, or when they are taught ethics according to the misguided "methods of ethics" approach, they can be tempted to adopt relativism. So let us next examine relativism.

Relativism may be defined as the view that there is no single, true ethical theory, but that many theories are true, because they are "true for" those who accept them. Relativism should be rejected because: (i) it involves sophistry and (ii) it is self-refuting; (iii) it easily deteriorates into nihilism; (iv) it presupposes its own falsehood; (v) it cannot be consistently held; and (vi) it is incompatible with professional ethics.

(i) *Relativism involves a sophistry*, since it depends upon a misuse of words. A relativist has to change the meanings of the words "true" and "false." In their usual senses, the words "true" and "false" are opposites. Hence, if one of an opposite pair of statements is true, the other must be false, and vice versa. For example, if "The cat is on the mat" is true, then "The cat is not on the mat," which is the opposite, must be false. Suppose that someone adopts relativism and asserts that both of those statements are "true." He is now using the word "true" in some different and new sense—in a sense in which it is not the case that "true" is opposite to "false." Consider the following comparison. Suppose you were trying to determine the meaning of a color word in another language—say, "*verde*"—and you found that speakers of that language applied that word to both light and dark objects. You would conclude that, whatever they meant by that word, the word could not mean "light" or "dark." In the same way, whatever a relativist means by "true," he does not mean the same thing as what we mean by the word. He has changed the meanings of words and is abusing language.

(ii) *Relativism is self-refuting.* Suppose a relativist asserts, "Nothing is absolutely true." Is that assertion itself absolutely true or not? If it is, then he has contradicted himself. If it is not, then what he asserts makes no claim on us—why should we be bound to believe anything which is not true, absolutely so? Or suppose I say "Relativism is false." But a relativist thinks that all views are true. So he must think that this view is true. And so he is committed to holding that relativism is false. Again, suppose a relativist asserts, "All truth is true only for the person who holds it." Is that assertion true only for him? If so, then he cannot say that anyone else ought to agree with his relativism. But if not, then he contradicts himself, because he thinks that at least one truth is true absolutely.

(iii) *Relativism easily turns into nihilism.* Suppose a relativist says that "All ethical theories are true." Does he actually mean that all are true, or rather that none is true? If, as seems correct, truth by its very nature is true absolutely (whatever is true, it seems, is true for everyone, and for all time) then to be a relativist is to deny that there is any truth at all. In that case, relativism changes into something else: it becomes nihilism, the view that there is no truth.

(iv) *Relativism presupposes its own falsehood.* No one could even understand relativism, unless it were false. The reason is that typically what may be called the *qualified* use of a word presupposes its *unqualified* use. For instance, I cannot understand the phrase "my cup" (a qualified use of the word, "cup"), unless I first understand what "cup" means, just on its own. Similarly, I cannot understand "next to me," unless I already understand what it is for me to have a location. Consider now that the relativist says that "all views are true, in the sense that they are true for the person who holds them." But how would it even be possible to understand the phrase "true for him," unless we understood already what "true" just on its own meant? And yet how could we understand the latter, unless we had learned it, and how could we have learned it, if nothing were really like that? Actually, in a world in which nothing was absolutely true, no one even could have imagined that some things were like that.

(v) *No one can consistently be a relativist.* No one is a relativist across the board. For example, no one is a relativist about mathematics ("Do not impose *your* arithmetic on me!" "That is merely *your* mathematics—it is true only *for you!*") or a relativist about physics ("It is merely true *for you* that a nuclear bomb can incinerate a city!"). Even in matters of ethics, no one is a consistent relativist. The most committed ethical relativist will still insist that rape and pedophilia are just plain wrong. People appeal to relativism in order to prohibit others from setting down prohibitions, but, when they do so, they are contradicting themselves. A good example would be those Parisian students who, during the student uprisings of 1968, adopted the slogan, "It is forbidden to forbid" (*Il est interdit d'interdire*). The slogan is based on relativism, and it is an obvious practical contradiction.

(vi) *Relativism is not compatible with professional ethics.* Relativism breeds uncertainty and indecision, which will undermine a practitioner's integrity in those cases where his commitment to professional standards require of him some kind of serious sacrifice. As G.K. Chesterton once noted, "A man must be certain of his morality, for the simple reason that he has to suffer for it." Relativism can also lead someone to give up in the search for truth. It would deflect an accountant from his role as truth-seeker. Why should someone struggle hard to figure out the truth, when, on his view, the very first idea that comes into his head is "true for him"?

We may well wonder: if relativism is self-defeating, incoherent, and self-contradictory, then why do people adopt it?

In personal relationships, people adopt relativism because it seems friendly. To disagree with someone is, after all, disagreeable. When two people disagree, they come into conflict, and someone has to give way. It can seem as if there has to be a "winner" and a "loser." In reality, that is not so. In reality, when **A** believes something false, and **B** points that out and corrects him, with the result that **A** changes his mind, then both of them actually come out winners. **A** comes out a winner, because he formerly believed something false, but now believes something true, and **B** comes out a winner, because he helped someone else, insofar as he helped **A** to reject a false view and acquire a true one.

Socrates used to say that people should enter a discussion wanting to be shown wrong. Each should thank the other for doing a great favor to him, if the other person refutes his view. However, when people do not care about truth, they tend to view a disagreement as like a contest or battle. They recognize that, if they both adopt relativism, then their conflict seems to go away. So relativism is a reasonable approach to adopt when people do not care much about the truth and want some way of resolving or avoiding disputes among themselves.

Relativism as practiced like that in personal relationships is actually flattery rather than friendliness, because each person is concerned to tell the other what he would *like* to hear, not what is *good*—and perhaps unpleasant—for him to hear. (A flatterer may be defined as someone who tells you what pleases you, not what is true.) As such, relativism is contrary to accounting ethics. It fosters a greater concern for the favorable opinion of others than for the truth—an attitude that can easily lead one astray in matters of accounting.

In serious matters, people often adopt relativism because they have been badly educated or do not have strong minds. They cannot see their way through to resolving a perplexing problem, where there are strong reasons on both sides. Hence they give up, and they rationalize doing so by saying that "all views are equally true." Obviously this attitude is at odds with the tenacity in seeking the truth which we said was one of the virtues of an accountant.

Finally, sometimes people adopt relativism because they believe it is a necessary foundation of democracy. They believe anyone who is convinced that he knows the truth—and that others do not—becomes inflexible, and that anyone like that will not listen to others, which leads to totalitarianism and oppression. They think, in contrast, that if someone adopts relativism, such a person will become convinced that no one has the truth, which will lead him to be flexible and open to others, which will lead in turn to tolerance and a free society. But there are many mistakes in this commonly accepted view. We shall mention only two.

First, it is the *content* of one's ideas, rather than one's certainty or uncertainty about those ideas, which is most important for whether one will favor freedom or oppression. Who knows whether the concentration camp guards who accepted Hitler's racial theories and marched prisoners to their death were "certain" of those views or not? Their degree of certainty was irrelevant: what mattered was *what* they believed, namely, they believed misguided theories of eugenics and Aryan supremacy. Again, Thomas Jefferson at the beginning of the Declaration of Independence wrote: "we hold these truths to be self-evident, that all men are created equal." That is, he held them as certain and was convinced that everyone else should accept them as certain. What Jefferson wrote in the Declaration presumably was praiseworthy because of the *content* of what he wrote. It would be absurd to say that the Declaration was in reality a totalitarian document because its author was not a relativist about its doctrines. At the same time, a relativist could never actually affirm "We hold these truths to be self-evident," because he does not hold that there are any truths at all. Thus, no relativist, if he is consistent, can affirm the necessary foundational truths of a free society.

Second, a consistent relativist will be less open to discussion, and to the ideas of others, than a non-relativist. There is no reason why a relativist should want to pay attention to anyone else. What he believes is already "true for him," and what anyone else believes is only "true for them," and so he has nothing he can learn from anyone. On the other hand, the non-relativist, who believes that some things are absolutely true, might reasonably doubt whether what he believes to be the truth actually is the truth. Thus he has a motive to inquire of others, in order to check the veracity of his own beliefs. He will suppose that people who hold differing views about some matter are grasping the actual truth imperfectly and in different degrees. So he would regard his task as that of uncovering the partial truth contained in each person's view.

Relativism is a powerful trend in contemporary society which nevertheless is corrosive of professional, accounting ethics. An accountant should recognize it as such and reject it.

Situation Ethics and Conventionalism

"Situation ethics" and conventionalism are two views which should be considered next, as they are similar to relativism.

"Situation ethics" is the view that there are no kinds of actions which are always right or always wrong in advance, but that right and wrong are shifting and depend on the situation. Situation ethics is a composite of two views, (i) a view about the classification of human actions, and (ii) a view about what makes actions right.

The view about classification is that human actions are unique and unrepeatable, and so no generalizations may be drawn which are true about classes of actions. In particular, situation ethics holds that there are no sorts of actions which are wrong just in virtue of the kind of action it is, "whatever the circumstances" and "whatever the consequences." A defender of situation ethics holds that, for any type of action which someone might think is always wrong, it is possible also to imagine circumstances in which it would be right to do that sort of action.

The view about what makes action right is that the agent's fundamental motive or intention in doing the action is alone decisive. Proponents of situation ethics often say that the only important factor in acting is to show love. Any action that shows love is good. Sometimes people cite a version of a famous saying of St. Augustine in support of situation ethics: "Love, and do what you will" (which was actually, "Love God, and do what you will"). Since in many cases an appeal to "love" seems to justify each of two opposite courses of action, situation ethics looks a lot like relativism. For example, suppose a professor is about to give a student a failing grade in the course, because the student did poor work and failed all of the exams. The student comes to the professor and begs to receive a passing grade: "If you fail me, I won't get into medical school." What is the "loving" thing to do in this instance? The professor can reason that failing the student shows love, as this teaches a lesson and is fair. But he can also reason that passing the student shows love, as this helps the student get into medical school.

Situation ethics is a very widely held view today. People often suppose that ethics is a matter of following some positive emotion, as when they think that morality is solely a matter of being "compassionate" or "nice." Often a sort of situation ethics is adopted in politics or international relations, and then it is referred to as "pragmatism" or "realism."

However, situation ethics seems incorrect both in its view about the classification of actions and in its view about what makes actions right or wrong. Actions are repeatable: particular actions are always members of broader kinds, as we said earlier. For example, in a baseball game a pitcher may throw 100 pitches. Each pitch is a repetition of the same "kind" of action, pitching. The pitches vary in their particulars, or what we called "circumstances"—high, low, outside, inside, curve ball, fast ball, and so on. But the basic "kind" of the action, its "moral kind," is the same for each pitch. Once we allow that there may be definite "kinds" of action, which admit of being defined or described, then the question arises as to whether it is possible to judge some actions to be right or wrong in advance, simply from their description. It seems that this is possible. For example, suppose envy is defined as "feeling sad and upset that someone else has received something good." Envy seems to be a kind of emotional response that we can judge in advance to be wrong, on the grounds that it is perverse and incompatible with human solidarity. Or again, consider the kind of action, "deliberately causing the death of an innocent person." This too looks like an action that may be judged to be wrong from the mere description of it, in advance, no matter how the incidental circumstances vary.

Situation ethics seems mistaken in its making the goodness of an action dependent on the goodness of an agent's motive, whereas in reality the reverse is often true. That is, we often assess and should assess the goodness (or badness) of the agent's motive from our assessment of the goodness (or badness) of the action. To take a clear example, suppose a physician removes someone's appendix, and we are wondering whether he was right to do so or not. We would not answer that question by looking at the physician's motive (did he *love* the patient?) but at what was achieved in the action. Did the patient need to have his appendix removed or not? If not, then the physician did not act rightly, no matter how "loving" the physician's motives might have seemed. Strictly speaking, to love means to wish good to someone. Hence, to say that one person "loves" another means very little if the person who "loves" is unclear or confused about what is truly good for that other person.

Situation ethics seems corrosive of accounting professionalism, just like relativism. An accountant needs to hold that there are some classes of action that are wrong in advance, regardless of the motive, such as fraud, false representations, and accounting treatments which are contrary to professional standards.

Also, someone who accepted a situation ethics approach to ethics would tend to "go over the line" in matters in which there was no clear line. Someone who thinks that everything depends on the situation would reason that, if one situation is fine, then another situation which was very close to that situation would also be fine. His disposition to reason in that way would make him vulnerable to committing what in logic is called a "sorites" fallacy. A sorites fallacy is when someone reasons that because a change in one step makes no difference, then a change involving many steps will make no difference. For example, it is a sorites fallacy to reason that, because a single seed makes no sound when it falls, then a whole heap of seeds will make no sound when it falls. (This is the original version of the fallacy, whence it gets its name, because the Greek word for heap is "sorites.") Or, again, the presence or absence of a single hair on a man's face cannot make the difference as to whether he has a beard or not; so the presence or absence of many hairs cannot make the difference (also a fallacy). It is easy to think of similar examples in accounting ethics, such as: a slight change in this variable would not be material; therefore, no change in this variable would be material.

Conventionalism is another view which is similar to relativism. Conventionalism is the view that nothing is right or wrong because of the nature of the action but solely because of human conventions. A clear example of something wrong solely because of convention is a one-way street. There is nothing about a street that, by its nature, makes it one-way in a certain direction. To make a street is by definition to make a pathway that can be traversed in either direction. As Heraclitus said, "The path up and the path down are one and the same." When a town or some other authority decides that a certain street is going to be a one-way street, then, purely as a result of that decision, it becomes wrong for people to go in the other direction on this street. The reason why this is wrong can be traced solely to the decision of the town, which is a human convention. "Conventionalism" is the view that all of morality is like that. Conventionalism resembles relativism, because it implies that the same action can be both right and wrong. After all, an action which was declared right one day by human convention, might be declared wrong the next day by human convention.

Conventionalism has been subjected to many criticisms in the history of thought. One interesting objection is that conventionalism cannot account for the moral uprightness of the reformers we mentioned earlier, such as Martin Luther King, Jr., because reformers by definition are advocating actions and ways of life that are contrary to existing conventions. Another objection is that, if conventionalism were true, then it would always be wrong to disobey a law passed by due procedures. But some procedurally correct laws should not in fact be obeyed, such as the laws in Nazi Germany which required that people report all Jewish citizens to the authorities.

Conventionalism can be a tempting view for an accountant, because many matters in accounting are matters of convention. For example, whether to use LIFO or FIFO accounting for inventory is sometimes a matter of convention, which gets settled on pragmatic grounds. Also, as mentioned in the last chapter, there is a lot of scope for convention in how accounting principles should get specified as particular, operationalized rules. But it does not follow that only conventions are relevant. Conventions cannot be sufficient, because, in accounting, conventions extend no further than the rules, yet, as we saw in the last chapter, rules are not enough. "Fair presentation in accordance with GAAP" is generally necessary, but not sufficient for truthful accounting. Ultimately, truth is the standard in accounting, but truth transcends conventions.

Scientism and Emotivism

Another misguided view which can be tempting for an accountant is emotivism, which is an approach to ethics which naturally goes along with scientism. So let us consider scientism and emotivism in this section.

Scientism may strictly be defined as the view that the only knowledge is scientific knowledge, that is, the only things we can claim to know are the results of the experimental sciences, such as physics, chemistry, and biology. Scientism denies that there is personal knowledge, or ethical knowledge, or religious knowledge, or even philosophical knowledge. It admits that people can have strong preferences or feelings in these realms, but not knowledge. Scientism is a tempting view for accountants, because accuracy and measurement are important both for accounting and for the experimental sciences, which can imply a certain sympathy towards the exact sciences on the part of accountants. Accountants may like to think of their own professional work as "scientific," reasonably enough.

Emotivism is the approach to ethics that naturally goes along with scientism. Emotivism presupposes a duality in human nature between thought and feeling— between cognition and conation. It holds that, on the one hand, we can *think* about something, which we express by formulating statements in the indicative mood, such as "The sun is shining outside" or "The wind is moderate." Indicative statements are descriptive, non-normative statements. They say how things are. Indicative statements include conditionals such as, "If someone attempts to fly a kite in current weather conditions, he will be successful." On the other hand, according to emotivism, we can have various *feelings* about things, which are either positive or negative. We have positive feelings towards things we favor, and negative feelings towards things we disfavor. We express our positive feelings, not through statements, but by expressions of enthusiasm, such as a cheer, "Hurrah for this!" Similarly we express our negative feelings with expressions of dismay, such as a boo, "Blah for that!"

According to emotivism, when we say that something is good or bad, or that an action is right or wrong to do, we are not actually saying how the world is— because, again, our only knowledge about the world is scientific knowledge, and the experimental sciences do not draw conclusions about such things. Rather, when we say that something is good or bad, we are only expressing our positive and negative feelings. According to emotivism, if someone saw that the sun was shining and the wind was moderate, and said that "Today is a good day for flying a kite," he would simply be expressing a positive emotion, along the lines of "Hurrah for kite flying today!" Or if someone looked at the same weather and said it would be bad for the crops, as there was a drought, he would merely be expressing a negative emotion, as if he had blurted out "Blah for another rainless day!"

Emotivism seems to be yet another example of a theory which misguidedly takes something which is sometimes true and overgeneralizes it, claiming falsely that this is always true. All of us have mere preferences, and sometimes we use the language of "good" or "bad" to express these preferences, as in the examples given above about the weather. When we do so, "good" and "bad" are words that are merely expressive of our preferences. But it does not follow that "good" and "bad" always have that sense. As we saw in chapter 4 above, "good" often means "having the virtues, or excellences, which a thing of that kind needs to have in order to carry out its distinctive work well," and "bad" often means the opposite of this. When good and bad are regarded in that way, then they are objective.

A common objection to emotivism is that it implies that no two people can truly disagree on any matter of morality. After all, a difference of preference is not a disagreement. If I say that I like vanilla ice cream but you say that you dislike it, we are not disagreeing but rather expressing different preferences. If ethical language were merely the expression of preferences, as the emotivist holds, then a supposed ethical disagreement would have exactly the same character as a difference in preference for vanilla ice cream. Similarly, there would be no possibility of any genuine ethical deliberation or debate. As the saying goes, "There is no disputing tastes." If emotivism were correct, it would be just as absurd to attempt to persuade someone by argument that something was wrong, as it would be to attempt to persuade him to like vanilla ice cream.

Another common objection to emotivism is that it trivializes ethics. Preferences are superficial; they tell us little about someone's heart and character. Because they are so superficial, we should give way in them whenever we can. When two persons have different preferences (movies or miniature golf for a date? beach or mountains for vacation? Italian or Chinese food?), it is considered polite for each to be willing to go along with the other's preference. But with ethics it is the reverse. We believe ethical views are highly revelatory of someone's heart and character, and we think that people should not give way on important ethical matters, merely to get along with others or "go with the flow."

Emotivism can be a tempting view for accountants, because of the premium placed on clarity, accuracy, and exactness in accounting. In an accountant's quest to achieve exactness, every other sort of consideration can look like a distraction that should be put to the side as part of one's "emotional" nature, including perhaps even ethical considerations. However, emotivism, like the other misguided views we have considered, is corrosive of accounting professionalism. Emotivism holds that a matter of conscience is just an irrational preference, like someone's preference for vanilla over chocolate ice cream. It would of course be absurd for someone to endure the loss of his job or the loss of a client over an irrational preference. Yet accounting professionalism requires that sometimes one should make that choice. Also, as we saw in chapter 4 above, an accountant needs to be "stubborn" and unyielding in matters of conscience, but we should not be stubborn and unyielding when mere irrational preference is at stake.

There is a joke about a client asking an accountant to do something for a fee of $10,000. The accountant replies that he cannot oblige, because what the client is asking him to do is unethical. The client then responds, "Well, in that case, would you do it for $100,000?" If, as the emotivist holds, a matter of conscience is nothing more than an irrational preference, then there really ought to be a price at which the accountant would reasonably go along with a client's improper request.

Utilitarianism

Utilitarianism, strictly and in its historic meaning, is the view that the right action to do in any circumstance is that which leads to the greatest pleasurable experience for the greatest number of people affected by that action. But nowadays the label "utilitarianism" is applied, more broadly, to any view which says that the rightness or wrongness of an action is to be evaluated solely in relation to its consequences. (Note: philosophers use the term "consequentialism" for this broader view.) Utilitarianism denies that the intrinsic character of an action is decisive or even relevant for evaluating that action. It looks only for the "use value" or "usefulness" of an action, hence its name.

Utilitarianism can be a tempting view for an accountant, because utilitarian reasoning is similar to a so-called "cost-benefit analysis." An accountant will sometimes employ a cost-benefit analysis in determining whether a particular analysis should be undertaken or a certain accounting treatment employed. Utilitarianism is basically the view we should submit all our actions to a cost-benefit analysis and do those actions in which the ratio of benefits to costs for society generally is the greatest.

Utilitarianism is a theory which arose after the scientific revolution and which has had much appeal because it offers the promise of making ethical reasoning similar to scientific prediction. The physicist Laplace once said, famously, that if you told him the position and velocity of every particle in the universe, then, by using physics he could predict every future state of the universe. (By the way, this claim turns out to be false, for a variety of reasons having to do with necessary inaccuracies in measurement and quantum indeterminacy.) Similarly, a utilitarian holds that, if you tell him the physical effects of an action, he can predict the future good and bad consequences of that action, and that, if the same calculation were performed for all of the actions available to an agent at any one time, it would then be possible to determine with scientific accuracy the *best* action for that agent to do at that time. The best action would be that which could be predicted to lead to the greatest sum of good over bad consequences.

Many books have been written exposing the flaws in utilitarianism. Literally dozens of good objections have been advanced against it. We shall mention only a few here.

A simple objection is that consequences are not the only basis on which we should evaluate actions. Consequences are forward-looking considerations involving the future, but there are backward-looking considerations involving the past as well, which need to be considered in the evaluation of an action. For example, suppose that you have the option of giving a gift either to a friend, who has given you a similar gift in the past, or to a stranger, who has never given you anything. Suppose that the consequences of each gift work out to be the same— that is, each gift would lead to the same ratio of good over bad consequences for society. In this case, it looks as though it would be preferable to give the gift to the friend, in view of the past favor that your friend did for you. That is to say, the backward-looking considerations have some weight too. Hence, there are considerations relevant to the evaluation of the action other than the action's consequences.

A similar argument can be made about punishment, which reveals another flaw in utilitarianism. Suppose that a horrible murder was committed in a town and the people are clamoring for justice. The police cannot find the killer. So the authorities get together and arrange for a show trial in which a man known to be innocent is convincingly framed for the crime and punished. The truth never comes out. Suppose that the consequences of punishing the innocent man work out to be the exactly the same as those of punishing the guilty man, if the guilty man had been caught (there is no contradiction in such a supposition). But clearly it would be wrong to punish the innocent man, and it would only be right to punish the guilty man—because punishment must have a "retributive" basis, which is a backward-looking consideration. This example shows not only that backward-looking considerations, as well as consequences, are relevant for evaluating an action, but also that utilitarian reasoning can be abused to justify grave injustices.

Similarly, on utilitarian grounds, there can be societies in which slavery is justified. Slavery would be justified whenever the consequences for society as a whole worked out better with slavery than without. It is not incredible that there be such circumstances; for example, Lincoln believed that once the cotton gin was invented slavery became profitable on a cost-benefit basis for cotton growing states. Today, similarly, "sweat shops" and child labor are justifiable on utilitarian grounds, and, if so, so much the worse for utilitarianism. Hence, another well-known objection to utilitarianism is that by utilitarian reasoning the grossest and most objectionable injustices may become justified.

In Chapter 4 we said that there were four aspects of an action: the tradition behind it; the character of the agent; the inherent character of the action itself; and the effects or consequences of the action. Utilitarianism is yet another theory which goes astray through overgeneralization. It takes only one aspect relevant to the evaluation of an action and claims that it is the sole aspect. As mentioned, it wishes to do this in the hopes of introducing precise measurements and exact calculation. However, utilitarianism fails to give precision, as can be seen if we raise the question, precisely what effects of an action are supposed to be measured and added up? Suppose we say, along with the classic utilitarians (Jeremy Bentham and J.S. Mill), that the relevant effects are the pleasant and painful experiences caused by the action. But then a host of unanswerable questions arise: How do we measure pleasures and pains? Is it really possible to compare reliably the pleasures or pains of two different persons, or even of one person with himself at different times? What sense does it make to sum together the pleasures or pains of multiple persons, when there is no subject who ever experiences that sum? Does it make sense to subtract the pleasures from the pains, when a pleasure does not really negate or diminish a pain? (Experiencing a very strong pain followed by a lesser pleasure is not the same as experiencing only a mild pleasure without any pain).

Utilitarianism is yet another theory which is corrosive of sound professionalism in accounting. Accounting professionalism is non-utilitarian. A fraud, or a patently unsound accounting treatment, would not be justified even if a cost-benefit analysis showed that it had better general consequences for society than a truthful approach. Moreover, a practitioner who embraced utilitarianism would seem more likely to take a "results-oriented" or "make the numbers" approach to accounting, where first the desired result is set down and later an accounting treatment is devised which gets to that result. Finally, utilitarianism is unable to account for the inherent worth of professional integrity in accounting (which will be discussed in Chapters 8-10 below).

Kantianism, or Legalism

Kantianism is the view that morality consists most basically in following a fundamental law, which is referred to as the "categorical imperative." This view is called "Kantianism" after its original formulator, an 18th century Prussian philosopher named Immanuel Kant. Sometimes it is called "deontology," from the Greek word for obligation or duty (*deon*), because on this view the most fundamental consideration in ethical reasoning is the discovery and carrying out of one's duty. It may also be called "legalism" because it regards lawfulness as the most basic ethical consideration, not goodness, nature, or "distinctive work," as in classical and medieval views.

The categorical imperative was formulated by Kant in various ways, which he regarded as equivalent, but they are not evidently equivalent. They include: "Always act in such a way that the maxim implicit in one's action could be made into a universal law, binding on all rational persons" and "Treat other rational persons as ends and never as means."[11] Kant regarded the categorical imperative as a more precise and more philosophical version of the Golden Rule, "Do unto others as you would have them do unto you." This fundamental law, or imperative, is called a "categorical" imperative to distinguish it from a directive that is conditional. A conditional directive has the form, "If you want to do this, then you ought to do that." In a conditional directive (or "hypothetical imperative"), the "ought" part of the statement has force only when your desire, mentioned in the first part of the statement, is in effect. That is why the imperative is only conditional. Kant held that the most basic moral law is always in effect, regardless of our wants or desires, and so he called it "categorical."

Kant's theory involved the deepest foundations of ethics and was meant to resolve certain subtle philosophical questions which are not relevant to accounting ethics and cannot be taken up here. Like utilitarianism, Kantianism has been the object of many critiques over the centuries. Perhaps the most serious objection against it is that the various versions of the categorical imperative on their own seem to give no concrete guidance about how to act. To consider an example that Kant himself raises: Is suicide against the categorical imperative or not? Why exactly would suicide be a matter of treating oneself as a "means" rather than as an

---

[11] The so-called "personalist norm" is also a version of the categorical imperative and is sometimes stated, "Always treat other human beings as those who similarly *have ends*, never as mere means."

"end"? Are we sure that there are no circumstances in which the maxim implicit in an act of suicide could not be posited as a law binding on all rational beings? We shall not go into the discussion here, but over the centuries the problems affecting Kant's view have seemed unanswerable.

However, there is a related and more popular view, sometimes inaccurately also called "Kantianism"—but which we shall refer to as "legalism"—which holds simply that the only consideration relevant for the assessment of an action is whether the agent is doing his "duty" or not. On such an approach, what people want or desire, and even what is "good" for them, is irrelevant; only the law governing an action, and what counts as the agent's duty, is relevant for assessing an action. Legalism, when defined in this way, can be seen to be the inverse image of utilitarianism. Utilitarianism says that the inherent character of the action should be ignored and that only the action's consequences matter; legalism says that the consequences of the action should be ignored and that only the action's legality or correspondence to duty matters.

Legalism can be tempting to accountants because of the importance of following the rules in good accounting practice. Also, as we saw, an accountant's concern for truth is not utilitarian. So a view which dismisses consequences altogether may seem appealing. Legalism is not false so much as only partially true, and so in some circumstances it is likely to be misleading. Like conventionalism, legalism can lead someone to think that following the rules is sufficient. Also, legalism might keep someone from exercising sensible professional judgment in the application of accounting standards.

Nietzscheanism

Friedrich Nietzsche was a 19th century classics scholar who revived certain Greek ideas, although in a distorted and ultimately unscholarly way, and used them to criticize the influence of Judaism and Christianity on European culture. As with Kant, a distinction may be drawn between the subtle views that Nietzsche actually held, and which have been appreciated, if at all, by only a handful of scholars, and the common and popular impression of his ideas. The scholarly and the popular interpretations may or may not be compatible. We shall not try to decide that question but will be concerned here more with the popular interpretation of Nietzsche, because of its influence.

The main idea of popular Nietzscheanism is a distinction between the few who are naturally talented and strong ("the Supermen"), and who are meant to dominate over others, and the many who are weak and should be dominated over by others ("the herd"). The weak are envious of the strong, because of the natural talents which the strong have but which they lack. So, out of envy, the weak band together and attempt, as a group, to dominate over and weaken the strong. They do so by making up "morality," an illusory system of rules, based on false ideals, especially the false ideal of "equality." The weak try—with some success—to convince the strong to accept this make-believe morality. If the strong accept the bounds of morality, they allow themselves to get duped into slavery to the weak. Morality is no more than a system of enslavement of the few strong persons by the many weak persons. The weak, who find it easy to act "morally," get to pat themselves on the back for being good and moral persons, unlike the strong.

For Nietzsche, morality is solely the expression of envy (what Nietzsche called "*ressentiment*," using the French word for envy), much like the story of sour grapes in Aesop's fables. Recall that in the story a fox saw a hanging bunch of very appealing and tasty grapes. The fox jumped and jumped as high as he could but could not reach the grapes. Eventually he gave up, and as he walked away, he tried to downplay and even deny his failure by downplaying the attractiveness of the grapes, "They were sour grapes anyway." According to Nietzsche, the weak want to be like the strong, just as the fox wanted to get the grapes, but they cannot. However, instead of admitting their weakness and failure—and submitting to the strong, who ought to dominate them—they use deceit and try to deny their weakness. The ultimate form of denial is claiming that weakness itself is strength, which is really a kind of nihilism, since it is claiming, in effect, that nothingness is something. Nietzsche even alleged that this sort of envy was the basis of the seemingly high ideals of Christianity, such as "turn the other cheek" and "blessed are the poor in spirit."

Like utilitarianism and Kantianism, Nietzscheanism has been subjected to many critiques over the years. Clearly any thoroughgoing critique would have to account for the reality of morality as something more than a system of rules devised by "the weak." A satisfactory reply would also need to establish the true "strength" implicit in virtue and spiritual ideals. (We have already developed in chapters 4-5 above such a reply.) Perhaps the best critique along those lines was offered by Max Scheler in his brief book entitled *Ressentiment*. We cannot go into Scheler's response here, except to say that it hinges on the notion of magnanimity, which we considered above. Scheler argues, in effect, that Nietzsche misinterprets Christianity, because he overlooks the importance of magnanimity in Judeo-Christian culture.

Nietzsche's philosophy is an "ethic of suspicion." Because Nietzsche views morality as an instrument by which the weak dominate the strong, his philosophy encourages a highly sceptical approach to any expression of idealism. A Nietzschean will tend to view any professed idealism as essentially a con job—as a mere front for some kind of scam—by which the idealist person conceals his interest in dispossessing a strong person of his power and resources.

Clearly a little suspicion, applied at the right times, is a good thing. On many occasions people who have given the appearance of being very upright and good have proved to be shysters and frauds. Similarly, an accountant sometimes needs to cultivate a professional attitude of scepticism, especially in circumstances in which misstatement or fraud would not be surprising. So to this extent some appreciation of Nietzsche could be useful to an accountant.

On the other hand, it is foolhardy to hold that all idealism is fraudulent. The love of a mother for her child is not a scam. Sometimes two people in love really do stay faithful to their commitments to each other, even at great personal sacrifice. Similarly, there is such a thing as heroic commitment to integrity among professionals: in chapter 12, we shall see an extraordinary example of this in the way the Dutch medical profession behaved during World War II, resisting the attempts of their Nazi occupiers to co-opt them. Accountants, too, need to believe in the reality of the professed ideals of accountancy and be prepared to make great sacrifices for those ideals. Thus Nietzscheanism, although it has an aspect of truth, ends up being grossly incompatible with accounting ethics.

Threats and Safeguards

The last alternative approach we consider briefly in this chapter is that of "threats and safeguards." This approach differs from the others we have considered because it has not been proposed as a general approach to morality, but rather as a specific way of understanding accounting ethics in particular. Moreover, the approach is used primarily almost solely as regards the evaluation of a practitioner's independence. Because the view is not a complete theory, but a fragment of a theory and somewhat *ad hoc*, we will not offer a detailed examination here, so much as mention the view in passing, for the sake of completeness of this chapter's discussion of alternative views.

The "threats and safeguards" approach was developed in response to the proliferation of rules governing the application of the "independence" principle for accountants (see chapter 10 below). From the discussion in the last chapter about how rules are not enough, we saw how one way to attempt to remedy the incompleteness of a rule is by adding more rules, and then rules for those rules, and so on. This is in fact what has happened as regards "independence." In an attempt to clarify the "principles" underlying the ideal of independence, the "threats and safeguards" approach was born.

The "threats and safeguards" approach holds that a practitioner's independence should be viewed as "at risk" of being impaired. Like anything else that is at risk, some factors tend to increase the risk, whereas other factors tend to diminish the risk. The former are "threats"; the latter are "safeguards." For the purposes of evaluating the approach, it does not matter much what these threats and safeguards are. An obvious threat to independence would be a practitioner's financial interest in an entity; an obvious safeguard would be a strong ethical culture in the practitioner's accounting firm. The "threats and safeguards" approach holds that a practitioner should look at the threats and safeguards that would potentially be in play in any engagement, and that he should proceed with the engagement only if he judged that the safeguards were sufficient in the face of those threats. What counts as "sufficient" on this approach will vary with the seriousness of the engagement: for example, an audit of a major public company would require a much more diminished risk than a certification of a minor privately-held company.

There are three general problems in the "threats and safeguards" approach. First, as mentioned, the approach is *ad hoc* and not part of any unified theory. It offers nothing like a basis or rationale for professionalism in accounting, so much as a rule of thumb for how to engage in self-examination in a relatively limited domain. Also, the conceptual scheme of threats which increase risk, balanced by safeguards which reduce risks, is highly simplistic. Admittedly, its simplicity makes it easy to grasp, but at the same time the approach is unlikely to yield any insights or deeper understanding, if employed by a thoughtful practitioner.

Second, the approach seems to instrumentalize the practitioner in relation to himself. It encourages the practitioner to view himself as something like a distinct object, buffeted about by "threats" yet steadied by "safeguards." In effect, it asks a practitioner to "manipulate" himself, by manipulating variables thought to impinge upon himself. Now there is no question that sometimes we need to deal with ourselves in such a way. A good example would be how Odysseus famously tied himself to the mast when his ship went by the Sirens. He did so in order that he would not jump ship when, like everyone else who heard their songs, he was made mad by their amazingly beautiful singing. However, as the example shows, we "manipulate" ourselves in that way, from the outside, only to the extent that we regard our motives as not governed rationally from the inside, through the influence of the relevant virtues. Thus, there is an important sense in which the "threats and safeguards" approach is at odds with a virtue-based approach. It seems actually to presuppose an absence of virtue in a practitioner. Indeed, it is noteworthy that, in the common formulations of this approach offered by the AICPA and IFAC, a practitioner's good character is not counted among possible "safeguards," and a practitioner's lack of character is not held to be the basis for a possible "threat."

Third, the guidance offered by the "threats and safeguards" approach is so vague as to seem to encourage some of the misguided views we rightly rejected earlier in this chapter. We are presupposing that typically ethical views do not float around in isolation. They look for a natural home, context, or foundation, and thus anyone who employed the "threats and safeguards" approach—unless he were using it in a purely *pro forma* way, merely to satisfy the demands of a supervisor or regulator—would implicitly supply some kind of rationale for it. But since it is impossible to measure the threats and safeguards, or to assign a probability to the risk, or to the significance of the engagement, or to the acceptable threshold of risk, to recommend the approach might look like an implicit recommendation of situation ethics, conventionalism, or even utilitarianism.

In addition to these three main problems, the following more particular criticisms may be raised:

(i) One obvious problem is that the "threats and safeguards" conceptual framework, as applied to independence, requires someone to assess whether his own independence has been compromised, and yet someone whose independence has been compromised would likely not be in a position to see this clearly. Compromised independence is analogous to intoxication—a person under the influence is usually not in a position to make the judgment that his judgment has been compromised, precisely because his judgment has been compromised! (It is perhaps on account of this problem that the AICPA seems to regard the "threats and safeguards" conceptual framework largely as a guide for its Professional Ethics Executive Committee, not the practitioner.) The problem is not avoided by appeal to what an imagined third party might say. A person under the influence, if he believes, wrongly, that his judgment is just fine, will also be convinced that a third party observer would regard his judgment as just fine. Hence, this difficulty involved in self-assessment is not helped by the conceptual framework's recommendation that a practitioner, who wonders whether his independence has been impaired, consider whether an "informed third party having knowledge of all relevant information" would consider independence to be impaired.

(ii) Another difficulty is that it is unclear that a "threats and safeguards" approach makes sense for the application of a principle which has the status of an ethical principle. We think of an ethical principle as a kind of "absolute"; furthermore, we think it is within our power to abide by an ethical principle. To see this, consider whether the "threats and safeguards" approach works well for a principle other than independence—take confidentiality as an example. Confidentiality looks like an absolute: unless the law requires it, you simply should not under any circumstances reveal information that is confidential to the professional relationship you have with your client. Furthermore, it looks to be within your power whether you reveal confidential information or not. Hence it would seem odd for someone to say, "I'm now in a circumstance in which I am at risk of revealing confidential information." Isn't it up to him whether he observes confidentiality? And either he abides by confidentiality, or he does not. If he does, then there is no "risk" that he'll breach confidentiality. Indeed, if someone said he considered himself "at risk" of violating someone's confidence, from that very admission we would likely conclude that he was unprincipled, untrustworthy, and could not keep information confidential.

(iii) A related difficulty is that it is strange to say, as regards an ethical principle, that it becomes more stringent the greater the harms that would result if it were not followed. Take honesty as an example. Someone who is honest, we think, tells the truth in small matters as much as in big matters. Indeed, we tend to think that people will fail to be honest in big matters, unless they are scrupulously honest in smaller matters. Another example would be fair judgment. It would be strange to say that judges sitting on lower courts did not need to care as much about justice and fairness as judges sitting on higher courts. Yet according to the "threats" and "safeguards" conceptual framework, an auditor can take bigger "risks" of not being independent with small companies than with larger companies, with private companies than with public companies.

(iv) A fourth difficulty is that the "threats" and "safeguards" mentioned in the AICPA's or IFAC's conceptual frameworks are stated in too general a fashion to be relevant to the actual facts and circumstances of any particular case. Consider, for example, one of the safeguards frequently mentioned, "a tone at the top that emphasizes the attest client's commitment to fair financial reporting." No doubt, a good "tone at the top" in an attest client makes it less likely, in general, that fraud or defalcation will take place in a company, but it does not absolutely preclude it. If the auditor is dealing with a member of senior management who is dishonest, and who shows signs of potentially being dishonest, then the putative safeguard, "good tone at the top," is completely irrelevant. The same is true of each of the safeguards. An auditor may, therefore, go through a checklist of such safeguards, confirm that all of them are in place, and nonetheless be quite mistaken in concluding that the "threat" to independence is at an "acceptable level."

(v) Difficulties beset not simply a practitioner's attempts to apply the conceptual framework to his or her own practice, but also efforts to understand the rules and rulings of the PEEC in relation to the conceptual framework. A review of those rules and rulings would raise all kinds of questions of how they are to be justified. For example, it would be difficult to see how, by applying the conceptual framework, one could arrive at the PEEC's ruling that an auditor's independence with respect to a municipality would be considered impaired simply as a result of his owning a bond issued by that municipality of trivial value (see chapter 10 below). But if the conceptual framework does not illuminate the basis for the rulings, what value is it?

(vi) The conceptual framework has an appeal because it appears sophisticated, analytical and rigorous. However, some of its key terms are poorly defined, rendering its rigor merely apparent. For example, "independence" and "attest engagement" are inter-defined: "attest engagement" is defined in terms of independence, because "an attest engagement is an engagement that requires independence" (92.01); but "independence" is defined in terms of attest engagement, since independence is that attitude which must be displayed for an attest engagement. Again, the conceptual framework calls for risks to be mitigated until they reach an "acceptable level," but "acceptable level" is not defined. The conceptual framework says that "Threats are at an acceptable level when it is not reasonable to expect that the threat would compromise professional judgment." But "it is not reasonable to expect" can mean any of several things. Is "not reasonable to expect X" the same as $P(X) = 0$? Or $P(X) < .5$? Or $P(X) \gg 0$? ("Acceptable level" is supposed to be a realistic standard, on the supposition that complete and absolute independence is unattainable, so presumably the first interpretation, at least, can be put aside.) An additional difficulty is that "acceptable level" looks as though it may be relative to circumstances; a level of risk may be more acceptable when the promise of reward is greater.

Finally, the conceptual framework states that "Risk is unacceptable if the relationship would compromise (or would be perceived as compromising by an informed third party having knowledge of all relevant information) the member's professional judgment when rendering an attest service to the client." (100.01) But, as we said, this consideration of what a third party might hypothetically say can add no new information. When a practitioner imagines what an informed third party might think, he can do no more than imagine what he himself, as informed as he is, does think. (Actually seeking the advice of a real, disinterested third party would be a different matter altogether.)

Recommended additional reading:

IFAC, *Code of Ethics for Professional Accountants*

Alasdair MacIntyre, *Three Rival Versions of Moral Enquiry*

C.S. Lewis, *The Abolition of Man*

PART III

THE MEANING OF ACCOUNTING PROFESSIONALISM

A New Profession: 8

"Trusted Because Truthful"

> "I believe that every high-minded accountant has accepted the principle that, once his conclusions are reached, the report or certificate which he issues, and which is designed to influence action, must be so worded that not only will every statement made therein be literally true, but every inference which could legitimately be drawn from the language will be warranted by the facts." —George Oliver May

ACCOUNTANCY IS A PROFESSION, GRANTED. BUT WHAT DOES THIS MEAN, and what makes a line of work count as a profession in the first place? The point of this chapter is to explain how that question was answered when accountancy first arose as a profession. After all, if accountancy today is at risk of turning into a "business" rather than a "profession," as some claim, then it becomes necessary today for accountants to engage in a kind of work of "recovery." They need to grasp the reasons why the founders of modern accountancy insisted that accountancy is a profession, not a business.

Is accounting indeed a profession? What makes a line of work a profession anyway? How exactly is a profession to be distinguished from a business? An accountant today should have ready answers to these questions.

The question of the meaning of professionalism is an important part of accounting ethics. Accounting ethics lies at the intersection of accounting, ethics, and professionalism, as in the diagram on the next page. To grasp accounting ethics, one needs to study its foundation in ethics generally, as we did in Chapters 4-7 above. One also needs to study the relationship between accounting ethics and accounting, as we do through the various cases studies, both large and small, that are presented in this book. But finally one needs to examine how accounting professionalism is an example of the broader phenomenon of professionalism, as we do in this and the next two chapters.

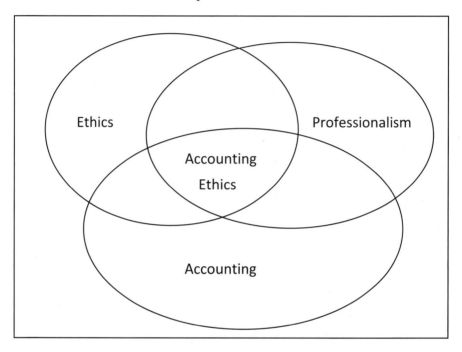

The Relation of Accounting Ethics to Accounting, Ethics, and Professionalism

Accountants in the United States first organized themselves into a professional association, in 1882, when the Institute of Accountants and Bookkeepers of the City of New York was formed, a forerunner of the American Institute of Certified Public Accountants (AICPA). Public accountants were licensed for the first time by the State of New York in 1896. The profession was not much older in England and Scotland, the countries from which it had been imported. The oldest firms there dated only from the mid-19th century. William Deloitte founded his firm in London in 1845; Samuel Price and Edwin Waterhouse joined together in a partnership in 1867; and William Peat began his practice in 1867. These men were among the founders of the first professional association of accountants in Britain, the Institute of Accounting, which received a royal charter in 1880, providing for the first professional designation, "Chartered Accountant."

Because of its relative youth, accountancy had to offer a deliberate, public argument as to why it should be considered as a profession. Unlike law and medicine, it did not have a history stretching back centuries that made its position as a profession obvious and unassailable. Consider the history of those major professions. The University of Bologna is credited with being the oldest university, founded in 1088. The University of Paris was second, founded in 1150. These original universities, like the other universities founded in the Middle Ages, typically had three professional faculties: law, medicine, and theology. When these universities were founded, law had already arrived at the status of a profession, out of its roots in a class of legal specialists who were important in the late Roman Empire. Theology, or the systematic study of matters of God and religion, which was the academic expression of the Catholic priesthood, at that time was about 1000 years old. Medicine had been practiced by a distinct class of specialists for over 1000 years.

In about 400 BC, Hippocrates had already formulated his famous Oath, which counts as the first code of professional conduct. One might say that the Hippocratic Oath made it possible for the concept of a "profession" to arise at all: a professional "professes," as he is someone who "professes" publicly to a commitment like that expressed in the Hippocratic Oath. Because of its antiquity and historical importance, it is worthwhile quoting it nearly in full.[12] We provide also brief guidelines as to the significance of each clause:

> [Commitment higher than law or convention] I swear by Apollo the physician, and Asclepius, and Health, and All-heal, and all the gods and goddesses . . .

> [Piety] to reckon him who taught me this Art equally dear to me as my parents, to share my substance with him, and relieve his necessities if required;

> [Gratitude] to look upon his offspring in the same footing as my own brothers, and to teach them this art, if they shall wish to learn it, without fee or stipulation;

---

[12] What follows is a translation of the oath used commonly by medical schools in the 19th century. In the late 20th century, medical schools began to modernize the oath and departed in significant ways from Hippocrates' original language and ideals.

[Expertise governed by values] I swear that by precept, lecture, and every other mode of instruction, I will impart a knowledge of the Art to my own sons, and those of my teachers, and to disciples bound by a stipulation and oath according to the law of medicine, but to none others.

[Best judgment] I will follow that system of regimen which, according to my ability and judgment, I consider for the benefit of my patients, and abstain from whatever is deleterious and mischievous.

[No harm] I will give no deadly medicine to any one if asked, nor suggest any such counsel; and in like manner I will not give to a woman a pessary to produce abortion. . . .

[Justice] Into whatever houses I enter, I will go into them for the benefit of the sick, and will abstain from every voluntary act of mischief and corruption;

[Moderation] I will abstain from the seduction of females or males, of freemen and slaves.

[Confidentiality] Whatever, in connection with my professional practice or not, in connection with it, I see or hear, in the life of men, which ought not to be spoken of abroad, I will not divulge, as reckoning that all such should be kept secret.

[High standards of conduct, self-regulation] While I continue to keep this Oath unviolated, may it be granted to me to enjoy life and the practice of the Art, respected by all men, in all times! But should I trespass and violate this Oath, may the reverse be my lot!

Thus the oldest professions can trace their roots back almost 2000 years. These professions accordingly have long-standing traditions and a relatively clear self-understanding, supported by a rich culture. They may not always be true to that tradition, or rely on that self-understanding and culture, yet these ancient realities exist and are available to them.

An example of the rich culture of the oldest traditions, is that there are an abundance of stories of great practitioners, "heroes" of medicine, law, and theology, such as Louis Pasteur and Albert Schweitzer in medicine; Thomas More and Abraham Lincoln in law; St. Thomas Aquinas and St. Edith Stein in theology. The lives of these "heroes" are well known outside of their professions. In contrast, although there have occasionally been calls to collect stories of "heroes" of accounting,[13] relatively few such stories seem to be available, and no exemplary accountants are widely-admired outside their discipline.[14]

It should be noted that the relative youthfulness of accounting as a profession provides an additional reason why ethics is so important to it. The trappings of tradition and culture provide reinforcement for ethical action. Accountants need to supply from within, through a strong ethical commitment, what they lack from without.

Is Accountancy a Profession? –A Sociological Approach

One way to consider what a profession is would be to study traits that are in common among professions. The question of whether accountancy is a profession may then be answered by seeing whether the traits that define a profession apply to accountancy as well.[15]

Over the years, sociologists have given lists of traits that putatively define a profession. A famous and influential account along these lines was developed by Abraham Flexner in 1915. Flexner said that it is a mark of professions that:

> They involve essentially intellectual operations with large individual responsibility. ("A free, resourceful, and unhampered intelligence applied to problems and seeking to understand and master them—that is in the first instance characteristic of a profession," as Flexner added.)

---

[13] As for example by Steven Mintz.: 1996, "The Role of Virtue in Accounting Education", *Accounting Education: A Journal of Theory, Practice and Research* 1, 67-91.

[14] There are good reasons, however, why few stories of heroism in accounting have been recorded. Usually client confidentiality prevents this. Also, heroic acts in accounting tend not to be *spectacularly* good; rather, they are noteworthy precisely because they prevent some spectacularly bad thing. Again, an accountant who is a good professional is not going to draw attention to his own good actions, and then usually those who benefit most from his good action will remain unaware that they have been benefited—that is, those many investors protected by his decision but who are unknown to him.

[15] A word on terminology: the words "accounting" and "accountancy" have basically the same sense, but they have a different emphasis. "Accounting" brings in the notion of the science, or the body of knowledge, used by accountants. "Accountancy" suggests rather putting this knowledge into practice. When we wish to put particular emphasis on the *practice* of accounting in contradistinction to the knowledge, we will often use the word "accountancy." But nothing much hinges on this distinction; it is a difference in emphasis only.

They derive their raw material from science and learning, worked up to some definite and practical end. ("No profession can be merely academic and theoretic; the professional man must have an absolutely definite and practical object," Flexner explained.)

They possess an educationally communicable technique.

They tend to self-organization.

They are becoming increasingly altruistic in motivation.

Some further criteria of a profession which have been added by sociologists since Flexner's time include:

Professions set down for themselves a standard for professional qualification, which governs admission to those professions.

They maintain certain standards of conduct among their members.

They have a recognized status in society at large.

They are constituted by associations devoted to the advancement of the social obligations of the profession.

They have a distinctive culture, involving customs, traditions, and symbols.

Other sociologists have tried to identify some single trait which most distinguishes a profession from a trade or business. For example, some have said that a profession is distinctive for its "autonomy." Others have said that the "altruism" of a profession is most distinctive.

Clearly, accountancy satisfies most of the criteria on the above lists. Therefore, from a sociological point of view, it may be considered as a profession. However, there are two reasons why we should be dissatisfied with this conclusion. First, this conclusion is not informative, because if the above criteria are interpreted loosely enough, nearly anything counts as a profession. Take plumbing as an example. Plumbing involves a body of knowledge. Its members organize themselves into trade unions and guilds. The state licenses plumbers, and so on. But if plumbing is a "profession," then nearly any line of work is.

Indeed, the word "profession" is sometimes used merely as an equivalent of "career" or "line of work." One sees lists of hundreds of "professions," such as golf course architect, landscaper, police officer, soldier, and so on. In short, there is a broad notion of "profession," which is not particularly interesting for our purposes. We want to know, rather, whether accounting is a "profession" in the relatively narrow sense in which medicine and law are.

Second, any conclusion we would arrive at by applying a list of traits assembled by sociologists would be merely descriptive, not normative. A sociologist can do no more than identify traits which are possessed by persons or groups that *are called* "professionals" by others. But whether these persons or groups *should be* called "professionals"—whether they *really are* professions, so that people who call them "professionals" are using the term *correctly*—this cannot be answered by the sociological approach. We do not want to know, merely, whether people happen to call accountancy a profession. Clearly they do. We want to know whether this label is justified. What is the nature of a profession, then, which justifies the application of that label?

Is Accountancy a Profession? –A Philosophical Approach

A profession may also be defined philosophically. Considered philosophically, a profession may be defined as a systematic and organized way in which persons, as a matter of their daily work, contribute an important good to society which is *incommensurable with market goods*, as being either higher in value than market goods, or presupposed by market goods.

In order to explain this definition, we must explain the distinction between a commensurable and an incommensurable good, and we need to explain the role of the market, and how there are goods that are both higher than and presupposed by it. The distinction between commensurable and incommensurable goods depends upon the notion of commensurability, so let us consider that first.

To say that X is *commensurable* with Y, is to say that X can be meaningfully expressed as some multiple of Y. Suppose in a barter economy that a shoemaker and a carpenter want to do business with each other. The shoemaker needs a kitchen table; the carpenter needs shoes for his family. They agree that the table made by the one will be equal to five pairs of shoes made by the other. In this case, then, the two goods (kitchen table, pair of shoes) are commensurated. We say that the table is commensurable with the pair of shoes, because its worth can be meaningfully expressed as a multiple of a pair of shoes (5/1). Suppose the shoemaker needs chairs for the table as well. He agrees with the carpenter to exchange four chairs with seven pairs of shoes. In that case also each chair is commensurable with a pair of shoes: a chair is 7/4 the value of a pair of shoes.

Generally, any two goods are commensurable if their relative value may be expressed in a proportion or fraction having the form X/Y. One might reasonably think that all goods used as instruments or tools are commensurable with one another, no matter what their size or role: a car, an office building, oranges, barrels of oil, a plasma TV, a microchip, and so on. Money is introduced and a market system operates precisely in order to work out a general system of commensuration among such goods, represented by their price in cash.

The notion of commensurability as applied to human transactions is analogous to a similar notion in mathematics. The ancient Greeks discovered in geometry that not all quantities are commensurable with one another. Consider a right triangle with base and height equal to one. The hypotenuse of the triangle has a length of $\sqrt{2}$, which is demonstrably incommensurable with the base and height, in the sense that no definite ratio of any unit used to measure the base or the height expresses its length. That is why $\sqrt{2}$ is referred to as an "irrational" number. That is, it is a "non-ratio" number, in the sense that it cannot be expressed as a ratio of the form X/Y. Similarly, there are some goods which cannot meaningfully be given a price, in the sense that their value is not a ratio of the value of other goods exchanged in the market. These may be called "incommensurable" goods, that is, goods that are not commensurable with typical market goods.

The market should be understood as a natural institution for the exchange of useful goods. As such, one would expect that there are goods which are both incommensurably "higher" than market goods, and many goods which are incommensurably "more basic" than market goods. We should expect that there are goods incommensurably "higher" than market goods, because market goods are useful goods. But useful goods must ultimately be valued for the sake of goods which are not merely useful but are valuable for their own sake—otherwise there would be an infinite regress. Suppose someone values money because of what he can buy with it. But suppose he buys useful goods with that money. Yet why does he value those useful goods? Eventually he has to stipulate goods which "money cannot buy" but which the goods he can buy with money are for—such as friendship, love, free time, knowledge, culture, worship, and so on.

Similarly, we should expect that there are goods incommensurably "more basic" than market goods, because the institution of the market presupposes that other goods are already in place. For example, the marketplace presupposes peace and stability in society, as markets deteriorate and even fail to function when these are absent. Again, a marketplace obviously presupposes the health of its participants, since at times of a great plague, markets will shut down.

Also, and most importantly for our purposes, a marketplace presupposes truthfulness and trust among its participants. A market transaction can take place only if each of the persons involved is convinced that he is engaging in a fair exchange. He knows the value of his own product. Therefore, he needs to know the value of the other product he would receive, and assess it as equal to what he is offering, if the exchange is to go through. But he knows that value only on the basis of truthfulness and trust. If, for all he knows, the other person's scales are inaccurate, if the product might very well have hidden flaws, if he has reason to think that the other person is ruthless or dishonest, if the coins are possibly counterfeit—that is, if some condition is present which erodes his trust in the other, or his truthful assessment of the other's product—then the exchange will not go through and the market will deteriorate.

Thus, a market should be depicted as an "intermediate" institution, which has goods above it, namely, those goods which marketplace exchanges are "for," and goods at its foundation, namely, those goods which make marketplace exchanges possible at all. We may illustrate the market's position in the following diagram:

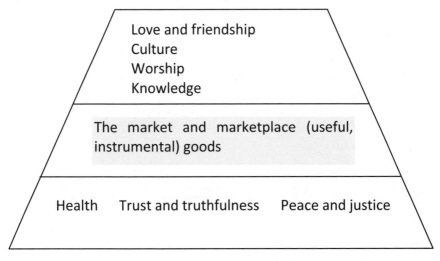

Location of the market between incommensurably higher and incommensurably more basic goods

Now, among incommensurably higher goods and incommensurably basic goods (those at the pinnacle and foundation of the above triangle), some are essential to human social life, whereas others are not. Among the latter are harmless diversions and pleasures. Consider, for example, the enjoyment we derive from spectator sports. This enjoyment would certainly be a "higher" good, in the sense it is one of the things that useful goods are for, and yet it is only a diversion. It clearly is not an essential or highly important good.

So, then, consider only those incommensurably higher goods, and incommensurably more basic goods, which are essential and important. Call these "honorable" goods (following the classical notion expressed in the Latin phrase, *bonum honestum*). Corresponding to each of these "honorable" goods a discipline has arisen, the purpose of which is to provide these goods for society. We regard such a discipline, together with its appropriate mode of association, as a profession. Basically, a business provides a commensurable good, appropriately exchanged with other useful goods in a marketplace; a profession provides an incommensurably higher or incommensurably more basic good—an "honorable" good, which does not strictly permit a marketplace exchange. We can mark out the professions by marking out the noteworthy honorable goods, as in the chart on the next page. It will be seen that this device of identifying essential, incommensurable goods is a helpful way of identifying professions in a strict and narrow sense. On this narrow understanding of a profession, accountancy should indeed be included as a profession, as it provides an honorable good essential to the working of the market:

INCOMMENSURABLE, ESSENTIAL GOOD	PROFESSION
Higher than the market	
Knowledge	Academic professoriate
Salvation, Worship	Theology, ministry
More basic than the market	
Health	Medicine
Justice	Law
Truth and trust	Accountancy

Accountancy is a profession, because it provides for truthfulness and the conditions of trust in a modern market economy. Commerce in general can work only insofar as there is trust. The commerce which marks a modern market economy—decisions to invest in public companies carried out by millions of investors acting independently, where the wealth available for investment often originates at great distances from the enterprises in which that wealth is applied—requires widespread trust in the truthfulness of financial information.

If, a thousand years ago, someone had foreseen the development of modern market economies, that person might likewise have predicted that a new profession would arise, to furnish an incommensurable good which was essential to that sort of society.

Three Corollaries

An important corollary of the preceding line of thought is that the payment received by an accountant has the character of an honorarium or stipend. Strictly speaking, the payment cannot be conceived of as payment in kind, since the good that the accountant provides (truthfulness and the conditions of trust) is incommensurably higher than the good received in payment (cash).

Consider once again the example of the shoemaker and carpenter described above: when they complete their trade they are "all even," and nothing remains to be given by one to the other. Each has transferred to the other a good that is meaningfully compensated for (as regards the use-value of the product rendered) by the agreed upon equivalence of the other good. But when for instance an auditor finishes an audit, the goods furnished—true information about an enterprise, and preservation of the conditions of trust required for a market economy—are not strictly compensated for by payment. That is why honor ("prestige," "standing," "status," "respect") are due to an accountant, just as with any other professional. People instinctively render honor when an incommensurably higher or more basic good has been provided. A good example is how we instinctively have feelings of honor and gratitude for our best teachers—a feeling which continues throughout life, even though we or our parents may have paid a hefty tuition that went towards our teachers' salaries. We feel that what we learned from those teachers is greater than money, and that we have a debt to them that can never be repaid. Or consider how we feel grateful towards doctors who treated us, even though the treatment, from the doctor's point of view, may have been entirely routine: this shows that we regard the doctor as standing in for "the art of medicine" in general, and we suppose that the healing we received is more valuable than any amount of money we paid in the exchange, even if that sum was quite large.

A second important corollary is that accountancy arguably has an even higher claim to be a profession, in some respects at least, than even medicine and law. If a profession is distinguished through its providing a good that is fittingly "compensated" for with honor, then the more that the good which it provides has the character of an honorable good, the more that that profession exemplifies the character of a profession. However, one thing that contributes to the honorability of a good is its altruism. Altruism seems to be a mark of all of the professions in the strict sense. For example, a minister is altruistic insofar as he will accept no payment whatsoever for his assistance. A physician is altruistic by being prepared to attend to his patient whenever necessary—even in the middle of the night, or by giving up sleep for many hours on end—and also by being willing to risk his own health in order to help his patients. (Many physicians have given up their lives by contracting the same disease they were treating their patients for.) But accountancy is especially altruistic in two ways. First, an accountant (and especially an auditor), in providing truthful financial information, typically serves persons who are entirely unknown to him. A physician sees his patient right before him; a lawyer meets and sees his client; but the investors or third parties helped by the accountant are typically unknown and anonymous. Second, the accountant as a matter of course has to be prepared to resign his livelihood rather than do anything dishonorable. A physician in contrast can simply refuse to go along with a patient's request (say, to give him drugs); a lawyer can simply refuse to take a client whose cause he thinks is unjust; but an accountant, in order to do what his profession requires, must be prepared to resign his job.

A final corollary is that an accountant's work, like that of any professional, is in an important respect *personal* rather than *impersonal*. The transaction between a professional and a client is not an exchange of products or services. It is not a matter of one person receiving some "thing" in exchange for some other "thing." Rather, what the professional principally offers is his "person": the client engages the person of the professional, especially his judgment and professed commitment. Correspondingly, the client entrusts himself and his affairs as a person to a professional. It is in the relationship among *persons* in the engagement of a professional that obligations of confidentiality have their basis.

Is Accountancy a Profession? –The Historical Approach

A third way of answering the question of whether accountancy is a profession would be to look at writings of the founders of accountancy. As mentioned, the founders of modern accountancy were intent to argue publicly that accountancy, as much as law and medicine, was deserving of the title of a "profession." They offered many considerations in favor of this view and proceeded with a definite understanding of what a profession was. From historical sources, we are therefore able to recover the profession's original understanding of itself. Although many sources would be serviceable for that task, here we shall look at only two: the original Rules of Professional Conduct of the American Institute of Accountants from 1917, and an influential book from 1931 summarizing thought up to that time about professionalism in accounting, entitled *The Ethics of a Profession*, by A. P. Richardson, a classic and elegantly written collection of essays, sometimes regarded as the first "textbook" on accounting ethics. We shall use the latter in part as a guide to interpreting the former.

The original 1917 rules were as follows:

(1) A firm or partnership, all the individual members of which are members of the Institute, may describe itself as "Members of the American Institute of Accountants," but a firm or partnership, all the individual members of which are not members of the Institute, or an individual practicing under a style denoting a partnership when in fact there be no partner or partners, or a corporation, or an individual or individuals practicing under a style denoting a corporate organization, shall not describe themselves as "Members of the American Institute of Accountants."

(2) The preparation and certification of exhibits, statements, schedules, or other forms of accountancy work, containing an essential mis-statement of fact, or omission therefrom of such a fact as would amount to an essential mis-statement shall be, *ipso facto*, cause for expulsion, or for such other discipline as the Council may determine, upon proper presentation of proof that such mis-statement was either wilful or was the result of such gross negligence as to be inexcusable.

(3) No member shall allow any person to practice in his name as a public accountant who is not a member of this Institute, or in partnership with him or in his employ on a salary.

(4) No member shall directly or indirectly allow or agree to allow a commission, brokerage, or other participation by the laity in the fees or profits of his professional work, nor shall he accept directly or indirectly from the laity any such commission, brokerage or other participation for professional or commercial business turned over to others as an incident of his services to clients.

(5) No member shall engage in any business or occupation conjointly with that of a public accountant, which in the opinion of the Executive Committee or of the Council is incompatible or inconsistent therewith.

(6) No member shall certify to any accounts, exhibits, statements, schedules or other forms of accountancy work which have not been verified entirely under the supervision of himself, a member of his firm, one of his staff, a member of this Institute or of a similar association of good standing in foreign countries which has been approved by the Council.

(7) No member shall take part in any effort to secure the enactment, alteration, or amendment of any state or federal law, or any regulation of any governmental or civic body, affecting the practice of the profession without giving immediate notice thereof to the Secretary of the Institute, who in turn shall at once advise the Executive Committee or the Council.

(8) No member shall directly or indirectly solicit the clients nor encroach upon the business of another member, but it is the right of any member to give proper service and advice to those asking such service or advice.

The Rules were amended in subsequent years to include rules forbidding poaching of employees, advertising, and contingent fees (1919); forecasting (1932); conflicts of interest and competitive bidding (1934); and violations of confidentiality (1942). Apart from these amendments, the Rules remained essentially the same until the 1960s. (Those later changes will be discussed in the next chapter.)

1919

(9) For a period not exceeding two years after notice by the Committee on Ethical Publicity no member or associate shall be permitted to distribute circulars or other instruments of publicity without the consent and approval of said Committee.

(10) No member shall directly or indirectly offer employment to an employee of a fellow member without first informing said fellow member of his intent. This rule shall not be construed so as to inhibit negotiations with any one who of his own initiative or in response to public advertisement shall apply to a member for employment.

(11) No member shall render professional service, the anticipated fee for which shall be contingent upon his findings and results thereof. This rule shall be construed as inhibiting only services in which the accountant's findings or expert opinion might be influenced by considerations of personal financial interest.

1932

WHEREAS, Estimates of earnings contingent upon future transactions should always be clearly distinguished from statements of actual earnings evidenced by definite records, and WHEREAS, An accountant may properly assist a client in estimating the results of future transactions, so long as no one may be led to believe that the estimates represent certainties, BE IT RESOLVED, That no public accountant should permit his name to be used in conjunction with such an estimate in a manner which might lead any one to believe that the accountant could vouch for the accuracy of the forecast.

1934

RESOLVED, That no member or associate shall certify the financial statements of any enterprise financed in whole or in part by the public distribution of securities if he is himself the actual or beneficial owner of a substantial financial interest in the enterprise or if he is committed to acquire such an interest.

RESOLVED, That the council of the American Institute of Accountants regards competitive bidding for professional accounting engagements as contrary to the best interests of members' clients and of the public generally and urges members of the Institute to endeavor by all means at their disposal to eliminate the practice of competitive bidding.

1942

A member or an associate shall not violate the confidential relationship between himself and his client.

There are five important observations to make about these rules:

(i) Note first of all that the above Rules are just that, namely, they are "Rules" rather than a "Code." The difference is not merely linguistic. The Rules given above are something like "rules of thumb." They are not meant to be comprehensive directives governing action in a given domain. They make no claim and adopt no pretence of being complete. In contrast, a "Code" would be something akin to a legal code. A Code is meant in principle to give comprehensive direction, just as a legal code must be continually clarified and specified, with more and more rules, covering finer and more specific cases, in the manner described in Chapter 6 above. "Rules" in contrast can remain basically unchanged, as these were for decades.

To see the difference between "rules of thumb" and a comprehensive code, consider an example from sports. When someone is learning golf, there are basically three "rules of thumb" he needs to keep in mind: keep your left arm straight, keep your eye on the ball, and keep your head still. (They could all be put in a negative, prohibitory form: Do not bend your left arm; Do not take your eye off the ball; Do not move your head.) These rules are by no means meant to be a complete description of all of the steps and movements involved in a golf swing, which would be very lengthy and complex, and would take a book to describe. They simply give a handful of directives which are such that any student who followed them would be on a good path and would be set in the direction of developing over time a proper golf swing.

(ii) The Rules of Professional Conduct are negatives, not positives. They rule out rather than command. Because they rule out, they can be sparse—since, as mentioned, they are merely meant to steer the practitioner in the right direction by ruling out some prominent or obvious ways of going wrong. Because they rule out, they leave lots of room for the practitioner's good judgment and discretion in all other, "positive" matters.

(iii) The Rules presuppose a basic ethical outlook and a good character in a practitioner. The Rules do not aim to make people moral. With one exception, they do not seem to care about ways in which people can act unethically. They are not concerned with what today is known as "compliance." Rather, they are concerned with behavior which does not accord with being a member of a profession. They are concerned to promote a certain refinement of action, not enforce a minimal core of ethics.

On this last point, Richardson's book is revealing. He says that a presupposition of the Rules of Professional Conduct is that an accountant will be a "gentleman" or a "lady":

> It is a tradition of the professions that all who practice them must be gentlemen or ladies. They must be people of education, refinement and that delicate, indescribable knowledge of what is proper which is called tact. They must be people to whom right is as natural as breathing. And above all they must be strong, steadfast, sure. Some are born with these qualities and many others acquire them. The man or woman who is to occupy a position in a learned profession must know the correct thing to do in all circumstances, and much of that knowledge must be instinctive. In the practice of a profession there will arise innumerable problems which will call for the nicest solution. Without a sense of the proprieties the practitioner will be fatally handicapped (p. 150).

(iv) Note that "independence," which today is widely regarded as the most important concept or ideal in accounting ethics, plays no role whatsoever in the original code, and it gets included later only in such a way as to rule out a noteworthy abuse.

(v) Finally, the Rules are rules, precisely, of *professional* conduct. They are not rules of ethics or ethical conduct. As said, ethical conduct is presupposed. The question the Rules address is: given that a practitioner is ethical, what further rules mark out what it means to act with "tact" as a member of the accounting profession. So the relevant contrast operative in the Rules is not that between ethical and unethical conduct—nor even between professional and "unprofessional" conduct (since "unprofessional" can often mean the same as "unethical")—but rather the contrast between conduct which suits a member of a profession and conduct which suits an entrepreneur or business man. Consider Richardson's observations in this regard:

> In accountancy, which is the newest of the professions, it has been rather easier to adopt high ethical standards than in any other profession, but that does not imply that those standards have been invariably observed. There are men and women calling themselves accountants who deride the argument that accountancy is a profession at all. They say, with a fair amount of apparent justification, that the accountant is merely engaged in a business service, very much like that of an appraisal company or a statistical venture; that he should perform his work honestly, of course,

and to the best of his ability, but that to consider himself on a plane with the lawyer, the physician or surgeon is preposterous (viii-ix).

The profitable nature of the practice of accountancy, especially during the great war and its aftermath, attracted many people poorly qualified, and there was a deal of so-called accountancy which was really nothing but a trade—and some of it execrably done. The profession was threatened with extinction because of the purely financial ambitions of some of its members. They even denied that it was a profession at all and toiled night and day to convert it into a matter of business (150-1).

In sum, the Rules of Professional Conduct are addressed to practitioners of good moral character, who have had a good upbringing, and are already intent on acting ethically. It presumes that there are certain points of conduct that suit a professional, and which are different from how a businessman acts, but which will not be obvious or easy to see, to someone who has a good character and was raised well. The Rules give "rules of thumb" which, if followed, will keep a practitioner on the path to developing a good sense of "tact" in acting as a professional.

The Original Conception of Accountancy as a Profession

Yet what is the concept of a profession, and of acting as a professional, which is implicit in the Rules? When Richardson and others were intent on maintaining that accountancy was a profession like medicine rather than a business, what were they insisting upon? The Rules convey a conception of a profession as:

- a fellowship of equal persons,
- who are equal in virtue of their shared competence.

Because of their equality:

- each can stand in for the other ("intersubstitutivity"), and
- "Golden Rule" type reasoning applies among them.

Because of their shared knowledge:

- their fellowship is marked by a regard for the dignity of each, and
- considerations of honor and fittingness are given great emphasis.

Consider for example the very first rule. One might expect that the original Rules of Professional Conduct would begin with a grand statement of principle, or some incredible high-sounding ideal. Yet at first glance Rule (1) looks rather legalistic and unimportant. (What is its purpose? The reader should study Rule (1) at this point and, before proceeding, try to figure out its meaning.) Upon further reflection it becomes clear that Rule (1) is concerned with something like "quality control." It draws a distinction between those who have expertise in matters of accounting, and those who do not, and it aims to reserve the label of the professional association to those who have expertise. In other words, Rule (1) represents persons with expertise claiming an exclusive authority in their domain.

Knowledge claims a prerogative for itself. Suppose that in a crowded room during a symposium a man falls down to the floor, apparently suffering from a heart attack, and people gather around him. They start loosening his tie and check his pulse, but otherwise they do not know what to do. Suddenly someone's voice is heard, "Please stand clear! I am a doctor!" He pushes everyone else aside and takes control: because he knows what he is doing, and the others do not, and he knows that he knows. Or imagine a group of men with only a layperson's knowledge is looking at a complicated engine, trying to figure out what is wrong with it, and then someone with real expertise comes along and says, "Let me in there. I'll show you what's wrong" and takes control. If in such situations there are two or more people with expertise, immediately they recognize each other as having expertise and take control together. Something similar happened at the beginning of the accountancy profession. There were some who had studied accounting in a scientific manner and who began to meet regularly to read papers and confer on difficult matters. They realized that they had an expertise which others lacked and, through forming a professional association, claimed a prerogative.

Some sociologists have viewed professional associations as a kind of power play: one group wants to dominate and consolidate control, so they create a special organization and convince society to appoint them the sole gatekeeper in a certain area. However, this reductionistic approach fails to recognize that knowledge always claims a prerogative for itself, and that knowledge is the basis for the special prerogatives claimed by professionals. Note that Rule (6) also springs from this conviction, but it emphasizes the responsibility of a professional that cannot be avoided, ruling out what today would be called the "subordination of judgment" of a professional to a non-professional in a matter falling under the professional's expertise.

Rule (8) is a good expression of the felt intersubstitutivity of professionals, one with another. It is the assumption of a professional association that all admitted members have an equal standing as experts. Thus, on this assumption, each professional is as good as any other. It follows from this that, if a client had to move from one city to another, a professional in the latter city might continue with the necessary service to the client that a professional in the former city had started. But it also follows that no professional, as a professional, has any reason to propose his own services as superior to that of his fellow professional—which is what Rule (8) rules out.

Rule (5) is a good example of the importance of considerations of dignity and fittingness in a profession. Part of the reason for Rule (5) originally was, in effect, to force members of the new profession of accountancy to make their living solely from their professional work, and to help them persevere in the usually difficult task of developing a professional practice. The American Institute of Accountants wanted it to be the case that accountancy alone was a viable profession, and if members took on other lines of work, the development of the profession in that direction would have been hindered. Another part of the reason for Rule (5) was to sharpen the distinction between a business and a profession, by keeping practitioners from confusing the two—which could happen if accountants carried on businesses on the side.

But another reason was the consideration of the dignity of the profession, which was regarded as pertaining to the *person* of the professional. A good example would be how it is thought that a physician is always a physician, even when not on call—so we would expect the medical vocation to manifest itself if, for example, a physician is driving by an accident and sees an injured stranger. Or we might think that generally, in all areas of his life, a physician would do things that fostered and promoted health in his own life and in those around him. A profession engages the entire person of the professional. It calls for a unity of life, whereby the professional sees his whole life as in some way harmonious with the ideals ("incommensurable goods") aimed at by his profession. Such an attitude would conceivably rule out lots of things: to pick just one example, we might think it was incompatible with the dignity of a profession that a professional hawk peanuts at a circus for extra money on his time off. This is an honorable line of work; yet for those alive to the dignity of a profession, and sensitive to considerations of honor and "fittingness," conceivably it might not seem fully compatible with the unity of life and dignity of a professional. (Similarly, accountants were forbidden to organize into corporations because that mode of organization was thought to nullify their distinctness as persons and preclude genuinely personal service.)

Because of the prerogatives of knowledge and the possibility of highlighting considerations of honor and fittingness, professions have had the appearance of being "elitist." Historically they have been "elitist" in the sense of being exclusive. Moreover, in affirming an equality among all who are admitted as members of a profession, a profession at the same time affirms an inequality between those members and "the laity" (to use the term used in Rule (4)). Recall that, after all, the concept of a profession originated in antiquity but was consolidated in the Middle Ages, where people were quite comfortable with differences in status in society, and where honor and dignity were highly important concepts. An important question to raise today is whether an institution such as a profession which, in its original concept at least, can be traced to the Middle Ages, can easily survive in modern commercial society. Perhaps the pressures of the marketplace and of regulation with a view to equalization are too great nowadays for a profession to withstand. We shall consider this issue in greater detail in the next chapter.

Ethics and the Rules

The only rule where "ethics" as opposed to "professionalism" comes into play would seem to be Rule (2). This rule gives the accounting profession's original understanding of its point and purpose, which is truth. The rule in effect requires the truth (as is implicit in "certification"), the whole truth (it rules out an "omission therefrom of such a fact as would amount to an essential mis-statement"), and nothing but the truth (it precludes "an essential mis-statement of fact"). The Rule's strength consists in its lack of precision. It is as if it binds the practitioner to swear in certifying accounts that, just as in a court of law, he was testifying as to "the truth, the whole truth, and nothing but the truth." That form of words is not without point in a court of law. Indeed, precisely because the formula is so general, it rules out exactly what it should rule out, namely, any kind of falsehood—even though what amounts to falsehood in particular facts and circumstances will vary. In just the same way, Rule (2) is uncompromising in ruling out any kind of falsehood. It mentions both negligence and criminal intent as possible motives for falsehood.

Observe what is missing in Rule (2) but which would be included in any similar rule today: there is no mention of "generally accepted accounting principles" (GAAP). Today, of course, an accountant certifies that financial statements "present fairly in accordance with GAAP," which is a subtly different notion from truth. The reason why Rule (2) does not mention GAAP, is that in

1917 GAAP did not exist. That is to say, more precisely, the term "generally accepted accounting principles" did not exist. Obviously there were best practices then, and a shared sense among practitioners of the principles of accounting, but this would have been referred to by a phrase such as "best professional judgment." The label, "generally accepted accounting principles" came later, in 1934, when it was used by the Securities and Exchange Commission and then became normative for the profession. But note the subtle difference. Rule (2) makes truth the normative conception and effectively requires the accountant to consider whether financial statements correspond to the truth. It has a substantive conception of truth as correspondence. But the phrase "presents fairly in accordance with GAAP" involves a procedural conception of conformity to GAAP, which in turn may or may not imply correspondence to truth. The difference may be depicted as in the diagrams below.

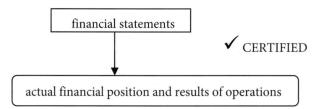

"no essential mis-statement of fact, or omission therefrom of such a fact as would amount to an essential mis-statement"

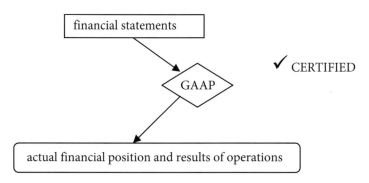

"presents fairly in accordance with GAAP"

Richardson observes as regards the truthfulness enjoined by Rule (2) that it presents especial difficulties to new practitioners, but that the remedy is to be found in the personal trait of courage: "It is particularly trying for the young accountant with only a few clients to be confronted with something which he does not approve and to know that if he condemns what he believes to be unworthy he will lose lucrative practice. It all resolves itself into a question of common honesty, and the accountant who is worthy of a place in his profession will tell the truth whatever befall. This is not to imply, however, that there may not be times when the temptation to be lenient will be almost irresistible. At such times the accountant must summon all his store of courage and stand firm" (p. 135).

Some Particular Rules

The rules against advertising, contingent fees, and competitive bidding were not arbitrary, and they were not expressions of a monopolistic intent, but rather they were the direct consequences of the concept of a profession which has been explained.

Advertising was ruled out for many reasons, including the following:

(i)   Given the presumed equality of any member of the profession with any other, there would be no grounds on which a member could recommend his own services in preference to those of any fellow member.

(ii)   Calling attention to one's own accomplishments and talents was incompatible with the dignity of a professional, especially for someone who was also a "gentleman," as a gentleman did not draw attention to himself or give the appearance of boasting. "Self-laudation is ever despicable and yet what can soliciting do without it? It is impossible to understand the mentality of a man who tells other men that he is exceptionally good. To get back to a good old-fashioned word which has been much misused, let it be said that the accountant should be a gentleman and a gentleman never praises himself," Richardson observes (p. 58).

(iii)   More than this, advertising requires both boasting, and the wish that others accept and rely upon one's boast, because that which is boasted of is not something tangible, which can be seen and examined, whether one is speaking of it or not, but rather it involves "immaterial" assets: "It is not merchandise nor commodity nor tangible thing, but merely something intangible, one's mental equipment and natural ability augmented by training and education—at least that is what is supposed to be offered. In order to convince the prospective buyer that these incorporeal assets exist, it is necessary to mention them in a laudatory way, which must be repugnant to anyone with a sense of propriety" (pp. 45-6).

(iv)   A professional is required to seek the interests of his client, which would include encouraging his client to conduct his affairs rationally; but it would be irrational for the client to engage a professional for the reason that he had seen that professional's advertisement (since an advertisement could provide no rational grounds for preferring one professional over another); thus a professional would not want to gain clients on that basis, since that would be to wish one's own clients to be irrational. In short, advertising depends upon and encourages client irrationality. As Richardson remarks: "One would not engage a lawyer to conduct a litigation because he had seen the lawyer's name advertised. Nor would anyone with a grain of intelligence engage an accountant by virtue of advertisement. The accountant is brought into touch with all the details of one's business, its trade secrets, its financial conditions, its prospects, its retrospects, and it is simply incredible that anyone would engage an accountant to do that sort of work without knowing something about the man engaged" (p. 61).

(v)   Advertising presupposes that the professional's services are available for purchase, but what the professional offers is his own person, as a qualified expert, rather than any service or commodity. Richardson regards advertising as a professional putting himself up for sale: "It is, of course, a totally different thing to attempt to sell merchandise or advertising. The men who devote their activities to the sale of things for which they are not themselves directly responsible or things which are the tangible result of another's labor, are pursuing a perfectly reputable and commendable vocation. It is only the sale or attempted sale of oneself that is anathema." (p. 46).

(vi)   Finally, and in any case, advertising had been shown by experience not to be effective for professionals.

Contingent fees likewise were ruled out on the basis of the concept of a profession. A contingent fee is payment which is not fixed in advance but is contingent upon and proportionate to the desired result, such as a fee for tax preparation which is paid only if the client receives a refund, and which is greater if the client's refund is greater. In contemporary discussions, contingent fees are looked at askance because they provide the wrong incentives, but this consideration, although important, was originally amplified by other arguments based on the concept of a profession:

(i)   A professional who is willing to work on a contingent fee basis shows a lack of self-dignity and a lack of appreciation for his self-worth as a professional, because he is prepared in some circumstances to work for no payment at all.

(ii)   Likewise, if an accountant in some circumstances works for no payment at all, in other circumstances, to balance things out, he must seek a payment which is greater than it should be, and then he would be treating that other client unjustly.

(iii)   An accountant who works on a contingent fee basis becomes essentially a sharer in the profits of the business of the client, in which case he stops acting like a professional and takes on the role instead of a businessman. "One expects the lawyer to be an advocate, in other words one who speaks for his client, but the accountant is in a different category altogether—his client really is the truth. He is engaged by the facts to make them known and it should matter not at all who pays the fees for the service rendered provided the fees are paid, for justice demands compensation," Richardson says (p. 102).

(iv)   Finally, an accountant working on a contingent fee basis loses the impartiality required of his role as "judge." As Richardson comments: "the accountant worthy of his calling is entirely impartial. His working tools are facts and he should never be an advocate, in any sense of the word. If he enters into a contract with a taxpayer he becomes the taxpayer's partner in the adventure and therefore loses the capacity for impartiality. He becomes a pleader in his own suit and when he appears before the department of internal revenue or the board of tax appeals or the courts he is perhaps usurping the prerogative of the lawyer, and surely repudiating his own status as an accountant, if he have any interest whatever in the outcome of the case. It is humanly impossible for any man, however upright he may consider himself, to escape the effect of personal interest" (p. 101).

Competitive bidding was also ruled out as incompatible with the concept of a profession. Along these lines, Richardson laments: "A great problem which confronts the accounting profession is the direct result of a prevalent and generally commendable practice in business. This is the custom of calling for bids or tenders for certain specified work which is to be done, and of course it involves competition. It involves in a profession many other things as well, but the problem's solution is rendered difficult chiefly by the fact that what is good in ordinary business is not good in the professions, and it is no easy matter to convince the public that there is such a distinction. As in the case of advertising or soliciting there are many good citizens who fail to see that business practices may be quite improper when dragged into the field of professional work. Bidding is in this category." (p. 135). Arguments against competitive bidding included:

(i)   Competitive bidding (like working on a contingent fee basis) shows a misguided willingness to receive fees that are higher than deserved in some cases and less than deserved in others; hence, it leads to fundamentally unjust results.

(ii)   No professional should encourage irrationality in his client, and it would be irrational for a client to engage an accountant because his fees were lowest (just as it would be irrational to choose an accountant based on an advertisement).

(iii)   It is unseemly and not worthy of the dignity of a professional and a gentleman to appear to be scraping up business by offering the lowest price.

(iv)   The competitiveness of competitive bidding—where one party benefits from the other's loss—is incompatible with the equal fellowship desired among members of a common profession. As Richardson comments: "the word 'competition' and the thing which it implies reflect no credit upon a profession. One can not think of professional men competing without coming to the conclusion that their professional claims are void and that they are in reality engaged in business. Competition, says the old proverb, is the life of trade. Nowadays people are not quite so sure of that; but at any rate, it is certain that competition sounds the death knell of a profession." (p. 25).

(v)   Competitive bidding (like advertising) can make it appear that a professional is selling a commodity, or that he is putting himself up for sale.

Recommended additional reading:

A.P Richardson, *The Ethics of a Profession*

Incipient
Legalism

9

"Truthful Because Trusted"

"If the accounting profession is to fulfill its public interest responsibilities, its own credibility must be restored. This is essential not only for the survival of the profession, but also for our free enterprise system itself."—Harvey Kapnick

TO UNDERSTAND THE CURRENT CODE OF PROFESSIONAL CONDUCT for accountants, one needs to see its history, how it developed, and the distinct stresses and determinants which imparted to it the form that it has today. Often the best way to understand something is to see its origin. Our goal over the next two chapters is to understand the shape of accounting ethics today, by seeing how the profession's main codes of accounting ethics developed during the last century.

One may distinguish four main periods in this development:

1917-1933	The period of "a newly-forged professionalism"
1933-1963	The period of "incipient legalism"
1964-1988	The period of "codification and restatement"
1988-present	The period of "a search for new foundations"

Here are brief descriptions of each period:

1917-1933: The period of "a newly-forged professionalism." As we saw in the preceding chapter, the first "Rules of Professional Conduct" were concerned with marking off accounting as a profession and distinguishing it from an ordinary business occupation. At that time, accountancy had existed for about 50 years and had worked hard to be recognized and established as a profession. But what does it mean to be a member of a profession? The Rules articulated various points of conduct, about how someone acts with propriety as a member of a learned profession, which would not be obvious already to a person of good character.

1933-1963: The period of "incipient legalism." During this phase, the Code[16] increasingly took on the appearance of a legal code, with rules, regulations, and interpretations. Like any legal code, it became increasingly articulated over time. The crucial force shaping the profession's conception of itself was governmental regulation. In the Securities Act of 1933 and the Securities Exchange Act of 1934, the Federal government required that publicly traded companies register their securities with the Securities and Exchange Commission (SEC) and file regular financial reports. Congress stipulated that these registrations and filings be audited by "independent public accountants." Thus, subsequent regulatory decisions by the SEC, especially decisions as regards "independence," exerted an enormous influence on accounting's understanding of its ethical responsibilities. The Securities Acts essentially established a reciprocal relationship between accounting and society: society (through the SEC) would require that public companies be audited by public accountants, and, in exchange, public accountants would strive to prove themselves worthy of that role. The main concern of the code therefore became: to clarify how accountants should act in order to justify this important role. At the same time, during this period, GAAP and GAAS were developing with increasing specificity, and they took the form of an increasingly articulated legal code. The Rules of Professional Conduct during that time, then, tended to be viewed in the profession as the same sort of thing as accounting standards, only at a higher conceptual level.

1964-1988: The period of "codification and restatement." During this time, the code underwent a major reorganization in 1964, a restatement in 1972, and a recasting in 1988, at which point it arrived at the basic form it has today—that is, it acquired a three-tiered structure involving not only "Concepts" (or "Principles"), but also "Rules," and "Interpretations." Until 1964, the Code was developed largely through amendments to the 1917 Code. But the old framework became recognized as no longer adequate, largely because of such factors as the rise of non-attest activity; the

---

[16] In this chapter and elsewhere, for the sake of simplicity, we use the label "Code" to refer to any of the accounting profession's statements of its own professional and ethical obligations, even though throughout most of the last century these statements were labeled "Rules" rather than a "Code", and even though, as we shall see, the change in labeling was not insignificant.

growing role of CPAs outside the context of public accounting and auditing; the growing complexity of accounting; and legal changes concerning advertising and bidding. All of these developments tended to erode accounting's understanding of itself as a distinct professional society in the traditional mode: instead of setting down rules about how to behave as a member of a learned society, the Code became concerned primarily with clarifying what counts as upright behavior of an individual accountant in particular engagements, both attest and non-attest, situated within a complex business environment. Additionally, the Code was increasingly viewed as an instrument of "compliance" and as a way of minimizing legal risk and "exposure," on the presumption that Codes of Conduct should play the role of inculcating and maintaining good conduct.

1988-present: The period of "searching for new foundations." This has been a period ineluctably shaped by major accounting scandals, which culminated in the massive frauds perpetrated by Enron and WorldCom (see chapters 11 and 12 below), in which accountants played a major role. During this time, people continue to look to the Code as a way to encourage and insure good conduct; yet it is evident that the Code is not functioning well as an instrument of "compliance." So people generally look to something more fundamental than a Code. For instance, some leaders in the field focus on the distinction between "principles" and "rules," and say that the problem is that the Code inculcates a concern only to follow rules—but at the same time it is said that only the "rules" are "legally enforceable." Others favor a "Threat-Safeguard" model, which tries to downplay the significance of rules and accord a large role to individual judgment. Others look to disciplines outside the accounting profession for guidance, such as philosophy, psychology or economics. A consensus forms that further education in ethics is necessary, but there is apparently little consensus about what that education should include, other than a review of the "principles, rules, and interpretations."

The current Code of Professional Conduct for accountants is the combined result of these four periods. There are still some slight vestiges within it of the period of "newly-forged professionalism," in the Code's mention of integrity, its reference to "the public interest," and its restrictions (now greatly attenuated) on advertising and soliciting. The period of "incipient legalism" is evident in the Code's highly legalistic approach to independence, its hundreds of interpretive opinions, and in the fact that generally, and lamentably, it does not give reasons for its particular holdings and interpretations. The period of "codification" is visible in the form and structure that the Code takes today. Finally, the period of searching for foundations—in which we find ourselves today—is evident in the very way that the Code is proposed and conceptualized: on the one hand, the Code is presented as a basic given, without any background or foundation; on the other hand, it is taught in accounting programs and for purposes of state relicensing, as if it were an indispensable solution to ethical problems in the profession.

In this and the following chapter, after a review of the first period (already covered in the preceding chapter), we shall look at the other periods in more detail.

The Period of "A Newly-Forged Professionalism" (1917-1933)

Accounting developed out of bookkeeping and began to establish itself as an independent profession in England and Scotland in the mid-19th century. By the early 20th century, similar developments had occurred in the United States, with the formation of the first professional associations and the rise of state licensure. It is important to emphasize that during this period "professionalism" meant something very concrete: there was no meaningful distinction between someone's holding himself out as a professional, and his belonging to a particular professional association. Thus, the Code of Professional Conduct was presented as an appendix to the bylaws of such an association; the code articulated ways in which a member of that association should act.

As mentioned, the early Rules of Professional Conduct make no reference to any of the concepts important for modern codes: there is no mention at all of "independence," "public trust," "due care," or "objectivity." Second, there is no reference to GAAP and GAAS. Rather, the purpose of the Rules is to mark off some noteworthy ways in which to practice as a professional in that sense is different from engaging in business; a sense of honor, fairness, and dedication are all presumed. This conception may be summarized by saying that a profession is presumed to be:

- a fraternity of equal learned experts;
- which takes pains to set itself apart from the "laity";
- the members of which are interchangeable as experts;
- who abide by Golden Rule type principles ("treat others in the profession as you would like to be treated yourself");
- whose association is cooperative not competitive;
- marked by unity; and
- the practice of which does not constitute engaging in a business or trade.

These points are closely connected with one another, and they largely hinge on the shared knowledge that members of a profession have, and the service to others to which members of a profession pledge themselves as having that knowledge. The reason a profession takes pains to set itself apart from other members of society, the "laity," is not some kind of proud quest for honor, but rather that it wishes to distinguish those who have some sort of expert knowledge from those who do not—the reason being that people are harmed unless the distinction between those who are knowledgeable and those who are not is clearly marked. The reason why a profession is jealous of its membership, is that it wishes to insure that only those who have the requisite expert knowledge and spirit of service are included within the profession. The reason professionals are conceived of as interchangeable with one another, and the judgment of one professional is regarded as freely substitutable with that of another, is that theoretically they are all equally qualified in virtue of sharing the same expert knowledge and spirit of service. The reason why they are expected to relate to one another through Golden Rule type reasoning, which would rule out encroachment among other things, is that professionals in principle conceive of themselves as interchangeable in the manner explained. The practice of a profession is inherently cooperative rather than competitive, as is the sharing of knowledge and service—a consideration which provides the most fundamental reason why competitive bidding is not consistent with the ideal of a profession and prohibited by later codes.

That a profession is not a business or trade is signaled precisely by the decisive role that considerations of honor and propriety play in how a professional organizes and conceives of his professional work. These considerations are and must be salient, because for a professional—according to the conception implicit in the above code—the governing consideration in his work is common membership in an association with others marked by shared knowledge and a shared spirit of service. This is not to say that considerations of honor and propriety play no role in a business or trade—indeed, they play an important role—but in a business or trade honor and propriety are important not as regards what one is making or what service one is providing, but as regards the manner in which one produces or provides a service—one "does business" with honesty and a sense of fairness and fair play. Furthermore, such considerations as operative within any business are common to any business, and they are continuous with ordinary human considerations of justice. In contrast, the practice of a professional is in an important way inherently a matter of honor, as explained in the preceding chapter.

Corresponding to this notion of a profession is an implicit portrait of a member of a profession:

(i) A professional has the character of a "gentleman." As Richardson stated, "They must be people of education, refinement and that delicate, indescribable knowledge of what is proper which is called tact. They must be people to whom right is as natural as breathing. And above all they must be strong, steadfast, sure" (p. 150).

(ii) A professional's service is inherently personal. "The service is one which is essentially personal" (Richardson, p. 30). Hence confidentiality is important, and accountants who practice together should not be organized as a corporation, since such a legal structure essentially removes individual responsibility.

(iii) A professional regards all fellow professionals as, ideally, equally qualified peers. "The ideal condition," Richardson explains, "which of course does not exist, would be for accountants generally to have such absolute confidence in the ability of their fellows that the man practising in Maine could trust with complete assurance the accountant in Arizona to undertake any work which might arise in Arizona for the client in Maine" (p. 25). Hence, the behavior of any individual reflects upon everyone: "If every practising accountant will remember that the name of the profession depends largely upon him and that every good deed will reflect honor upon his calling and every weakness will weaken it there will not be much need of a written law or rule" (p. 153).

(iv) What a professional offers is something mental and not tangible, closely identified with himself, rather than a product or service which is distinct from himself. It follows that soliciting and advertising must be avoided by professionals, because these require that a professional make unseemly claims about himself.

(v) Professionals are inherently cooperative, not competitive. The reason is that, for a professional, it is more important that the work be done well, than that he in particular do that work. A corollary is that no professional should deliberately aim to expand his own practice to the detriment of a colleague's practice.

(vi) A professional takes full responsibility for his work. "The accountant who would escape responsibility by fleeing in the cloak of incorporation is unworthy of membership in the profession. If he can not conduct his practice and accept whatever liability may attach to his work he does not belong to the profession and should divert his energies into some other channel. The man who seeks to evade the burden of responsibility is never much to be esteemed. Cowardice, everyone admits, is the most contemptible of failings" (p. 29).

(vii) A professional occupies a position of leadership and service generally. A professional intends and succeeds at having a widespread beneficial influence, such as, for instance, speaking up for the interests of employees of an audit client when appropriate; using one's auditing expertise for the oversight of local government; even running for office. "When a young man selects the district in which he will work he assumes a responsibility for the welfare of that district. This is true, not only of accountants, but of all men. It is a truism to say that every resident of a city has a distinct, far-reaching influence upon the affairs and the future of that city. Those who are engaged in occupations which are professional and bring one in touch with the people generally, have a more powerful effect upon the community than any others," Richardson writes (p. 33).

(viii) A professional, aware of the dignity of his profession, accepts an engagement only if fairly stringent conditions have been satisfied, which insure that the work will be rendered well and (importantly) received correctly. These conditions include: you have the required expertise; you will be compensated to a degree that enables you to do it well; and you will not be asked or expected to do or consent to anything improper. Furthermore, the client's motivation must be entirely correct and proper: you would not wish to work for another on any condition other than that you are qualified to do a job well and that your client wants that job done well.

Because honor was so important in professional practice at the time, "independence" was not. One reason is that objectivity and impartiality, which independence is meant to insure, are necessarily already involved in the rendering of a judgment based on expert knowledge, just as a scholar or scientist needs to be objective and impartial in reaching a conclusion based on a consideration of the relevant evidence. Another reason is that it is presumed that accountants will have good character, and they will not easily be swayed from rendering a well-grounded judgment. Finally, motives involving honor tend to "crowd out" those involving supervision and fear of punishment, and vice versa. People who wish to abide by an honor code tend to resent provisions for supervision as implicitly accusatory, just as people who wish to apply provisions of supervision tend to push aside reliance upon honor.

In sum, the first Rules of Professional of Conduct were both idealistic and practical. They were idealistic because they presupposed integrity and appealed implicitly to a professional's sense of honor. They were practical because they articulated fine points of conduct involved in practicing as a member of a professional association. Accounting ethics was conceived of as essentially courageous action, by persons of good character, in cooperative action with other like-minded experts, in the service of truth in financial matters.

The Period of "Incipient Legalism" (1933-1963)

In this period, the form taken by the Rules of Professional Conduct remains basically the same; however, the way the Rules are understood begins to change. At the beginning of this period, "professional ethics for accountants" means fine points of conduct related to the practice of a learned profession in an association of peers; by the end of this period, it means conformity to a system of rules which has the character of a legal code. The beginning of this period is marked by the Securities Acts of 1933 and 1934, which were a crucial contributory cause in the increasing "legalistic" approach to accounting ethics. By the end of this period, the accounting profession began to recognize clearly that the old formulation of the code was no longer adequate, and it soon thereafter began to attempt a series of reformulations and new codifications. Just as Richardson's book, *The Ethics of a Profession*, crystallizes the outlook of the earlier period, so John Carey's 1946 text, *Professional Ethics of Public Accounting*, captures well the spirit and approach of this second period.

Our phrase "incipient legalism" refers to a cluster of three trends affecting accounting ethics:

(1) A changed understanding of "professionalism." The question of professionalism ceases to be, "How does a man or woman of good upbringing work as a member of a profession instead of as a business person?" and it becomes, instead, "How should an engagement of a public accountant be done ·in a 'professional manner'?", where the purpose of a code of professional ethics is regarded as analyzing and spelling out what it means to show integrity in one's work. The focus shifts from what it means to be a member of an association to what it means for an individual to do a particular task well.

(2) Good character is accorded a diminished role. In the earlier period, as we saw, it was presupposed that an accounting professional have good character and the outlook of a "gentleman." It was recognized that occasionally someone who presented himself as having good character would turn out to be a crook, but it was thought that little could be done to prevent this. But in this second period it was increasingly thought that statements of accounting professionalism should help to create "compliance;" moreover, it is tacitly presumed that the remedy for someone's transgressing a set of rules is an increase in those rules, as though an

ideally crafted and highly articulated legal code could largely eliminate wrongdoing.

(3) The goal of the profession begins to be conceived of procedurally rather than substantively. As we saw, in the earlier period it was natural for practitioners to speak of their devotion to truth. However, in this second period, talk of truth tends to be replaced by talk of "independence." This is to replace a substantive and goal-related conception of the profession with a procedural conception. (When substantive considerations do need to be introduced, these are glossed as "the interest of the public.") With the development of GAAP and GAAS, there is an increasing temptation to say, not that the accountant's role is to "get it right"— which GAAP and GAAS assist in—but rather to say that the accountant's role is to follow a correct procedure by giving a report in conformity with the relevant rules.

What do we mean by saying that there was a replacement of "substantive" conception of the goal of the profession (truth) with a "procedural" one (independence)? Let us define terms. A "substantive" conception puts a certain result first and judges a procedure as acceptable depending upon whether that procedure reliably attains that result. A "procedural" conception puts a certain procedure first and says that whatever results from that procedure is acceptable. Here is an example. Suppose that two persons want to divide a cake to share between them. If one of them were to say, "Let's measure it carefully to determine equal portions and then cut it accordingly," he would be proposing a *substantive* conception, since he has a clear idea of the desired result (equal portions) and he proposes a procedure which he regards as acceptable (cutting the cake in accordance with the measurement) precisely because it yields that desired result. But suppose one were to say instead, "Let's divide it this way: you cut the cake in two, and then I'll pick which piece I want," he would be proposing a *procedural* conception, since he would be saying, in effect, that whatever distribution of cake resulted from such a procedure would be fine with him (and not necessarily an equal distribution).

In accounting, to give increasing emphasis to independence goes along with giving increasing emphasis on a procedural conception of the goal of the profession, since one would be saying, in effect, that any professional judgment rendered by an independent expert would be an acceptable result.

The period we are considering (1933-1963) was generally, for philosophy and thought, a period in which procedural conceptions were increasingly preferred to substantive ones. This is evident in the popularity during that period of "Ideal Observer" theories in ethics, which held that an ethical judgment was valid if it was the sort of judgment that would be rendered by someone ideally situated to make such a judgment (that is, someone who was entirely impartial and completely knowledgeable). At the same time, enormous attention was given to John Rawls' theory of justice, which proposed a procedural conception of justice, namely, that the basic laws of a society are just if they would be chosen by ideal deliberators in an ideal procedure for deliberation. So the change in outlook in accounting ethics followed a broader current in philosophy in general. Of course, this shift toward preferring a procedural conception in accounting ethics was also encouraged by the increasing complexity of business and contractual relationships (multinational business; conglomerates; derivatives)—and the corresponding increasing complexity of GAAP and GAAS—which could make it seem as if accounting was not so much a matter of representing how things are (truth) but rather of conforming one's judgment to a (sometimes seemingly arbitrary) standard.

What were some reasons for these changes? As mentioned, the Securities Act of 1933 and the Securities Exchange Act of 1934 were an important precipitating cause. Those acts required that an offering of a security be registered, and that a company whose shares are publicly exchanged file periodic reports with the SEC. The acts specify explicitly that these registrations and filings need to be audited by an "independent" public accountant. However, regulatory agencies such as the SEC must carefully define terms, since the entities they regulate must have a clear idea of what they need to do in order to satisfy the requirements of the law. Thus, it was necessary and inevitable that the SEC define what it understood the word "independent" to mean, as occurring in the Securities Acts, and it did so through Rule 2-01 of Regulation S-X. The SEC's definition had both the form and the force of law; furthermore, as an implementation of Federal law, its definition governed, shaped, and influenced the laws and outlooks of subsidiary associations and agencies. In particular, the SEC's definition, and its approach in general, had an enormous influence on the accounting profession. "Independence" soon became the central notion of accounting ethics, and the attempts of the SEC and the accounting profession to specify independence, through the detailed articulation of rules having the character of a legal code, was taken to be the paradigm of "accounting ethics" in general.

Another important cause of the changes in this period was the changed outlook of society as a result of World War II. The United State's waging of that war required an enormous expansion in government bureaucracies; likewise the country's astounding success in the war lent tremendous prestige to those bureaucracies. The rise of bureaucracies was a social phenomenon that became the subject of many commentaries and books. For the accounting profession, what this change implied is that it was no longer natural for accountants to regard themselves as "gentlemen" who were voluntarily associated with a "learned society," but rather as trained individuals linked together essentially through a bureaucracy. This was the period in which the large firm effectively replaced the "profession" as the basic unit of association for a professional accountant. However, whenever the form of something remains the same but the substance changes, legalism is a predictable result, since in that case it becomes difficult to assign reasons for the old forms, and so the old requirements become viewed as a system of somewhat arbitrary impositions and "rules." By the end of the period we are considering, the accounting profession found itself with a code that increasingly failed to make sense given large-scale changes in society and in the business world, and, not being able to give an account of the reasons, it identified ethics with a kind of legal code.

As mentioned, in the period we are considering, the form of the code does not change very much. But resolutions of 1932 and 1934, adding rules proscribing "forecasting" and competitive bidding, are interesting for our purposes. We give those resolutions again:

> WHEREAS, An accountant may properly assist a client in estimating the results of future transactions, so long as no one may be led to believe that the estimates represent certainties, BE IT RESOLVED, That no public accountant should permit his name to be used in conjunction with such an estimate in a manner which might lead any one to believe that the accountant could vouch for the accuracy of the forecast.

> RESOLVED, That the council of the American Institute of Accountants regards competitive bidding for professional accounting engagements as contrary to the best interests of members" clients and of the public generally and urges members of the Institute to endeavor by all means at their disposal to eliminate the practice of competitive bidding.

One already begins to see the breakdown of the older understanding of accountancy in the resolution against forecasting. The resolution as given makes little sense: if what one wants to avoid is the impression that an accountant can judge anything with "certainty," then there could be no problem in an accountant's vouching for a merely probabilistic forecast. Also, the resolution confuses "certainty" with "accuracy": a forecast which estimates a probability could be highly accurate and yet—because it offers a probability—not "certain." What the resolution actually wishes to say is that an accountant's judgment issues from the knowledge that he or she has, and that it therefore carries with it all kinds of implicit qualifications and caveats, such that it would be hazardous, and potentially misleading, if a layperson wished to put that judgment to use on his own, as if the judgment could be coherently separated from the expertise which gave rise to it. But this sort of justification for the rule depends heavily on the conception of accountancy as a learned profession, which was already being eroded.

The second resolution merely asserts, without explaining why, that competitive bidding is contrary to the interests of clients and the general public. This is apparently a utilitarian justification. The resolution declines to rule out competitive bidding by an appeal to the nature of a profession. Note that if competitive bidding really were to be proscribed on the grounds that it was against the interests of the general public, it would be most surprising for the general public to fail to see this, and yet the general public has tended to favor competitive bidding.

A similar complaint may be raised against the various "Numbered Opinions of the Committee on Professional Ethics," originally published in the *CPA Journal*, which begin to be included with the Rules in 1958. By 1963 over ten such Opinions get included. These resolutions of problem cases are of some value, as revealing where thoughtful professionals will come down in each matter; however, the Opinions are generally offered without reasons, which tends to encourage the thought that a practitioner should avoid what is proscribed in an Opinion *because the Committee says so*, rather than because the Committee is discerning what any practitioner with a refined sense of professional conduct would likewise have independently decided.

For instance, consider how the Committee deals with the issues addressed in Opinion No. 1. The question is whether it is "improper" for a member to furnish clients and others with "tax and similar booklets prepared by others" and imprinted with the firm name of the member. That is, is such a practice to be avoided, because it is a form of advertising, or rather is the practice acceptable, because it involves simply the offering of a legitimate client service? Here is the Committee's opinion. We add numbers to the paragraphs, not found in the original, for ease of reference:

> (1) In the opinion of the committee, imprinting the name of the accountant on newsletters, tax booklets or other similar publications which are prepared by others and distributed by a member of the Institute does not add to the usefulness of the material to the reader.

(2) Use of the imprint, in the committee's opinion, is objectionable in that it tends to suggest (and has been interpreted by many as a means of) circumventing Rule 10 of the rules of professional conduct, which says that a member shall not advertise his services.

(3) It is the conclusion of the committee that distribution of newsletters, tax booklets or similar publications, prepared by others, when imprinted with the name of the accountant furnishing the material, is not in the interest of the public or the profession.

(4) The committee sees no grounds for objection to furnishing material of the type indicated to clients or others provided that such material does not carry the imprint described and provided that such distribution is limited in a manner consistent with Rule 7.

Paragraph (1) is highly disputable: one might think it would be useful to inform the reader of the professional who thought the literature valuable enough to distribute, and who would presumably be prepared to answer, with expert opinion, any further questions the reader might have. Paragraph (2) seems weak: someone might object that what is at issue is not whether the practice "tends to suggest" or is "interpreted" as advertising, but whether it really is that. The weight of the opinion therefore seems to rest on paragraph (3), and yet no grounds are given there at all, besides the bare assertion that the practice "is not in the interest of the public or the profession"—a merely utilitarian justification which has not been substantiated.

A Re-Interpretation of Accounting Professionalism

A careful examination of Opinion No. 1 shows an attempt to discuss the case under the headings: "interest of the public," "interest of the client," "interest of the profession." That schema reflects the influence of John Carey and his books on accounting ethics, especially *Professional Ethics of Public Accounting* (1946), but also the later, substantial revision of the same, *Professional Ethics of Certified Public Accountants* (1956).

Carey was born in Brooklyn, New York and attended Yale University. Although not a CPA himself, he was a staff member of the AICPA for 40 years, before his retirement in 1969, serving as assistant secretary, secretary, executive director, and vice president. He gave hundreds of speeches and authored many books including *Professional Ethics of Public Accounting, Ethical Standards of the Accounting Profession*, and *The Rise of the Accounting Profession*. Carey was also closely involved with the AICPA's official periodical, *The Journal of Accountancy*.

He was the first non-CPA to receive the AICPA's Gold Medal Award. His thought was enormously influential on the AICPA and therefore the profession.

Carey's two books capture well the changes in accounting ethics typical of the period of "incipient legalism." The 1946 text is dedicated to Richardson and purports to follow in Richardson's footsteps. It is presented as a commentary on the Rules of Professional Conduct. However, those rules are organized according to the three mentioned headings, as evident in its table of contents:

I. Introduction
II. The Interest of the Public
    1. Independence
    2. False or Misleading Statements
    3. Contingent Fees
    4. Financial Interest in Client's Affairs
    5. Auditor as Director
    6. Occupations Incompatible with Public Accounting
    7. Occupations Followed Simultaneously with Practice of Public Accounting
    8. Commissions, Brokerage, and Fee Splitting
    9. Forecasts
III. The Interest of the Client
    10. Confidential Relationship
    11. "Professional Dignity"
    12. Commissions, Brokerage, and Fee Splitting
    13. Practice by Corporations
    14. Use of Accountant's Name by Another
    15. Certification of Statements Audited by Others
IV. The Interest of the Profession
    16. Advertising
    17. Solicitation
    18. Competitive Bidding
    19. Offers to Employees of Other Accountants
    20. Use of Professional Description with Firm Names

The 1956 code in its turn anticipates the reformulations and codifications which will mark the third period of accounting ethics after 1963. It announces that "An entirely new plan of discussion has been adopted in this book. Instead of devoting a separate chapter to each of the existing Rules of Professional Conduct, an effort has been made to follow a more logical pattern." Carey then introduces "fundamental principles of professional ethics," including "the public interest, professional competence, independence and integrity, and the professional attitude" (p. xi). He does not understand accounting ethics as concerned with articulating the "rules of conduct" which go along with membership in a learned profession—Carey in fact impugns such rules for not being "logical"—but rather his concern is to state abstract "fundamental principles," which he believes captures "the professional attitude."

The 1946 text, although purporting to follow Richardson, and presented as a commentary on the Rules of Professional Conduct, is sharply discontinuous with Richardson's approach. This is clear from Carey's remarks on his threefold schema for organizing the Rules, in which he effectively dismisses Richardson's main interests as involving no more than "etiquette":

> It was said earlier in this book that the rules of professional conduct of the accounting profession were essentially of two types: the first designed primarily to protect the interests of the public, including clients (or perhaps rather to reassure the public that the profession is vitally concerned with protection of the public interest); the second designed primarily to advance the interests of the profession itself. Even in the second category there is evident the basic motive of encouraging the kind of behavior on the part of professional accountants which will inspire public confidence and respect. This means essentially the kind of behavior which is good for the public, and that is what the rules in the first category prescribe.
>
> It might be more meaningful to say that the first, and larger, group of rules is mainly concerned with ethics, and the second with etiquette. The first group is surely the more important—violations are regarded as much more serious than in the second. Actually violations of rules within the second group are more frequent, which indicates that the concepts inherent in the rules of the first group are so fundamental that accountants instinctively comply with them—their intelligence would warn them against the actions proscribed even if the rules did not exist. It doesn't require a formal pronouncement to tell a professional certified public accountant that he should be independent, that he should not be negligent, that he should keep his clients' secrets, and so on. The rules on these subjects are intended more for the information of the public,

perhaps, than of members of the profession, whose personal experience will soon inform them adequately (pp. 83-4).

That is to say, what Carey regards as the substance of accounting ethics was hardly addressed by Richardson, and the sorts of concerns that Richardson focused on hardly interest Carey at all.

Note how strange it is for Carey to say in the above passage that an accountant's actions in the "interests of the client" involve "assuring the client of the accountant's being in service of the public interest." One might wonder why the client should be concerned to employ for himself someone who is serving the interest of some other entity, the "public." Also, it may seem puzzling why an accountant should be preoccupied with making it *seem* to someone that he is acting in a certain sort of way, which seems a departure from the earlier conception, that an accountant is simply a knowledgeable expert who does his work by rendering an expert opinion.

These and other oddities in the above passage reflect what might be called the "social contract" understanding of the accounting profession which Carey puts forward in his books. On this view, the accounting profession exists because of an implicit agreement it has with society in general, namely, society renders "confidence" in accountants, and, in exchange, the accountants "protect the public interest":

> The very existence of the accounting profession depends on public confidence in the determination of certified public accountants to safeguard the public interest. This confidence can be maintained only by evidence of both technical competence and moral obligation. One item of evidence is promulgation and enforcement of rules of professional conduct.
>
> These rules, then, are not meaningless mouthings of idealists remote from reality; they are not arbitrary dogma imposed by a professional hierarchy upon a helpless rank and file; they are not inspired by a sadistic pleasure in the irritation of those who have to observe them. The rules of professional conduct of the accounting profession are in part a pledge to the public that in consideration of public confidence the profession will protect the public interest; and in part a code of behavior designed to protect the profession itself against the selfish impulses of individual members (Carey, 1946, p. 2).

The "social contract" conception of the accounting profession represents a shift in accountancy's understanding of the relationship between truthfulness and trustworthiness. In the first period we considered, the profession claimed that it was worthy of being trusted by others because of fellowship of knowledge and expertise which it represented. Accountants were reliable experts belonging to a profession, and for that reason one should trust them. In a word, accountancy regarded itself as "trusted because truthful." In this second period, however, where the "social contract" understanding dominates, the relationship is reversed, and the profession regards itself as needing to be truthful—or, more importantly, needing to give the impression of being truthful—precisely because society places great trust in their work. In other words, the profession now begins to conceive of itself as "truthful because trusted."

What were the sources of this "social contract" concept of the profession. No doubt philosophical and sociological views played a role. Carey like many Americans was probably influenced by political philosophers, such as Thomas Hobbes and John Locke, who regarded society and law as founded on social contracts. Again, according to some sociologists, a profession is distinguished from a business only because of a social contract: according to this view, certain means of employment (such as medicine and law) are picked out by society because of their great importance, and their practitioners are then granted public honors and a higher "status," in exchange for the service that these practitioners provide.

But it would seem that the greatest influence on Carey's thought was the new relationship between the United States government and the accounting profession following the Securities Acts of 1933 and 1934. These Acts effectively established a reciprocal relationship between government (specifically, the SEC) and the accounting profession, and it was natural to view this as a reciprocal relationship between society and the accounting profession, insofar as the government presumably represented and served society. The terms of the reciprocal relationship, or "contract," as implicitly contained in those Acts, was that the accounting profession would be accorded the continuing role of certifying a public company's legally mandated filings with the SEC—a highly lucrative role, which gave the accounting profession considerable prominence and prestige—on condition that the accounting profession acquitted itself well in its task of correctly verifying those companies' representations of their financial position in those filings. The accounting profession would continue to be "trusted" in this capacity by the SEC, only so long as it carried on in a "truthful" way: thus accountants should very much signal their commitment to being "truthful," so that they might continue to be in this way "trusted."

A kind a partnership between government and the accounting profession was indeed part of the SEC's original mandate and was envisaged by the Securities Acts. In writing the original Acts, Congress, with the approval and concurrence of President Franklin D. Roosevelt, deliberately rejected a proposal that would require that financial statements be certified by government accountants, and instead specified that financial statements submitted to the SEC be certified by "independent public accountants":

> At the time when Congress was considering the Securities Act of 1933, Col. Arthur Carter, representing the accounting profession, testified that the bill should include a requirement that financial statements be audited and reported on by independent accountants. Such a provision was ultimately added to the Act before passage. In addition, the Act did not follow the example of companies acts throughout the world which generally define required financial statements in considerable detail but rather gave authority to an independent agency to set forth accounting and disclosure requirements. Thus Congress created the necessity of the partnership between agency and profession that has since existed.[17]

The SEC likewise, from its beginning, acted in recognition of such a partnership and with a view to fostering it:

> During its early years the Commission considered undertaking the establishment of a uniform system of accounting standards, but determined in 1938 that the primary responsibility for accounting principles should remain in the private sector with those who practice the accounting profession.[18]

---

[17] John C. Burton, Chief Accountant of the SEC, "The SEC and the Accounting Profession: Responsibility, Authority and Progress," Accounting Colloquium III, University of Kansas, May 10-11, 1973.   Burton goes on to say: "In the years since its creation, the Commission has looked to the profession to assume the leadership in setting accounting principles. Authority and responsibility have been delegated and have been accepted by the profession."

[18] John R. Evans, Commissioner of the SEC, "The SEC, the Accounting Profession, and Self-Regulation," Distinguished Speaker Series, Department of Accounting, University of Kentucky, Lexington, Kentucky, Feb. 28, 1979.

For example, in 1938, in Accounting Series Release No. 4, the SEC recognized "substantial authoritative support" for financial statement disclosures deriving from the judgments of accounting professionals. Similarly, the SEC from its inception relied upon and showed deference to the accounting profession in the formulation of sound accounting principles. This was manifested in the SEC's active efforts to help establish and then recognize professional bodies responsible for formulating authoritative principles (the Committee on Accounting Procedures; the Accounting Principles Board; the FASB), as well as its use of a light hand in oversight, and its being reluctant directly to contravene considered professional judgment.

Note that this historical relationship was, in its origin, not a matter of a government entity's designating, perhaps in the interest of efficiency, some group of experts to specify accounting principles, but rather of the deliberate cooperation of a regulatory authority with a pre-existing profession. One SEC Chairman even referred to this cooperative endeavor as "The Great Treaty":

> In both the Securities Act and the Exchange Act . . . Congress gave us the authority to establish accounting principles. The Commission declined to exercise this authority in what I like to refer to as the Great Treaty. We would accept statements prepared in accordance with generally-accepted accounting principles, which would be principles having substantial authoritative support, except that where several inconsistent principles had substantial authoritative support, we might insist on one rather than another.[19]

The influence of SEC regulatory actions on the development of accounting ethics are already clearly evident in Carey's discussion of independence in his 1946 textbook. Carey begins by giving a definition of independence which correctly puts truth first: "It means, in simplest terms, that the certified public accountant will tell the truth as he sees it, and will permit no influence, financial or sentimental, to turn him from his course" (7). In the interest of showing that independence is not merely of "academic" interest, Carey then turns to the SEC regulation then in effect about independence, the original rule 2-01 of Regulation S-X. The regulation draws an implicit distinction between "independence" and "independence in fact," where

---

[19] Ray Garrett, Jr., Chairman of the SEC, "The Accounting Profession and Accounting Principles," Second Annual Robert M. Trueblood Memorial Conference, Illinois CPA Foundation, Palmer House, Chicago, Illinois, October 3, 1975.

the former means "not corrupt; judging with integrity," and the latter means "not entangled (with financial interests)." On account of S-X 2-01, the latter becomes more important than the former for purposes of risk, exposure, and legality, since the SEC declares that it regards itself as entitled to dismiss a claim of the first sort of independence if there is evidence of lack of the second sort:

> (a) The Commission will not recognize any certified public accountant or public accountant as independent who is not in fact independent. For example, an accountant will not be considered independent with respect to any person in whom he has any substantial interest, direct or indirect, or with whom he is, or was during the period of report, connected as a promoter, underwriter, voting trustee, director, officer, or employee.
>
> (b) In determining whether an accountant is in fact independent with respect to a particular registrant, the Commission will give appropriate consideration to all relevant circumstances including evidence bearing on all relationships between the accountant and that registrant, and will not confine itself to the relationships existing in connection with the filing of reports with the Commission.

That is to say, the regulation treats "independence in fact" as if it were a necessary condition of true independence, when clearly it is not. Moreover, given clause (b), in which the SEC claims a wide discretion in determinations of "independence in fact," the regulation gives the impression that preserving "independence in fact" in some broad sense would be sufficient, when clearly too it is not. What one would have ideally liked the SEC to say is that "independence in fact" may nonetheless still not amount to true independence, and that determining whether the one amounts to another requires judgment and discretion in different facts and circumstances. Perhaps the SEC reasoned that that sort of statement would not have constituted clear guidance to practitioners about what counts as abiding by the law. In any case, the direct result of this regulation is that it became widely believed, mistakenly so, that true independence (which, as we saw, Carey had rightly defined as a determination to discover and declare the truth at all costs) can be analyzed as "independence in fact" together with adherence to GAAP.

A Changed Understanding of Professional Rules

Another example of how Federal regulatory agencies exerted an influence on accounting ethics is in Carey's discussion of the ethics of contingent fees in tax practice. Here, once again, it is illuminating to contrast Richardson's treatment of the subject with Carey's. As we saw, Richardson held that the arguments for contingent fees depend upon the misguided assumption that a profession is the same as a business, especially, he thought, through an implicit analogy with piece work, where the worker gets paid depending upon how much he produces for the client. Richardson pointed to various reasons why contingent fees were incompatible with the ideal of professionalism and summed up his view by saying, in a passage quoted earlier, that the client of an accountant "really is the truth," that "it should not matter at all who pays the fees for the service rendered," and that it is incidental that someone who derives a particular benefit from that particular service pays for it (pp. 101-2). All of Richardson's arguments would apparently apply to any professional in any capacity, including tax practice: contingent fees are never acceptable for any member of a learned profession, and accountants need to adhere to the highest standards for a profession.

In contrast, Carey gives only one argument: through a contingent fee arrangement, Carey says, an accountant "forfeits[s] his independent status, and therefore his value to prospective investors"; such an arrangement "destroy[s] his usefulness to all concerned." The argument is implausible since Carey must exaggerate for the argument to be decisive. As for whether accountants can accept contingent fees for tax work, Carey is initially undecided. It seems initially plausible to him that contingent fees are permissible in that circumstance, because the accountant's opinion is subject to government review and does not count as final. Carey states: "The government does not rely on the accountant's findings but makes whatever investigations it considers necessary before reaching its own conclusions." Carey then settles the matter by appealing to a regulation, namely, Treasury Tax Circular 230. Carey interprets the regulation as holding that practitioners "may serve clients on a contingent-fee basis, but they may not exploit a client by claiming an exorbitant fee, regardless of the outcome of the case, and the determination as to what is reasonable should be subject to review by a court or other official authority." Given the holding of Circular 230, Carey concludes: "These precedents provided powerful support for those who contended successfully that the prohibition against acceptance of contingent fees by members of the American Institute of Accountants should not apply to fees for tax practice." That is to say, Carey was willing to settle a question of propriety for the accounting profession by appealing to a government regulation.

Whether this way of settling such a question is legitimate or not may be debated, but that it represents a departure from how such questions were handled in the earlier period cannot be doubted.

We noted that Richardson's primary concern in accounting ethics, the differentiation of the profession of accounting from an ordinary business, is effectively dismissed by Carey as falling within the realm of "etiquette." However, it is still possible to find in Carey a residual concern with professionalism, in his brief treatment of what he calls "professional dignity" (chapter 11 in the 1946 text). Strangely, however, Carey places his discussion of this topic under the heading of "the interest of the client," and he keeps it separate from his discussion of "independence."

Carey begins his discussion by expressing sympathy with those who look with skepticism on a profession's claim to some kind of distinctive status or honor. We belong to a "debunking" age, he says, when anyone who makes such a claim is likely to be ridiculed. Furthermore, he says, arguments which appeal to propriety— which Carey interprets as a mindless appeal to tradition, along the lines of "that sort of thing isn't done"—have little weight in the present day and age. Rather, everyone acts in a self-interested manner, Carey says, and so you cannot explain someone's behavior, until you have shown how a person's behavior serves that person's own interests. That is why Carey wants to re-interpret what Richardson said about professionalism as a matter of accountancy pursuing its own self-interest.

What is the point of rules intended to mark out an occupation such as accounting as a "profession"? Such rules, Carey explains, were necessary:

> to persuade businessmen that the accountants were interested in serving society as well as making a living ... The problem was, if you like, a public-relations problem. The rules of professional conduct were an important medium for advertising the profession's intentions ... This was a way of enabling businessmen to distinguish the professional motive of pride in service from the commercial motive of profit. Professional dignity is a constant reminder to the public that the certified public accountant regards himself as engaged in a profession, not a business, (pp. 67-8).

In this passage, Carey seems to be saying that the social contract that accountants have engaged in is a kind of beneficent deception. Everyone acts in their own self-interest, Carey believes, accountants no less than anyone else. So then why should anyone entrust his own interests to accountants? According to

Carey, accountants adopt the trappings of professionalism precisely in order to convince others to trust them. Professionalism, then, is a matter of "public relations" and "advertisement" rather than of making a commitment and pursuing a mode of life that transcends egoistic self-seeking.

A similar approach is reflected in Carey's explanation elsewhere in his text as to why accounting ethics is constituted by rules. Carey is a big proponent of rules: the opening section of his book is entitled, "Why Rules are Needed," and he argues that the very "definition of civilized society" is "a mass of rules." "Rules are absolutely essential to organized cooperation," Carey says, because "The nature of the individual is instinctively egoistic and selfish." Thus, "to protect the interests of the group as a whole against the anti-social instincts of the individual," society imposes rules.

Here too an implicit social contract is at work, seemingly inspired by the philosophy of Thomas Hobbes: "Each member of the group, accepting the discipline [of the rules of the group] over his own selfish impulses, receives in return protection against the selfish impulses of others" (p. 1). On this picture of the accounting profession, accountants like anyone else have egoistic and selfish impulses. Without rules, they would presumably defraud others whenever they had a chance. They could not be trusted to give a fair account of anything, but would twist facts as it suited them, to advance their interests. Thus a group forms—calling itself "the accounting profession"—which imposes strict rules on itself, requiring its members to give a fair accounting of financial statements. These rules "advance the group interest of those who constitute the profession" because "the opportunity of a profession to serve the public will be widened if the public is convinced that members of the profession are required to protect the public interest" (pp. 1-2). Carey thus regards rules of professional ethics as a means of social control, because he thinks that people are naturally selfish and egoistic.

Yet for all Carey's enthusiasm for rules, he almost immediately draws attention to the inadequacy of rules. He points out that the by-laws of the AIA provide for the expulsion from the profession of anyone committing "an act discreditable to the profession," which is not comprehensively defined. Carey warns: "While the rules enumerate many prohibited acts they do not purport to be all inclusive, and a member is bound to exercise his judgment and his conscience in doubtful areas not covered by the rules" (pp. 3-4).

We said that in the period of "incipient legalism" the Rules of Professional Conduct remained largely unchanged, although some additional rules were added. The most important change in an earlier rule itself was the change of former Rule 2 into what became Rule 5 in 1942. Rule 2, it will be recalled, was the rule dealing with an accountant's obligation to the truth. It stated that:

> (2) The preparation and certification of exhibits, statements, schedules or other forms of accountancy work, containing an essential misstatement of fact or omission therefrom of such a fact as would amount to an essential misstatement or a failure to put prospective investors on notice in respect of an essential or material fact not specifically shown in the balance-sheet itself shall be, ipso facto, cause for expulsion or for such other discipline as the council may impose upon proper presentation of proof that such misstatement was either wilful or the result of such gross negligence as to be inexcusable.

The new form of this rule, adopted in 1941 and included in the Code from 1942 onward, stated instead:

> (5) In expressing an opinion on representations in financial statements which he has examined, a member or an associate shall be held guilty of an act discreditable to the profession if:
>
>   (a) He fails to disclose a material fact known to him which is not disclosed in the financial statements but disclosure of which is necessary to make the financial statements not misleading; or
>   (b) He fails to report any material misstatement known to him to appear in the financial statements; or
>   (c) He is grossly negligent in the conduct of his examination or in making his report thereon; or
>   (d) He fails to acquire sufficient information to warrant expression of an opinion, or his exceptions are sufficiently material to negative the expression of an opinion; or
>   (e) He fails to direct attention to any material departure from generally accepted accounting principles or to disclose any material omission of generally accepted auditing procedure applicable in the circumstances.

There are some minor changes in choice of words in the new rule; for example, it speaks of "material" rather than "essential" misstatements or omissions. The term "essential" is unclear (essential to what?), but "material" means "would make a difference for someone's decision" and is much clearer. Rule 5 largely breaks out conditions that were compressed and put together in the old Rule 2. Omissions are dealt with separately in (5)(a); misstatements in (5)(b). In Rule 2, "gross negligence" was censured only insofar as it contributed to an essential misstatement or omission; in (5)(c), in contrast, gross negligence is itself made a reason for censure. (5)(d) is important because it is the first time what would now be called "due diligence" finds its way into the code: someone who failed to acquire "sufficient information to warrant expression of an opinion" would have failed to exercise due diligence. That someone should not include so many exceptions to an opinion as to "negative" the expression of an opinion rules out an accountant's seeming to give an opinion but not really doing so—thus abusing the weight of his or her professional qualifications.

But the really new aspect of Rule 5 is its reference to GAAP and GAAS in clause (e). However, note that GAAP and GAAS are not introduced as replacing the notion of truth or as defining what it means to be truthful. The notions of "omission" and "misstatement" are prior and given first, in clauses (a) and (b). This is important because it shows the profession's understanding of GAAP and GAAS when they are first introduced into the Code. As we have seen, the question will later arise as to whether an accountant acts ethically and legally if he certifies a financial statement fully in accordance with GAAP and GAAS, and yet that statement leaves out information which investors would reasonably be interested in. In such circumstances, common sense and courts have held, that following GAAP and GAAS is not itself sufficient to exculpate an accountant. In Rule (5) we find a role accorded to GAAP and GAAS which is fully consistent with such a holding.

Conclusion

We may summarize the approach to accounting ethics in the period of "incipient legalism" as follows:

1. Accounting ethics is no longer conceived of as the articulation of diverse "Rules of Professional Conduct," which deal with those fine points of conduct which serve to mark out a member of a learned profession from a businessman, but rather as rules intended to suppress (or "discipline") someone's inborn egoism and selfishness, thereby making it possible for such a person to participate in a social contract, whereby he is accorded confidence (especially, prestige and a high salary) in exchange for the service he provides to the "public interest."

2. Ethics essentially requires the statement of rules. Ethics is the articulation of a law code or rule book, rather than the imparting of a certain conception of

"being a professional" through example and through attention to anecdotes and case studies. Whereas Richardson would clearly regard rules as derivative and secondary in importance to someone's having a sound conception of a profession, under Carey's influence rules become primary—while Carey at the same time admits that rules are not sufficient.

3. The Rules of Professional conduct for accountants, when not disparaged as illogical "etiquette," are regarded as instruments of social control, to suppress selfishness which may threaten the implicit social contract by which society looks to services from accountants for pay.

4. As a result of the influence of government regulation, those areas of accounting ethics which are most easily approached through the articulation of complex rules begin to assume the greatest importance, especially, rules about "independence."

5. A "principle," in contrast to a "rule," is conceived of as a broad category under which a rule falls. Rules should be articulated to "reveal" principles. There are three "principles" in this sense: "the interest of the public"; "the interest of the client"; and "the interest of the profession." Given this presupposition about "principles," accounting ethics is taken to consist of rules which have the form of a legal code, but which do not function like a legal code—as a practitioner could in theory be held guilty of and punished for acts "held to be discreditable to the profession," even if he has violated no rules.

Recommended additional reading:

John L. Carey, *Professional Ethics of Public Accounting*

Stephen A. Zeff, "How the U.S. Accounting Profession Got Where it is Today: Part I," *Accounting Horizons* 17(3), 2003: 189-205.

Codifications and New Foundations

10

"[O]ver the years, attestation has come to account for only about one-third of the $26 billion of revenues of today's 'Big Five' accounting firms, with tax services accounting for one-quarter. The remainder, not far from one-half of revenues, is derived from consulting, management, and advisory services. The potential problem that arises from this trend, obviously, is that the desire to garner or retain a highly-lucrative consulting contract from an audit client could jeopardize the auditor's independence....

"It must also be clear that, whether or not the auditor has the backbone to maintain its independence under these circumstances, many management and consulting arrangements could easily be perceived as representing a new element in the relationship between auditor and corporation—a business relationship with a customer rather than a professional relationship with a client. Surely this issue goes to the very core of the central issue of philosophy that I expressed earlier: The movement of auditing from profession to business, with all the potential conflicts of interest that entails."—John Bogle, Founder, The Vanguard Group

The '60s, '70s, and '80s were a period of reformulation for the Rules of Professional Conduct. We mentioned the major changes which the accounting profession had undergone, especially the increasing complexity of transactions and accounting standards, the influence of regulation, and the growing importance of non-attest work done by accountants, especially management consulting. These changes and others made the old Rules seem unsuited to modern conditions: for instance, the Rules had no rule dealing with independence, which had come to be viewed as the most fundamental ethical requirement binding on an accountant. At the same time, under the influence of John Carey and his concern to discover "principles" underlying the various rules which had accreted over time, it was felt that some more fundamental basis of the Rules had to be set down. The accounting profession found itself faced with a case of "new wine in old wineskins": new wineskins needed to be fashioned, and there were three main attempts along these lines in the period we are considering: a preliminary codification in 1964; a major reformulation in 1972; and the recasting or revision of the code in 1988, by which the code attained essentially the form that it has today.

The Preliminary Codification of 1964

The spirit of the 1964 codification may be gleaned from an inspection of the new, systematic organization of the Rules which it offered. The enumeration of the Rules had previously been essentially chronological: when a rule was added it was given the next number, regardless of its conceptual connections with other rules. In the 1964, the Rules were basically kept the same as before—the most significant exception being the addition of a rule concerning independence—but they were now organized according to main concepts:

Article 1 – Relations with Clients and Public
      Rule 1.01 — Independence
      Rule 1.02 — Discreditable Acts
      Rule 1.03 — Confidential Relationship
      Rule 1.04 — Contingent Fees
Article 2 — Technical Standards
      Rule 2.01 — Reliance on Other Accountants
      Rule 2.02 — Reports — Responsibility and Disclosure
      Rule 2.03 — Reports — Opinions and Disclaimers
      Rule 2.04 — Forecasts
Article 3 — Promotional Practices
      Rule 3.01 — Advertising
      Rule 3.02 — Solicitation
      Rule 3.03 — Competitive Bidding

The Rules are preceded by an introduction proposing, as in Carey's textbook, that the ethical obligations of the accounting profession derive from an implicit, reciprocal contract:

> The reliance of the public and the business community on sound financial reporting and advice on business affairs imposes on the accounting profession an obligation to maintain high standards of technical competence, morality and integrity. To this end, a member or associate of the American Institute of Certified Public Accountants shall at all times maintain independence of thought and action, hold the affairs of his clients in strict confidence, strive continuously to improve his professional skills, observe generally accepted auditing standards, promote sound and informative financial reporting, uphold the dignity and honor of the accounting profession, and maintain high standards of personal conduct.

Again, it should be noted that this sort of recount reverses the order of justification which was given in the first period (1917-1933). In the first period, it was held that because accountants were knowledgeable experts, their opinions were objective and could be relied upon by businessmen ("trusted because truthful"); now it is claimed that because their opinions are relied upon, accountants should be objective ("truthful because trusted").

Rule 1.01 on independence was elegant and brief:

> Neither a member or associate, nor a firm of which he is a partner, shall express an opinion on financial statements of any enterprise unless he and his firm are in fact independent with respect to such enterprise.

Obviously the rule is unsatisfying, because it does not define "independent." Interpreted as a definition, it would be circular. One might even argue that the rule has no content whatsoever, taken on its own. No doubt sensing this, the 1964 codification then includes a lengthy explanation of the rule. Yet we should pause to appreciate how extraordinary this is. What is the use of a rule which gives no guidance on its own? Also, why should only the rule on independence need such an explanation? (Indeed, no similar explanation is given for any of the other 20 rules in the Code.)[20]

The first thing the Code says by way of explanation is that "Independence is not susceptible of precise definition, but is an expression of the professional integrity of the individual," which is unhelpful, as it is presumed but not explained why "professional integrity" is not the sort of thing that admits of a precise definition. Also, none of the other terms used in the code admit of a precise definition ("act discreditable to the profession," "confidential," "purporting to express," etc.), and yet apparently serviceable rules may nonetheless be articulated with respect to such things.

Next by way of explanation the Code states:

> A member or associate, before expressing his opinion on financial statements, has the responsibility of assessing his relationships with an enterprise to determine whether, in the circumstances, he might expect his opinion to be considered independent, objective and unbiased by one who had knowledge of all the facts.

One might ask: is this additional comment offered as a definition of independence, or is it discussing something else in addition to independence? Clearly it is not a definition of independence, since it would be a circular definition, as it says basically that someone is independent if he would be regarded as independent. (It is unclear how someone who was in doubt about his own independence could be helped by thinking about whether some other person would be in doubt as to his independence.) So this paragraph should presumably be interpreted as introducing

---

[20] Note furthermore the use of the expression "in fact independent", which could potentially be confused with the SEC's notion of "independence in fact."

another notion, perhaps, "the appearance of independence": someone has the *appearance* of independence, if an onlooker with knowledge of the facts would regard him as *in fact independent*. And yet as a definition of "appearance of independence" the paragraph fails, because it stipulates that the relevant onlooker be someone who has knowledge of "all the facts," and yet it never happens that onlookers know all the facts. Onlookers form their impressions on the basis of limited facts, and so it is irrelevant to the appearance of independence whether someone knows all the facts. To see this, imagine a man of enormous integrity— call him "Jack"—who steadfastly and earnestly takes his duties to be of the highest importance, and who is therefore capable of rendering, and typically does render, objective judgments about the financial position of a company, even if he has a substantial interest in a company. Suppose Jack audits Company X, in which he has a large investment. His audit is perfectly sound, as he is a man of the highest integrity. Such a person, clearly, lacks the appearance of independence as regards Company X, and, surely, if an auditor is bound to decline an engagement in which he lacks the appearance of independence, then Jack should decline to audit Company X. And yet someone who "knew all the facts" about Jack would know that he was a person of the highest integrity and would consider him "independent, objective, and unbiased," even in his audit of Company X.

So the above paragraph serves to clarify neither "independence," since then it would be viciously circular, nor "the appearance of independence," since then it would be incorrect.

Finally, a further paragraph is added which says that:

> A member or associate will be considered not independent, for example, with respect to any enterprise if he, or one of his partners, (a) during the period of his professional engagement or at the time of expressing his opinion, had, or was committed to acquire, any direct financial interest or material indirect financial interest in the enterprise, or (b) during the period of his professional engagement, at the time of expressing his opinion or during the period covered by the financial statements, was connected with the enterprise as a promoter, underwriter, voting trustee, director, officer or key employee.

This language in contrast is reasonably clear; yet it is simply an elaboration of the previous Rule 13. Thus one can say that the 1964 codification adds nothing new with respect to independence, despite its attempt to set down independence as the fundamental notion of accounting ethics.

It should be emphasized once again that "independent" in the first period we considered (1917-1933) was primarily an attribute of the profession and derivatively an attribute of a practitioner. An "independent accountant" was simply a member of the independent accounting profession, that is, a profession which set itself apart from business interests because, like any learned society, it was interested in discerning and reporting on a certain kind of truth. The opposite of "independent" in this sense would be "under the employ of, and devoting one's efforts to, some business enterprise." In contrast, by 1964 "independence" comes to signify a subjective frame of mind, which in the first instance is an attribute of individuals, not a profession, and which is applied to the profession only derivatively, if at all. The opposite of "independent" in this new sense would be "biased."

One consequence of this shift in meaning of "independence" is that it changes where one would locate the crux of the ethical difficulty or struggle typically faced by an accountant. Under the older meaning, the main ethical difficulty faced by an accountant was understood to be that of *declaring the truth once it had been discerned*, as there are many circumstances in which it would be difficult to state a truth which was disadvantageous to a business.[21] That is why "courage" was uniformly cited, by the founders of accountancy, as the character trait that an accountant should especially have. However, under the newer understanding of independence, the main ethical difficulty faced by an accountant comes to be understood as that of *discerning the truth in the first place*, on the grounds that self-interest introduces a distorting bias, which would cause someone to judge differently in ways that he himself would fail to recognize. We saw that Carey in his textbook was sympathetic with those who tended to "debunk" idealism and claims of probity. His discussions presuppose that each person pursues his selfish interests and is kept to a standard of objectivity only by "rules" imposed from without, which as it were force him to act in disinterested way. On this approach one really must deny that there is such a thing as a practitioner's fundamentally

---

[21] This is not to deny that sometimes it is correct not to declare the truth when doing so would be disadvantageous for a business and indeed for the common good. To take the obvious example of a "self-fulfilling prophecy": there are sometimes circumstances in which a bank might irresponsibly encourage a "run on the bank" if, without serious reasons, or due cause, it disclosed a precarious but not inevitably disastrous position.

disinterested regard for the truth, and appeals to such a motive must be "debunked."[22]

Once independence is in this way turned into a subjective state which is in practice unattainable—because we are all inherently selfish anyway—then, precisely as a subjective state, it becomes practically speaking irrelevant. Paradoxically, the attempt to make independence the fundamental concept of accounting ethics also renders it in a real sense irrelevant. This is evident in Opinion No. 12 on independence, included in the 1964 codification. The question which the Opinion aims to answer is whether providing tax or management services to an enterprise renders a practitioner no longer independent of that enterprise. In reply, the Committee on Professional Ethics cites at first a statement on independence which was issued in 1947 by the Council of the AIA: "Independence is an attitude of mind, much deeper than the surface display of visible standards." The Committee immediately goes on to say:

> While endorsing the Council's statement that independence is an attitude of mind, the committee recognizes that it is of the utmost importance to the profession that the public generally shall maintain confidence in the objectivity of certified public accountants in expressing opinions on financial statements. In maintaining this public confidence, it is imperative to avoid relationships which may have the appearance of a conflict of interest. It is this reasoning which led the Institute to include in Rule 1.01 of the Code of Professional Ethics the statements that members should not have any financial interest in, or serve as officers or directors of, clients on whose financial statements they express opinions.

That is to say, independence as an attitude of mind is put aside. However, the "reasonable observer" criterion for assessing the appearance of independence is also put aside, or at least it plays no evident role in the Committee's Opinion:

> The committee does not intend to suggest, however, that the rendering of professional services other than the independent audit itself would suggest to a reasonable observer a conflict of interest. For example, in the areas of management advisory services and tax practice, so long as the

---

[22] This shift was consistent with the growing importance, in the fields of psychology and social science, of the theory that all human agents are inherently "biased" and cannot on their own transcend the coloring and slant which they place on things in the service of their own interests.

CPA's services consist of advice and technical assistance, the committee can discern no likelihood of a conflict of interest arising from such services. It is a rare instance for management to surrender its responsibility to make management decisions. However, should a member make such decisions on matters affecting the company's financial position or results of operations, it would appear that his objectivity as independent auditor of the company's financial statements might well be impaired. Consequently, such situations should be avoided.

In summary, it is the opinion of the committee that there is no ethical reason why a member or associate may not properly perform professional services for clients in the areas of tax practice or management advisory services, and at the same time serve the same client as independent auditor, so long as he does not make management decisions or take positions which might impair that objectivity. But note that the Committee draws a conclusion about what a "reasonable observer" would think based upon what the Committee itself thinks, not the other way round! It is because the Committee believes that "there is no ethical reason why a member or associate may not properly perform professional services for clients in the areas of tax practice or management advisory services, and at the same time serve the same client as independent auditor," that it expects that a "reasonable observer" would have the same view. Presumably and naturally enough, an observer who thought differently would be "unreasonable." Note too that what really gives weight to this Opinion has little or nothing to do with independence as a state of mind, or what a reasonable observer would judge. What really is decisive for the Opinion is the simple principle that an auditor should not audit his own work: because if the auditor has made management decisions, then the audit either will, or can potentially, involve results which he himself is responsible for. That is, the argument underlying the Opinion rests merely on the concept of what it is actually to *review* something.

The 1972 Restatement

The very title of the 1972 Restatement is informative: it is a "Restatement of the Code of Professional Ethics," which includes "Concepts of Professional Ethics" and "Rules of Conduct." The old artifice that the Code marks off fine points of behavior that pertain to acting as a member of a learned profession has now finally been dropped: the Code is clear that it no longer offers rules of professional conduct. Rather it gives rules of conduct, and professionalism has become a "concept." The Introduction explains the new structure of the Code as follows:

> This document consists of three parts. The first part, the Concepts of Professional Ethics, is a philosophical essay approved by the Division of Professional Ethics. It is not intended to establish enforceable standards since it suggests behavior beyond what is called for in the Rules of Conduct.
>
> The second part, the Rules of Conduct, consists of enforceable ethical standards and requires the approval of the membership before the Rules would become effective. It is printed on colored pages to facilitate identification.
>
> The third part, Interpretations of Rules of Conduct, consists of interpretations which have been adopted by the Division of Professional Ethics to take the place of the present Opinions of the Ethics Division upon adoption of the restated Rules of Conduct.

So "Rules" carry the major burden, because they are "enforceable" and adopted by vote of the membership. They are printed on colored paper to distinguish them.

What these changes tend to suggest, if not strictly imply, is that accounting ethics is juridical and risk-related. When later in the Code it is stated that, "The Institute's Code of Professional Ethics derives its authority from the bylaws of the Institute which provide that the Trial Board may, after a hearing, admonish, suspend or expel a member who is found guilty of infringing any of the bylaws or any provisions of the Rules of Conduct" (p. 19), the assimilation of accounting ethics to a legal code is complete. Accounting ethics is conceived of as a system of laws passed by the AICPA membership, which apparently have no authority beyond the bylaws of that association. Such an approach would have had little justification even when the profession accepted "Rules of Professional Conduct," since what makes an occupation a "profession" is objective and prior to any system of rules articulating what that amounts to. But it clearly has no justification when accounting "ethics" is at issue. "Ethics" cannot possibly be identified with rules that happen to have been passed by a majority of members of a particular association.

The first part, a "philosophical essay," is in effect presented as dispensable, for the curious reason that to follow what is promoted by that essay would require behavior "beyond what is called for in the Rules of Conduct." Nonetheless the essay repays study. The two fundamental notions from the first period of accounting ethics (1917-1933), professionalism and character, get short shrift: the

1972 Code makes no attempt to define a profession, or explain what sets accounting apart as a profession; and although it says, correctly, that people "have a right to expect … that [a CPA] is a person of competence and integrity" (p.7), it stipulates nothing which is aimed at insuring this.

The essay, although ostensibly about the "concepts" of accounting ethics, shows no small degree of conceptual confusion. The "concepts" are alternatively called "principles," as if these were the same. It mentions five "concepts," which it gives as follows:

> *Independence, integrity and objectivity.* A certified public accountant should maintain his integrity and objectivity and, when engaged in the practice of public accounting, be independent of those he serves.
> *Competence and technical standards.* A certified public accountant should observe the profession's technical standards and strive continually to improve his competence and the quality of his services.
> *Responsibilities to clients.* A certified public accountant should be fair and candid with his clients and serve them to the best of his ability, with professional concern for their best interests, consistent with his responsibilities to the public.
> *Responsibilities to colleagues.* A certified public accountant should conduct himself in a manner which will promote cooperation and good relations among members of the profession.
> *Other responsibilities and practices.* A certified public accountant should conduct himself in a manner which will enhance the stature of the profession and its ability to serve the public (p. 7).

But the first two of these are manifestly not unities, and the last seems a miscellaneous category, raising the question of whether there are not in fact at least eight "concepts" or "principles." Thus, the codification gives a false impression of greater system than it actually provides.

Similarly, there is great confusion in its discussion of independence. After asserting, incorrectly, that "Independence has always been a concept fundamental to the accounting profession, the cornerstone of its philosophical structure" (p. 8), it goes on define independence as "the ability to act with integrity and objectivity"—which actually makes "integrity" and "objectivity" fundamental, rather than independence. Integrity in turn is not defined. On the other hand objectivity is defined as the "ability to maintain an impartial attitude on all matters which come under his review." Thus, when all the definitions are put together, independence ends up being the ability to have an ability.

The essay generally takes an approach to accounting ethics that it is a matter of risk minimization. That is, it suggests that a practitioner should view himself as always liable to act improperly, and that he should therefore view his task, if he is to succeed at acting ethically, as a matter of minimizing the chances that he will in fact act improperly. For example, the essay states that:

> CPAs cannot practice their calling and participate in the world's affairs without being exposed to situations that involve the possibility of pressures upon their integrity and objectivity. To define and proscribe all such situations would be impracticable. To ignore the problem for that reason, however, and to set no limits at all would be irresponsible.
>
> It follows that the concept of independence should not be interpreted so loosely as to permit relationships likely to impair the CPA's integrity or the impartiality of his judgment, nor so strictly as to inhibit the rendering of useful services when the likelihood of such impairment is relatively remote (p. 8).

The approach the essay favors, given this reality, is a kind of "physics" of countervailing forces—an approach that foreshadows the "threat and safeguard" approach which was mentioned in Chapter 7 above. Recall that, on this approach, a practitioner should enter into any engagement only after sizing up the threats to his integrity which the engagement might pose, and assessing whether his resources, including his character traits, are sufficient safeguards to withstand those threats. Only after he judges that the safeguards are sufficient should he reasonably proceed. As we said, such an approach is laudable insofar as it attempts to move away from dealing with independence in the manner of a baroquely articulated legal code. However, the approach is puzzling if the practitioner's character traits, such as honesty or integrity, are counted among safeguards. Consider the odd sound of this paragraph:

> The more important question is whether a CPA would deliberately compromise his integrity by expressing an unqualified opinion on financial statements which were prepared in such a way as to cover up a poor business decision by the client and on which the CPA had rendered advice. The basic character traits of the CPA as well as the risks arising from such a compromise of integrity, including liability to third parties,

disciplinary action and loss of right to practice, should preclude such action (10).

The reason this is puzzling is that we expect a virtue such as honesty to rule out in advance certain temptations. We suppose that an honest person will simply not even contemplate fraud. That sort of thing is "out of the question for him"; he "wouldn't even think of it." If you were to suggest something dishonorable to him, he might even get angry, or leave and wish to have nothing to do with you in the future.[23]

After its lengthy discussion of independence, the philosophical essay of the 1972 codification turns into an informal and discursive overview of the various rules. This discussion is noteworthy chiefly for its lack of resourcefulness in giving reasons for those rules, which is probably to be explained by the restatement's aforementioned lack of any clear conception of a profession. Consider for example the following explanations given of the impropriety of solicitation and advertising:

> Solicitation to obtain clients is prohibited under the Rules of Conduct because it tends to lessen the professional independence toward clients which is essential to the best interests of the public. It may also induce an unhealthy rivalry within the profession and thus lessen the cooperation among members which is essential to advancing the state of the art of accounting and providing maximum service to the public.
>
> Advertising, which is a form of solicitation, is also prohibited because it could encourage representations which might mislead the public and thereby reduce or destroy the profession's usefulness to society (14).

Solicitation is ruled out relative to independence, and yet solicitation for non-attest employment had traditionally been ruled out as well. Note too that nothing is said here which would serve to rule out truthful advertising.

---

[23] The inflexibility we attribute to virtue is well illustrated in a humorous exchange often attributed to Winston Churchill and a young socialite: "Madam, would you sleep with me for five million pounds?" –"Well ... I suppose I would."—"So then would you sleep with me for five pounds?"—"Mr. Churchill, what kind of woman do you think I am?!" — "Madam, we've established that already. Now we are haggling about the price."

Changes in Rules concerning Advertising and Competitive Bidding

Two important changes in the Code during the 1970s were the abandonment by the profession of the longstanding rule against competitive bidding, in 1972, and of the rule against advertising, in 1977. Both of these changes were forced upon the accounting profession by governmental action, and yet the profession found itself unable to make a strong defense of these rules, in part because of various changes which we have noted in the understanding of accounting professionalism prior to that time.

It should be said that the accounting profession in much of the 20th century was conflicted about whether to prohibit or allow competitive bidding. At times the national profession took the view that it would not itself proscribe the practice, yet it would support those state associations which did so. At other times it entirely proscribed it, as in Rule 3.03 from the 1964 codification:

> A member or associate shall not make a competitive bid for a professional engagement. Competitive bidding for public accounting services is not in the public interest, is a form of solicitation, and is unprofessional.

The common arguments against competitive bidding are alluded to in this rule. The argument that the practice is inherently objectionable because it is not worthy of a profession (in contrast to a business) goes back to the first period of accounting ethics. With respect to bidding, as we have seen, Richardson had argued that "what is good in ordinary business is not good in the professions," that bidding was simply "improper," and that there was no "excuse whatever for perpetuating in the professions something which seems to be inseparable from business" (112). He proposed the example of surgeons competing for the business of a wealthy patient and exclaimed that "the spirit of the profession would be outraged at the thought of it" (114-5). These are arguments based on fittingness and propriety. Along similar lines the AIA in an official statement at the time additionally argued that bids among accounting professionals in principle cannot be compared, because professionals are offering something intangible:

> The accountant's opinion is far from being a mere intellectual abstraction. The readiness with which bankers, creditors, federal and state governmental agencies and taxing authorities, and all other third parties who must rely on accounting statements accept them is a definite and concrete matter on which the success or failure of important business

transactions may depend. Decisions may be taken by the owners or managers of enterprises on the strength of an accountant's opinion and statements which may have serious and far-reaching results. There is no comparative measure of such results either on a qualitative or quantitative basis.

In the second period of accounting ethics various "public interest" arguments were also developed. One such argument was that competitive bidding would result in professionals working for fees so low that they would be tempted or even disposed to do substandard work. Another was in line with Carey's "professionalism as public relations" idea, that accounting professionals would best signal to the public that their motives were altruistic, if they kept clear of practices associated with businesses: "One way of avoiding the impression that money-making is the primary interest is to avoid behavior commonly associated with commercial activities—for example, advertising and solicitation, competitive bidding, and the giving and receiving of commissions and brokerage."

But it was also urged, against the rule, that enforcement of the rule was impossible. Already in 1946 Carey had made this point, as well as that the rule can give the impression, at least, of violating antitrust laws:

> An accountant is entitled to work for as little as he pleases, or for nothing if he wishes. A client is entitled to have some estimate, however tentative, of the probable cost of an engagement. Such an estimate is not competitive bidding unless another accountant has made a similar estimate on the same work. The existence of an earlier estimate, however, cannot always be known. It is not easy to define and prohibit competitive bidding without appearing to "combine in restraint of trade," or to expose the public to exorbitant charges.

Carey also argued that accountants who belonged to a professional association which forbade competitive bidding would be undercut by those which did not, as the public would generally favor and seek out competitive bids, if it had the opportunity.

All these questions became moot when the AICPA abandoned Rule 3.03 in 1972 and signed a "consent agreement" in response to threatened litigation from the Federal Trade Commission (FTC) and potential action by the U.S. Department of Justice:

The former provision of the Code of Professional Ethics prohibiting competitive bidding, Rule 3.03, was declared null and void by the United States District Court for the District of Columbia in a consent judgment entered on July 6, 1972, in a civil antitrust suit brought by the United States against the American Institute. In consequence, no provision of the Code of Professional Ethics now prohibits the submission of price quotations for accounting services to persons seeking such services; and such submission of price quotations is not an unethical practice under any policy of the Institute. To avoid misunderstanding it is important to note that otherwise unethical conduct (e.g., advertising, solicitation or substandard work) is subject to disciplinary sanctions regardless of whether or not such unethical conduct is preceded by, associated with, or followed by a submission of price quotations for accounting services.

What happened was that in the early 1970s, for the first time, the FTC and Justice initiated suits against the various professions, on the grounds that the restrictions against competitive bidding, common to nearly all self-identified professions, violated the federal antitrust acts, especially section 1 of the 1890 Sherman Act, which reads: "Every contract, combination in the form of trust or otherwise, or conspiracy, in restraint of trade or commerce among the several States, or with foreign nations, is declared to be illegal." Lawyers for the AICPA advised that the accounting profession, if it tried to resist these enforcement efforts, would turn out to be the loser, and so the AICPA proactively agreed to drop its proscription against competitive bidding. This legal advice proved to be correct, because those professional associations which did try to defend the proscription eventually lost in court.

The chief case along these lines was a decision by the U.S. Supreme Court against the engineering profession, *National Society of Prof. Engineers v. United States*, 435 U.S. 679 (1978). The entire case repays study, but the essence of the Court's opinion is that:

> ... on its face, the canon in question [that is, the engineering profession's rule] restrains trade within the meaning of § 1 of the Sherman Act ... Petitioner's affirmative defense confirms rather than refutes the anticompetitive purpose and effect of its canon, and its attempt to justify ... the restraint on competition imposed by the canon on the basis of the potential threat that competition poses to the public safety and the ethics

of the engineering profession is nothing less than a frontal assault on the basic policy of the Sherman Act.

A decision by the Supreme Court's interpretation of the Sherman Act is final and can be overturned only by the Court's reversing itself or a new act of Congress.

Nonetheless, we may still ask whether the Court's reasoning in such cases is correct, especially in relation to the considerations of the nature of a profession presented in earlier chapters of this text. There are three reasons which at least make the case that it is not. First, laws need to be interpreted in accordance with their legislative intent, and the historical record suggests that Congress was not aiming in the Sherman Act to regulate the distinctive practices of learned professions; indeed, some professions were established already in 1890, when the Sherman Act was passed, and none viewed themselves as potentially falling within the intention of that law. Second, the language of the Sherman Act refers to restrictions on "commerce" and "trade," but, as we saw, it is precisely the claim of a profession that it is distinct from a business and not engaged in commerce or trade. Third, the Court's interpretation of the historic restrictions on competitive bidding among professionals seems skewed. The Court effectively assimilates an ostensibly high and honorable practice—the collegiality and commonality which is sought among members of a learned profession—with a lawless attempt to extort money unjustly from customers, by exploiting relationships of power. That is, the Court fundamentally misconstrues an honorable practice as a dishonorable practice. In effect, the Court holds that professions are illegal, insofar as a profession wishes to play a role in the marketplace yet constitute itself as different from a business.

The Court rightly senses that a profession presupposes notions of "hierarchy" in the marketplace, that it sets itself apart from and above ordinary businesses, and that it claims prerogatives based on that position. However, the Court seems to be mistaken in interpreting this higher position as a relationship of pure, exploitative power. It fails to recognize that a profession in the traditional sense advances a claim of authority based upon the expert knowledge possessed by members of a profession. At the same time it should be said that by 1972 the accounting profession was hardly in a position to put forward arguments defending its status as a profession in the traditional sense.

Unlike the rule against competitive bidding, the longstanding rule against advertising for members of the accounting profession was never controversial and was always widely accepted. "The general prohibition against advertising is accepted today without much question," Carey wrote in his 1966 version of his textbook, co-authored with Doherty, "To be sure, there is nothing illegal or immoral about advertising as such, but it is almost universally regarded as unprofessional." Carey and Doherty give three reasons against advertising, including an appeal to the nature of a profession, which are worth repeating:

> In the first place, advertising would not benefit the young practitioner. If it were generally permitted, the larger, well-established firms could afford to advertise on a scale that would throw the young practitioner wholly in the shade. Secondly, advertising is commercial. Professional accounting service is not a tangible product to be sold like any commodity. Its value depends on the knowledge, skill and honesty of the CPA. Who would be impressed with a man's own statement that he is intelligent, skillful and honest? Lastly, advertising does not pay. The accountants in the early days who tried it agreed for the most part that it did not attract clients (pp. 47-8).

The 1964 codification gave the rule against advertising (Rule 3.01) as follows:

> A member or associate shall not advertise his professional attainments or services.
>
> Publication in a newspaper, magazine or similar medium of an announcement or what is technically known as a card is prohibited.
>
> A listing in a directory is restricted to the name, title, address and telephone number of the person or firm, and it shall not appear in a box, or other form of display or in a type or style which differentiates it from other listings in the same directory.
>
> Listing of the same name in more than one place in a classified directory is prohibited.

But this was changed in 1977 to prohibit only untruthful advertising:

> Rule 502—Advertising and Other Forms of Solicitation
> A member shall not seek to obtain clients by advertising or other forms of solicitation in a manner that is false, misleading, or deceptive.

What was the reason for the change? Once again, governmental pressure originating from outside the accounting profession forced the change, this time in the form of a Supreme Court decision involving advertising by lawyers—*Bates v. Arizona State Bar* (433 U.S. 350 (1977)) —which was regarded as extending to any profession whatsoever. The Court held that advertising by lawyers was "commercial speech" protected by the First Amendment. In its comments the Court showed that it was also rejecting the distinction between a business and a profession. In fact, the Court could not even understand the distinction. Rather, it offered a dubious history of rules of professional conduct, in order to debunk them:

> It appears that the ban on advertising originated as a rule of etiquette, and not as a rule of ethics. Early lawyers in Great Britain viewed the law as a form of public service, rather than as a means of earning a living, and they looked down on "trade" as unseemly (see H. Drinker, *Legal Ethics* 5, 210-211 (1953)). Eventually, the attitude toward advertising fostered by this view evolved into an aspect of the ethics of the profession. Id at 211. But habit and tradition are not, in themselves, an adequate answer to a constitutional challenge. In this day, we do not belittle the person who earns his living by the strength of his arm or the force of his mind. Since the belief that lawyers are somehow "above" trade has become an anachronism, the historical foundation for the advertising restraint has crumbled.

The Court's invidious characterization of a rule of professional conduct as merely a rule of "etiquette," as we have seen, is quite mistaken. In any case, one might argue in reply that the longstanding restriction against advertising in various professions showed precisely that the historical foundation for it had not entirely "crumbled"; also, that when foundations are crumbling one is always faced with a choice between, on the one hand, helping to destroy that foundation entirely, as the Court apparently favored—on the basis of its particular theory of the history of professionalism—or, on the other, taking care to preserve whatever remains of the integrity of the foundation, and rebuilding from there.

1988 to the Present: "A Search for New Foundations"

Today's Code of Professional Conduct is a direct descendent of the restatement of the Code from 1988. In the 1988 codification, the break from the original 1917 Code is complete. The Code is no longer recognizable as mainly a reclassification or reorganization of fine points of conduct relative to acting as a member of a learned profession. Rather, the Code is presented as a set of abstract "principles," together with rules, interpretations, and rulings, all of which are putatively applications of these principles. The principles are:

Public Interest
Integrity
Objectivity and Independence
Due Care
Scope and Nature of Services (including Competence and Confidentiality)

Note that the Code gives no distinct principle of "Professionalism." As we have seen, the rules of the 1917 Code were mainly intent on conveying a concept of professionalism. Thus, we can say that today's Code differs essentially in what it regards as central to accounting ethics. In today's Code, professionalism gets briefly addressed only in a prefatory paragraph entitled "Responsibilities":

As professionals, certified public accountants perform an essential role in society. Consistent with that role, members of the American Institute of Certified Public Accountants have responsibilities to all those who use their professional services. Members also have a continuing responsibility to cooperate with each other to improve the art of accounting, maintain the public's confidence, and carry out the profession's special responsibilities for self-governance. The collective efforts of all members are required to maintain and enhance the traditions of the profession.

However, although the paragraph mentions or alludes to various responsibilities of an accountant— to society, to investors, and to fellow accountants—none of these "responsibilities" is given separate attention, or, evidently, deemed worthy of the status of a "Principle."

Because of this major change, it is fair to say that today's Code is an attempt to give what might be called an "ethics of an action" rather than "ethics of professional association." That is, it is an attempt to say how a particular engagement should be carried out well, not what it means to belong a certain kind of association. Its unit of analysis is the *action*, not a professional *life* and the cultivation of a certain *character* as a member of a certain kind of association.

This can be seen by considering the nature of the claims or requirements which it does mark out as "Principles." Suppose we were to ask the question: What is necessary if a particular engagement is to be carried out well? One might answer that a particular engagement is carried out well if, in the end, the accountant articulates a fair (true, sound) representation of the financial condition of a company. In order to do this, he needs to form a sound judgment and articulate what he has judged, which requires "Integrity." In order to arrive at a sound judgment, he needs to look at all of the relevant evidence ("Due Care") with an impartial attitude ("Objectivity"). In order to be able to do that, he needs to approach the engagement in a position of being disinterested ("Independence"). The relationship of these requirements may be illustrated by the following flow chart:

THE ETHICS OF AN ENGAGEMENT

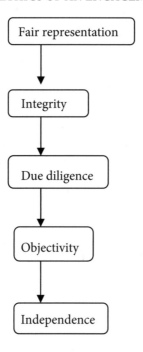

That is, the requirements picked out in today's Code as "Principles" evidently represent the various steps or aspects involved in carrying out a particular engagement well. Note that the "Principles" are stated with so great a degree of generality and abstraction, that they would apply to any act having a "judicial" character, not simply the practice of accountancy. A physician making a diagnosis, a judge handing down a judgment, an assessor offering a valuation, a scientist or scholar drawing a conclusion from evidence—all would be bound by the very same "principles." This is far from inappropriate, as an accountant does exercise a "quasi-judicial" role in giving his or her professional judgment. However, it seems that the "principles" of a code of professional conduct for *accountants* should offer something specific to accountancy. But these are more like "principles of sound judgment" rather than an explication of the profession of accountancy.

What are the reasons for this final shift in the 1988 codification from an "ethics of professional association" to an "ethics of professional action"? There would seem to be three central reasons, all involving the erosion of accountancy as a distinct, learned profession, and the consequent loss of a clear sense of professional identity.

The first reason has already been mentioned, namely, that in the later part of the 20th century the non-attest work of accountants began to dominate over attest engagements, yet attestation and truth-telling represent the reason for the existence of the accounting profession in the first place. If the essence of accountancy is found in attest work and truth-telling, and yet work of that sort represents only part of what an accountant does, then a "professional ethics for accountants" needs to focus more on particular engagements than on the professional practice of accountants as a whole.

The second reason, also mentioned, would be various forces and influences which had the tendency of changing the nature of accounting into a "business" rather than a "profession." Perhaps chief among these would be regulatory and judicial decisions which eliminated longstanding professional restrictions on advertising and competitive bidding. Yet once accountancy is viewed as a "business," then "accounting ethics" is no longer a matter of how to behave as a member of a learned profession; at best it consists of guidance as regards engaging in business relationships "with a professional attitude."

But the third and perhaps most important reason involves a factor which has not yet been touched upon, namely, the accounting profession's loss of authority to determine its own accounting principles and standards. This change took place in the 1970s, but it is appropriately discussed here, because the ramifications of this change were not felt until the 1988 recodification.

Here a brief review of the history of accounting standards (GAAP) is in order. As we saw, through the Securities Acts the SEC was effectively granted by Congress the authority to determine accounting principles. This would be an odd function for a government agency to perform on its own, if one thinks about it, since governmental employees as such have no particular technical expertise—just as it would be odd for a government agency to attempt to determine best practices in medicine or engineering, or to try to say what counted as "settled science" at any particular time. Government is simply not competent to make such judgments. Fortunately, Congress had the wisdom to stipulate in the Securities Acts that the SEC should rely upon and largely defer to the authority of the accounting profession—as professional accountants were the standing experts in this domain. Accordingly, from 1939 until 1973, with the SEC's approval, accounting standards for public companies were determined by the AICPA, first through its Committee on Accounting Procedures (CAP, 1939-1959), and then through the Accounting Principles Board (APB, 1959-1973).

However, in the 1960s there was a growing sense among business leaders, regulators, and the accounting profession itself that the APB, an unpaid and unwieldy board of 18 part-time members, was incapable of keeping up with rapid and increasingly more complex changes in business. "A rapidly growing accounting profession, an abundance of public offerings, intricate new business practices and greater corporate reliance on mergers and acquisitions created an urgent need for timely accounting standards that addressed the new conditions. Doubts grew that the recognized standard setter, the AICPA Accounting Principles Board, could satisfy this requirement."[24] The AICPA therefore appointed a committee, called the "Wheat Committee" after its chairman, former SEC Commissioner Francis M. Wheat, which was charged with recommending changes that would enable accounting standards to be formulated more efficiently, that is, "how to get better results faster." In the following year the Committee issued the "Wheat Report," which recommended the formation of a leaner board of seven members, who served full time and were commensurately compensated. The Report also emphasized that the board should be independent of any private interests which would conflict with the need to formulate accounting standards which served the public interest.

The Wheat Committee's recommendations were accepted by the AICPA, and so in 1973 the Financial Accounting Standards Board (FASB) was created. All of the members of the APB were CPAs. In contrast, the FASB was originally required to have only four of its seven members chosen from the accounting profession. However, even this requirement was dropped in 1977, because it was felt that those four could form a voting block and control the determination of accounting standards. As mentioned, the FASB was meant to be an "independent" board, and, interestingly enough, it was thought that CPAs who represented big accounting firms could not be independent judges of professional standards.

---

[24] "Francis M. Wheat, 1921–2000," *Journal of Accountancy*, October, 2000.

Thus by 1977 even this indirect link between the accounting profession and the determination of accounting standards was effectively severed. These changes are represented in the following chart:

WHO SETS ACCOUNTING STANDARDS?

1939-1959	Committee on Accounting Procedures (CAP)
1959-1973	Accounting Principles Board (APB)
1973-present	Financial Accounting Standards Board (FASB)

One remarkable consequence of this development was the *dissociation of technical expertise and ethics* in accounting. The locus for technical standards became the FASB, regarded now as independent of the accounting profession; and the locus for accounting standards became the Professional Ethics Executive Committee (PEEC) of the AICPA, founded in 1971. However, such a dissociation is a problematic state of affairs for a profession, because of the inherently ethical character of a profession. To be an "expert" in a profession implies having both technical expertise and ethical integrity. Professional service is precisely technical expertise in the service of an ethical ideal. Thus, when technical expertise and ethics are dissociated, each becomes weakened. Technique becomes "mere" technique, open to being used for unethical purposes: in accounting, technical "form" may dominate over the "substance" of a transaction or position. Ethics, on the other hand, when uncoupled from technical expertise, loses its prestige and authority. Ethics begins to look like a frivolous "extra," ultimately irrelevant to technical competence; it attempts to retain its importance only by taking on the aspect of a legal code.

The post-1988 Code has parts which appear to be frivolous "extras" and other parts which are evidently legalistic. The "Principles" which it articulates may easily appear to be "extras," because, as the Code states, they are not "enforceable." The by-laws of the AICPA require only that the rules be followed. On the other hand, the rules and associated interpretations and rulings look to be legalistic, because they are presented without supporting reasons. They are presented in such a way as to give the impression that there is no reasoning, no understanding, no shared grasp or agreement expressed in the Code; rather, following the Code involves merely the mastery of decisions (for who knows what reason) made by an authoritative body. As illustration of this last point, consider the following AICPA ethics questions:

.021 Question—A member has been designated to serve as an executor or trustee of the estate of an individual who owns the majority of a client's stock. Would independence be considered to be impaired with respect to the client?

What would be the correct way of answering these questions? One may think of plausible reasons which point in different and conflicting directions. Actually serving as executor or trustee in the circumstances described would presumably be incompatible with independence, as an executor or trustee in fact has an obligation to advance the interests of the estate, which would imply seeking as high a valuation of that stock as possible. However, it is not so clear whether simply being designated executor or trustee would similarly impair independence. Someone might argue there are some circumstances in which it would: consider for instance a case where the reason one was so designated was one's friendship with that individual, but where that friendship would not itself be so close as to count as impairing independence.

Yet the ruling given in the Code seems not to contemplate this or other scenarios:

.022 Answer—The mere designation of a covered member as executor or trustee would not be considered to impair independence, however, if a covered member actually served in such capacity, independence would be considered to be impaired.

Perhaps that is the correct ruling after all; but then again perhaps it is not. The point is that we have no way of telling, since no reasons are given for this answer. Moreover, the fact that no reasons are given suggests that what the Code seeks from practitioners is not reasoned adherence, deriving from a shared grasp of the reasons, but rather "compliance" with the decisions of the AICPA and its Professional Ethics Executive Committee.

Or, again, consider the following:

.057 Question—Would independence be considered to be impaired if a member owned an immaterial amount of a municipal authority's outstanding bonds?

One would ostensibly answer this question in the negative, if the amount really were immaterial. Suppose a senior partner in a Big Four firm with a yearly compensation in the seven figures owns a $100 municipal bond which he bought out of a sense of public service. Suppose his expected return from the bond is about

$3/year. There are no reasonable grounds on which his independence could be considered impaired. Yet the ruling reaches a different answer:

> .058 Answer—Ownership of a client's bonds constitute a loan to that client. Accordingly, if a covered member owned such bonds, independence would be considered to be impaired.

However, it is unclear why a municipal bond should be analogized to a personal loan. Also, the answer seems to deny a premise of the question, since the answer is saying that there is no such thing as an "immaterial" amount of ownership in a bond. But, again, the important point is that no reasons are given, and the ruling is presented as a rule which a practitioner needs to memorize and follow legalistically.

Accounting Ethics in Crisis?

If the fate of the accounting profession in the years following the 1988 codification is any indication, then that version of the Code must be judged a failure, as the 1990s and the early years of the new millennium marked a period of profound crisis, unparalleled in the history of the profession. Some of these reasons were discussed in Chapter 1, but the chief marks of that crisis would be the following:

➢ Accounting scandals and restatements of a scope and magnitude not seen before: Enron, WorldCom, Adelphia, Global Crossing, Qwest, Tyco, Xerox, Martha Stewart, HealthSouth, Royal Ahold, Parmalat, AIG, and Lehman Brothers, among others.

➢ The profession's repeated failure to regulate itself effectively. The late 1970s saw the formation of various self-regulatory entities in the accounting profession, none of which proved to be effective. These included the Public Oversight Board (POB), founded in 1977; the Quality Control Inquiry Committee (QCIC), founded in 1979; the peer review provisions related to the AICPA's SEC Practice Section (SECPS), enacted in 1989; and the Independence Standards Board (ISB), established in 1997.

➢ An increasing sense that accounting had made a transition from being a profession to being a business, as evidenced by many comments by observers and business leaders, and as perhaps most clearly seen in the controversy over the AICPA's proposal in 2001, ultimately defeated after a heated battle, of a "Global Business Credential" (also referred to as the "XYZ" credential), which would have been shared between CPAs and non-CPAs.

➢ Government actions against the accounting profession, including a criminal prosecution which caused one of the Big Five accounting firms to cease practicing, and the eventual imposition of far-ranging regulations on the accounting profession by Congress in the form of the Sarbanes-Oxley Act and the establishment of the PCAOB.

➢ An unfortunate deteriorating public opinion of accountants, and lessened public prestige, as shown by numerous studies.

One may identify four ways in which accounting ethics has developed in response to this crisis:

1) attention to principles over rules;
2) adoption of a risk/safeguard "conceptual framework" for independence;
3) institution of ethics courses in accounting education and as part of Continuing Professional Education (CPE) for relicensing; and
4) adoption within firms of internal codes of professional conduct and creation of the position of a "Compliance and Ethics Officer."

We have discussed the first two already but will add further considerations, when we consider these four responses at the beginning of Chapter 15 below.

Recommended additional reading:

Bates v. Arizona State Bar (433 U.S. 350 (1977)). The Supreme Court opinion which led to the rescinding of restrictions on advertising among the professions.

National Society of Prof. Engineers v. United States, (435 U.S. 679 (1978)). The most important Supreme Court decision applying antitrust law to professions.

Olson, W.E. (1999), "The accounting profession in the 20th century," *The CPA Journal*, Vol. 69 No.7, pp.28-33. A brief overview of changes in the accounting profession corresponding to some of the changes in the Rules of Professional Conduct discussed in this chapter.

Zeff, Stephen A. "How the U.S. Accounting Profession Got Where it is Today: Part II," *Accounting Horizons*, 17:4 (2003), 267-86. A comprehensive overview of changes in the accounting profession for the period covered by this chapter.

PART IV

HIGH PROFILE CASES

Enron:
Rules Trumping Principles

11

"Mr. Delainey goes up to Mr. Causey's office. He says, 'What are we going to do? We've got $200 million in losses. There's no way to deal with it.' The accountants suggest moving all of the contracts in the risk management from EES to wholesale.—That's an interesting thing to note, ladies and gentlemen. The suggestion, according to Mr. Delainey's testimony, actually came from the accountants, not the guys who are running the business."

—From the government's closing statement in *U.S. vs. Jeffrey Skilling and Kenneth Lay* (May 15, 2006).

Background

The sudden and unexpected collapse of Enron was a financial cataclysm. A company which at the start of 2001 employed 25,000 people and was the 7th largest U.S. company by revenues—repeatedly voted by readers of *Fortune* magazine as one of the most admired and innovative companies in the country—after a restatement of November 8, 2001, which recognized 1.2 billion dollars of theretofore hidden debt, filed for bankruptcy on December 2, 2001.

Enron's collapse was caused by accounting improprieties. It used about 3,500 Special Purpose Entities (SPEs, also known as "Special Purpose Vehicles") to manipulate earnings and transfer "off-balance sheet" approximately 40 billion dollars of debt. Because many of these SPEs were not truly independent, either in control or in financing—they were managed, directly or indirectly, by Enron employees, and funded, directly or indirectly, almost solely by Enron stock—they should not, for accounting purposes, have been treated as off-balance sheet, but should have been consolidated.

In its restatement, Enron itself gives a serviceable, if terse, explanation of one such irregularity:

> Enron's previously-announced $1.2 billion reduction of shareholders' equity primarily involves the correction of the effect of an accounting

error made in the second quarter of 2000 and in the first quarter of 2001. As described in more detail below, four SPEs known as Raptor I-IV (collectively, "Raptor") were created in 2000, permitting Enron to hedge market risk in certain of its investments. (LJM2 invested in these entities, but the related-party nature of the transaction is not relevant to the accounting correction.) As part of the capitalization of these entities, Enron issued common stock in exchange for a note receivable. Enron increased notes receivable and shareholders' equity to reflect this transaction. Enron now believes that, under generally accepted accounting principles, the note receivable should have been presented as a reduction to shareholders' equity (similar to a shareholder loan)....

... In the first quarter of 2001, Enron entered into contracts with Raptor that could have obligated Enron to issue Enron common stock in the future in exchange for notes receivable. Enron accounted for these transactions using the accounting treatment described in the preceding paragraph. This resulted in an additional overstatement of both notes receivable and shareholders' equity by $828 million. As a result of these errors, shareholders' equity and notes receivable were overstated by a total of $1 billion in the unaudited financial statements of Enron at March 31 and June 30, 2001....

The 1.2 billion dollars of additional debt acknowledged in the restatement was not itself crushingly large for Enron—although admittedly Enron's debt-to-capital ratio was close to 50% at the time. The restatement led to Enron's demise because it led to Enron's loss of credibility among creditors and investors: How much other debt was perhaps hidden by SPEs? What other irregularities were yet to be revealed? How much more of the investing public's confidence in Enron would prove to be unfounded? Its credibility had been the very thing sustaining Enron's business.

Although the configuration of the Raptors was extremely complex, the underlying idea was simple—and flawed. Because the Raptors were not truly distinct entities, Enron's transactions with them were sham transactions that the company engaged in with itself. A "payment" from a Raptor or similar SPE could not in substance count as income; a Raptor or similar SPE could not in substance serve to control risk, lower debt, or hedge losses—any more than an individual can "pay" himself for services or "hedge" his own investments. As the Powers report remarked: "The fundamental flaw in these transactions was not that the price was too low [i.e. Enron accepted terms disadvantageous to itself, because one of its own officers was representing the Raptors]. Instead, as a matter of economic substance, it is not clear that anything was really being bought or sold."[25] The Raptors and other SPEs had no legitimate business purpose; their purpose was simply to improve the *appearance* of the health of the company.

Given that these SPE arrangements were viciously circular, and that Enron's dealings with them were sham transactions, how might any intelligent person at Enron, or its auditors, have thought that they could work? They would have "worked"—in the sense of hiding Enron's degree of indebtedness, until such time as that presumably improved—if Enron's stock value had continued to increase. If Enron's stock continued to rise, then the SPEs would have remained well "funded," and presumably the debt that they were designed to hide would have been lowered, over time, by actual payments, or it would have been simply rendered insignificant in relation to Enron's increasing capitalization. But when Enron's stock in fact fell, and dropped below certain limits required for the sham transactions to be viable (about $45/share for the Raptors, which was about half of Enron's share price at the beginning of 2001), then the viciously circular character of the SPEs had to be dealt with—and this is what led to Enron's restatement.

There was something of the character of a self-fulfilling prophecy for the SPEs: they would work, just in case they worked. The SPEs hid Enron's debt and allowed the recognition of sham earnings; this in turn made Enron continue to appear to be an attractive company to investors; that it appeared attractive implied a high or increasing share price; that the share price was high or increasing implied that the debt, hidden by the SPEs, could be successfully hidden—which in turn kept Enron appearing attractive. Contrariwise, if the share price of Enron began to fall, then the SPEs would begin to unravel; the debt they hid would be uncovered; this would make Enron appear unattractive, contributing to a greater fall in share price; and so on. Since investors holding shares in Enron would ostensibly be helped by rising share prices, and hurt by falling share prices, it is natural that the "success" of these SPEs in hiding Enron's debt would seem (misguidedly) a very good thing and even a grave duty to those who devised them. Perhaps this helps to explain why Enron executives, such as CEO Ken Lay, continued to represent Enron in analyst conferences as a profitable company, even as he was being briefed with increasingly dire internal reports on Enron's financing: it might have seemed to him that the only way of saving the company would be by sustaining investors" unfounded confidence in Enron stock.

Enron's use of SPEs is frequently referred to, metaphorically, as a "shell game." But this is not an entirely appropriate metaphor. A shell game is a confidence trick,

---

[25] Powers, Jr., W.C.: 2002, *Report of the Special Investigative Committee of the Board of Directors of Enron Corp* ("Powers Report"), p. 171.

where a ball is quickly moved from shell-to-shell by the con-artist, and then actually removed, by sleight of hand, to be placed deliberately and at will, in some shell not selected by the "mark." But the confidence trick to which the Enron SPEs are better likened is a "Ponzi scheme" (recently made familiar to the American public because of a similar scam perpetrated by Bernard Madoff). A Ponzi scheme, named after Charles Ponzi, an Italian immigrant to the U.S., is a fraudulent investment operation that involves paying returns to investors out of the money raised from subsequent investors. In 1919-1920, Ponzi claimed to offer returns of up to 400% by taking advantage of an arbitrage that then existed in International Postage Coupons. His business grew from $5,000 in March 1920 to $420,000 in May, to millions in the summer, until eventually it became clear that Ponzi was not buying and selling Postage Coupons at all, but using the surplus of increasing funds invested to pay off past investments (indeed, most of his clients chose to reinvest their profits). Ponzi's "business" collapsed nearly overnight after a series of critical *Boston Post* stories in the late summer of 1920, which pointed out that there were not even enough postage coupons in existence to justify the amounts that people had invested with him! When Federal agents later raided Ponzi's offices, they found, in fact, no postage coupons at all. The profitability of Ponzi's "business" was based solely on the appearance of its profitability, not on any sound business practice. And this was largely the situation eighty years later with Enron.

From the Investor's Point of View

Ponzi was a crude con-artist who, prior to starting his "business," had worked odd jobs as a waiter and bank clerk and even spent time in prison for forgery and petty crimes. He had no legal advisors; he published no company report or prospectus; his business was never audited. Presumably his business could not have endured a public audit. In contrast, Enron was a public company, and its business was regularly examined and reported upon by Arthur Andersen, historically one of the most prestigious and reliable accounting firms. How could Andersen have signed off on Enron's Ponzi scheme? Well, they not only signed off on it, they helped to design it, and they billed Enron 1.3 million dollars for doing so. To appreciate the wrongness of this, let us approach the matter from the point of view of an investor, the interests of whom, as we have seen, Andersen was charged to serve.

Imagine an investor in middle-America in early March of 2001, burned by the dot.com bust, and wearied by a prolonged bear market, who has cashed out many of his equity positions, but who by that point has regained some of his confidence and is wanting to buy a good growth stock. He picks up the latest issue of *Fortune* magazine (Mar. 5, 2001) and finds there an article by Bethany McLean entitled, "Is Enron Overpriced?" The subheading of the article states, "It's in a bunch of complex businesses. Its financial statements are nearly impenetrable. So why is Enron trading at such a huge multiple?" Our imaginary investor has so far not purchased Enron shares, and Enron stock is expensive, but he wonders whether he is "missing the boat." Should he now take a position in Enron? Although the stock price, at almost $90, has a p/e ratio of about 55, in late January of 2001 Enron executives met with Wall Street analysts and argued, convincingly to many, that its stock ought really be valued at $126.

In this thought exercise, keep in mind the classic definition of "materiality" which we saw above: that is, information about a company is material and should be reported if an investor would reasonably decide to invest or not in that company on the basis of that information.

The article begins by acknowledging Enron's popularity among investors, due largely to Enron's remarkable returns in a relatively dismal investment period. But then McLean raises some concerns. Above all, there is the problem of Enron's debt: in the first 9 months of 2000, Enron's debt increased dramatically by $3.9 billion, making its debt-to-capital ratio now 50%, as opposed to 39% at the end of the previous year. Then there is an apparent problem of cash flow: during the same period, the company showed nearly a negative cash flow. But more fundamentally, there is the problem that hardly anyone seems to understand Enron's business: "How exactly does Enron make its money?," McLean wonders, "Details are hard to come by because Enron keeps many of the specifics confidential for what it terms 'competitive reasons.'"

When McLean raises these concerns with Enron executives, they give an apparently plausible explanation:

> But Enron says that extrapolating from its financial statements is misleading. The fact that Enron's cash flow this year was meager, at least when compared with earnings, was partly a result of its wholesale business. Accounting standards mandate that its assets and liabilities from its wholesale business be "marked to market"—valued at their market price at a given moment in time. Changes in the valuation are reported in earnings. But these earnings aren't necessarily cash at the instant they are recorded. [Jeff] Skilling [Enron's CEO] says that Enron can convert these contracts to cash anytime it chooses by "securitizing" them, or selling them off to a financial institution. Enron then receives a "servicing fee," but Skilling says that all the risks (for example, changes in the value of the assets and liabilities) are then transferred to the buyer. That's why, he says, Enron's cash flow will be up dramatically, while debt will be "way down, way down" when the company publishes its full year-end results, which are due out soon.

In retrospect, in this passage it looks as though Skilling is indirectly referring to Enron's use of SPEs to "sell off" risky investments, and he is claiming, in effect, that these structures are capable of resolving any apparent difficulties Enron faces with indebtedness or cash. That is, the SPEs are effectively being relied upon in an argument that investors should purchase Enron stock.

Enron's Hidden Debt, 3rd Quarter 2001

Reported debt per 3rd qtr 10Q $ 12.9 b

Actual debt per 3rd qtr $ 38.0 b

Where hidden:

Unconsolidated affiliates	$ 10.7 b
Commodity transfer w/fin. inst.	$ 4.8 b
Share trusts	$ 3.4 b
Minority Interest financings	$ 1.7 b
FAS 140 transactions	$ 2.1 b
Structured assets	$ 1.5 b
Leases	$ .6 b

Equity forward contracts $ .3 b

Source: AccountingMalpractice.com

Recall that this is March of 2001. This is Enron's public face. But how did the financial health of the company appear internally? The best evidence we have for this is the famous "whistle blower" letter of Sherron Watkins, an Enron internal auditor. The letter is sent to the new CEO of Enron, Ken Lay, in August 2001, the day after Skilling's abrupt resignation. "To the layman on the street," Watkins writes, expressing concerns about the true nature of Enron's SPEs, "it will look like we recognized funds flow of $800mm from merchant asset sales in 1999 by selling to a vehicle (Condor) that we capitalized with a promise of Enron stock in later years. Is that really funds flow or is it cash from equity issuance?" As regards Raptor, "It sure looks to the layman on the street that we are hiding losses in a related company and will compensate that company with Enron stock in the future...Raptor looks to be a big bet, if the underlying stocks did well, then no one would be the wiser. If Enron stock did well, the stock issuance to these entities would decline and the transactions would be less noticeable. All has gone against us." She adds, "I am incredibly nervous that we will implode in a wave of accounting scandals....I realize that we have had a lot of smart people looking at this and a lot of accountants including AA & Co. have blessed the accounting treatment. None of that will protect Enron if these transactions are ever disclosed in the bright light of day."

Watkins suggests that her observations were widely appreciated in the company but left largely unstated by those who knew of the SPEs. "I have heard one management level employee from the principle [*sic*] investments group say, 'I know it would be devastating to all of us, but I wish we would get caught. We're such a crooked company.' The principle investments group hedged a large number of their investments with Raptor. These people know and see a lot. Many similar comments are made when you ask about these deals."

Now think again about Skilling's sales-pitch for Enron with McLean of *Fortune* magazine.

Andersen and Independence

It is natural enough for an executive of a company to promote his company's interests, even if he is aware of grave problems facing the company, and so long as he does not exceed the boundaries of honesty. In a sense, that is his job. But what about that company's auditors, who are in theory independent and have a responsibility to the public interest? Their job is to render an objective report as regards anything within their purview that may be "material" to an investor's reasonable investment decision. One would expect that, long before the summer of 2001, Andersen auditors would have said to Enron executives, "Look, these SPEs need to be consolidated and are supportable only if Enron is operating as a Ponzi scheme. We will not sign off on a financial report which does not consolidate the debt that these SPEs conceal."

In fact, the question of whether to adopt this position seems to have been raised internally by Andersen, in a conference call among 14 of its officers of February 6, 2001, which an internal Andersen memo refers to as an "Enron Retention Meeting." (Keep in mind that many Andersen documents related to Enron were destroyed in a concerted shredding project of late 2001. What remains is perhaps only a slight indication of the reality.) From the language of the memo, it is clear that the Andersen auditors discussed and shared concerns about the Enron SPEs that were exactly of the character of the (later) Watkins letter:

> A significant discussion was held regarding the related party transactions with LJM [a general name for two Enron SPEs, one of which had ownership in the Raptor SPEs] including the materiality of such amounts to Enron's income statement and the amount retained "off balance sheet."

> …We discussed Enron's reliance on its current credit rating to maintain itself as a high credit rated transaction party.

...We discussed Enron's dependence on transaction execution to meet financial objectives...

...Ultimately the conclusion was reached to retain Enron as a client citing that it appeared that we had the appropriate people and processes in place to serve Enron and manage our engagement risks. We discussed whether there would be a perceived independence issue solely considering our level of fees. We discussed that the concerns should not be on the magnitude of fees but on the nature of fees. We arbitrarily discussed that it would not be unforeseeable that fees could reach a $100 million per year amount considering the multi-disciplinary services being provided. Such amount did not trouble the participants as long as the nature of the services was not an issue.

The decision arrived at by the group was apparently that things should continue as before, since the "To Do" items at the end of the memo included nothing about challenging the accounting treatment of the SPEs or restating past financials. Rather, action items included such things as making sure the SEC would not have concerns about SPE control (but not SPE accounting); placing more responsibility on the Enron Board of Directors; and shifting more responsibility to Enron officers. The items are all procedural. None deal with, or show signs of taking responsibility for, the substantive difficulties evidently raised and discussed in the meeting:

Take away To Do's

Inquire as to whether Andy Fastow [Enron CFO, who effectively controlled the LJM entities] and/or LJM would be viewed as an "affiliate" from an SEC perspective which would require looking through the transactions and treating them as within the consolidated group.

Suggest that a special committee of the BOD be established to review the fairness of LJM transactions...

Focus on Enron preparing their own documentation and conclusions to issues and transactions.

AA [Arthur Andersen] to focus on timely documentation of final transaction structures to ensure consensus is reached on the final structure.

Note that in the year 2000, Andersen received $25mm in fees for auditing from Enron, and an additional $27mm for consulting services. As mentioned, Andersen helped to structure the Raptor and LJM SPEs, and was paid over $1mm for its work in doing so. Moreover, many internal accountants for Enron were former employees of Andersen. Jeff Skilling in fact was known to have remarked that the best reason for using Andersen as auditors was that they were a good source of talent for recruiting for Enron. (Sherron Watkins was an Andersen accountant, hired by Enron in 1993.)

In light of these facts, it would be reasonable to hold that Andersen was incapable of maintaining the independence that is required of auditors. As we saw, this concern was raised in the Andersen phone conference: "We discussed whether there would be a perceived independence issue solely considering our level of fees." Put aside the consideration that there were issues of independence that arose from other matters besides simply the level of fees. For our purposes, note the fuzziness in even this language. A "perceived independence issue" might mean either:

(a.) The perception, that is, the thought or judgment, that Andersen lacked independence;

(b.) The appearance (to a reasonable observer, aware of the relevant facts) of a lack of independence.

The ambiguity is important, because (a.) is defeasible, but (b.) is not. Someone might judge or think, "Andersen is not independent in its Enron engagement" and be wrong about that—which was the line of thought taken by the Andersen accountants in the conference call. Recall: "We discussed that the concerns should not be on the magnitude of fees but on the nature of fees. We arbitrarily discussed that it would not be unforeseeable that fees could reach a $100 million per year amount considering the multi-disciplinary services being provided. Such amount did not trouble the participants as long as the nature of the services was not an issue." The Andersen accountants are effectively saying: *Although someone might think the level of our fees compromises our independence, in fact it does not, because it is the nature of those fees which is important—and therefore there are no ethical concerns, and we should carry on as before.*

But this is to apply the wrong ethical standard. The correct standard, rather, concerns (b.) above: under the Code which was applicable at the time, a practitioner should not undertake an engagement, if there would be even an appearance, to a reasonable observer, of compromised independence. This concern is not similarly defeasible: if there simply appears to be a lack of independence (to a reasonable person), then, whether there is a lack of independence in reality is not relevant. So the distinction drawn between the "level" and the "nature" of fees was irrelevant. Andersen should have recognized—indeed, they apparently did recognize it, in the conference call—that there was an appearance of compromised independence, and this should have been sufficient to reach a judgment to disengage.

One reason why it has been thought that the mere appearance (to a reasonable observer) is decisive, is that we are poor judges in our own case. We are not suited, in our own case, to judge whether our judgment is really compromised, when it appears that it might be—precisely because, if it is compromised, we will lack the judgment to recognize that it is so. This would seem to be what happened with Andersen in relation to Enron. Andersen regarded itself as competent to decide that a reasonable claim of compromised judgment in fact had no substance. In hindsight we can see that that claim was correct, and that Andersen was wrong in dismissing it. And in hindsight we strongly suspect that it was precisely the unconscious, distorting motive of strong economic self-interest that had corrupted Andersen's judgment.

Andersen's lack of objectivity in expression is also apparent in the internal memo. The memo states that, "A significant discussion was held regarding the related party transactions with LJM, including the materiality of such amounts to Enron's income statement and the amount retained 'off balance sheet.'" If one considers this remark alone, one might think that Andersen had concluded that the debt concealed in the SPEs was so small as to be immaterial to a company the size of Enron. That judgment would not have been entirely unreasonable. But objectivity in expression implies thinking about the effect of one's representation on the intended audience. And in connection with this, a subsequent remark becomes telling: "We discussed Enron's reliance on its current credit rating to maintain itself as a high credit rated transaction party." That is to say, Andersen directly recognized that Enron's representations were sustaining a trust in the company, which was not however justifiable in substance. Enron's financial representations therefore lacked objectivity in expression, yet Andersen continued to certify them.

Note that Enron's reluctance to disclose in its annual reports the details of SPE transactions, and the time and care it put into saying as little as possible about these, should have been a concern to Andersen, given its responsibility to the public interest. Indeed, Andersen should have been intent on clarifying for others precisely these obscure areas: "That impulse to avoid public exposure, coupled with the significance of the transactions for Enron's income statements and balance sheets, should have raised red flags for Senior Management, as well as for Enron's outside auditors and lawyers. Unfortunately, it apparently did not" (Powers Report, 201).

Andersen, Integrity, and Professionalism

We mentioned that altruistic service follows fairly directly from the "distinctive work" of an accountant, involving service to the creditors and investors, actual or potential. This orientation of service is often referred to today as a concern for the public interest.

A concern for the public interest at first seems to be shown in the Watkins letter: "To the layman on the street, it will look like we recognized funds flow of $800mm from merchant asset sales in 1999 by selling to a vehicle (Condor) that we capitalized with a promise of Enron stock in later years....It sure looks to the layman on the street that we are hiding losses in a related company and will compensate that company with Enron stock in the future." And yet Watkins, although hailed as a "whistle-blower," does not seem to rise to the level of a concern for the public interest. Her remarks seem more concerned with "how it will look," and not so much with whether Enron's actions are harming others.

For instance, later in the letter, where she puts forward possible scenarios for resolving the problem, she writes:

> Develop clean up plan:
>
> a. Best case: Clean up quietly if possible.
>
> b. Worst case: Quantify, develop PR and IR campaigns, customer assistance plans (don't want to go the way of Salomon's trading shop), legal actions, severance actions, disclosure.

Watkins is an employee of Enron, but as a professional CPA, she has a responsibility the public interest that transcends her employment there. It is not clear, however, that her concerns for her own standing ever rise to the level of professional integrity; they seem to be phrased more in terms of her career: "My 8 years of Enron work history will be worth nothing on my resume," she writes to Lay, "the business world will consider the past successes as nothing but an elaborate accounting hoax."

The point of these remarks is not principally to criticize Watkins, who showed a praiseworthy candor in writing to Lay, and who in doing so certainly put her job at risk in the Enron culture, where notoriously 10% of staff were fired each year, regardless of performance. It is rather to establish a point of comparison. Watkins is universally regarded as the "good guy" in the Enron scandal, rightly so, yet even her expressed remarks fall short of the standards expected of a CPA. (Note: this is an observation about her expressed remarks to Lay. Of course one cannot judge to what extent her own thoughts were different, and whether her way of describing the problem to Lay was shaped by "tactical" considerations.)

In examining the Andersen memos, we do not even see the level of Watkins' concern reaching as far as how the Enron SPEs would appear to an informed investor. As we saw, the memo very briefly mentions the materiality of Enron's concealed debt. But its preoccupation is with Andersen and its interests, not the interest of the public. How much does the Enron engagement place Andersen at risk? What are the potential exposures? How much may nonetheless be gained from a continuing relationship? How much responsibility and therefore risk can be shifted to Enron or its Board of Directors? The Andersen memo displays not the slightest concern for the public interest.

In relation to this, think once more of McLean's piece in *Fortune*, and consider the sort of correction or restatement that Andersen in February 2001 ought to have insisted upon, given investors' reliance upon their audits. Not a single "To Do" item coming out of the conference call had anything to do with Andersen's responsibility to the public interest.

Andersen's Role in Non-Economic Hedge Transactions

- Advising as to the establishment of Enron SPEs.
- Approval of these transactions as satisfying GAAP.
- Advising audit committee that transactions were properly recorded.
- Auditing the transactions for fairness.

Source: AccountingMalpractice.com

Rules vs. Principles

We explained in chapter 6 above that adherence to rules is not sufficient for propriety. This is clear from Andersen's handling of the Enron SPEs. The relevant accounting rule at the time stipulated that SPEs, to be truly independent, had to have at least 3% outside equity. But this stipulates a "necessary condition," not a "sufficient condition" of independence. If an entity cannot be regarded as independent if it fails to have 3% equity, it does not follow that it will always be independent if it does have 3% equity. The rule must be treated as a good starting point, which guides but does not substitute for professional judgment. By using good sense and good professional judgment—rather than merely being concerned to adhere to the rules—Andersen might have judged that the Enron SPEs were not truly independent and therefore, to avoid misrepresentation, had to be consolidated on the Enron balance sheet.

Note that, as the restatement acknowledged, Andersen in fact signed off on Enron SPEs where the outside equity was less than 3%. What this shows is that when someone is not trying to follow the principle underlying the rule, then he will not even reliably follow the rule. It is necessary to see rules as expressions or applications of principles, and to follow them in that spirit. If rules are in the service of principles, then the transaction gets recorded as it is, whatever the consequences for a company's financial report. Enron's practice in contrast was to determine in advance what was expedient and then find some way of making accounting rules allow for it.[26]

Andersen's treatment of Enron SPEs also verifies the maxim that good character and good culture require that one follow high standards of conduct in small matters and in new circumstances. People rightly wonder how Andersen could have arrived at the dismally corrupt outlook shown in its February 2001 memo, and even more so its actual destruction of documents later in the year, after the SEC had announced its intent to launch an investigation. But small indiscretions lead to large ones. Perhaps the fatal false step was Enron's use of an SPE in the early 1990s to move the liability of its Houston headquarters off-balance sheet. This arrangement had some color of justification then, but a conservative application of the principles underlying the construal of SPEs would have decided against it. Yet once this doubtful expedient was found to "work," it was relied upon later, in more pressing circumstances, when Enron desperately needed to hide its mounting debt. Andersen could not later argue consistently against the device, without thereby implicitly judging itself to have been irresponsible in signing off on its use earlier. And by 2001 Andersen was eagerly cooperating with Enron to devise even more elaborate SPEs, effectively to cover for the failure of earlier ones. At every later step, it became more difficult and more costly to reverse course. Eventually Andersen took the reckless step of destroying Enron documents rather than straightforwardly admit its accumulating responsibility for the Enron fraud.

Andersen's Assumption of Enron Internal Auditing Functions

We mentioned above the hefty consulting fees that Andersen was receiving from Enron, amounting in the year 2000 to about $27 million, roughly equal to what the firm was receiving in auditing fees. The incentives that would naturally arise from such an arrangement, as we have seen, were already enough to raise a question of, at least, whether the firm was maintaining the appearance of independence.

But also problematic was the close working relationship between Enron and Andersen, which was such that Andersen played something of the role of a partner and collaborator, rather than objective judge and critic, relative to Enron's financial structures. This close relationship, at the time, was presented by Enron management as a praiseworthy innovation. For instance, here is how Kenneth Lay explains it in retrospect, in his testimony of April 24, 2006, under direct

---

[26] See Baker, R. C. and R. Hayes : 2004, "Reflecting Form over Substance: The Case of Enron Corp," *Critical Perspectives on Accounting* 15, 767-785.

examination by his attorney, when on trial for conspiracy to commit wire and securities fraud:

> Q. Did the audit committee also oversee the way the company prepared financial statements and the way the company complied with SEC requirements and that kind of thing?

> A. Yes. And even further—and Enron's one of the first companies—one of the few companies early on to do this, but—but we, basically, turned over all of our internal and external audit functions (and I call them that; sometimes the auditors call them something else)—but audit functions to an outside audit firm; and we turned them over to Arthur Andersen.

> In the process, we—they—had over a hundred auditors on site in one of Enron's buildings. And indeed it was made known to them, and made repeatedly known to them, that they had access to anything and everything they needed at Enron.

> Now, one reason we did that was because we wanted them current enough on everything we were doing that if, in fact, there were problems or there were rumors of problems, as there were from time to time, in our—particularly in our wholesale trading business, they would be current enough that, certainly overnight, or in a few hours, they could respond as to whether there was a problem or wasn't a problem.

> So they, basically—we, basically—had a real time audit by Arthur Andersen ongoing all the time.

It is an interesting philosophical question whether the notion of a "real time audit" is possible or in fact makes sense. Is it possible to judge or evaluate something continuously, while preserving an adequate distance from what is being judged? Typically, judgments and assessments come only at intervals, and they involve clearly defined objects of judgment: a professor gives a test once a week, or a final examination at the end of the semester; a scorekeeper in a sport registers and evaluates only definite plays which purport to be scores. Moreover, would not the degree of collaboration required for a "real time audit" raise the question of whether the audit firm in spite of establishing so-called chinese walls, was sometimes being asked to audit its own work? Again, the degree of collaboration required for "real time audit" might easily lead to an alignment of interests between auditor and client, as shown, tellingly, in the fact that Lay twice in his testimony refers to Andersen as "we," as if there were no distinction between Enron and Andersen.

On a more basic level one might also ask whether the Andersen "internal audit" personnel were even competent to provide the necessary internal audit work services. It seems fairly reasonable that by utilizing the Andersen personnel to provide all internal audit services, that short of a strong ethical orientation, they were creating even more barriers to detecting fraud. A junior Andersen accountant would have to overcome not only the authority of Enron executives, but Andersen's as well. At least, later with respect to WorldCom, an outlet existed for internal auditors to raise concerns about accounting issues, to the largely independent Andersen partners on the WorldCom audit.

Enron's "innovative" relationship with Andersen was an extreme example of what was occurring throughout the business world, which led the SEC in 2000 to propose a rule on auditor independence:

> [T]he Commission looks in the first instance to whether a relationship or the provision of a service:
> (a) creates a mutual or conflicting interest between the accountant and the audit client;
> (b) places the accountant in the position of auditing his or her own work;
> (c) results in the accountant acting as management or an employee of the audit client; or
> (d) places the accountant in a position of being an advocate for the audit client.

The relationship between Andersen and Enron was problematic as regards all four considerations.

As it happens, Ken Lay sent a comment in response to the proposed rule on auditor independence, in a letter to SEC Chairman, Arthur Levitt, dated September 20, 2000:

> For the past several years, Enron has successfully utilized its independent audit firm's expertise and professional skepticism to help improve the overall control environment within the company. In addition to their traditional financial statement related work, the independent auditor's procedures at Enron have been extended to include specific audits of and reporting on critical control processes. This arrangement has resulted in qualitative and comprehensive reporting to management and to Enron's audit committee, which has been found to be extremely valuable. Also, I believe independent audits of the internal control environment are valuable to the investing public, particularly given the risks and complexities of Enron's business and the extremely dynamic business environment in which Enron and others now operate.

... The proposed rule would preclude independent financial statement auditors from performing "certain internal audit services." The description of inappropriate activities included in your current proposal is so broad that it could restrict Enron from engaging its independent financial statement auditors to report on the company's control processes on a recurring basis as the company has now arranged. I find this troubling, not only because I believe the independence and expertise of the independent auditors enhances this process, but also because Enron has found its "integrated audit" arrangement to be more efficient and cost-effective than the more traditional roles of separate internal and external auditing functions. Frankly, I fail to understand how extending the scope of what is independently audited can be anything but positive.

Lay here incorrectly characterizes the relationship between Andersen and Enron, presenting Andersen's work in internal audit as periodic and "specific," as if it were simply a more frequent and more detailed scrutiny, the same in kind as an external audit. In the end the SEC rejected the concerns of Lay and others and ruled out an auditor's providing of internal audit services, (except for small companies and under limited circumstances)—a restriction which mirrored independence rules already adopted by many professional associations and which, in 2002, was incorporated into Federal Law by the Sarbanes-Oxley Act.

Ethics and Legality

It is sometimes thought that, in business and professional work, ethical considerations are a kind of nice window-dressing, a luxury, whereas in contrast considerations of law (liability, risk) and profitability are inescapable and crucial. But in reality lawfulness and profitability follow naturally from a solid and unswerving commitment to ethical ideals. Honesty is the best policy over the long haul; and the best way to avoid doing something illegal is to aim to avoid doing anything unethical. As a result, once a person or a firm adopts practices which are dubious from an ethical point of view, it frequently happens that criminality, and eventually lack of profitability and true business value, follow close behind.

This sequence was very clear in the case of Enron. Its management and some of its accountants began to disregard basic ethical principles of accounting, such as the priority of substance over form, and this led very quickly to fraudulent and criminal behavior. One reason for this is that to place form before substance is to favor already a kind of deception or misrepresentation; and deception is the essence of fraud. Thus someone who displays this incorrect preference in accounting may, by a slight change of circumstances, and in only a few steps, begin to engage in actual fraud. This slide was clearly exhibited, for instance, in the actions of Enron's Treasurer, Ben Glisan, who was a CPA and former Andersen employee. Consider the statement which he gives in his plea agreement (*U.S. v. Glisan*, Sept. 10, 2003), where he admits to conspiracy to commit wire and securities fraud:

> I was the Treasurer of Enron Corporation from the spring of 2000 until October 2001. Beginning in the spring of 2000, I and others at Enron engaged in a conspiracy to manipulate artificially Enron's financial statements. LJM enabled Enron to falsify its financial picture to the public; in return, LJM received a prearranged profit. Specifically, I and others caused the creation and use of a Special Purpose Entity (SPE) known as Talon to engage in illegal transactions, including the use of Talon as an off-balance-sheet vehicle that I knew in fact did not qualify for such treatment and should have been included on Enron's books.
>
> Talon, which was created in April 2000, was designed by me and others to protect Enron's balance sheet from decreases in value of certain investments. Talon was funded mainly by Enron through a promissory note and Enron's own stock. The remainder of Talon's funding came from a $30 million "investment" from LJM. This alleged third party funding served as the supposed 3% outside equity that I knew was required for Talon not to be reflected in Enron's financial statements, which I knew were publicly filed with the Securities and Exchange Commission and relied on by the public.
>
> As I knew, this transaction violated existing accounting principles in that its form was misleading and was accounted in a manner inconsistent with its economic substance. As I also knew, Talon was not properly off-balance-sheet. I and others arranged for Enron to pay $41 million to LJM before Talon entered into a "put," that is, a transaction that purportedly served to hedge Enron against a decline in its own stock value. Although there was no true business purpose, the "put" option was purchased by Enron for $41 million. The put was designed by me and others as an ostensible reason to make a distribution of $41 million to LJM, economically providing a return of and return on capital. Since the put failed to have a true business purpose, Talon failed to meet the minimum equity test as required by applicable accounting rules. As a result of this failure, LJM lacked substantive control of Talon. This failure, in turn, led to the substantive control of Talon by Enron.
>
> As part of the scheme, I understood that the use of the interstate wires would be made in the form of, among other things, payments and filings by Enron with regulators of misleading financial statements.

Arthur Andersen and Document Destruction

Enron's November 2001 restatement was an attempt to give the correct accounting treatment to a $1.2 billion dollar reduction in shareholder equity that Enron had already announced in a third quarter earnings release of the month before, on October 16 ("ENRON REPORTS RECURRING THIRD QUARTER EARNINGS OF $0.43 PER DILUTED SHARE; REPORTS NON-RECURRING CHARGES OF $1.01 BILLION AFTER-TAX," the release was titled.) There was a debate within Enron, and with Andersen, as to whether this reduction should be presented as recurring or non-recurring. Andersen wished that it be called recurring, as accounting principles required; however, it did not object or withdraw from its relationship with Enron, when Enron reported these as non-recurring. Enron CFO, Andy Fastow, also wanted the reduction to be reported as recurring—not, as he later testified, because this was the correct accounting, but rather because the businesses to which the reduction was attributed had been reporting "recurring" earnings previously, and Fastow thought that the match of recurring losses (currently) to recurring earnings (previously) would be less likely to raise suspicion. In the end, Lay directed that the reduction be represented as non-recurring, presumably on the grounds that this would inflict less damage on Enron share-price.

That the press release was debated beforehand among Enron and Andersen is important, because this shows that even before October 16th Andersen would have been aware that an SEC investigation was imminent. And, indeed, on October 17th, the day after Enron's press release, the SEC opened an informal investigation of Enron, informing Enron of this in writing. Over the following few days, Andersen accountants convened at Enron for discussions of the matter; and, on October 23, Andersen initiated a company-wide action of destroying documents related to Enron. As recounted in the indictment that was brought against Andersen:

> During the next few weeks, an unparalleled initiative was undertaken to shred physical documentation and delete computer files. Tons of papers relating to the Enron audit were promptly shredded as part of the orchestrated document destruction. The shredder at the Andersen office at the Enron building was used virtually constantly and, to handle the overload, dozens of large trunks filled with Enron documents were sent to Andersen's main Houston office to be shredded. A systematic effort was also undertaken and carried out to purge the computer hard-drives and E-mail system of Enron-related files.

On October 31, the SEC opened a formal investigation against Enron. Andersen halted its document destruction only when it received a subpoena in connection with this investigation, on November 9.

The following year, on March 14, Andersen was indicted on the criminal charge of obstruction of justice. Even before this, Andersen began to lose clients, with its employees beginning to defect to other accounting firms. By May of 2002, Andersen had been fired by over 500 of the 2300 clients it had audited the year before. On June 14 the firm was found guilty of obstruction of justice (a felony) and prohibited as a matter of regulation from serving publicly registered clients before the SEC. No longer able to audit public companies, Andersen's demise was all but guaranteed.

Andersen was convicted under a Federal witness-tampering statute, which prohibited anyone from "knowingly" and "corruptly" persuading someone to destroy evidence relevant to a Federal investigation. There were two weak points in its conviction, which Andersen aimed to exploit in its appeals: first, the bulk of its document destruction took place when the SEC was conducting only an informal, not a formal, investigation; second, Andersen's destruction of documents technically fell within its stated, and at that time lawful, document retention policy, so that it was unclear whether those who ordered the destruction actually had the criminal mentality that the statute required (that is, "knowingly" and "corruptly" persuading another). On May 30, 2005, the US Supreme Court overturned the Andersen conviction principally on the second ground. It held that the trial judge in her instructions to the jury gave too weak an interpretation of the word "corruptly": the trial judge had said that this might amount simply to an intent to impede an investigation, but the Supreme Court held that it additionally had to include an intent to impede an investigation unlawfully.

What are the ethical, as opposed to the legal, considerations that bear upon document destruction and retention for accountants? The following seems to be the correct ethical principle: if storage were infinite in capacity and free, then an auditor would have no reason at all to destroy work papers and supporting documents, and these should be retained ad infinitum. That is, the default policy for such papers is to retain them; some reason is needed to destroy them; and the only relevant motives for this, from an ethical point of view, are practical considerations of storage limitations and expense. When these limitations and expenses grow sufficiently, and there is no realistic probability that there could be any need to consult the documents, then, from an ethical point of view, it would be acceptable to destroy documents. But otherwise they should be retained.

That this is the correct principle seems to follow from the nature of accounting. As we have pointed out, the role of an accountant is to secure the conditions of trust, necessary for the good functioning of the marketplace, by giving an accurate, reliable, and verified representation of the financial condition of an enterprise. Three considerations therefore follow:

(1) An accountant, when performing an attest-like or truth-telling function, is therefore something like a scientific researcher or scholar. His work papers serve as evidence and justification for conclusions reached in the audit (or review or compilation). Just as a scientist or scholar, if storage were infinite and inexpensive, would retain the data that supported his published findings, so an accountant should retain work papers.

(2) Accounting by nature is an activity of verification. It does not give findings, so much as verify findings. In this way an audit is similar to a proof in mathematics. A proof is not simply an argument or a line of thought: it is an argument the reliability of which has been checked and verified. Thus, verification and checking is of the nature of accounting. But an accountant's work papers are indispensable for verifying and checking his work. Hence the default policy is that these should be retained, as they are essential to the sort of work that an accountant does.

(3) As has been mentioned repeatedly, an accountant as a professional should aim to serve altruistically those others, perhaps unknown or anonymous, who may need to rely on the results of his work. The basic attitude of accountancy is therefore service, not self-seeking or self-protection. Clearly the retention of work papers is more consistent with this attitude, whereas their destruction looks like self-protection rather than altruism.

These ethical reflections have largely been embodied in law in the wake of Andersen's document destruction in the Enron scandal. The current state of the law is that documents should be retained so long as they might reasonably be expected to be relevant to any inquiry as to the validity of the findings of attest work. Sarbanes-Oxley stipulated that, minimally, "Any accountant who conducts an audit of an issuer of securities ... shall maintain all audit or review workpapers for a period of 5 years from the end of the fiscal period in which the audit or review was concluded." (Sect. 1520 (a)(1)). It also gave the SEC authority to set more stringent standards, which extended the retention period to seven years.[27] The SEC

---

[27] § 210.2-06 Retention of audit and review records.

(a) For a period of seven years after an accountant concludes an audit or review of an issuer's financial statements ... the accountant shall retain records relevant to the audit or review, including workpapers and other documents that form the basis of the audit or review, and memoranda, correspondence, communications, other documents, and records (including electronic records), which:

(1) Are created, sent or received in connection with the audit or review, and

rule alludes to two distinct grounds for document retention: (i) so that the audit firm itself may be in a position to check or correct its own work; and (ii) so that public authorities, in cases of dispute, may have access to information that might reasonably call into question the validity of an auditor's findings. The second ground corresponds to the auditor's duty to serve the public interest. This duty exposes an auditor's work, rightfully so, to a certain degree of public scrutiny.

Criminal Trials

A month after Enron filed for Chapter 11 bankruptcy on December 2, 2001, Federal prosecutors began to bring charges against Enron executives under the 1932 Securities Act and the 1934 Securities Exchange Act. They used a domino strategy, developing cases first against lower-level figures, and putting pressure on these to turn state's witness, in exchange for the possibility of a reduced sentence. This led to eventually to indictments against Andrew Fastow, Jeff Skilling, and Ken Lay.

Michael Kopper was the first to plead guilty, in August 2002. His case is especially interesting as providing a clear illustration of the maxim, "rules are not enough" (see Chapter 6 above). Among the many frauds in which he participated was one involving an SPE called RADR. This was a sham transaction by which Enron pretended to divest itself, for regulatory reasons, of wind farms in California, while still maintaining control over those wind farms. In order to accomplish this, Enron CFO, Andy Fastow, secretly loaned $16 million to Kopper, who in turn loaned this money to his domestic partner, William Dodson, the nominal manager of RADR, for purchase of the wind farms. Eventually Enron bought back the wind farms at a much higher price, generating handsome profits for Kopper, Dodson, Fastow, and others. In his testimony later, in the trial of Skilling and Lay, Fastow described the deal as follows:

Q. What did the RADR transaction pertain to?

---

(2) Contain conclusions, opinions, analyses, or financial data related to the audit or review.

...(c) Memoranda, correspondence, communications, other documents, and records (including electronic records) described in paragraph (a) of this section shall be retained whether they support the auditor's final conclusions regarding the audit or review, or contain information or data, relating to a significant matter, that is inconsistent with the auditor's final conclusions regarding that matter or the audit or review. Significance of a matter shall be determined based on an objective analysis of the facts and circumstances. Such documents and records include, but are not limited to, those documenting a consultation on or resolution of differences in professional judgment.

A. Well, like most of these transactions, Enron had a problem. And the problem at the time was that it needed—it wanted to acquire—a utility; but when acquiring that utility, it had to dispose of a couple of assets called wind farms, the windmills that generate power, in order to complete the merger. Enron wanted to complete the merger; they did not want to give up control of the wind farms; and so the RADR transaction was a structure to try to sell them and keep control at the same time.

Q. And what was your role going to be in the RADR transaction?

A. Well, originally, my role was discussed as being the general partner, like in LJM. But it was determined that I could not be general partner, because then Enron would not be deemed to have sold the wind farms.

Q. Well, let me just stop you there. Did anyone have a problem with you doing this RADR transaction until it was determined that you'd have potentially this issue you're just describing?

A. No. In fact, I recall working at length with people to try to find various structures that would make it possible for me to do that.

Q. Okay. So what is it that came up that caused a problem for you to remain involved personally in that transaction?

A. … If Enron continued to own those wind farms, it would stop getting the tax rebates. So we wanted to have some other company own those wind farms for Enron, so that it could keep getting tax benefits, if you will. I couldn't do that, because, if I did that, it was determined that Enron wouldn't get the tax benefits any longer. So instead, I arranged with Mr. Kopper to secretly have an interest in RADR.

Q. All right. And by the way, what was the solution to getting someone involved in RADR instead of you? What was the idea? Who was going to be substituted in for you?

A. Someone very close—you know, that we felt would go along with anything that we, at Enron, wanted to do with those wind farms.

Q. And who was that person? …

A. Mr. Dodson.

Q. Who was Mr. Dodson?

A. Mr. Dodson was Mr. Kopper's domestic partner.

Q. Okay. Was Mr. Skilling aware of Mr. Dodson's relationship with Mr. Kopper?

A. Yes.

Q. And was this discussed with Mr. Skilling; namely, putting Mr. Dodson in the transaction?

A. Yes, it was.

Q. What do you remember being said about that?

A. We talked about …how there was this anomaly, if you will, in the law; that if it were the spouse of someone, that wouldn't work, because that would be a related party, if you will. Or if Mr. Kopper were married to a woman, his wife couldn't be the general partner, because it would be deemed to be like Mr. Kopper being the general partner; but under the law, the Texas law, Mr. Dodson wasn't recognized as his spouse. So notwithstanding they had a very similar relationship to a spousal relationship, technically, it worked under the law.

Here Fastow recounts how he made the mistake of confusing a necessary with a sufficient condition (which was explained at length in Chapter 6). It was a necessary condition for the RADR transaction to count as a sale, that the buyer not be the spouse of an Enron executive. But this was not a sufficient condition; rather, the buyer could not have any sort of relationship to an Enron executive which was such that, in substance, Enron retained control over the wind farm.

Fastow pled guilty in January 2004 to securities and wire fraud, and accepted a sentence of 10 years. Richard Causey, Chief Accountant at Enron, and a CPA and former Andersen employee, pled guilty in December 2005, accepting a sentence of 7 years. Skilling and Lay continued to maintain their innocence. Their trial ended on May 25, with the jury finding Lay guilty of all six counts against him, and Skilling guilty of 19 of 28 counts. Skilling received a 24 year sentence on October 23, 2006. Ken Lay received no sentence in a Texas court: he died of a heart attack on July 5.

The various guilty pleas, and especially the testimony of Fastow, substantiated what was already clear from the Powers report, namely, that the fraud at Enron took place in a context of a company culture in which employees were rewarded more for meeting analyst's projections, and therefore boosting share price, than for actually contributing genuine economic value. "At Enron, the culture was, and the practice seemed to be: do transactions that maximized financial reporting earnings as opposed to maximizing the true economic value of transactions," Fastow said in testimony. Complaining about this, Steve Kean, Enron chief of staff, wrote in a now famous e-mail to Ken Lay (August 17, 2001):

> We should do the economically rational thing in every transaction and business and let the chips fall where they may. Instead of tying ourselves in a knot about managing earnings or write downs or avoiding an asset sale because it's on the books for more than the market, we should just make the rational economic decision ... If we make the economically rational decisions over and over, the stock price will come along.

The culture of Enron was primarily focused on share price; share price depended on what analysts and investors thought about the company (rather than the actually state of the business); it therefore took as its primary goal the appearance that the company presented; and this led to a favoring of form over substance. Management decided upon desired earnings goals and results in advance, according to what would make the most favorable impression on investors, and then accounting was used to insure these results, regardless of the economic substance of the transactions. As Neal Batson, the court-appointed examiner in the Enron bankruptcy proceedings observed in his report:

> In many cases, the Enron officers appeared less concerned about making the correct or best decision, and more focused on finding some justification for their desired result. That is, their primary concern seems to have been to ensure that they had an explanation if someone challenged their position, rather than to determine whether their decision was correct or was justified in light of the risks assumed. Examples of this strategy include: (i) using accounting rules that did not directly address the accounting question at issue but simply provided an argument to justify an aggressive position; (ii) searching for ways to avoid public disclosure; and (iii) obtaining professional opinions or advice merely as a necessary procedural step.

On the first point, Batson remarked:

> Evidence suggests that Enron officers often took aggressive accounting positions with little direct GAAP support. Rather than using accounting principles to achieve a fair presentation of Enron's financial condition, both as a means of fulfilling their disclosure obligations and as an effective management tool, it appears that Enron officers (often with the support of Andersen) focused their efforts on using hyper-technical and strained judgments to justify aggressive and misleading financial presentation.

An auditor's loss of objectivity of judgment is typically associated with some deficiency in character: a failure in sound professional judgment does not occur in a vacuum. Yet one should take care not to suppose that such a deficiency need be purely personal or private. Rather, it is typically part of a culture, or social context, with skewed motivations and incentives. That is why many persons working together may fail simultaneously to reach appropriate and sound judgments—as happened with the dozens of Andersen accountants, and Enron internal accountants, who reviewed the misleading accounting of Enron SPEs and failed to voice any objection to them.

Greed is perhaps the most common deficiency of character which can skew a person's judgment in financial matters. Greed is often understood in a simplistic way; we perhaps think of it as like the attitude of a miser, who sits in front of mounds of gold, and is filled with irrational glee at the prospect of having more and more. But greed is a subtle attitude, often an attitude of elation or pride, which consists essentially in the expectation of gaining something for oneself for nothing—the gain of wealth for no reason at all, neither in exchange for work nor as a gift, and therefore the gain of wealth apart from intrinsic or extrinsic limits.

The culture in Enron of preferring the appearance of economic value over the reality was a culture of greed. To look for profit—from an increase in value of the shares that one owns; from bonuses attached to boosting the price of the stock—for little reason other than that, through manipulating appearances, you have caused analysts and investors to think highly of the stock, is essentially an attitude of greed.

Andy Fastow's testimony (under cross examination from Jeff Skilling's defense attorney) provides perhaps the best commentary on this point:

Q. You want the jury to believe that Mr. Skilling is consumed by greed as you are, right?

A. I didn't say that, sir. You did.

Q. I asked you. It's a question. Answer it.

A. My answer to that question is I spent a lot of time up here already saying that I stole from Enron. I did steal from Enron. We stole from Enron. That was why it was difficult for me when you posed your question to me directly.

Q. Who's the "we"?

A. Myself and other members of senior management of Enron.

Q. Did they steal that 120 million?

A. No. They stole in different ways related to this 120 million.

Q. Now, you say, "They stole in different ways," other members of senior management. What you're saying is that other members of senior management committed fraud to make their stock go up, then they would sell their stock and get away with the booty that way. That's what you're suggesting, right?

A. Are you asking me?

Q. I'm asking you.

A. What I'm saying is when you misrepresent the nature of your company, when you artificially hide losses, when you do things like this to cause your stock price to go up so you can sell your stock to cause yourself to make earning targets, that otherwise you'd be unable, to make it so you get high salaries and bonuses, that is stealing.

Q. Okay.

A. I stole one way, and I stole that way. All I'm saying is that we stole.

Illustrative Legal Case

We saw in *Feit v. Leasco* that the court regarded as settled fact that the Securities Acts were designed with the primary purpose of protecting the ordinary investor. In *U.S. v. Arthur Young*, the Supreme Court attributed to accountants, consistent with professional standards and codes of conduct affirmed by accountants themselves, the public role as a kind of "watchdog," in their work of auditing publicly traded companies. This role is additionally reinforced through the creation of the PCAOB, which was established by a provision of the Sarbanes-Oxley Act,[28] which became the basis of the mission statement of PCAOB:

> The PCAOB is a private-sector, non-profit corporation, created by the Sarbanes-Oxley Act of 2002, to oversee the auditors of public companies in order to protect the interests of investors and further the public interest in the preparation of informative, fair, and independent audit reports.

Given that Sarbanes-Oxley makes PCAOB the highest authority as regards auditing standards for public accountants, it seems correct that the "public watchdog" role

---

[28] "There is established the Public Company Accounting Oversight Board, to oversee the audit of public companies that are subject to the securities laws, and related matters, in order to protect the interests of investors and further the public interest in the preparation of informative, accurate, and independent audit reports for companies the securities of which are sold to, and held by and for, public investors."

articulated in *U.S. v. Arthur Young* is thereby given greater definiteness and reinforcement.

In light of these matters, it is interesting to look at the dissenting opinion in *Bily v. Arthur Young* 834 P. 2d 745 (Cal 1992), as indicating a certain tension in the law relative to the Code of Conduct accepted by accountants. Bily decided as regards California state law the scope of duty of care, and thus liability for negligence, for accountants as regards persons other than their clients. It did so by proposing a compromise as regards the three recognized standards: the traditional privity doctrine; the Restatement of Torts standard; and the Reasonable Foreseeability approach. The California court held that each standard was relevant, depending upon the nature of an accountant's work and the degree of breach of the standard of care alleged: accountants have no general duty of care to anyone other than to their clients or restricted other parties as would be recognized under privity, for any work other than auditing; for negligent misrepresentations in an audit report, they are liable to the extent allowed under the more liberal Restatement approach; and finally, for misrepresentations in an audit report that amount to fraud, they are liable under the most expansive standard of the Reasonable Foreseeability approach.

The dissenting opinion in *Bily* argued that the expansive Reasonable Foreseeability standard should instead be used for negligent misrepresentation in an audit report. Here is a passage from its conclusion:

> The majority recognizes that accountants acknowledge a responsibility to third parties who foreseeably rely on audit reports in their business dealings with the audited company. Yet the majority adopts a rule that betrays the expectations of third party users whose reliance makes the audit report valuable to the audited company. Under the majority's rule, the audit report is made a trap for the unwary, because only the most legally sophisticated and well advised will understand that the report will not deliver what on its face it seems to promise: a qualified professional's actual assurance that the financial statement fairly states the financial situation of the audited company. An assurance with no legal recourse is essentially a hoax. Under the rule the majority adopts, any value that third parties place on the unqualified opinion is mistaken, because the law now insists that reliance upon the opinion, no matter how reasonable and foreseeable, is unjustified.
>
> Finally, and perhaps most importantly, the majority pays too little attention to the importance of negligence liability as a means of preventing bad financial data from entering and polluting the waters of commerce. Without a liability rule that enforces the reasonable

expectations of third party users of audit reports and provides an adequate incentive for due care, we may expect less careful audits, inefficient allocation of capital resources, increased transaction costs for loans and investments, and delay and disruption in the processes of lending and investing.

In the dissent we find first an argument based on the nature of the accountant's role, and then an argument appealing to consequences. The first argument is interesting because it effectively calls attention to the "expectations gap," that is, the gap between what the ordinary investor thinks is certified by an unqualified audit report, and what the accounting profession commonly and appropriately regards itself to be certifying. The second argument, it would seem, has effectively been adopted by the U.S. Congress, since a similar line of thought underlies Sarbanes-Oxley and the formation of PCAOB.

The dissenting opinion in *Bily* highlights an apparent incongruence between the ethical standards accepted by accountants and the scope of liability allowed by the majority in that decision. Because an accountant's moral, ethical, and professional responsibilities extend to foreseeable users of audit opinions, such as lenders and investors, an accountant whose carelessness causes economic loss to a foreseeable user is arguably as morally blameworthy as an attorney who negligently drafts a will or contract, or a broker or escrow holder who negligently mishandles important documents in a real estate transaction. In each instance, the breach of a professional responsibility through lack of due care should presumably result in liability or at least some accountability to those to whom the professional owes an established moral and ethical obligation. Although defendant and the majority advance various arguments against this conclusion, none is entirely persuasive from a professional ethics perspective. In the end, the majority's argument becomes one of expediency or public policy; they are recognizing at least indirectly that, because accounting professionals have such an altruistic calling or responsibility, and play such an important role in a free market economy, the profession must be protected in way so as to ensure its continuance. This protection is necessary because the number of parties that might be relying on any given audit report is so great that even an unintended negligent act could cause the failure of a firm. Alternatively, to overcome this failure potential, an accountant's compensation might need to be so high as to make the service uneconomical for those new companies that most need the audit opinion to advance growth prospects.

The profession's standards propose a general responsibility to the public, but the majority recognizes an exposure to liability that falls short of that. Whatever the force of this consideration as a matter of law, one might expect that it would have weight at trial, before a jury. Members of a jury, one may suppose, would share in the same "expectations gap" as the public at large and impute a correlative duty of care. And it is in the particular circumstances of each case that this balance of responsibility and obligation are weighed. Hence, the existence of restrictions on auditor liability does not reduce the necessity for ethical conduct or accountability but in fact increase its necessity in considerations of professional development. No accountant wants to find himself needing to explain dubious conduct before a jury generally not made up of his peers.

From this consideration, perhaps, the following important lesson can be gleaned, as an incidental conclusion: the argument that an accountant's liability in law should be more restricted than the extent of public reliance upon an accountant's work, can ultimately make sense only if there exist strong and demonstrably effective safeguards already in place, internal to the profession of accounting itself, so that legal protection of the investor's reasonable expectation becomes unnecessary. This, clearly, is one of the things meant by the "obligation of self-discipline above and beyond the requirements of laws and regulations," inherent in the profession, referred to at the opening of the current Code.

Recommended additional reading:

Baker, R. C., and R. Hayes : 2004, "Reflecting Form over Substance: The Case of Enron Corp," *Critical Perspectives on Accounting* 15, 767-785.

Bazerman, M. H., G. Loewenstein, and D. A. Moore: 2002, "Why Good Accountants Do Bad Audits," *Harvard Business Review* 80(11), 97-102.

Berenson, A.: 2004, *The Number* (Random House, New York).

Bily v. Arthur Young

Powers, Jr., W.C.: 2002, *Report of the Special Investigative Committee of the Board of Directors of Enron Corp.*

Staubus, G.J.: 2005, "Ethics Failures in Corporate Financial Reporting," *Journal of Business Ethics* 57(1), 5-15.

WorldCom:
Complicity of Internal Accountants

12

"In October, Mr. Yates convened a meeting with Ms. Vinson and Mr. Normand in the accounting department, which occupied a corner of the fourth floor at WorldCom's headquarters. He told them that Mr. Myers and Mr. Sullivan had asked them to dip into a reserve account set aside to cover line costs and other items for WorldCom's telecommunications unit, fish out $828 million and use it to pay other expenses, according to people familiar with the meeting. In doing so, they would reduce expenses for the quarter and boost earnings. ...

"Ms. Vinson and Mr. Normand were shocked by their bosses' proposal and the huge sum involved. All three accountants were worried that the adjustment wasn't proper, according to the people familiar with the conversation. Under accounting rules, reserves can be set up only if management expects a loss in the unit where the reserve is established, and there must be a good reason to reduce them. The transfer would violate those rules, the accountants believed, because there was no business reason for depleting the reserve account.

"Ms. Vinson and Mr. Normand told their boss that the transfer wasn't good accounting, according to a person close to Ms. Vinson. Mr. Yates replied that he wasn't happy about it either. But he said that Mr. Myers had assured him that it would never happen again and that he had agreed to go along. Finally, so did Ms. Vinson and Mr. Normand. They made the transfer."[29]

IN WORLDCOM, AS IN ENRON, securities fraud was initiated at the highest levels of management. Accounting fraud was a result of this. At first, WorldCom may seem less egregious because, as we have seen, Andersen actively collaborated with Enron in designing its ultimately fraudulent use of off-balance sheet entities. External auditors in the WorldCom case, in contrast, were kept in the dark. Yet in WorldCom one sees a lapse in professional responsibility that, taken altogether, seems equally grave. How is it that Andersen was able to issue an unqualified audit

---

[29] From: "Over the Line: A Staffer Ordered To Commit Fraud Balked, Then Caved —- Pushed by WorldCom Bosses, Accountant Betty Vinson Helped Cook the Books —- A Confession at the Marriott By Susan Pulliam." *Wall Street Journal*. (Eastern edition). New York, N.Y.: Jun 23, 2003. pg. A.1.

report for WorldCom, when it was consistently denied access to the company's General Ledger? How is it that many CPAs internal to the company assisted management in committing fraud with very little protest or complaint? If Enron presents us with a failure of objectivity and independence, WorldCom shows a similarly serious failure in integrity and professionalism.

History of WorldCom and Its Business

"Bernie was out of his league," a telecom executive from the deep South commented after the precipitous fall of WorldCom. "He wasn't qualified to be the CEO of a global telecom company. You can try to spin it any way you want, but the bottom line is that he's a peddler. He likes to peddle and make deals...." The executive added:

> He didn't surround himself with good people to run the company. He personally couldn't do it. He was more intrigued with more mergers, more acquisitions, and more deals than he was with actually making money. They're just fortunate they experienced a period that we all did in our industry of "crazy money," that 1995-2000 time-frame where even idiots could make money. You didn't have to outsmart the other guys. You didn't have to be that good. When that counted and mattered, people started falling left and right. WorldCom was no exception.[30]

This comment summarizes the nature of WorldCom's business and the key to its phenomenal growth. WorldCom was, so to speak, the breakup of AT&T but in reverse. In 1983, Judge Harold H. Greene ordered the breakup of AT&T, then the world's largest corporation. A condition of the breakup was that AT&T make available for lease its long-distance lines at substantial discounts. Entrepreneurs immediately saw the potential to make money quickly. Among these was a group of nine investors from Mississippi, including Bernie Ebbers, who started Long Distance Discount Services. Ebbers, with a net worth then of about $2 million from a hotel business, had formerly been employed as a milkman, bartender, bar bouncer, car salesman, truck driver, garment factory foreman, and high school basketball coach. Ebbers and the others were drawn to the argument of Murray Waldron, one of the original nine:

> If, for example, a customer could be charged $1 for a 50-cent phone call, and a simple piece of switching equipment required for routing the calls could handle 40 calls at once, the potential to make $20 a minute was

---

[30] Jeter, L.W.: 2003, *Disconnected: Deceit and Betrayal at WorldCom*, (John Wiley & Sons, Inc, Hoboken, NJ), p. 161.

extremely alluring. Using that example, if the switcher was maxed out around the clock, a phone company could make $28,800 a day, just for starters.[31]

Of course other investors had the same idea, creating a competitive environment which pushed down prices. It became clear to Ebbers and his associates that success required that they quickly attain economies of scale. This required in turn the purchase of increasingly more expensive switching equipment, to provide service for large clients, such as business and public agencies. The strategy that eventually worked was acquisition and merger, underwritten by stock value after the company went public with the acquisition of Advantage Companies, a NASDAQ listed company, in 1989.

Deal-making was a great strength of Ebbers, who was elected CEO of LDDS in 1985. Ebbers put the company in the black and increased revenues to almost $100 million within three years:

> He had learned a very simple acquisition formula that guaranteed success. A reseller who was interested in selling to LDDS called the office and was faxed a short questionnaire, requesting a financial statement and a few other items. "We could look at it in no time and decide what we could pay," said a former LDDS accountant. "If his revenue was good and he was priced right, paying him six times annual revenues for his company was standard. The best he could get on his own was three or four multiples. We got to take, say, 12 times revenue off our next quarter's bottom line. It was a beautiful deal. And we found people like that all day long." [32]

Larger LDDS acquisitions in the early 1990s included Mid-American Communications, AmeriCall, FirstPhone, Advanced Telephone ($850 million), World Communications, Dial-Net, TRT, and Metromedia together with Resurgens ($1.25 billion). By now the company was called WorldCom and it was poised for truly phenomenal growth, with a series of major acquisitions and mergers. Then WorldCom acquired Williams Telecom (1995, $2.5 billion), MFS (1996, $12.4 billion), MCI (1998, $40 billion), and Intermedia (2001, $6 billion).

WorldCom's growth came to an end with the sagging of the telecom industry, its loss of customers through the bursting of the dot.com bubble, and, perhaps most importantly, its failed merger with Sprint. "The kiboshing of the Sprint merger was, for all intents and purposes, the end of WorldCom," remarked accounting

---

[31] Ibid, p. xxiv.

[32] Ibid, p. 42.

watchdog Howard J. Schilit, "When you have companies that have to make acquisitions to survive, once the music stops, the dance is over."

In early 2002, WorldCom, with 60,000 employees, was reporting $30 billion in revenues and $104 billion in assets. But troubles were breaking out. In the wake of the failed Sprint merger, its stock price kept falling. In March, the SEC launched an investigation into alleged business improprieties. In May an article entitled, "Accounting for Anguish" appeared in the *Fort Worth Weekly* about Kim Emigh, who alleged that he was laid off from his job with WorldCom because he complained about shady financial practices, such as the company's decision in November 2001 not to pay vendors for the rest of the year, and the improper re-classification of labor in capital projects as an operating expense. The article included this prescient paragraph:

> "The larger picture for WorldCom and MCI is that they are in a business that is in trouble and getting worse," said Pat Brogan, a telecom analyst with the Precursor Group, an investor-side research firm. "The economics of the industry are miserable. The spotlight being shined on its accounting practices is putting a drag on the industry. A lot of the growth and hype that was surging the industry in the late '90s may have been fueled by accounting practices."[33]

Ebbers resigned as CEO in April 2002 and was succeeded by John Sidgmore. In early June, internal auditor Cynthia Cooper presented to the WorldCom audit committee evidence of widespread accounting fraud perpetrated by management. WorldCom stock dropped soon thereafter to pennies per share. Various state and federal criminal probes were launched. Finally, WorldCom filed for Chapter 11 bankruptcy protection on July 21, 2002. Many of its executives and several internal accountants were indicted. Its external auditor, Andersen, by that point had ceased to exist. On the Ides of March in 2005, Bernie Ebbers was convicted of securities fraud, conspiracy, and false filings. The following day, the *Wall Street Journal* in its editorial pages opined that Ebbers' conviction might prove more salutary for corporate accounting than the entire apparatus of Sarbanes-Oxley regulation.

It was an astonishing spectacle—WorldCom's phenomenal rise and even faster fall, all within 20 years from the time that Ebbers and his friends put up $600,000 to start LDDS. That WorldCom's business would slow down was inevitable, and that its stock price had to sag was understandable. But that the company would crash

---

[33] Reaves, G.: 2002, "Accounting for Anguish", *Fort Worth Weekly*, May 16, 2002, available at *Fort Worth Weekly Online*, http://www.fwweekly.com/issues/2002-05-16/feature.html /page1.html.

and burn as it did, with substantial harm to investors and the nation's economy, was unnecessary, and purely the result of dishonesty, misrepresentation, and accounting malfeasance.

The Nature of the Fraud

WorldCom's fraud was designed to boost reported revenues in a depressed telecom market, so that the company might appear to satisfy a 42% "line cost expenditure to revenue" (E/R) ratio set down as a criterion by industry analysts.

As we have seen, in the competitive telecom market of the late 1990s, companies such as WorldCom thrived by exploiting economies of scale that came from more extensive access to telecommunications lines through leasing—so-called "line costs." This strategy of expansion worked well so long as demand was increasing. Once demand fell, however, WorldCom and its competitors found themselves in a dilemma. On the one hand, they could not extricate themselves from these leases, which involved punitive termination fees. On the other hand, industry analysts judged that the stock of a telecom company such as WorldCom would remain a good investment only so long as it maintained the E/R ratio that it showed in 2000, before the deterioration of the telecom market.

This was an industry-wide dilemma, not peculiar to WorldCom. It is important to stress this, because sometimes one might suppose that WorldCom's fraud constituted a harm principally against its own employees and investors in WorldCom stock. But the fraud was equally a harm against—because an unfair advantage relative to—the company's competitors, which for the most part faced the same difficulties as WorldCom, but which did not avail themselves of dishonest means. Admittedly, WorldCom was probably less able to deal with the difficulties than many of its competitors. Because it had acquired so many companies so quickly, it lacked good internal organization: it had to try to harmonize, for instance, dozens of different billing procedures and price plans. Furthermore, the main reason for its success never was good telecom business practice, but rather, as we have seen, a shrewd strategy of rolling up other companies.

The effort to maintain a 42% E/R ratio in a down market placed WorldCom employees at every level under tremendous pressure:

> WorldCom marketed itself as a high-growth company, and revenue growth was clearly a critical component of WorldCom's early success. As market conditions throughout the telecommunications industry deteriorated in 2000 and 2001, WorldCom nevertheless continued to post impressive revenue growth numbers, and Ebbers and [CFO Scott] Sullivan continued to assure Wall Street that WorldCom could sustain that level of growth. In essence, WorldCom claimed it was successfully

managing industry trends that were hurting all of its competitors. These promises of double-digit growth translated into pressure within WorldCom to achieve those results. As one officer told us, the emphasis on revenue was "in every brick in every building." [34]

This intense pressure to boost reported revenue would help to explain the dubious practices that Kim Emigh complained about. It also led WorldCom management and some employees to commit or be complicit in serious fraud.

WorldCom sustained its 42% E/R ratio through a series of fraudulent or questionable practices: the improper release of accruals (2Q 1999 through 2000); one time, top-side entries of undocumented revenue, recorded as "unallocated corporate" revenue (beginning 4Q 1999); a "close the gap" approach to day-to-day accounting decisions (beginning 2Q of 2001-through 2002); and finally, and most audaciously, the capitalization of line costs (beginning 3Q 2000):

How WorldCom Kept a 42% E/R Ratio
1. Improper release of accruals.
2. One time, top-side entries.
3. A daily "close the gap" approach to accounting.
4. Capitalization of line costs.

Accruals, or revenue set aside to cover anticipated costs, were important for WorldCom's business. WorldCom was typically billed months afterwards for leased lines that it was utilizing for business and revenue. Funds sufficient to make these payments would therefore be put aside in accrual accounts and counted toward line costs. It would be proper to release these funds, only if they were not needed to cover definite future expenses. From early 1999 until late 2000, at the direction of WorldCom CFO Sullivan and David Myers, the company Controller, approximately $3.3 billion was released improperly from accrual funds. Note that the effect of a release of accruals is to decrease line costs and to increase revenue correspondingly, thus shoring up the E/R ratio.

The improper releases of accruals had several features in common. They were directed by senior members of the corporate finance organization. They did not occur in the normal course of day-to-day operations, but instead in the weeks following the end of the quarter in question. The timing and amounts of the releases were not supported by contemporaneous analysis or documentation. Most significantly,

---

[34] Dennis R. Beresford, Nicholas de B. Katzenbach, and C. B. Rogers, Jr.: 2003, "Report of Investigation", Special Investigative Committee of the Board of Directors of WorldCom, Inc..

WorldCom employees involved in the releases generally understood at the time that they were improper. Some even raised concerns at the time of the releases.[35]

WorldCom's improper release of accruals was fraudulent, because it is impossible to use funds properly dedicated to line costs to "pay down" line costs.

WorldCom's second fraudulent tactic lacked any finesse: increase the revenue of your company, simply by writing in numbers on your ledger as income:

> Beginning in 1999, WorldCom personnel made large revenue accounting entries after the close of many quarters in order to report that it had achieved the high revenue targets that Ebbers and Sullivan had established. Most of the questionable revenue entries were booked to "Corporate Unallocated" revenue accounts....The questionable revenue entries included in Corporate Unallocated often involved large, round-dollar revenue items (in millions or tens of millions of dollars). They generally appeared only in the quarter-ending month, and they were not recorded during the quarter, but instead in the weeks after the quarter had ended.[36]

Apparently WorldCom booked almost $2 billion of "income" in this manner in 1999-2000. (If Ebbers had been able to make money like that in 1983, there would have been no need for all the trouble of starting a company.) Eventually Sullivan seems to have become concerned by how freely they were relying on this method to "make the numbers," as evidenced in this voice message he left for Ebbers:

> "Hey Bernie, it's Scott. This MonRev [monthly revenue report] just keeps getting worse and worse. The copy, um the latest copy that you and I have already, has accounting fluff in it ...all one time stuff or junk that's already in the numbers. With the numbers being, you know, off as far as they were, I didn't think that this stuff was already in there...We are going to dig ourselves into a huge hole because year to date it's disguising what is going on on the recurring, uh, service side of the business...[37]

What Sullivan's message reveals is that, once they had resorted to lying on a single occasion, it became easy for them to do so repeatedly, so that they now actually had to rely on lying ("stuff or junk" in revenue statements). It wasn't long before they were just as badly off, after the lies were already factored in (the "stuff or junk" is

---

[35] Ibid., p. 65.

[36] Ibid., pp. 13-14.

[37] Ibid., p. 15.

"already in the numbers"), than they were before, when they were not telling lies. Note too that Sullivan apparently engages in the self-deceit that this dishonesty is only a short-term matter, which they will eventually compensate for: he refers to the unjustified entries as a "hole" which, presumably, they will eventually "fill in" with legitimate income. Finally, note Sullivan's concern that their reliance on deceit now makes it less necessary for them to remedy the poor business practices which the deceit was originally meant to compensate for. (When he refers to "what is going on, on the recurring, uh, service side of the business," he means the telecom business, of course.)

The third questionable accounting practice was referred to within WorldCom as "Close the Gap." Here's how it worked:

> Throughout much of 2001, WorldCom's Business Operations and Revenue Accounting groups tracked the difference between projected and target revenue and kept a running tally of accounting "opportunities" that could be exploited to bridge that gap. What emerged was a coordinated and institutionalized process in which revenue "opportunities" were identified, measured and booked in the amount needed to hit the Company's external growth projections. [38]

This is an excellent example of the manipulation and exploitation of accounting rules in order to represent a company's condition in the way that the management wants it to be represented, regardless of whether this gives a fair or true picture ("form over substance"), rather than letting principles control the use of accounting rules, so that those rules serve as constraints and correctives ("substance over form"). The result is determined not with a view to truthfulness and fair presentation, but with a view to targets and interests set from the outside. The "Close the Gap" program seems to have been responsible for constructing about a billion dollars of questionable revenue.

The fourth and most egregious accounting malfeasance at WorldCom, however, was its shift in 2001 to capitalizing line costs. Of course a lease can sometimes be treated as an operating expense and sometimes as an expenditure on capital. Also, there can be close calls, and the relevant principle is, roughly, that a lease can be capitalized if, in leasing the item, one assumes in substance the benefits, risks, and burdens of ownership. The lease of a telecommunications line is clearly not like that, and therefore it must be treated as an operating expense, as indeed all telecom companies besides WorldCom were doing, and as WorldCom itself was doing, until, curiously enough, faced with extreme business pressures—

---

[38] Ibid., p. 14.

and all accrual accounts had been depleted—Sullivan and Ebbers came to the sudden realization that a different accounting treatment would then be warranted.

It would be very *favorable* to WorldCom if line costs could reasonably be capitalized: this would have the effect of decreasing line costs (which are operating expenses) and therefore the E/R ratio, and, correspondingly, increasing the company's assets. How extensive was WorldCom's reliance on this hoax? The Table 6-1 below from the SEC complaint against two of the accountants who made the illicit entries tells the tale.

WorldCom's False Statements in Filings with the SEC Third Quarter 2000 Through First Quarter 2002[39]				
Form Filed With the Commission	Reported Line Cost Expenses	Actual Line Cost Expenses	Reported Income before Taxes and Minority Interests	Actual Income (Loss) before Taxes and Minority Interests
10-Q, 3rd Qtr 2000	$3.867 billion	$4.695 billion	$1.736 billion	$908 million
10-K, 2000	$15.462 billion	$16.697 billion	$7.568 billion	$6.333 billion
10-Q, 1st Qtr 2001	$4.108 billion	$4.879 billion	$988 million	$217 million
10-Q, 2nd Qtr 2001	$3.73 billion	$4.29 billion	$159 million	($401 million)
10-Q, 3rd Qtr 2001	$3.745 billion	$4.488 billion	$845 million	$102 million
10-K, 2001	$14.739 billion	$17.754 billion	$2.393 billion	($622 million)
10-Q, 1st Qtr 2002	$3.479 billion	$4.297 billion	$240 million	($578 million)

Let us call a "disinterested judgment" a decision we reach when there are no reasons of self-interest to decide one way or another. Let us call an "interested judgment" a decision we reach, when there are pressures or incentives to decide in a certain way, and we happen to decide in the way that matches our self-interest. In July 2000, an internal accountant for WorldCom, Tony Minert, CPA, who had been given the task of looking into the reduction of line costs, floated a proposal to Sullivan and Myers:

> I have been making some phone calls trying to find out why our cost[s] are increasing for this quarter and from what I am gathering it sounds like we are starting to get a network out there that has a lot of extra capacity...If we could somehow take that...underutilized network...into an inventory or prepaid account and only booked it as expense when we have the revenue to match it, then this might help with our e/r numbers. I

---

[39] Source: United States District Court for the Southern District of New York 02 CV 8083 (JSR) COMPLAINT (Securities Fraud) *Securities and Exchange Commission, Plaintiff, v. BETTY L. VINSON, and TROY M. NORMAND, Defendants.*

would think that our cost would be at a 42% e/r. ...I am definitely going to go down this alley because this would help out our cause tremendously, and I have got to think that there is something we could do.[40]

In July 2000 accrual accounts had not yet been depleted, and "Corporate Unallocated" revenues were working well enough. In these circumstances, where there were yet no self-interested reasons for deciding one way or another, Myers and Yates considered Minert's idea of capitalizing the network's unused capacity and, rendering a disinterested judgment, quickly rejected it as unsupportable under GAAP. After Minert raised the issue several more times in July, Yates wrote to Myers: "David, I might be narrow minded, but I can't see a logical path for capitalizing excess capacity. Your thoughts?" Myers agreed. Yates informed Minert that his idea had no accounting support: "Tony, David [Myers] and I have reviewed and discussed your logic of capitalizing excess capacity and can find no support within current accounting guidelines that would allow for this accounting treatment."

However, within a few months Scott Sullivan had decided that line costs for underutilized lines *should* be capitalized, and he directed that entries be made accordingly, in the amounts listed in Table 6-1. That Sullivan's judgment was "interested" and not made in good faith is clear for five reasons.

1. Sullivan had no plausible argument for that change in accounting treatment. When the fraud was discovered in the summer of 2002 by Cynthia Cooper, and the WorldCom Audit Committee asked Sullivan to give a justification, the two-page "White Paper" that he wrote for them explaining the practice was entirely ad hoc, citing irrelevant accounting rules, and containing no remotely plausible arguments.

2. The adjustments to line costs and balance sheets mandated by Sullivan bore no relation to actual underutilized capacity but were exactly what was needed to meet the 42% E/R criterion.

3. The capitalizations were not placed in their proper categories but distributed randomly throughout the balance sheet, as if to hide the fact.

4. Sullivan never discussed the change of accounting treatment with the external auditors, as would be usual with a judgment call made in good faith.

---

[40] Ibid., p. 98.

5. If the accounting change had been introduced in good faith, then presumably it would have been disclosed openly in public filings, but it wasn't. [41]

People usually do not act dishonestly unless there is some patina of justification, some stretch of a plausible argument, which rationalizes what they are doing. The capitalization of line costs, which as if by magic converts an expense into an asset, looks so ludicrous, that one wonders how it might in any way have appeared justifiable. We suggest that an underlying fallacy was at work. Recall once again that a lease can be capitalized if, through the lease, one assumes the burdens and risks of ownership. WorldCom was certainly burdened by the transmission lines it had leased but was not utilizing, and one might feel that the burden was analogous at least to the burden of an asset that one purchases for use on a future date: for instance, Jones purchases in the summer a snow blower that is on sale at a good price, since he anticipates using it in the winter, and in the meantime he has the burden of owning it (that is, he assumes the costs of storage, insurance, depreciation, and so on). But the analogy fails, because a burden devolved upon WorldCom not because of the leased lines, but because of their (mistaken, overly optimistic) decision to lease the lines in advance of demand. Suppose Jones buys 10 snow-blowers, because he expects a hard winter, and he wants to start a small snow-removal business, but it turns out to be a mild winter, and he can make use of only one. Then he has two distinct burdens: (i) the burden of storing and insuring, etc., so many snow blowers, and (ii) the "burden" on his resources of having committed (as it turns out mistakenly) so much capital to acquiring snow-blowers. The second burden is a consequence of a mistaken judgment, not ownership, and that is the sort of burden that WorldCom had to bear in connection with unused lines. It is a fallacy to mistake that for the burden of ownership.

But one might wonder still about the entire policy of fraud adopted by WorldCom's executives. Could they not see that they were being dishonest, through and through? And how could they dare to do what they did, if they saw it squarely as fraudulent? But we may speculate that they thought their desperate steps were for a good cause. In the preceding chapter, we noted that Enron actually had the salient characteristics of a Ponzi scheme: Enron's core businesses in the 1990s became unimportant compared with its energy futures trading. That business, because of its success, fostered unrealistic investor confidence and resulted in Ponzi-like structures and incentives. In a Ponzi scheme, there is no real business, and income derives rather from growth, that is, from signing on new customers, who pay in advance in expectation of a service or return. A Ponzi

---

[41] Beresford et al, p. 98.

scheme by its nature requires growth; it cannot sustain itself in the absence of growth. Moreover, we saw that, in such an arrangement, the very expectation of growth ends up being essential to growth, and the fostering of that expectation becomes essential to the business. Enron was like that, which helps to explain why, in such circumstances, its management might have come to think of fraud as a positive good. Fraud (it can appear) will actually benefit employees and investors, on the grounds that it preserves the expectation of success that is essential to the company's success. Moreover, management can successfully fool itself that the fraud is only a temporary expedient, useful for getting a company through a slow period, until the company can resume once more its successful strategy of growth.

WorldCom, because its explosive growth came from mergers and acquisitions, not from its core business, similarly developed something of a Ponzi-structure. Its continued success depended upon continued expansion; but that depended upon acquisitions; but that required a strong stock price; but that in turn required the expectation of continued success. "It seems clear that WorldCom's ability to borrow monies was facilitated by its massive accounting fraud," according to Richard Thornburgh, "which allowed the Company to falsely present itself as creditworthy and 'investment grade.' It also seems clear that the Company's ability to borrow vast sums allowed it to perpetuate the illusion of financial health created by its accounting fraud." In these circumstances, it would be natural for WorldCom management, when faced with what, for all they knew, was a brief downturn in the telecom market, to try to prop up or puff up expectations, until the market strengthened and the company could resume its earlier pattern of success. Fraud would appear an unpleasant expedient, necessary only for the short-term, which in the long run would benefit thousands of employees and millions of investors, not to mention the local economy.

Ebbers presented a substantially false picture to the market, to the Board of Directors, and to most of the Company's own employees. At the same time that he was projecting, and then reporting, continued vigorous growth, he was receiving internal information that was increasingly inconsistent with those projections and reports. Moreover, he did not disclose the persistent use of non-recurring items to boost reported revenues. Ebbers was aware, at a minimum, that WorldCom was meeting revenue expectations through financial gimmickry. Yet he kept making unrealistic promises, and failed to disclose the existence of these devices or their magnitude.

The Complicity of Internal Accountants

One sees a kind of fool's parade of accounting tricks carried out by WorldCom management over a period of roughly three years, and this in circumstances which should have prompted suspicion, since it was puzzling that WorldCom should continue to achieve double-digit revenue growth, when all the other telecoms were barely avoiding losses. What role did accountants play in this? Why did internal auditors fail to detect the fraud? Why were internal accountants complicit? How did a fraud of this magnitude, and which lacked the complexity of Enron's SPEs, escape detection by Andersen, WorldCom's external auditors? We might speculate that not a few internal accountants in WorldCom were aware of the disparity between Ebbers' representations to the market and the internal picture of the company. How did they understand their own role as regards these misrepresentations?

The WorldCom scandal was made possible because some accountants failed to live the virtues of accountancy, and failed to adhere to the principles and ideals of their profession. Worse than this: Ebbers, Sullivan, and Myers presumed that it would be so. Even in a post-Enron environment, they acted on the presumption that the accountants whose cooperation they needed to perpetrate their fraud would not oppose them (at the price of losing their jobs), or would turn a blind eye, or would even assist them—and, sad to say, they were proved right in this. Let us consider in turn the internal accountants, external auditors, and internal auditors of WorldCom.

How *should* internal accountants have acted at WorldCom? The answer is that they should have refused from the start to cooperate with accounting practices that had even the appearance of deceit or impropriety, even if this implied the loss of their jobs—just as we expect policemen, firefighters or physicians to carry out their professional obligations even if that implies personal risk. Moreover, they should have been prepared to do so as a "united front," so that it would have seemed hopeless to Sullivan or Ebbers that they could ever induce members of the accounting profession to "budge" from the highest standards.

An excellent although extreme example of that kind of professionalism is found in the actions of the physicians of Holland under the Nazi occupation in World War II. Their heroic stance is described in a classic study of the failure of professionalism in German medicine, Dr. Leo Alexander's "Medicine Under Dictatorship," first published in the *New England Journal of Medicine*, July 14, 1949, pp. 39-47. Dr. Alexander writes the following:

> There is no doubt that in Germany itself the first and most effective step of propaganda within the medical profession was the propaganda barrage against the useless, incurably sick... Similar, even more subtle efforts were made in some of the occupied countries. It is to the everlasting honor of the medical profession of Holland that they recognized the earliest and most subtle phases of this attempt and rejected

it. When Sciss-Inquart, Reich Commissar for the Occupied Netherlands Territories, wanted to draw the Dutch physicians into the orbit of the activities of the German medical profession, he did not tell them "You must send your chronic patients to death factories" or "You must give lethal injections at Government request in your offices," but he couched his order in most careful and superficially acceptable terms. One of the paragraphs in the order of the Reich Commissar of the Netherlands Territories concerning the Netherlands doctors of 19 December 1941 reads as follows: "It is the duty of the doctor, through advice and effort, conscientiously and to his best ability, to assist as helper the person entrusted to his care in the maintenance, improvement and re-establishment of his vitality, physical efficiency and health. The accomplishment of this duty is a public task."

Without exception, the physicians of Holland refused to obey this order. They understood what it really meant. Despite the superficial appearance of being a mere bureaucratic formality, the order implied that physicians were to become subordinate to the utilitarian purposes of the state, by rehabilitating the sick for useful labor. It also encroached upon the relationship of trust between patient and physician, violating confidentiality. Sciss-Inquart in retaliation threatened to revoke their licenses. The Dutch physicians, in their turn, subsequently mailed in their licenses and unilaterally took down their shingles. They continued to see patients privately, in secret, but no longer wrote birth or death certificates. Sciss-Inquart saw his mistake and tried to persuade them gently, to no avail. Losing his patience, he tried the harsh step of arresting 100 Dutch physicians and sending them to concentration camps, to teach a lesson. But this step likewise had no effect:

> The medical profession remained adamant and quietly took care of their widows and orphans, but would not give in.
>
> Thus it came about that not a single euthanasia or non-therapeutic sterilization was recommended or participated in by any Dutch physician. They had the foresight to resist before the first step was taken, and they acted unanimously and won out in the end. It is obvious that if the medical profession of a small nation under the conqueror's heel could resist so effectively, the German medical profession could likewise have resisted had they not taken the fatal first step. It is the first seemingly innocent step away from principle that frequently decides a career of crime. Corrosion begins in microscopic proportions.

The Dutch physicians, and their shrewd resistance to subterfuge, even to the point of death, serve as an example of professionalism at its best. In this connection, it is important to remind ourselves that fraud at WorldCom was carried out with the assistance of many accountants. And one might reasonably presume that, for these accountants likewise, the first, small step of compromise was the fatal step:

> Awareness of this financial fraud was not confined to just two or three people. Others at WorldCom either knew or suspected that senior financial management was engaged in improper accounting. These included not only people in the General Accounting group…who ordered or implemented the entries, but people in other financial reporting and accounting groups whose responsibilities were affected by them. Employees in several such groups suggested, made or knew of entries that were not supportable, or prepared reports that were false or misleading as a consequence. Remarkably these employees frequently did not raise any objections despite their awareness or suspicions that the accounting was wrong, and simply followed directions or even enlisted the assistance of others. Some of them complained to their supervisors or, in a handful of cases, refused to take actions they considered inappropriate. However, none took effective action to try to halt or expose these practices until the Spring of 2002. Employees in the financial and accounting groups believed that forcefully objecting to conduct that they knew was being directed by Sullivan would cost them their jobs; few of them were prepared to take that risk.[42]

Admittedly, because of the byzantine organizational structure of WorldCom, it was possible for supervisors to deflect concerns about undocumented entries. More than one employee described WorldCom as a series of isolated "silos" where each group knew and understood its own costs and revenues but had no knowledge about other groups and never shared information with the others. When employees raised concerns about reductions of their accruals or other apparent misconduct, senior management could always—and frequently did—say that the issue was resolved and acceptable at the consolidated, total company level. Ebbers and Sullivan no doubt benefited, too, from the principle of the "big lie," namely, if a lie is outlandish enough, no one will believe that you are lying, because it would seem too easy for the lie to be found out. Yet, on the whole, WorldCom accountants were "simply following orders," so to speak, and they did what they were told, not even bothering to consider whether what they were asked to do met standards of

---

[42] Beresford et al., p. 7.

truthfulness and integrity: "Many, even those with accounting degrees and CPA designations, told us that they viewed their job as simply entering numbers."[43]

People usually need to employ euphemisms to hide misconduct from themselves. For instance, as mentioned, there was a ripple effect that resulted from the imposition by highest management of the capitalized line costs: "The accounting entries necessary to shift line costs to capital accounts were relatively simple for the General Accounting group to make, but they had ripple effects in other areas of the Company." Property Accounting, in charge of expenditures, and Capital Reporting, responsible for tracking assets, had to reconcile their books as regards these "capital assets" that unaccountably were added to their inventory, as they did for authorized and reported acquisitions. They euphemistically referred to these dubious adjustments as "non-cash adjustments": "Employees in those two groups described regular conversations about the capitalization entries, which they called 'non-cash adjustments'."[44]

The Failure of the External Auditor

Andersen as the external auditor apparently failed as regards independence and due-diligence. It might be thought that the latter followed from the former.

Andersen's doubtful independence is evident in language the firm used to describe its relationship to WorldCom:

> Andersen told the [WorldCom] Audit Committee in its Year 2000 Audit Proposal that it understood the business issues and risks associated with WorldCom's operations, and that it considered itself "a committed member of [WorldCom's] team." …Indeed, in a presentation to the Audit Committee on May 20, 1999, Andersen stated that it viewed its relationship with WorldCom as a "long-term partnership," in which Andersen would help WorldCom improve its business operations and grow in the future.[45]

Needless to say, "partnership" and "team member" are phrases suggestive of an advocacy or collaborative role, and are inappropriate to the position of an independent auditor, which has a responsibility to render objective judgment in the service of the public interest. This language and outlook was mirrored in the close business relationship of Andersen with WorldCom: from 1999 to 2000 WorldCom

---

[43] Ibid.

[44] Ibid., p. 104.

[45] Ibid., pp. 223-4.

paid Andersen $7.8 million in audit fees but about $50 million for other services, including tax services and consulting.

In its presentations to the WorldCom Audit Committee, Andersen stated explicitly that it would not use a "traditional audit approach" which would involve verifying the information on accounting records and financial statements, and a focus on account balances. Rather, Andersen told the Audit Committee that it would provide a new kind of audit, a "controls-based" or "risk-based" approach. Such an approach depends heavily on internal controls, the reliability of which is the responsibility of management. In fact Andersen requested from management the same 20 to 30 schedules each quarter, a predictability which would make its work especially vulnerable to manipulation by management.

Andersen failed to cultivate an appropriate attitude of skepticism about WorldCom management. They used software which gave the result that WorldCom was only a "high" risk client. Andersen partners overrode this result and rated WorldCom as "maximum" risk. Yet Andersen failed to take the steps that the firm required for maximum risk clients, and they failed to inform the Audit Committee that they regarded WorldCom in this light. In their audit of the highly relevant area of capital expenditure,

> Andersen's auditing methodology was in large part premised on the assumption that capital expenditures would arise through proper means—specific capital projects that could be tracked—and, based on the work papers, does not appear to have implemented any procedures to address the possibility that they would be created through accounting fraud.[46]

In a June 2001 "fraud brainstorming" session, Andersen auditors met to discuss possible problem areas regarding WorldCom. They specifically identified improper capitalization and top-side adjustments as issues to be concerned about for WorldCom. Yet the firm apparently took no special steps to test these areas.

Andersen repeatedly asked to be able to examine the General Ledger of the company, and their request was uniformly denied. Of course, had they been able to examine the General Ledger, they would likely have quickly discovered the sizeable, whole number top-side entries. One might wonder how they could have issued an unqualified audit report on WorldCom without access to the General Ledger.

Andersen also overlooked tips and clues which, if interpreted with an appropriate concern over fraud, might conceivably had led them to detect the WorldCom accounting irregularities. For instance, in October 2000 a WorldCom

---

[46] Ibid., p. 225.

employee told Andersen UK that, over his protestations, he was required by a US WorldCom office to release, without documentation or explanation, an accrual to the amount of $33.6 million dollars, as a result of which he regarded himself as underaccrued. Andersen UK reported the matter to Andersen's WorldCom engagement team, which apparently failed to follow up on the matter, having accepted a WorldCom executive's cursory explanation as satisfactory.

The Internal Auditor

Internal auditing at WorldCom reported directly to Scott Sullivan, the mastermind of the frauds, and thus we may suspect, as was indeed the case, that their activities were directed by Sullivan in such a way as to keep them from discovering anything that might alert them to the fraud. And because they reported directly to Sullivan, employees who saw something doubtful or suspicious would be reluctant to approach them.

Internal audit is the closest thing to a hero in the WorldCom decline. The story was told in major media, and Cynthia Cooper, head of internal audit, became something of a celebrity, even being named a *Time Magazine* Person of the Year for 2002. Cooper and some colleagues in May and June of 2002 pressed forward with an audit of Capital Expenditures, downloading data late at night to avoid raising suspicions. Once they gained access to the General Ledger, they quickly identified the large, round number capitalization entries. When they approached Myers about them, who said he could give no justification, they went to the audit Committee, and that is how the WorldCom fraud came to light.

And yet even internal audit is not an unblemished hero. Internal audit had commenced a Capital Expenditures Audit the preceding year, in December 2001. In the course of the audit, they sought information from Capital Reporting. The employees there, who knew all about "non-cash adjustments," were unsure what to do. Should they include these adjustments in what they sent to internal audit or not? (Needless to say, they should not have hesitated to inform internal audit about them.) By some fluke or mistake, the "non-cash adjustments" were included. These totaled $2.3 billion dollars, under the heading "Corporate"! (Compare: during the same time period, WorldCom's entire expenditures on telecommunications equipment was only slightly more, at $2.9 billion.) Internal audit asked for an explanation ("Just so I have an answer," an internal audit Manager wrote, "What kinds of projects make up the bulk of Corporate?"); apparently what they heard satisfied them; and in their final report the $2.3 billion is simply omitted. Thus internal audit failed to follow up on a big clue that, by some fluke, was placed directly in their path.

Conclusion

If Enron, with its complicated system of SPEs, is a failure in ethics of accountants working at a very high level of technical expertise—"the smartest guys in the room"—WorldCom provides a sobering example of how massive fraud may be perpetrated when ordinary practitioners lose sight of professionalism, and of the sacrifice of self-interest that true professionalism sometimes requires, and instead they excuse their own complicity in fraud on the grounds that they were "following the rules."

Epilogue

Bernie Ebbers was sentenced on September 22, 2005 to 25 years in Federal prison for securities fraud, conspiracy and filing false documents with regulators. At his trial, his lawyers argued that accounting fraud at WorldCom was masterminded by Scott Sullivan and that Ebbers was ignorant of the details. But the jury was convinced rather by the prosecutors' arguments, that Ebbers was a proven hands-on manager, fabled for his attention to cost-saving details, who could not have been ignorant of such a massive fraud, and that Ebbers had a motive to uphold the WorldCom share price, because most of his own wealth was tied up in WorldCom stock. Ebbers is currently serving his sentence in a Louisiana prison and is likely to die in jail.

Scott Sullivan turned state's witness against Ebbers and, although the judge acknowledged that Sullivan was the chief architect of the fraud, was rewarded with a relatively light sentence of only five years. "Mr. Sullivan's offenses were of the highest magnitude," the judge said, but "his cooperation was the key factor in the case of Mr. Ebbers, without which Mr. Ebbers likely would not have been indicted much less convicted."

David Myers and Buford Yates were each sentenced to one year in prison. Betty Vinson, an accounting department manager, was sentenced to five months in prison, and five months of house arrest.

Cynthia Cooper, after being voted a *Time Magazine* person of the year in 2002, has served as an advisor to the PCAOB and is a sought-after public speaker.

Recommended additional reading:

Alexander, Dr. L.: 1949, "Medicine Under Dictatorship," *New England Journal of Medicine*, July 14.

Beresford, D.R, and N.B. Katzenbach, and C. B. Rogers, Jr.: 2003, "Report of Investigation," Special Investigative Committee of the Board of Directors of WorldCom, Inc., March 31.

Kaplan, R.S., and D. Kiron: 2004,"Accounting Fraud at WorldCom," *Harvard Business School case study*, 9-104-071, July 26.

United States District Court for the Southern District of New York 02 CV 8083 (JSR) COMPLAINT (Securities Fraud) Securities and Exchange Commission, Plaintiff, v. BETTY L. VINSON, and TROY M. NORMAND, Defendants.

Lehman Bros:

What If the Principles Are Misguided?

13

"These transactions are well understood in the marketplace as financing arrangements, and the existing financial reporting of them as financing transactions has served users of financial statements well."—Ernst & Young, comment on SFAS 125 exposure draft, January 1996

"The Board determined that the criterion pertaining to an exchange of collateral should not be a determining factor of effective control. The Board believes that the assessment of effective control should focus on a transferor's contractual rights and obligations with respect to transferred financial assets, not on whether the transferor has the practical ability, by way of a collateral maintenance agreement, to exercise those rights or honor those obligations."—FASB, exposure draft amendment of SFAS 140, March 2011

THE ENRON AND WORLDCOM SCANDALS, discussed in the two previous chapters, led to the passage of the 2002 Sarbanes-Oxley Act and increased attention to the priority of principles over rules. But what are an accountant's professional responsibilities if the principles themselves seem to be misguided, or if an accounting standard itself seems to promote a purely rules-based approach? The case presented in this chapter, Lehman Bros's accounting for Repo 105s, is problematic for precisely these reasons. We contend that no approach to accounting ethics besides that explained in this book is adequate for properly reflecting upon such a case.

The Lehman Bankruptcy

Lehman Bros. Holdings Inc. ("Lehman") was one of the great historic companies on Wall Street and before its demise the fourth largest investment bank. Its bankruptcy on September 15, 2008 was the largest in history at that time.

Lehman began as a cotton trading company in Alabama in the 1840s, founded by a young immigrant from Bavaria, Henry Lehman, who was joined later by two brothers. After the Civil War its headquarters was moved to New York City, where Lehman's business was as a commodities house, and it played a key role in founding the New York Cotton Exchange. In the 1900s its business shifted to being a house of issue, and Lehman went on to underwrite or help to underwrite the initial public offerings (IPOs) of many of America's most prominent companies, including Sears Roebuck, Macy's, B.F. Goodrich, Endicott Johnson, RCA and Digital.

Like other investment banks, Lehman tried to take full advantage of what in retrospect appeared as a housing bubble by leveraging itself to the greatest extent possible. Leverage multiplies the payback of profitable investments but becomes problematic as the value of one's assets declines. Also, like other investment banks, Lehman took large positions in the subprime housing market through CDOs. However, its exposure was greater than other financial institutions. Commentators differ over whether Lehman's management simply did not recognize the deterioration in the subprime market early enough, or they did but deliberately adopted a contrarian strategy and "doubled down" on those investments. In any case, Lehman found itself with deteriorating, illiquid assets (or "sticky" investments, as they were referred to), while relying heavily on short term financing. Its counterparties would continue to provide such short term financing only so long as they had confidence in Lehman's solvency and continued liquidity.

As the bankruptcy examiner's report explains:

> Lehman's business model was not unique; all of the major investment banks that existed at the time followed some variation of a high-risk, high-leverage model that required the confidence of counterparties to sustain. Lehman maintained approximately $700 billion of assets, and corresponding liabilities, on capital of approximately $25 billion. But the assets were predominantly long-term, while the liabilities were largely short-term. Lehman funded itself through the short-term repo markets and had to borrow tens or hundreds of billions of dollars in those markets each day from counterparties to be able to open for business. Confidence was critical. The moment that repo counterparties were to lose confidence in Lehman and decline to roll over its daily funding, Lehman would be unable to fund itself and continue to operate.

During 2008, Lehman tried unsuccessfully to raise cash and to lessen its degree of leverage. When Bear Stearns avoided bankruptcy by a sale to JP Morgan Chase in March 2008, analysts viewed Lehman as highly vulnerable and the investment bank most likely to fail next. Paradoxically, lack of confidence in Lehman may have been exacerbated by claims that Bear Stearns almost failed only through lack of confidence, as captured in the remark by SEC Chairman Christopher Cox, "Notwithstanding that Bear Stearns continued to have high quality collateral to provide as security for borrowings, market counterparties became less willing to enter into collateralized funding arrangements with Bear Stearns"[47] –since, after all, if a bank could fail solely through lack of confidence, then what would keep Lehman from failing? When Korea Development Bank pulled out of a deal to buy Lehman in August, Lehman's share price fell by 45%. The New York Fed was stymied in its search for some kind of third-party solution:

> ... senior Federal officials, including President Geithner, continually pressed Lehman to find workable solutions for its capital and liquidity problems from March to September 2008. Lehman executives pursued potential merger partners. They engaged in discussions with potential Korean buyers and approached Warren Buffett. At no time did the New York Fed tell Lehman that it would be bailed out with taxpayer money, nor did the New York Fed instruct Lehman to act as if such an option was available.[48]

Various counterparties, especially JP Morgan, made demands for additional collateral, which Lehman was unable to meet. Lehman filed for bankruptcy on Sunday evening, September 15, when it was clear that it could not avoid being illiquid during the next business day.

Lehman's bankruptcy was regarded as one of the sparks that ignited the worldwide financial crisis. Some observers estimate that the bankruptcy resulted in losses to counterparties and investors that totaled $700 billion. Particularly controversial was the decision of the Federal government not to intervene, by lending money to Lehman on an emergency basis, or otherwise mitigating its failure. After the fact Hank Paulson (Secretary of the Treasury) and Ben Bernanke (Chairman of the Federal Reserve Board) defended the decision on the grounds that in pre-TARP days they had no legal basis for injecting capital; that that strategy would have been ineffective anyway in staving off the "run on the bank" against Lehman, which was clearly looming; and that Lehman needed to serve as a lesson about "moral hazard" to other financial institutions. ("Moral hazard" in this context refers to how an agent may fail to amend irresponsible behavior if he

---

[47] Chairman Cox Letter to the Basel Committee in Support of New Guidance on Liquidity Management, March 20, 2008.

[48] Testimony to the FICI of Thomas C. Baxter, Jr., Executive Vice President and General Counsel, Federal Reserve Bank of New York, September 1, 2010.

reckons that he will be saved from the consequences of his actions by others.) But critics charge that every kind of assistance that would have helped Lehman was provided to other institutions later in the same week, such as AIG, and that the costs of the Lehman bankruptcy to the public in general have been much greater than any taxpayer funds which might have been at risk in a rescue of Lehman.

Repo 105 Transactions

A "repo" transaction is a repurchase and resale transaction, typically among banks, which is used to secure low-risk short-term financing. In a typical repo, at the end of the business day the "seller" transfers securities to the "purchaser" in exchange for cash, and, at the beginning of the next business day (but sometimes after a longer period), the "purchaser" (now "reseller") returns the securities and receives back in exchange his cash (from the "repurchaser") plus an agreed upon charge representing what is in effect the interest charged. Typically the securities have a greater fair value than the cash received in the initial sale, the percentage difference constituting the so-called "haircut" in the transaction. The transaction has the *form* of a sale and subsequent repurchase: the "seller" parts with securities in exchange for cash and "buys back" those securities a short time later. But in *substance* it is a financing and has traditionally been accounted for as such, in which the securities which are transferred function as collateral; the difference between the purchase and repurchase price is the interest; and the haircut is a protective overcollateralization. Lehman, like other investment banks, relied upon ordinary repo transactions for most of its short-term financing, borrowing up to hundreds of billions of dollars in this way on a daily basis.

A so-called "Repo 105" is a repo transaction in which the haircut is 5 percent, that is, for every 100 dollars of cash received, 105 dollars worth of securities is transferred.[49] Lehman accounted for Repo 105 transactions as true sales rather than as financings, that is, in accordance with what might seem to be the form of the transaction, not the substance. Lehman did so with some warrant under the relevant accounting standard, SFAS 140. We will consider below in more detail whether Lehman actually was justified in understanding SFAS 140 in that way. But briefly the rationale for that sort of accounting treatment has to do with the extent of overcollateralization. Under SFAS 140, a transfer of securities should be accounted for as a sale if the initial seller surrenders "effective control" over the transferred securities. Surrender of effective control is understood as the negation of the maintenance of effective control. Maintenance of effective control, in turn, is

---

[49] Note that technically when the repo is overcollateralized by 5% the haircut is strictly 105 — (100/105), or 4.76%.

understood as meaning that the seller, through the proceeds of the sale, is able to buy replacements for the securities it surrendered, even if the purchaser "defaults" and fails to resell them. If the overcollateralization is sufficiently high, then, arguably the seller is unable to do so; the seller has in some definitive sense surrendered control over the securities and therefore has truly "sold" them.

A Repo 105 transaction, when viewed as a sale, generally has no effect on the balance sheet, as it involves merely an exchange of one type of asset for another. But Lehman engaged in such transactions at the end of a financial quarter (with Repos having terms of 7-10 days), using the cash received to pay down other liabilities, and not disclosing as liabilities any commitments to pay back that cash.

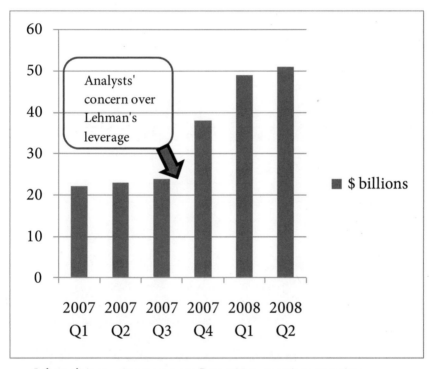

Lehman's increasing recourse to Repo 105 transactions over time

Lehman began to make minimal use of Repo 105 transactions immediately after SFAS 140 was issued in September 2000, when lawyers and accountants at Lehman recognized, as did other accounting experts, that SFAS 140 could potentially be interpreted to permit accounting for sufficiently overcollateralized repos as true sales. But Repo 105s came in handy as Lehman's subprime investments began to deteriorate and Lehman was under pressure to lower its leverage ratio, since, as we have seen, when relied upon at quarter's end they could be used to decrease reported debt. The chart above shows Lehman's increased reliance on Repo 105s, in billions of dollars, as its troubles increased.

Lehman's use of Repo 105s in this way was not known until the bankruptcy examination conducted by Anton Valukas (chairman of the Jenner & Block law firm in Chicago). Valukas in his extensive, multi-volume report concluded that "sufficient evidence exists to support colorable claims" of accounting malpractice against Lehman's external auditor, and that likewise "sufficient evidence exists to support colorable claims" that particular Lehman officers, including its CEO:

> breached their fiduciary duties by engaging in one or more of the following: (1) allowing and certifying the filing of financial statements that omitted or misrepresented material information regarding Lehman's use of Repo 105 transactions and their accounting treatment, thus exposing the firm to potential liability; and/or (2) failing to disclose to Lehman Directors information about the firm's Repo 105 program.[50]

As regards materiality, Valukas presented a chart showing the achieved difference in Lehman's leverage ratio through the use of Repo 105s:

Date	Repo 105 Usage	Reported Net Leverage	Leverage without Repo 105	Difference
Q4 2007	$38.6 B	16.1	17.8	1.7
Q1 2008	$49.1 B	15.4	17.3	1.9
Q2 2008	$50.4 B	12.1	13.9	1.8

Lehman's auditors advised specifically that "Materiality is usually defined as any item individually, or in the aggregate, that moves net leverage by 0.1 or more (typically $1.8 billion)." But then, Valukas argued, Lehman's failure to report its use of Repo 105s constituted a material omission, as "according to former Global Financial Controller Martin Kelly, a careful review of Lehman's Forms 10-K and 10-Q would not reveal Lehman's use of Repo 105 transactions" (p. 734). Moreover, Valukas charged, there was a colorable claim that Lehman made misleading statements in its financials, since in its Notes to its financial statements, Lehman

[50] The phrase "colorable claim" is a technical legal term, explained by Valukas at the beginning of his report as "one for which the Examiner has found that there is sufficient credible evidence to support a finding by a trier of fact... The identification of a claim by the Examiner as colorable does not preclude the existence of defenses and is not a prediction as to how a court or a jury may resolve any contested legal, factual, or credibility issues" (volume I, pages 17-18).

stated that it treated all "repurchase and resale agreements" as "collateralized agreements and financings for financial reporting purposes"; and that "Other secured borrowings principally reflect transfers accounted for as financings rather than sales under SFAS 140."

Valukas' conclusions led to speculations about forthcoming malpractice complaints against the auditor and potential criminal charges against Richard S. Fuld, Jr, the former Lehman CEO. On December 21, 2010, then New York Attorney General Andrew Cuomo filed a complaint against the auditor, Ernst & Young, alleging that it:

> substantially assisted Lehman Brothers Holdings Inc. ("Lehman," or the "Company"), now bankrupt, to engage in a massive accounting fraud, involving the surreptitious removal of tens of billions of dollars of securities from Lehman's balance sheet in order to create a false impression of Lehman's liquidity, thereby defrauding the investing public. Called "Repo 105," these transactions, hatched in 2001, allowed Lehman to park tens of billions of dollars of highly liquid fixed income securities with European banks for the sole purpose of reducing Lehman's balance sheet leverage, and painting a false picture of an important financial metric for investors, stock analysts, lenders, and others involved with Lehman.

As of May 2011, the SEC had given indications that it would not pursue a case against the auditors, presumably for reasons connected with those that will be explained below, and, if so, then it would be highly unlikely that the Justice Department would pursue any criminal charges. Yet the NY State AG's office has stated that it intends to persevere with its case.

SFAS 140 Accounting "Rules"

Lehman's use of Repo 105s looks at first glance to be exactly the same type of scandal, the same trumping of principles by rules in order to hide debt, which characterized the Enron case (discussed in Chapter 11 above), and which we castigated in our discussion of the proper relationship of rules to principles (in Chapter 6 above). But upon a fuller consideration it will be seen that the Lehman case involves an extra twist. Therefore, in the discussion that follows, first, we consider the "rule" that Lehman relied upon for its Repo 105 transactions; second, we look again at the (correct) view that an accountant cannot take refuge in a rule when the rule yields a misleading representation; but, third, we consider the extra wrinkle in this case, which is that Lehman's accounting was in accordance not simply with an accounting "rule" but also with the underlying pertinent "principle."

One might reasonably wonder how the treatment of a repo transaction as a true sale could be in accordance with the relevant underlying principle, since a repo would seem to be in substance a sale. But, as we shall see, in this case the highest relevant accounting authority (FASB) had endorsed and imposed, over the objections of the profession, a principle that precisely implied a divergence between the form and the substance. That is why, it turns out, Lehman's treatment of Repo 105s was arguably correct both with respect to "rules" and with respect to "principles." This is not to say that that treatment is immune from any criticism, but it is to say that it is immune from all *typical* criticism, and that a justified criticism of the treatment would have to reach to the very fundamentals of accounting professionalism. In that sense, the Lehman case serves as an argument for the indispensability of the approach urged in this book.

The relevant "rule" of SFAS 140 applying to repos, in paragraph 9, reads as follows:

> The transferor has surrendered control over transferred assets if and only if all of the following conditions are met:
>
> a. The transferred assets have been isolated from the transferor— put presumptively beyond the reach of the transferor and its creditors, even in bankruptcy or other receivership ...
>
> b. Each transferee ... has the right to pledge or exchange the assets (or beneficial interests) it received, and no condition both constrains the transferee (or holder) from taking advantage of its right to pledge or exchange and provides more than a trivial benefit to the transferor.
>
> c. The transferor does not maintain effective control over the transferred assets through either (1) an agreement that both entitles and obligates the transferor to repurchase or redeem them before their maturity ... or (2) the ability to unilaterally cause the holder to return specific assets, other than through a cleanup call ...

Lehman published an internal "Repo 105 Accounting Policy"[51] manual, used firm-wide, which explains that "there are circumstances under which a repo should be re-characterized from a secured financing transaction to a sale of inventory and a

---

[51] Reproduced in its entirety as Appendix 17 of the bankruptcy examiner's report.

forward to repurchase securities, provided certain criteria in SFAS 140 are met. This policy addresses such situations." The manual then goes on to give a detailed account about when the three conditions given in SFAS 140, paragraph 9, are satisfied.

As regards the first criterion, the manual states, "Repos generally cannot be treated as sales in the United States because lawyers cannot provide a true sale opinion under U.S. law." Lehman therefore provided for the execution of all Repo 105s through a London affiliate, so that the transactions would be governed by English law. The manual states that "The U.K. law firm of Linklaters has issued us true sale opinions covering Repo 105 and Repo 108 transactions documented under a GMRA ["Global Master Repurchase Agreement"] under English law." Thus the first criterion would be satisfied for Repo 105s.

The second condition was met straightforwardly and as something of a formality, so long as the transferred securities were relatively liquid and the clearing bank in a tri-party repo had made the appropriate arrangements. The manual states, for example, that: "This ability to pledge or exchange must be a legal right and an operational capability. For transactions involving third-party custodians such as in tri-party arrangements, the counterparty's re-use or re-hypothecation options in Tri-party Services Agreement must be executed to ensure the transferee has the legal right to pledge or exchange the transferred assets."

It was to satisfy the third criterion that the rationale of overcollateralization was employed. The manual's entire discussion of this criterion is worth quoting here:

> Re-characterization of a repo from a secured financing transaction to a sale of inventory and a forward to repurchase assets is allowed only if we can demonstrate we have relinquished control of the transferred assets. We retain control over a transferred asset if we are assured of the ability to repurchase or redeem the transferred asset, even in the event of default by the transferee. Our right to repurchase the transferred asset is assured only if it is protected by obtaining collateral (i.e., cash) sufficient to fund substantially all of the cost of purchasing the same or substantially the same replacement assets during the term of the contract. If we can fund substantially all of the cost of purchasing the same or substantially the same replacement assets, we are viewed as having the means to replace the assets, even if the transferee defaults, and we are considered not to have relinquished control of the assets. For purposes of this requirement, we have retained control of the transferred assets if a fixed income security is margined at less than 105% of the cash received ....

> Transfers in which we transfer fixed income securities valued at a minimum of 105% of the cash received ... are considered to be sales with a forward agreement to repurchase the securities rather than secured financing transactions. The assets transferred (i.e., sold) should be valued and margined frequently for changes in the market price of the assets to ensure the assets transferred equal or exceed 105% ... of the cash received. When both the foregoing criteria are met, the assets transferred are removed from our balance sheet and an asset under a derivative contract is recorded to reflect that we will repurchase, under a forward contract, the transferred assets.

The argument here, again, is that for the seller or "transferor" of the securities to have succeeded in selling those securities, it must not continue to control them; and it continues to control them so long as it can buy back those securities, or substantially the same securities, with precisely the cash that it received in exchange for them. Overcollateralizing the loan to the extent of 105%, it is maintained, puts those securities beyond the reach, or control, of the transferor.

One might reasonably wonder why the figure of 105% overcollateralization would be enough to negate control. Why not 106% or 110%? Also, the argument depends upon regarding the cash received in the exchange as a fixed parcel, whereas cash is fungible. It would be absurd to claim that an investment bank with the vast resources of a Lehman Bros would have lost "control" over those securities in an overcollateralized repo simply because it could not repurchase those securities with only that bundle of cash it received in exchange for them. Moreover, suppose, as seems correct, that the cash would suffice to buy back 95% of the transferred securities: then why not say that the transferor maintained "effective control" over that 95% and succeeded in losing "effective control" over, and therefore sold, only 5% of the securities?

The argument does not make a great deal of sense. Nonetheless, as mentioned above, that sort of reasoning seems to be invited by the FASB in its own guidance as to how to interpret paragraph 9 of SFAS 140:

> 218. The Board also decided that the transferor's right to repurchase is not assured unless it is protected by obtaining collateral sufficient to fund substantially all of the cost of purchasing identical replacement securities during the term of the contract so that it has received the means to replace the assets even if the transferee defaults. Judgment is needed to interpret the term *substantially all* and other aspects of the criterion that the terms of a repurchase agreement do not maintain effective control over the transferred asset. However, arrangements to repurchase or lend readily obtainable securities, typically with as much as 98 percent

collateralization (for entities agreeing to repurchase) or as little as 102 percent overcollateralization (for securities lenders), valued daily and adjusted up or down frequently for changes in the market price of the security transferred and with clear powers to use that collateral quickly in the event of default, typically fall clearly within that guideline. The Board believes that other collateral arrangements typically fall well outside that guideline.

The Lehman internal accounting manual clearly draws upon FASB's own interpretation. However, note the following logical point, involving the important difference between necessary and sufficient conditions (discussed in Chapter 6 above). What FASB says is that collateralization of 102% or lower is *sufficient* for retaining effective control. What Lehman's interpretation requires is that collateralization of 102% or lower (or, strictly, lower than 105%) is *necessary* for retaining effective control. From "if the collateral is less than 102% then control is retained" it does not follow that "if collateral is greater than 102% then control is not retained"—a step of false inference which is known as the fallacy of "denying the antecedent."

Here is another way of putting the same point. All of the following conditional statements are endorsed by FASB:

- If collateralization is 102% or less, then the transferor retains the ability to repurchase the securities.
- If the transferor retains the ability to repurchase, then it retains control over the securities.
- If it retains control, then the transfer may not be re-characterized as a sale.

From which only the following conclusion may be drawn:

Hence, if collateralization is 102% or less, then the transfer may not be re-characterized as a sale.

When one looks carefully at the first paragraph of the Lehman argument quoted above, nothing more is supplied than various versions of the above conditional statements, (although with 105% used as the boundary rather than 102%).[52] However, what Lehman wishes to conclude, and does conclude, but may not logically conclude, is:

---

[52] To construe the statements in the paragraph properly, recall that "Q, if P" is the same as "if P then Q", but "P only if Q" is the same as "if P then Q."

Hence, if collateralization is not 102% or less, then the transfer may be re-characterized as a sale.

That is, the Lehman manual argues fallaciously from "If P, then Q" to "If not P, then not Q."[53] (We include, as an appendix to this chapter, a logical analysis of the paragraph, to prove this point.)

It would not be a fallacy, indeed, for someone trying to interpret SFAS 140, to reason that, if FASB in paragraph 218 was unwilling to say with assurance that, for collateralizations higher than 102%, the transferror retained effective control, then a collateralization of 105% would plausibly be clear of any grey area and might potentially be among the "other collateral arrangements" contemplated by FASB which "fall well outside that guideline." Presumably Lehman was implicitly relying on just that sort of consideration. Yet reasoning of that sort is not reflected in its argument; moreover, such an argument would yield at best only a likely conclusion, not a reliable or definitive interpretation.

Then FASB Chairman Robert Herz seems to be articulating a similar objetion in a letter of April 9, 2010, addressed to Congressman Barney Frank, Chairman of the House Financial Services Committee, about Lehman's Repo 105 accounting treatment:

> The accounting guidance emphasizes the need for understanding the terms of a repo agreement and applying judgment in other situations to determine whether a company maintains effective control over the transferred securities. That example [sc. in paragraph 218] was not intended to, nor does it, create a "bright-line" for making that determination. Rather, the example describes typical collateral arrangements in repurchase agreements involving marketable securities indicating that these typical arrangements clearly result in the transferor maintaining effective control over the transferred securities.

And yet at the same time Herz is unwilling to say outright that Lehman misinterpreted SFAS 140, stating:

> while we have read the report of the Lehman Bankruptcy Examiner, press accounts, and other reports, we do not have sufficient information to assess whether Lehman complied with or violated particular standards relating to accounting for repurchase agreements...

---

[53] To see that this is a fallacy, consider for example that from "If it is raining, the ground is wet" it does not follow that "If it is not raining, then the ground is not wet."

This seems an odd assessment, given the detail of the bankruptcy examiner's report and the availability of Lehman's public filings.

If Lehman's interpretation of SFAS 140 was not correct, at least it was not obviously incorrect, as Herz' letter might be taken to show. Or one might cite the way in which SEC staff dealt with sale accounting of repos in staff comment letters on financial statements filed with the SEC. For instance, a staff comment on AIG's 2008 10-K filing asked the following:

> [Y]ou disclose that in connection with certain securities lending transactions, you met the requirements of sale accounting under SFAS 140 because collateral received was insufficient to fund substantially all of the cost of purchasing replacement assets for the securities lent to various counterparties. Please explain why this would result in a deemed sale under SFAS 140 as indicated by your disclosure. (UPLOAD, 4/2/2009)[54]

In reply, AIG gave the same reasoning as Lehman:

> [T]he securities lending transactions ... were accounted for as sales because they met all of the criteria set forth in paragraph 9 of FAS 140 ...
>
> [They met] Paragraph 9(c), because AIG no longer maintained effective control over the transferred assets. While AIG is both entitled and obligated to reacquire the securities before maturity pursuant to the terms of these securities lending agreements, AIG will not be able to reacquire the securities on substantially the agreed terms in the event of default by the transferee because collateral obtained during the contract term was not sufficient to fund substantially all of the cost of purchasing replacement securities lent to the various counterparties.[55]

Although silence from the SEC does not imply consent, nonetheless AIG's accounting was not so egregious as to provoke any objections or even requests for further clarification in subsequent staff comment letters.

"Rules are Not Enough," Once More

Thus, although Lehman's accounting treatment for Repo 105s was not strictly implied by the accounting "rules" given in SFAS 140, still, that treatment was not an implausible interpretation of those rules. If so, on what basis could Lehman's accounting or the auditor's role be criticized?

---

[54] Mark Cheffers and John A. Smillie, "SEC Comment Letters: Accounting for Repurchase Agreements," AuditAnalytics report, July 2010, page 10.

[55] Ibid.

At first glance, as was said, it looks as though Lehman's accounting would be at fault in the just the same way as Enron's, namely, Lehman's accounting treatment trumped principles by rules in order to hide debt and present a misleading picture of its financial condition. It might be argued that even if Lehman were following the rules, it would be at fault for not following the relevant "principles;" it placed form above substance; and it relied on GAAP even when it realized that such reliance would yield a misleading representation.

For instance, the New York AG's complaint appeals (at n. 61) to some of the most basic concepts of GAAP, with the implication that less basic provisions of GAAP should yield when they conflict with the most basic concepts:

> Lehman's accounting for the Repo 105 transactions failed fundamental tenets of financial reporting under GAAP. GAAP requires that the overall impression created by financial statements be consistent with the business realities of the company's financial position and operations, so that the financial statements are useful and comprehensible to users in making rational business and investment decisions. (See, e.g., Financial Accounting Standards Board – Statement of Financial Accounting Concepts ("FASCON") No. 1, ¶¶ 9, 16, 33-34; No. 5, ¶ 5.) FASCON 1 states that "[f]inancial reporting should include explanations and interpretations to help users understand financial information." (Id. at ¶54.) Under GAAP, "nothing material is left out of the information that may be necessary to [ensure] that [the report] validly represents the underlying events and conditions." (FASCON No. 2, ¶¶ 79-80.)

The AG also faults Lehman and its auditors for incomplete and misleading disclosures:

> 62. Lehman's accounting treatment for the Repo 105 transactions, and the absence of any disclosures about Repo 105, created a false impression of Lehman's financial condition. Readers of Lehman's reports could not have learned about the Repo 105 program and therefore received an erroneous impression of Lehman's leverage. Further, Lehman falsely stated in its audited financial statements that all its repurchase agreements were treated as financing arrangements, not as sales.

Finally, it charges that Lehman's accounting placed form over substance:

> 64. GAAP rules require that financial statements place substance over form. FASCON No. 2, Qualitative Characteristics of Accounting Information, for example, states in relevant part: "The quality of reliability and, in particular, of representational faithfulness leaves no

room for accounting representations that subordinate substance to form ...." (FASCON 2, ¶ 59). Additionally, AU § 411 states, in relevant part: "Generally accepted accounting principles recognize the importance of reporting transactions and events in accordance with their substance" (AU § 411.06).

65. Lehman's Repo 105 transactions lacked substance as "sales." Elevating form over substance, Lehman engaged in tens of billions of dollars of Repo 105 transactions at the end of the fiscal quarters simply to improve the appearance of its balance sheet and mislead the public as to its leverage ratio.

The bankruptcy examiner's report additionally argues, as has been emphasized throughout this text, that accountants cannot rest satisfied with mere "technical compliance" with GAAP:

Even if Lehman's use of Repo 105 transactions technically complied with SFAS 140, financial statements may be materially misleading even when they do not violate GAAP. (*United States v. Ebbers*, 458 F.3d 110 (2d Cir. 2006), cert. denied, 127 S.Ct. 1483 (2007)) The Second Circuit has explained that "GAAP itself recognizes that technical compliance with particular GAAP rules may lead to misleading financial statements, and imposes an overall requirement that the statements as a whole accurately reflect the financial status of the company."

Similarly, as noted in *In re Global Crossing Ltd. Securities Litigation*, even if a defendant established that its accounting practices "were in technical compliance with certain individual GAAP provisions . . . this would not necessarily insulate it from liability. This is because, unlike other regulatory systems, *GAAP's ultimate goals of fairness and accuracy in reporting require more than mere technical compliance.*"(*In re Global Crossing, Ltd. Sec. Litig.*, 322 F. Supp.2d 319, 339 (S.D.N.Y. 2004) (emphasis added)) The court explained that "when viewed as a whole," GAAP has no "loopholes" because its purpose, shared by the securities laws, is "to increase investor confidence by ensuring transparency and accuracy in financial reporting." Technical compliance with specific accounting rules does not automatically lead to fairly presented financial statements. "Fair presentation is the touchstone for determining the adequacy of disclosure in financial statements. While adherence to generally accepted accounting principles is a tool to help achieve that end, it is not necessarily a guarantee of fairness. Moreover, registrants are *required to provide whatever additional information would be necessary to make the statements in their financial reports fair and accurate, and not misleading"* (emphasis added).

So, on the basis of these astute and pertinent arguments, there would seem to be parity between Enron and Lehman Bros.

"Presents Fairly in Accordance with GAAP"

However, as mentioned, there is an additional, complicating wrinkle in the Lehman Bros case, which is that, arguably, Lehman's accounting for Repo 105s was not a matter of mere "technical compliance," but had a more solid basis. Lehman's accounting treatment:

- was in accordance with the "principles" inherent in SFAS 140 and not simply that standard's "rules";
- was originally proposed, or at least suggested, by the most authoritative "standard setter" and interpreter of GAAP, the Financial Accounting Standards Board (FASB);
- was proposed, or suggested, by FASB precisely as the best expression and realization of the fundamental accounting concepts which FASB had articulated in its statements of financial accounting concepts (FASCON 1 and 2);
- was even insisted on by FASB over the objections of the accounting profession.

If so, then the criticisms of the sort raised by the NY AG and the bankruptcy examiner—essentially amounting to the idea that Lehman's accounting for Repo 105s was "rule based" to the exclusion of principles—become highly problematic.

SFAS 140, "Accounting for Transfers and Servicing of Financial Assets and Extinguishments of Liabilities," was a replacement of the earlier FASB Statement No. 125. Both standards were ambitious attempts to unify a variety of disparate phenomena under the notion of "control": in a transfer of financial assets, an entity should recognize assets if and only if it "controls" them. "Control" or "effective control" was not defined except by the three conditions given under paragraph 9, which we have already seen.

For our purposes, the important point is that this "control" approach initially suggested to FASB that *all* repos should be accounted for as sales, on the grounds that the "sale" of securities in a repo is distinguished from putting up collateral for loan precisely on the grounds that in the former the transferor gives up "control."

The big firms objected strenuously to the underlying philosophy and concrete implications of the SFAS 125 exposure draft. Some firms, such as Coopers &

Lybrand, criticized FASB's attempt to formulate a comprehensive system, which they took to be an example of wrongheaded overgeneralization:

> We do not believe that the proposed Statement should extend the control-based concept to the accounting for other financial instruments such as repurchase agreements, securities loans, and similar transactions ("repos"). In our view, as noted above, the primary objective of this project is to address the current inconsistent accounting for securitization transactions and not to attempt to establish a "universal" set of criteria for the derecognition of all financial assets that would change current accounting practices that we believe are conceptually sound and that have been generally understood and long accepted by the financial markets.[56]

The firms had generally favored a "risks and rewards" approach to asset recognition rather than FASB's favored notion of "control."

Andersen objected to the criterion of paragraph 9(a)—as if it could foresee Lehman's eventual recourse to the Linklaters firm in England—both on accounting grounds and from the point of view of the auditor:

> Under the Board's overall approach, we agree in concept with its criterion in paragraph 9a, "presumptively beyond the reach of the transferor and its creditors, even in bankruptcy or other receivership." However, the Board needs to determine its operationality. We have received conflicting signals on the matter, with some saying that frequently it cannot be determined objectively, while others have said it can be. The question is "Can the lawyers deliver?" In the U.S.? Among different legal jurisdictions within the U.S. (we understand differences exist)? The U.K.? Japan? For certain financial institutions not covered by the bankruptcy laws? Etc. We believe it will be a new concept for accountants (at least as an explicit accounting standard) and perhaps for lawyers. ... How are the preparer and auditor to have any idea whether paragraph 9a is met?[57]

But FASB brushed aside these difficulties and retained the objectionable language nonetheless. Could one reasonably object, then, if a company such as Lehman used to its own advantage a characteristic of the standard which FASB was aware of and had decided not to change?

Note that the firms objected specifically to the way in which repurchasing agreements would be dealt with under the proposal. Andersen argued:

---

[56] Coopers & Lybrand, LLP, Letter on Exposure Draft of SFAS 125, January 19, 1996, page 2.

[57] Arthur Andersen, LLP, Letter on Exposure Draft of SFAS 125, January 22, 1996, page 10.

Current practice in this area generally has not been a problem and conforms with what most participants believe is the "economic substance." The FASB's objective should be to improve financial reporting. In our judgment, the ED [exposure draft] would not be an improvement in this area. ... The Board's proposed accounting is strained and unnatural. .... While legal differences may exist between repurchase agreements and securities lending, they are more similar than different to the party with the repurchase obligation. The business purpose seems clear and the subsequent cash flows (interest and principal payments, etc.) between the parties would be easier to understand, explain, and account for. Accounting for these transactions as borrowings would be more consistent with what we believe is the expectation of the majority of users and other constituents of the Board.[58]

Deloitte & Touche added:

The risks and rewards approach was rejected primarily because of the subjectivity of assessing the extent to which the retention of certain risks would preclude derecognition. In this situation, however, there is no subjective assessment to be made because none of the risks and rewards are transferred. We believe the retention of all risks and rewards of ownership, along with a forward commitment to buy back the transferred financial asset, should preclude derecognition.[59]

KPMG Peat Marwick criticized the proposed standard for its failure to link the sale and repurchase in a repo:

We believe the current non-sale treatment used for most securities-lending transactions and repurchase agreements is appropriate and should be continued. Non-sale treatment of these transactions recognizes the need to link the agreements to re-acquire the assets or substantially the same assets or to re-exchange the loaned securities for the assets received as collateral with the initial exchange to determine the appropriate accounting.[60]

In the SFAS 125 draft, FASB had begun to retreat from its original idea that all repos should be accounted for as sales. As a compromise with the firms, it allowed

---

[58] Ibid, pages 3-5.

[59] Deloitte & Touche, LLP, Letter on Exposure Draft of SFAS 125, January 24, 1996, page 7.

[60] KPMG Peat Marwick, LLP, Letter on Exposure Draft of SFAS 125, January 25, 1996, page 2.

that repos with a term of less than 90 days might be accounted for as financings. But the firms objected that such a line would be arbitrary and create artificial opportunities for market arbitrage. Ernst & Young criticized among other things the arbitrary nature of the compromise:

> Paragraph 24 also provides that securities loans, repurchase contracts and other contracts qualify as assuredly temporary transfers only if they have maturities less than three months or are for an indefinite period and meet other specified criteria.
>
> We agree with the intention of the Board in establishing this requirement to continue the historical treatment of certain securities lending and securities repurchase transactions as financing transactions. The nature of these transactions are well understood in the marketplace as financing arrangements, and the existing financial reporting of them as financing transactions has served users of financial statements well. However, we do not believe that an arbitrary three month criterion appropriately distinguishes between sales and financing arrangements, and would result in many transactions being reported as sales which we believe, in substance, are financing arrangements.[61]

Arthur Andersen complained with evident frustration that its repeated attempts to persuade FASB to adopt another approach had been rebuffed:

> Our views on the conceptual derecognition issues have been expressed to the Board in various correspondence over the years (see Appendix 1). Representatives of our firm have authored articles on these topics expressing our views (for example, see the August 1986 issue of the *Journal of Accountancy*). We have also expressed our views at various FASB task force meetings. In addition, our views have been included in our responses to the exposure drafts issued by the International Accounting Standards Committee on financial instruments (E40 and E48), copies of which have been sent to the Board. Our views have been consistent over the years—we have supported a risks and rewards approach to derecognition, an approach we believe is consistent with the FASB's conceptual framework.[62]

Andersen concluded that the best it could achieve in the circumstances was to encourage FASB to operationalize the standard in such a way that the accounting

---

[61] Ernst & Young, LLP, Letter on Exposure Draft of SFAS 125, January 22, 1996, page 5.

[62] Andersen Letter, page 1.

treatment required by SFAS 125 (and later SFAS 140) would align for the most part with what Andersen regarded as the proper treatment:

> We believe our best course of action at this point is not to continue to debate the overall issue but rather work with the FASB to make its approach more operational and produce more understandable results that conform better to the economics.[63]

A word about the notion of "operationalize": this term is taken from philosophy of science, where some philosophers have held that a concept or principle has no content and is meaningless until the *use* of that concept or principle in practice is spelled out in such a way that one can measure, or otherwise exactly determine, whether the concept or principle applies in any particular case. In accounting, to operationalize a concept is to develop accounting "rules" for its application, and the concept which gets operationalized corresponds to the relevant "principle." What Andersen is saying, then, is that it has given up trying to persuade FASB of the correct principles to apply and has become reconciled, instead, to simply trying to get FASB to stipulate the rules of SFAS 125 (and later SFAS 140) in such a way that someone who followed those rules, without a view to the underlying principle (as one *should* do in this case, Andersen thinks, because the principle is mistaken), would for the most part use accounting treatments which would give the same results as someone who selected an accounting treatment based on the correct principles.

That is, in the above quotation, Andersen is in effect saying that it regards the FASB as having compelled the profession to adopt a rules-based approach to repos, with the rule in this case running contrary in many instances to the true economics of the arrangement. As mentioned, FASB's principle of "control" originally implied that all repos should be accounted for as sales. Through pressure and insistence from the firms, FASB agreed to "operationalize" the notion of control in the case of repos such that—and here the significance of paragraph 218 becomes clear—repos that were collateralized between 98 and 102 percent should be accounted for in manner that mimicked how they would be accounted for by someone who was relying upon the alternative "risks and rewards" approach.

Given that this is so, when Lehman accounted for Repo 105s as sales, it was simply reverting to the baseline, "usual" accounting for repos implicit in SFAS 125/140. Lehman's Repo 105 accounting treatment was not a matter of taking advantage of a "loophole" relative to SFAS 140; rather, SFAS 140s allowance that some repos could be treated as financings was itself the "loophole"! It would be

---

[63] Ibid.

difficult to object, then, that Lehman was ignoring the principle of "substance over form," since the criticism of the firms as against SFAS 125/140 was just that its use of the notion of "control" for repos itself misconstrued the substance of the transaction. Likewise, to object that Lehman used an accounting "rule" to trump a "principle" would be to ignore the telling fact that Lehman's Repo 105 treatment was in accord with the relevant principle of SFAS 125/140. Moreover, FASB's adoption of that standard over the well-grounded objections of the firms might reasonably be interpreted as FASB's asserting that it was looking precisely for a solely "rules based"—that is to say, fully "operationalized"—accounting for the transactions covered by that standard.

One might argue, too, that the external auditor could not easily have advised Lehman's to reject SFAS 140's rules: the venerable grounds that an accountant should depart even from GAAP when GAAP leads to misleading results would not be available in this case, as the big firms had *already* voiced their disagreements to this aspect of GAAP, in the long periods of exposure drafts and commentary preceding SFAS 140's promulgation. To dissent from the newly promulgated standard would have looked like lawlessness and a recipe for chaos.

But what about issues involving disclosure? Even if, for all the reasons mentioned, the accounting treatment cannot easily be criticized, should not Lehman have fully *disclosed* that treatment, at least? And yet how much of the sense that the *disclosure* was faulty derives from the sense that the *accounting* was faulty? If you can manage to think yourself into the point of view from which the accounting is perfectly correct, then why would the absence of *special* disclosure— for this correct accounting (as we are assuming)—be wrong?

But in any case it is not clear that there was any failure to disclose, as it seems that Lehman disclosed everything as it should have been disclosed. True enough, in the notes to its financial statements for the year 2007 10-K, Lehman states that "repurchase and resale agreements" are "treated as collateralized agreements and financings for financial reporting purposes." But that remark is preceded by the explicit assertion that "In accordance with SFAS 140, we recognize transfers of financial assets as sales, if control has been surrendered. We determine control has been surrendered when the following three criteria have been met." Then the three conditions of SFAS 140, paragraph 9 are given. That is, it would be futile to object that Lehman failed to disclose that some of its repurchase and resale agreements were accounted for as sales, because, strictly, according to SFAS 140, such transactions were not actually repos but rather "transfers of financial assets," which should in fact be "recognized as sales," because "control has been surrendered." And they *were* recognized as sales!

Our claim that Lehman's accounting and disclosure were both "correct," given SFAS 140, seems now to have been implicitly supported by FASB itself, which in early 2011 put out an exposure draft to repair the corresponding deficiency in SFAS 140. Here is FASB's explanation on the need for the fix:

> The Board determined that the criterion pertaining to an exchange of collateral should not be a determining factor of effective control. The Board believes that the assessment of effective control should focus on a transferor's contractual rights and obligations with respect to transferred financial assets, not on whether the transferor has the practical ability, by way of a collateral maintenance agreement, to exercise those rights or honor those obligations. The Board believes that the remaining criteria are sufficient to determine effective control. Consequently, the proposed amendments would remove the transferor's ability criterion from the consideration of effective control for repos and other agreements that both entitle and obligate the transferor to repurchase or redeem financial assets before their maturity.

Talk about closing the barn door after the horse has escaped!

No Authority Higher than Truth

Suppose Lehman was correct that if collateralization was 105% or higher in a repo, then, on the terms of SFAS 140, the transferor had "surrendered control." Then, on the terms of SFAS 140 once again, *the transaction would have to be accounted for as a sale*. Given the criteria of paragraph 9, and its "if and only if" definition of "control," sale accounting would not be an *option* for the transaction but rather a *requirement*. The same holds for the auditor, which would be obliged to sign off on such an accounting treatment—as the only other alternative would be to proceed as if FASB had no authority to settle the argument which the auditor had carried out with FASB during the period of exposure drafts and commentary. To be sure, the auditor might have insisted that Lehman disclose the discrepancy between the required accounting treatment and the auditor's own understanding of the proper way to account for the transactions. But, again, this would have been carrying over the disagreements of the comment letters into the financial statements, and it is hard to locate the auditor's fault in not taking this approach.

Yet Lehman's engaging in such transactions was optional in the first place. Given that that was so, then it seems that the one remaining basis for criticizing Lehman would be something like the following. One might argue that a company should not engage in an optional transaction if it would consequently be obliged (under GAAP and given the highest relevant legal authorities) to apply an accounting treatment which someone who had a proper regard for truth and truthfulness would be obliged to reject. Likewise, one might maintain that an auditor should refuse to take as a client any company that persisted in engaging in optional transactions of the sort just described, that is, transactions which it would consequently be obliged to account for in ways that would be rejected by someone who had a proper regard for truth.

These highly refined grounds for objecting to Lehman's Repo 105s are hardly available today, when the unit of analysis for accounting ethics, as we have seen, is the particular engagement or even particular audited representation, and when "presents fairly with GAAP" is the decisive standard. However, a member of the accounting profession when it was originally founded, whose standard was simply truth and truthfulness, as articulated in the original Rule 2 from 1919, and who tended to assess his practices within a big picture, in terms of how they comported with the dignity of the profession as a whole within an integrated professional life— that sort of person might very well have kept clear of Repo 105s.

Recommended additional reading:

Report of Anton R. Valukas, Examiner, *In re Lehman Brothers Holdings, Inc.*, Section III.A.4: Repo 105, Volume 3 of 9, March 11, 2010.

Appendix

Logical Analysis of the Argument in the Lehman Brothers Accounting Manual to Justify Its Treatment of Repo 105s

First step: present separately and number each of the sentences in the relevant paragraph:

1)   Re-characterization of a repo from a secured financing transaction to a sale of inventory and a forward to repurchase assets is allowed only if we can demonstrate we have relinquished control of the transferred assets.

2)   We retain control over a transferred asset if we are assured of the ability to repurchase or redeem the transferred asset, even in the event of default by the transferee.

3)   Our right to repurchase the transferred asset is assured only if it is protected by obtaining collateral (i.e., cash) sufficient to fund substantially all of the cost of purchasing the same or substantially the same replacement assets during the term of the contract.

4)   If we can fund substantially all of the cost of purchasing the same or substantially the same replacement assets, we are viewed as having the means to replace the assets, even if the transferee defaults, and we are considered not to have relinquished control of the assets.

5)   For purposes of this requirement, we have retained control of the transferred assets if a fixed income security is margined at less than 105% of the cash received

Second step: Assign statement letters to each of the distinct statements in conditionals given above.

     S = The repo may be re-characterized as a sale of inventory.
     E = Lehman has retained control.
     ¬E = Lehman has relinquished control.
     R = Lehman is assured of the ability to repurchase
     C = Lehman has collateral sufficient to fund substantially all of the cost of purchasing the same.
     ¬O= Lehman has not overcollateralized at 105% or more.

Third step: Using this assignment, give the logical form of each of the conditionals in the argument.

1) $S \rightarrow \neg E$
2) $R \rightarrow E$
3) $R \rightarrow C$
4) $C \rightarrow \neg E$
5) $\neg O \rightarrow E$

Fourth step: State the argument which is definitely licensed by SFAS 140, paragraphs 9 and 218.

a) If there is 102% or less collateralization, then there is sufficient collateral to fund substantially all the cost of purchasing the same. [Nearly equivalent to $\neg O \rightarrow C$.]

b) If there is sufficient collateral to fund substantially all the cost of purchasing the same, then the transferor retains the ability to repurchase. [Nearly equivalent to $C \rightarrow R$.]

c) If the transferor retains the ability to repurchase, then the transferor retains effective control. [Nearly equivalent to 2) above.]

d) If the transferor retains effective control, then the repo may not be re-characterized as sale. [Nearly equivalent to 1) above.]

e) Thus, if there is 102% or less collateralization, then the repo may not be re-characterized as sale. [Nearly equivalent to 5) above.]

Analysis:

What Lehman wishes to prove is:

If there is overcollateralization at 105% or more, then Lehman does not retain control. $(O \rightarrow \neg E)$.

The considerations and arguments in SFAS 140, paragraphs 9 and 218, support only the claim that a collateralization of 102% suffices to retain control. From this it does not follow that a collateralization of 105%, or more than 102%, suffices to negate control. The fallacy is hidden by the sheer repetition and multiplication of claims in the Lehman argument, also by the tendency to conflate "only if" with "if."

PART V

ACCOUNTING ETHICS IN PRACTICE

Cases from Practice

14

"A doctor seems not even to study health in this way, but the health of man, or perhaps rather the health of a particular man; it is individuals that he is healing."—Aristotle

THE PRESENT CHAPTER GIVES TEN CASES taken from auditing and forensic accounting practice. Each case study below begins with a brief scenario or "fact pattern," which we call The Situation. This description of the case is then followed by a Question, and, after that, four preliminary suggestions for action.

The cases may be studied in either of two ways:

(I) They may be considered according to the usual case-study method, in which case one would, first, review the facts presented in The Situation; second, identify possible solutions (which may or may not coincide with those offered here); and, third, debate and decide upon possible solutions. In this context, one ought to consider links between these cases and the discussions of accounting ethics and professionalism offered in preceding chapters of this text. The traditional case study approach is perhaps the best to adopt in a seminar or classroom setting.

(II) Alternatively, the cases may be considered as a kind of "quiz" about accounting ethics. If this approach is adopted, consider the four possible resolutions presented in the section entitled "Looking for an Answer." Try to reach two judgments about the proposed answers: decide whether any answer is simply unacceptable, as being incompatible with accounting ethics or professionalism, and then, among the remaining not unacceptable answers, provide a rank ordering from best to worst (and formulate reasons for your rank ordering). Then check your answer against the suggested resolutions given later in the chapter. This quiz-type approach is the best to adopt for self-study.

Besides offering suggested resolutions of each case, we explain how the case actually played out in real life. It will be seen that an attractive advantage of considering cases from forensic practice is that inevitably there is a legal consequence, which helps to check and confirm which resolutions truly are better. It will be seen that each case carries with it a cautionary lesson, which emphasizes the connections among sound professionalism, limitation of exposure, and good business practice.

SCENARIO 1 ~~ THE AGE-OLD DILEMMA

You are not told to cheat, but your job may be on the line.

The Situation Suzanne Striker, a staff accountant recently hired by AccuSuccess accounting firm, is participating in the audit of E-Z Company. She needs to check 60 loan files against 15 different criteria, to draw a conclusion in each case about E-Z Company's assessment of collectability. The senior accountant for the job, Will Smythe, has a similar job. Over the course of a week, Will consistently gets through his work and is able to leave on time every day. But Suzanne has been working late to finish the job on time, and even then she is falling behind. Suzanne begins to think that she is too slow at her work and that she risks being reprimanded. At the rate she's going, it will take her almost 80 hours to do a job for which 40 hours were budgeted.

One evening late in the week, Suzanne catches up with Will after work at the local watering hole. "How do you do it?" she asks. "Your loan files are even bigger and more complex than mine. I can't see how to get through this work on schedule." "You don't seem to get it," Will says in reply. "Don't you know that the real risk assessment for this job has already been done by the audit manager and partner? We're here just to make sure the work papers look good. What do those guys *really* want, after all? They want the job to be done on time and within budget."

Suzanne was trying to take this in.

"Don't get me wrong. I'm not saying you shouldn't look at all the files," Will added, firmly, "But it should take you a lot less time to get through them. The loan portfolio isn't material anyway. If you keep taking nearly twice as long as budgeted, they won't keep you."

Suzanne couldn't help thinking that the implicit message was in what he said was: *I'm not looking at every file. I'm sampling them and making my own risk assessment.*

Question What should Suzanne do about her quandary, if anything?

Looking for an Answer After this conversation, which both relieved and disturbed her, Suzanne called some friends and asked their advice. Should Suzanne dismiss any of this advice as unacceptable? And, as regards that advice which is acceptable, which is the best alternative? Is there an even better alternative than the four suggested by her friends?

Andrew, an entrepreneur who had some accounting background, said to her, "If I were you, I'd just do what your senior accountant seems to be implicitly suggesting. Look carefully at two files, then 'scan' two, and so on. That is, adopt an intelligent risk-assessment approach. You have a sense of where the risks are. 'Transaction testing,' as they say—you're simply 'sampling loans receivable.' That's a perfectly respectable accounting practice."

Boris, a friend who was still completing his accounting studies, said, "Shouldn't you just do the job as you were directed, with all of the procedures? Okay, so you'll have to work double the hours. Suck it up. And don't bill for those extra hours, if you want to keep your job. Also, don't say anything about the senior. Despite your suspicions, you don't know whether he is actually doing his job properly or not. Saying something will almost certainly cause you problems."

Cathy, an accountant friend at another firm, said, "I agree you should do the job without skipping anything. But if you have to work 80 hours to finish it, then bill for 80 hours. Won't the audit manager be able to see that not enough time was budgeted for this job? And your billing might cause the manager to reconsider the senior accountant's work."

Drew, another accountant friend, said, "Here's what I would recommend. When you reach the budgeted time of 40 hours—suppose you've gone through only half the loan files—then go to the audit manager and explain the situation. Ask him whether he wants you to finish the job. Don't say anything about what the senior accountant said. And if the audit manager asks you why you are going to him rather than to the senior accountant—have some kind of 'cover' available that doesn't implicate the senior accountant."

(See page 365 below for a suggested resolution and discussion.)

SCENARIO 2 ~~ THE NEW PARTNER

How do you make yourself look good?

The Situation A new partner in an accounting firm was put in charge of an acquisition audit. The seller was a long-time friend of a name partner in the accounting firm. The acquisition represented the end of a long-time business rivalry between seller and buyer.

About two months after the deal closed, the buyer sent a claim to the seller, alleging that the financial statements had been manipulated, with the result that the seller overpaid by about $3 million. The buyer insisted that the seller remit the difference.

Even before this claim had arrived, the new partner who was in charge of the audit had suspected that a lawsuit might be in the works. The reason? A couple of weeks before the buyer's claim arrived, he had received a request from the buyer to examine the work papers for the audit. Specifically, the buyer was interested in the representation of the collectability of accounts receivable and the potential impact of this on historic and projected cash flows.

The partner was confident that the buyer's claim was spurious and that, if necessary, the firm should be able to defend against it successfully in trial. This became clear to him in his own review of the work papers, which he undertook when he became aware of the buyer's complaint. However, when he was carrying out that review, he also noticed that the work papers had been prepared in a very sloppy manner. In fact, their sloppiness was such that, just conceivably, they could be subject to misinterpretation, and taken to reflect deceit, incompetence or bias.

It was not that the sloppiness could be directly construed as a manipulation of the financials, but rather that it would make the financials more difficult to defend. The firm was therefore unnecessarily exposed to risk. Furthermore, the partner was concerned about the sloppiness, because he recognized that, if he had exercised proper due diligence as being in charge of the audit, he would have discovered this problem earlier. The sloppiness showed him up as lacking due care.

Question What should this new partner do, if anything?

Looking for an Answer As the partner was reviewing the work papers, various courses of action occurred to him. Which do you think is best? Which must be excluded? How would you rank the permissible courses of action? Can you think of something better?

Note that at this point no legal claim had yet been filed, and no documents had been subpoenaed.

1. The partner's *first thought* was: "I should simply do nothing about this. There's a slight chance that this sloppiness will escape notice. That's the best I can count on. It's not material anyway."

2. His *second thought* was: "But I'm going through these work papers right now and can easily correct them. I wouldn't be changing anything of substance, but just making the form, the appearance of the work papers, align with the substance."

3. Then he thought, *third*: "Or maybe I should bring this problem to the attention of the senior partners. I should claim responsibility for the sloppy audit and accept the consequences."

4. Finally, and *fourth*, he thought: "But if I'm going that route, why don't I bring the problem to the attention of everyone at once—not only the senior partners, but also the seller and buyer? I'll write a comment on the current status of the work papers and copy this to all the parties of the transaction. That might clear the air and help everyone to see that the sloppiness doesn't touch the substance of the transaction."

(See page 366 below for a suggested resolution and discussion.)

SCENARIO 3 ~~ TO BUNDLE OR NOT TO BUNDLE

What counts as true conservativism?

The Situation A public company is faced with the necessity of a significant write-down of intangible assets associated with a previous share-based acquisition. Much work and expertise has been brought to bear in looking at this problem; there is no escaping this conclusion.

After the meeting in which this is decided, the company's CFO calls the Financial Controller aside and says, "Why don't we look at this circumstance as an opportunity to write down the value of all kinds of questionable asset values on our financial statements, and record them all as one big extraordinary item? If we take that approach, we can position ourselves for much higher profitability later. You see what I mean? So that's what I would like you to do."

Question The Financial Controller finds this reasoning very appealing from the point of view of the company, but he is a CPA and also regards it is questionable. How should he respond to the CFO's suggestion?

Looking for an Answer The Financial Controller has the following train of thoughts. Which do you concur with? What is not permissible for him? What is his best course of action among permissible alternatives?

1. His *first thought* is simply to do what the CFO wants, but to dress it up so that it can pass muster: "An accountant can always book an asset in a 'conservative' manner if he wants," he says to himself, "It's likely that a conservative treatment of the aforementioned intangible and other assets, as manifested in an extraordinary

item write-down, would work out to be roughly the same as the bundled write-down the CFO wants. So I can do what he wants and still, in a sense, make it fall within GAAP under conservative treatment principles"

2. He then thinks, *second*: "But wouldn't that be manipulative—to bundle unrelated write-downs without both obtaining an independent valuation and fully declaring the actions? I think I'll just ignore what the CFO said, and, if someone questions me later about it, I'll simply say that I didn't think he was serious, but just testing me."

3. He then thinks, *third*: "But maybe I can have my cake and eat it too. I'll assemble the write-downs of other assets, as the CFO wants, but I'll disclose them separately in various places in the financial statement as to make them difficult to understand. In this way, we can have the write-downs, while making the disclosures extended, opaque and complex. The result may be the same result except without any real regulatory exposure."

4. Finally, and *fourth*, he thinks: "But really, such a course of action wouldn't help the long-term interests of the company very much, even if this treatment remains hidden from exposure and investigation; and, after all, it is in the share-holders' interest to know the true financial circumstance of the company. So I'll prepare the write-downs, but submit the decision to the auditors and the audit committee for their approval."

(See page 367 below for a suggested resolution and discussion.)

SCENARIO 4 ~~ "EXCEPTIONAL CLIENT SERVICE"

How does one act in the best interests of one's client?

The Situation A senior accountant is working on the audit of a distribution company. The company is a big client of the office of the managing director of the firm, who has instructed his team to provide "the greatest level of service" to this client.

One day the audit manager approaches the senior accountant and asks him to prepare the company's Federal tax return. A significant part of the tax return is the valuation of inventory, using a LIFO/FIFO standard of valuation— the choice of the standard being contingent on the legal tax benefits that can accrue. Because the distribution company has thousands of products, the manager suggests that the senior accountant use a statistical sampling method of valuing the inventory for tax purposes. The senior accountant has not done anything like this before. Knowing this, the manager offers his assistance, saying, "When you get to that point of the tax return, let me know, and I'll show you how to do it."

Later, when the senior accountant asks for this help, the manager shows him how to use the relevant software for statistical samples. He then adds: "I'll set this up for you so that it runs 1000 samples. You can then pick the sample that is most advantageous to our client's tax position and use that for the tax return."

The senior accountant at first shows some hesitation. Seeing this, the manager reminds him of what the managing director had requested, namely, that this client should be given "exceptional client service." The manager suggests that to do 1000 samples, and not merely one, is to go through the trouble of finding the sample that best advances the interests of the client. This is the way to provide "exceptional client service."

Question The senior accountant continues to have doubts about the suggested procedure. And yet this sort of tax return is new to him, and, as far as he knows, the procedure of searching through 1000 samples to find the best one for his client is not forbidden by the letter of the law. So then, what should he do in such a circumstance?

Looking for an Answer Which of the following is not permissible? And, of the permissible alternatives, which is the best course of action?

1. The senior accountant's *first thought* is simply to do what the manager tells him. After all, the manager is in charge, and if he decides upon something, then that is surely his responsibility. Also, the senior accountant recognizes that he is not a tax expert. Maybe there is something about this that he does not understand, but which the manager knows. As far as he is aware, nothing in the letter of the law forbids that sort of sampling. And, if is not forbidden, then he should do it, because that would be in the best interests of his client.

2. On *second thought*, the senior accountant comes to think that it's likely that to pick the most advantageous of 1000 samples crosses the line between tax avoidance and tax fraud. He thinks that, if he takes a number of samples, he should give the average of them, not select out a sample, which would make the result no longer random. He therefore decides that he should separate himself from any responsibility for the tax return. He will tell the senior manager that he'd prefer that someone else do it—perhaps coming up with some excuse about his lack of knowledge in the area. He recognizes that he will possibly suffer bad consequences from taking this position, but this seems the right thing to do nonetheless.

3. However, then he has a *third* idea, which is that simply to remove himself is not enough: he should be more proactive and speak with the managing partner about

the manager's suggested procedure. He should suggest to the partner that, in his view, to select out a sample is tantamount to fraud. He should seek the managing partner's agreement that to call this sort of procedure "exceptional client service" is a misnomer. To use a procedure which is fraudulent, or borders on the fraudulent, puts the firm's reputation at risk and exposes the client to penalties and interest—which is definitely not "advantageous" to the client.

4. But then *fourth*, and finally, the senior accountant considers whether it wouldn't be good enough, after all, if he simply spoke with the head of his firm's tax department. He could seek that person's opinion as to the legitimacy of the sampling procedure and abide by that advice. And he could just leave it with that person to deal with the manager.

(See page 368 below for a suggested resolution and discussion.)

SCENARIO 5 ~~ "WHO AUTHORIZES YOUR PAYCHECK?"

To whom does an internal auditor report?

The Situation William McGee is an internal auditor for Premiere Printers, a book printing company. It's of the nature of the book printing business that a printer will be constantly distributing books and then taking books back in return. That is, from an accounting perspective, the company is constantly creating receivables and crediting against receivables. Furthermore, if books are printed with flaws, then there will be a run of books such that a customer has a claim against the company. The customer will regard himself as not obliged to pay the full amount of the original invoice. The accounts receivable clerk (who, at Premiere Printers, is a CPA) will therefore be constantly adding receivables and crediting receivables, without knowing exactly how many are valid, and to what extent, at any time. Thus, an important job for the internal auditor of such a company will be to insure that the accounts receivable clerk is accounting for these appropriately.

When William McGee is doing his review of accounts receivable at Premiere, he discovers many instances, in large accounts, in which a customer alleges a claim against the company for flawed book production and therefore pays less than the original invoice. (For instance, the customer is billed $50,000 but pays only $45,000, regarding this as in complete satisfaction of the original invoice.) But this lesser payment has been accounted for, not by crediting it against the original invoice, thus revealing a shortfall, but rather by crediting it against the carried over receivable from a prior impaired transaction, thus hiding potential write-offs. McGee sees that this has been going on for some time and that the receivable balance has become less and less collectible.

When McGee investigates further, he discovers that the accounts receivable department is understaffed and for some time has lacked the resources to determine the extent and validity of customers' claims. Moreover, he learns that the CFO, in light of this, has instructed accounts receivable to regard all invoices as collectible and to apply current payments to carried-over balances. The CFO has set down this policy in part because he is hard-nosed and dismissive of customers' claims, thinking that they lack basis, and in part because the policy leads to a reporting of strong profits for the company, for which the CFO has already received several large bonuses.

McGee approaches the CFO and tells him that the policy is misguided and should be changed. "You can't do that," McGee insists. The CFO in reply says to McGee: "Oh can't I? Tell me, McGee, who authorizes your paycheck?"

Question What should McGee do? In this company, the CFO is his boss. Should he do what the CFO tells him, or should he do something else?

Looking for an Answer Which of the following courses of action are permissible for McGee, and, of those which are permissible, how would you rank order them?

A. McGee should do what the CFO instructs. After all, the CFO knows better, since he has responsibility for the finances of the company as a whole. Also, he has both the authority and the responsibility for this decision. McGee should let it play out; time will tell whether the CFO's policy is a good one.

B. McGee should go directly to the president and say something like the following: "The company has a major problem here, which is being covered up. We've lost control of the receivable balance. The loss we will have to sustain, which will be entirely unsuspected, could be catastrophic for the business—and for your and my livelihood." Of course, in speaking so plainly to the president, McGee risks being fired, whether the president agrees with him or not.

C. It would be better for McGee to go the external auditor. He should speak with a partner in the external audit firm and explain the accounting irregularity. This could be done in such a way that no one in Premiere will know that the external auditor has been tipped off. But the external auditors will certainly flag the problem in their next audit.

D. McGee should speak with the owners or Board of Directors of the company and explain how the accounting irregularities in Premiere are effectively misrepresenting the true financial condition of the company.

(See page 369 below for a suggested resolution and discussion.)

SCENARIO 6 ~~ INTIMATE CONFLICTS

You've seen it. Now what do you do?

The Situation Ralph Judson is a CPA who is the head of internal audit of a mid-sized bank with about $500 million in loans. One evening he just happens to walk into a bar on the outskirts of town at 10 pm to meet someone, and, as he walks in—the bar is very crowded—a face catches his eye, and it is the face of a female senior loan officer in his bank, Nancy Draper. He sees that she is having a fairly intimate drink with a major borrower, one of the largest developers in town.

Judson freezes; he moves out of eyesight and is not quite sure what to do. The more he looks on at the scene, the more it seems obvious that this is not an "extended business meeting." He decides to go out to the parking lot, because he knows what Draper's car looks like. His plan is to learn more by observing what happens next. Draper's car is parked in a poorly lit back section of the parking lot. Judson therefore moves his car into position among the shadows, where he can have a good view.

Not fifteen minutes later, Draper and the major borrower come out, and, walking to her car, even before they put the key in the door, the developer acts in such a way that there can be no doubt as to the intimate relationship that exists between them. They next get into the car, steam up the windows, and half an hour later he gets out and leaves. Judson stays and observes until Draper drives off.

Question The next day Judson sees Draper at work and is not sure what to do. Draper's relationship with the major borrower/developer is a serious violation of bank policy. However, Judson is very concerned because he has heard rumors that Draper has also been intimate with the bank President—and Draper reports to the bank President. As head of internal audit, Judson has the authority to initiate a review of the loan relationship, but this would look suspicious and strange. He might of course contrive to review "certain lending relationships that the bank has"—which would just "happen" to include this particular loan relationship, picked "accidentally" for extensive review. However, that path is effectively closed to him, since a fairly comprehensive review of that sort was just completed, and for him to initiate a new review at this time would be regarded as inappropriate and perhaps even as a kind of harassment.

What should Judson do?

Looking for an Answer What follows are various possible courses of action. Are there any that should be excluded? Of those that are permissible, which is best? How would you rank them?

First possibility: Judson should make an appointment with the bank President. He should explain what he has seen, and he should recommend that the bank undertake a serious, objective review of its lending relationship with that borrower/developer—to be carried out by internal audit, or by whatever independent means the President decides (such as an outside consultant; another loan officer; or the president himself). Judson recognizes that by taking this action he might precipitate his own dismissal, since the President might conclude that his observations of Draper constituted "spying" and were inappropriate. Also, if the President still had affection for Draper, he might be more willing to believe that Judson was the problem than that Draper acted badly.

Second possibility: Judson should do nothing, on the grounds that he really should not have "observed" the loan officer in the way that he did, and that his doing so has, arguably, created in his own mind a certain level of bias, and even paranoia. He has so compromised any objectivity he might have had, that he is no longer in a position to deal with this issue as head of internal audit.

Third possibility: Judson should go to the Chairman of the Board and explain the problem. Because the Chairman and the bank President have been good friends in the past, Draper regards this as a risky course—he might need to explain why he is going over the head of the President.

Fourth possibility: Judson should deal with this directly and personally. He should approach the senior loan officer directly and say something like: "At the ____ Bar last night, I saw what seemed to be a serious violation of company policy, as regards your relationship with one of the bank's major borrowers. As head of internal audit, I must insist that you either break off this relationship, or resign from your position at the bank, or both."

(See page 371 below for a suggested resolution and discussion.)

SCENARIO 7 ~~ LIFE CAN BE BUSY

How do you do your job—when you don't have time?

The Situation Susan York is an experienced partner in a regional CPA firm, whose largest audit client is a mental health provider, Health Plus. The president of the healthcare system, Dirk Eliot, was a good friend of hers from college. York admired

Eliot greatly, because she was aware that, for humanitarian reasons, Eliot had given up a well-paid and prestigious job in order to take on the management of Health Plus.

Health Plus's system relies heavily on Medicare reimbursements for its revenue. York, understanding the importance of these reimbursements to the vitality of this healthcare business, would prudently aim to review personally the Medicare reimbursement and claims documentation provided by the healthcare system, as part of the audit.

It was a June 30th audit. Health Plus's financial statements had to be delivered to their primary creditor, a financial institution, by the end of the day on August 15th, or their fairly substantial loans could be put into default.

In past years, because of the nature of this critical part of the audit engagement—the evaluation of the propriety of the Medicare reimbursements—York would not get the client papers to review until around August 10th. This was acceptable to her, since she was happy to put other work to the side in order to do this task for her friend, and four or five days would be sufficient time.

This year, however, on the 10th of August, York receives a call from her friend, who explains that a key person in the preparation of the papers has been ill for a week, and that he will therefore need a few extra days to get the papers to her. Eliot emphasizes once again how important this work is for his business, and York once again repeats how much she is committed to helping with this crucial part of the audit.

A couple of days later, Eliot calls again and says that the papers are still delayed; again he and York reaffirm their shared commitment to getting this work done in time.

However, now it is August 14th, one day before the review is due at the financial institution. In the late morning, Eliot calls and says that, at last, he has the work papers in his possession and has read through them, and he is ready to have them sent over by courier. He apologizes and begs forgiveness for their tardiness. He emphasizes his need to have the review delivered by the end of the 15th and wonders aloud whether the partner can complete the review on the morning of the 15th.

When York receives the papers in the late morning, she is in a bit of a fix. She cannot look at the papers then, since she is just going out the door for lunch with her son, who has just returned from an overseas trip and who has stopped in at her office to surprise her. But when she gets back to the office in the early afternoon, she is told that an interview candidate has been waiting for her for at least 25 minutes—she had completely forgotten that this was on her agenda. Her evening is already committed to a party and reception for her husband in a nearby city. She is unwilling even to consider breaking that "date," since she and her husband have been having some rocky times recently, such that missing this could be just about the "last straw."

Question Is there anything York can do to escape her dilemma?

Looking for an Answer It seems to York that she has only four options. Which should she do? Or has she overlooked an even better way out?

First, she can sign off on the papers without reviewing them. After all, she knows her friend and trusts him. She can probably rely on his assessment and on her own intuition that the work papers represent the true condition of the health care system, as they have in the past.

Second, she can call up her friend and say that, unfortunately, she cannot do the review, since she has not been left with enough time.—Yet she is reluctant to do so, because her friend might say that she broke her promise. Also, she might even end up jeopardizing his health care business, by hurting his relationship with his creditor.

Third, she could take the fairly extreme measure of calling on one or more of her fellow partners and ask them to work late into the night on the 14th in order to meet the creditor's deadline.

Finally, she could make some effort to contact the creditor, to seek an extension on behalf of her client and friend.

(See page 372 below for a suggested resolution and discussion.)

SCENARIO 8 ~~ WHAT YOU DON'T KNOW...

You didn't even know that there was a chain, never mind that someone is yanking it.

The Situation Kathleen Currie is a CPA who recently started a business valuation firm. After working twenty years in audit and tax practice, it became clear to her that what she really enjoyed was the element of business valuation. She ultimately became skilled enough in this area to start her own firm.

One day Currie receives a call from a longtime friend, Jim Lawson. Lawson is the owner of a medium-sized business ($20 million in sales, 400 employees). Currie's former audit firm used to audit Lawson's business, and Currie was the audit partner in charge of those audits. Besides being Lawson's friend, then, she is very familiar with his business.

Lawson says, "I've been thinking about doing some estate planning, and I would like to get a business valuation done, so that I can examine the various possibilities, including estate taxes, as regards the distribution of my 75% ownership shares." They agree upon a reasonable fee for this, and Currie begins work on the valuation. Understanding that the valuation is intended for the purpose of an estate valuation, she looks at the various inputs into the valuation with a critical eye, so that she can value the estate as low as reasonably possible, thus minimizing taxes upon it. She writes a nicely produced and professional report, and sends it to Lawson.

Currie does not hear from Lawson for a few weeks, and, in particular, she has not received payment. She therefore decides to call Lawson and ask what he thinks of the valuation. When she poses the question, she is greeted by silence. After a long pause, Lawson says: "To tell the truth, in my view you've been overly aggressive in the valuation of this business. Remember, this is for an estate valuation. Frankly, I don't understand how you can pick some of the ranges you picked for discount and growth rates; and some of your assumptions about capital expenditures are unjustifiable."

Question When Currie hears this, she is disappointed and perplexed. She does not want to disappoint Lawson. He is her friend (Currie even went to the wedding of Lawson's daughter recently). And this assignment represents the first major appraisal job of her fledgling practice. (The fee they had agreed upon was $25,000.) Besides, Lawson is important in the business community; his opinion of her will have a lot of weight. Nonetheless, Currie's initial reaction is that she had given an objective if conservative valuation, and she hesitates to change it. What should she do?

Looking for an Answer What follows are four ways in which this might play out. Which is best, and are any excluded? Can you think of a better alternative?

1. Currie tells Lawson, in response, "Well, I could probably refine what I've done a bit." She then goes back and gives the "refining" job to one of her senior managers, who prepares some addendum work papers, where he sets the basis for the valuation by making use of the lowest end of the range for all the relevant inputs. They re-run the valuation and give it to Lawson—who, they expect, will be very happy and will pay the fee promptly.

2. Currie takes into account what the owner has said, and tries to give it as much credit as possible, but in the end she only tweaks a few things and fundamentally does not change her valuation.

3. When Lawson expresses his unhappiness with the valuation, Currie says in reply, "That's my professional opinion. I've spent a great deal of time on this and incorporated lots of comparables, looking at economic data and considering the various risk factors. This is a good and proper valuation. It's my best work, and I have to stand by it."

4. Currie decides to withdraw from the agreement, saying, "I understand what you're asking me to do, but that is improper, and I can't be involved in anything like that. The mere fact that you've asked me to produce a valuation which would be, in my opinion, unjustifiably low, implies that I can no longer undertake to do this for you."

(See page 373 below for a suggested resolution and discussion.)

SCENARIO 9 ~~ CASCADING ATTEST WORK

If you are asked to do less, should you insist on doing more?

The Situation Burt Lang is an audit partner who has as one of his clients EZ Duzzit, a medium-sized manufacturing company. (EZ Duzzit in past years has paid a yearly audit fee in the neighborhood of $200,000.) Recently EZ Duzzit has been struggling financially, to the point that Lang insists upon, and goes through a process, that results in his firm's giving the company a going-concern opinion. This does not come as a surprise to the owner of the company, Sweety Bill Leonard, since he and Lang in the past have had extensive discussions about this possibility.

The next year, Sweety Bill comes to Lang and says, "This past year has been much better for us," and he hands him the draft financial statements, which indicate a 20% increase in sales. The company is back in profitability. The line of credit reflected in the books has declined. Sweety Bill adds that he is pleased that his company has cut back on its expenses and has been more efficient in sales. "Getting that going-concern was a real wake-up call and spurred our managers really to get 'going,'" he jokes, thanking Lang. "We've started to turn things around. Everything looks so much more positive. And because we're on a very tight cost control plan, we've solicited and received approval from the bank to seek this year only a review, not a full-fledged audit." Sweety Bill views this as contributing to the "tighter ship" that his company has become, since a review will cost about $40,000, rather than the $200,000 fee of past audits.

Lang congratulates him on doing such a good job. However, he is somewhat concerned, because it is not obvious to him that it is wise to substitute a review for an audit. Yet he can see why the newly cost-conscious company might favor it, and why the bank might regard a review as a justifiable, if temporary, expedient.

When Lang's firm does the review, he notices that a few ratios seem not quite right. The gross margin seems to be lower than the previous year, although not by much. He's not sure that that makes sense. Also, interest expense is higher—but perhaps that is to be explained by the fact that interest rates are slightly higher. But these niggling concerns are no obstacle to his firm's completing the review.

Another year passes. This time Sweety Bill approaches Lang and says, "The turnaround is continuing. For one year more we want to forego an audit, as part of the 'tight ship' policy at our company. This year, in fact, we are seeking only a compilation, which we figure would cost only $15,000, instead of a review." When Lang inquires as to the wisdom of this, Sweety Bill asserts that a review would only be so much unnecessary work. He explains that bank auditors have already been in to look at inventory and receivables. They've already subjected the business to far greater scrutiny than a review, he says, and even the bank agrees that it would be unnecessary to seek a review. "In these circumstances," Sweety Bill says, "EZ Duzzit's number one priority should be—and is—to pay down its debt." At the end of the conversation, almost as an afterthought, he adds that in the coming months he may need some expert witness work done, which could result in upwards of $100,000 in fees for Lang's firm.

Question Lang is somewhat perplexed by this. He is aware, for instance, that Sweety Bill has left the country club. Sweety Bill also had his son switch colleges from a private school to a state school, and he put his summer home up for sale. These incidental facts might suggest that EZ Duzzit has not yet reached profitability and perhaps has not turned around to the extent that Sweety Bill claims. But then Lang thinks that there could be some other, good explanation— perhaps, even, Sweety Bill accepted a drastic pay reduction to help the company attain profitability. Furthermore, the bank apparently feels comfortable with skipping an audit for one more year.

Looking for an Answer In this context, four courses of action present themselves to Lang. Which is excluded, and which is best for him to do?

1. Lang should tell Sweety Bill that he is not comfortable with doing anything other than a full audit. He should refuse to do only a compilation and withdraw from the engagement if Sweety Bill continues to insist on a compilation.

2. He should withdraw from the engagement entirely, but he should do so with a so-called "noisy withdrawal": that is, he should make it clear to Sweety Bill that major creditors will get copies of his firm's letter refusing to do the requested compilation.

3. He should confer directly with the financial institutions, the creditors of EZ Duzzit, and discuss the wisdom of not doing an audit for a second straight year.

4. He should go ahead with a compilation, on the grounds that it is the client's responsibility, and therefore in his domain, to determine what level of attest function he wishes to seek. His firm's responsibility, on the other hand, is to carry out, with professionalism and competence, the job that his client requests.

(See page 375 below for a suggested resolution and discussion.)

SCENARIO 10 ~~ HOW MANY ENTITIES DO YOU NEED TO LOOK THROUGH?
You didn't look before, but maybe you need to look now.

The Situation Starburgh Investments is an investment advisory firm which manages 20 investment funds for various local labor unions—welfare funds, health funds, and so on. The funds vary from $50 million to $200 million in capital. Roughly 25% of each fund (the exact percentage varies from fund to fund) is invested in Mortgage Equity, a related entity, which generates private equity mortgages.

Your firm, Danvers Accounting LLP, audits three of these funds. You are the partner responsible for these audits, and this is your second year doing so. The funds are relatively easy to audit and involve minimal risk. They have almost no debt; they show limited activity and carry few expenses. You need to confirm, through the report of an actuary, that what the funds are obligated to pay out is properly represented in the financial statements. You also need to confirm the validity and value of the assets that the fund invests in. You need to verify that Starburgh is properly carrying out its fiduciary responsibility, by investing in a manner consistent with the charters set down by the union directors of the various funds. And you need to obtain a SAS 70 review of the holder of the securities (a group employed by Starburgh), to confirm that the securities actually held represent the securities owned. These audits, then, are overall fairly low-risk engagements, since you are relying on reports of the relevant experts at nearly every point.

In the course of the audit, the audit manager approaches you and asks whether your firm should seek an independent valuation of the funds' investments in Mortgage Equity. You are caught off guard by the question, because Danvers has not once in the last twenty years sought such a valuation. Generally, mortgages are not a particularly risky investment, since they have real estate as collateral. Moreover, the funds' investments in Mortgage Equity have been scrutinized and approved by the directors of the three union funds. You are unaware of GAAS requiring an independent valuation in such circumstances; in fact, you are fairly confident that it does not. And besides, each year Starburgh provides a valuation of those investments, produced by its own expert. So for all these reasons an independent valuation looks completely unnecessary to you.

You recognize, of course, that Starburgh would have an incentive to hide a problem in those investments, since they might be fired as fund managers if those investments implied a substantial overall loss. Also, the union directors have an incentive to ignore problems that might arise. The reason is that some of the union funds are health and welfare funds, where the return on investment has a direct effect on dues to be charged to union members in future years. The higher the rate of return of the funds, the more the directors can reduce dues, thus keeping the support of rank-and-file and keeping their jobs. On the other hand, if the funds were to lose value, the union fund directors would be held responsible by union members and would probably lose their jobs.

Compounding all of this is that, soon after your manager asks you the question about an independent valuation, you remember that a few months ago the newspapers were reporting charges made by minority investors in Starburgh that Starburgh's president had defrauded them. You did not give much credit to these charges; they seemed motivated because of personal enmities and jealousy. More importantly, perhaps, the union directors dismissed the claims as unfounded. Ultimately it would be the union directors who would have to approve the added expense of obtaining an independent valuation. And if you were to insist on this expense—and especially if you were to express any doubts about the integrity of the president of Starburgh—you might endanger the retention of these audit engagements.

Question What should you do, then? All things considered, should you seek an independent valuation or not?

Looking for an Answer What follows are four possible actions you can take. Which of these are excluded, and which is best?

1. There is no need to do anything in particular. It is best, and safest, to do what your firm has always done in the past. You think: this option has the weight of experience and the credibility of past practice on its side. You see no decisive or determining reason to do anything differently.

2. You should organize meetings with the investment directors of the three union funds. At these meetings, you should express your skepticism and explain that your firm will not give an audit opinion until it can reach a greater comfort level about the valuation of the investments in Mortgage Equity.

3. You should go ahead and require the independent valuation, approaching Starburgh and asking them to have it done, using a recognized and independent expert. This would be done without consultation with the fund directors.

4. You should initiate a conversation with the three or four other audit firms which audit the other seventeen funds managed by Starburgh, to find out what these firms are doing and why. You hope in this way to confirm your interpretation of GAAS. As mentioned, you believe that GAAS does not require the valuation, but perhaps your interpretation is incorrect or not up to date.

(See page 376 below for a suggested resolution and discussion.)

SUGGESTED RESOLUTIONS OF CASES

Note: The explanations given in the resolutions below rely largely on the principles articulated in the current Code of Professional Conduct, especially the principles of *integrity, objectivity, independence, due care,* and *public interest,* as, despite potential shortcomings, discussed above in chapter 10, these provide the framework within which accounting ethics will typically be considered today.

SCENARIO 1

Suggested Resolution We consider that Andrew's advice is unacceptable and should not be followed. As regards the other answers, depending on other factors, it seems that Cathy or Boris's advice is the best. The least-best course, but still acceptable, would be Drew's recommendation.

Reasoning The difference between a blameworthy omission—or sloppiness—in an audit, and legitimate "risk assessment," is that the latter is justified and made on proper authority. For the staff accountant to engage in unapproved "risk assessment" would be against integrity, since the job would not be done in the way it was described as being done. It would also be contrary to due care, because the staff accountant's work would not be providing to the audit manager and partner all of the information that was thought to be needed for an objective judgment of the company's representation of its financial condition.

With respect to informing on the senior accountant, it seems that one would first need to have clear evidence of a failure to perform the work. The senior accountant was careful not to advise the staff accountant explicitly not to do the work. He may very well have done the work. Perhaps additional conversations with various personnel would make a clear judgment about this possible. If there were definite evidence that the senior accountant was not doing his work properly, then it might become necessary to inform the audit manager about this, on the grounds that the firm would be exposed to risk and its reputation could potentially be damaged.

Potentially a better resolution than the four mentioned here would be for the new hire to go to the manager or partner and explain her difficulty straightforwardly, as it is possible that her workload really is unreasonable and needs to be adjusted.

In Real Life This scenario is based on a real-life case in which the staff accountant followed "Andrew type" advice. Later on, in litigation, a forensic accountant went through the loan files properly and discovered deficiencies. The staff accountant had to admit under oath in a deposition that she did not do the steps that she said she did.

An admission such as that can have the effect—and it did—of destroying the entire credibility of the auditors. As we have seen, the role of accountants and auditors is precisely to insure the conditions of trust in the marketplace. Their professional standing, therefore, collapses if they are not themselves credible. It is important to understand also that all directed steps in an audit need to be done thoroughly, since otherwise there can appear to be a weak link in that "chain" which constitutes an audit; and a weak link can compromise the credibility of the entire audit.

SCENARIO 2

Suggested Resolution We consider that the partner's first two thoughts should be rejected. Of the remaining options, it is probably best that he aim to inform all concerned parties of the poor audit work.

Reasoning The partner's second thought—to clean up the work papers after the fact—seems to be contrary to integrity, because it would misrepresent the work that was actually done. It would furthermore seem to be contrary to professionalism, because it would bespeak the partner's unwillingness to suffer a penalty for poor work rather than risk damage to his firm or clients.

The partner's first thought should probably also be rejected as contrary to professionalism. His fellow partners deserve to understand the issues that face both them and the firm.

Considerations of independence might tend to suggest that the fourth option would be best: the partner should inform all parties, after first discussing the circumstance with his partners and potentially counsel, since both the buyer and seller are his clients.

The third option seems acceptable but less preferable.

In Real Life The scenario is based on a real-life case in which the partner followed Option 2, that is, he went through the work papers and "cleaned them up." In litigation, a forensic accountant examined the work papers carefully and discovered discrepancies. The partner was then put in the difficult position of having to explain under oath in a deposition why it was *not* a fraud that, when he corrected the work papers, he wrote on the papers the initials of the other people who had originally done sloppy work.

The case demonstrates the peril of a relationship that appears to compromise independence. The buyer probably recognized that his claim was weak on the merits, but he was trying to exploit the appearance of bias that came from the friendship between the seller and a name partner in the accounting firm.

SCENARIO 3

Suggested Resolution We consider that the first and third thoughts would have to be excluded, as contrary to integrity, objectivity and professionalism. The second and fourth thoughts might be acceptable, depending upon additional considerations.

Reasoning The "very conservative" estimates of the other assets constituting the extraordinary write-down would seem not to be justifiable if standing on their own. The rationale for doing so is to prepare the financial statements to be overly positive for the future. But this rationale, by its nature, seems contrary to the duties owed the shareholders and corporation. To act on such a rationale, and follow the CFO's suggestion, would be contrary to an accountant's objectivity, in that there is nothing objective in determining in advance an outcome or representation, simply because that is the outcome that you want. To act on such a rationale would also seem to be contrary to professionalism, since it would ignore the interests of investors or other third-parties who might rely on the Financial Controller's representations related to the write-downs. Note that the Financial Controller, as a CPA, has a professional obligation to serve the public interest and not only the interests of the company that employs him.

In Real Life About six months later the company entered bankruptcy because of a quality control failure at one of their manufacturing facilities. The Federal authorities ended up getting involved, and, in their efforts to identify improprieties, they found the work-papers and journal entries that identified and increased the write-off amounts. This bright line accounting manipulation was used as leverage to force the CFO and Financial Controller into criminal plea deals that netted them each two years in a Federal penitentiary.

The accounting manipulation had little or nothing to do with the demise of the company; in fact the company emerged strongly from its Chapter 11 bankruptcy filing. But the public exposure, criminal plea deals, and the general cloud of accounting improprieties had raised issues about management integrity; these things brought an end to the careers of most of the company's senior management and all of its board members.

SCENARIO 4

Suggested Resolution We consider that the first course of action should be excluded as impermissible. Of the remaining alternatives, the best seems to be for the senior accountant to approach the managing partner (Option 3). Next best would be for him to approach the head of the tax department (Option 4). Least acceptable, and barely permissible, is simply for him to detach himself from preparing the tax return (Option 2).

Reasoning It is not open to the senior accountant, we think, simply to go along with what the manager says. Given that, reasonably so, he has concerns that the suggested procedure is improper, then, because of due diligence, he should investigate this further.

If he did so, he would discover that, as he suspected, it is indeed improper to represent a highly improbable and artificial result (which represents the far end of the bell curve) as if it were a sample arrived at by random methods. Once he becomes entirely clear about this, and even before he does so, it seems that the senior accountant cannot disclaim responsibility, and attempt to pass on all the responsibility to the manager ("after all, he is in charge"), because this would seem to constitute subordination of judgment, which would be at odds with an accountant's integrity as a professional.

The best course of action would presumably be for him to approach the managing partner. The reason is that a fraudulent practice, or even a practice which has the appearance of being fraudulent, harms the firm as a whole and therefore should be brought to the attention of those who have direct responsibility for the welfare of the firm as a whole. Also, the managing partner had set the standard of "exceptional client service," and therefore he would be in the best position to clarify that this could not mean acting improperly. (If the managing partner supports the manager, then this raises difficulties which go beyond the scope of this particular case.)

An accountant's preparation of a tax return involves, in part, a fiduciary relationship which the accountant has with respect to the client. This means that the accountant must be committed to serving the true and long-term interests of the client. But this in turn implies recommending to the client only positions and actions which are such that they could be defended as legitimate and fair, if subjected to open scrutiny.

Alternative (4) is good, but it seems not the best, for the reasons given. Alternative (2) looks to be only barely acceptable. The reason is that, according to the principle of integrity, an accountant is responsible for seeing that accounting work is done properly, not only by himself, but also by those whose work he supervises or is responsible for. By extension, the senior accountant should not detach himself from the project of preparing a tax return, if he has no confidence that the work will be done properly by those in the firm who take his place. But he cannot have this sort of confidence until the impropriety of the manager's proposed "sampling" method is somehow directly addressed.

In Real Life This scenario is based upon a case in which the senior accountant chose alternative (1). That is, despite his misgivings, he simply went along with what the manager said. Shortly thereafter, the senior accountant lost the workpapers for the audit, when they were stolen while he was at a bar. (This sort of freak and unexpected detail is common in cases as they occur in real life.) Thus the audit had to be largely done over again.

Because of the loss of the papers, the managing partner announced that he was going to dismiss him summarily without severance, explaining that he should be grateful that the firm was not suing him for damages. The senior accountant then raised the illicit manner in which the inventory valuations were originally calculated, and he hinted that, if he were dismissed without severance, he would go to the tax authorities and report the firm for tax fraud.

Thus it was that the managing partner changed his mind and came to propose a new and generous severance package—and no amendment was ever made to the original tax return.

The lesson to be drawn from this is not that, by being complicit in fraud, an accountant can arm himself with material for blackmailing his firm if necessary (!), but rather that a firm needs to foster a culture which precludes this sort of exposure to risk and vulnerability to internal blackmailing.

SCENARIO 5

Suggested Resolution We consider that it is not open to McGee to follow the instructions of the CFO. The CFO's policy, a form of "kiting," is not in accordance with sound accounting principles and cannot be supported or cooperated with by an accounting professional.

Of the other alternatives, that which is best would seem to depend upon which persons, among those who supervise the CFO, McGee is able to report to. If he has the ability to report directly to the Board (or an audit committee of the Board), he should go directly to them. Otherwise he should alert the president first and, if he gets no satisfaction, then he might go to the Board. To alert the external accountant would be good but least preferable, as this course of action would not allow for Premier to correct the problem of its own accord first; moreover, the auditors should presumably be informed by the proper authorities at the company.

Reasoning Internal auditing is responsible for seeing that a company's representation to itself of its financial condition is accurate and truthful. The CFO's kiting scheme creates a false impression of profitability while obscuring losses. Moreover, the problem has grown to such an extent that it could affect the very survivability of the company: for instance, when the necessary write-offs are taken into account, this could affect the "performance ratios" which the company's lenders abide by, leading them to call their loans to the company. There is nothing that the CFO knows, and that an internal accountant does not know, which could change this. Thus, it is not open to McGee to "let it play out." He must turn to someone who has responsibility for the company as a whole—president or owners.

As a last resort, he should turn to the external auditors. An internal auditor, as an accounting professional, has a responsibility that extends more widely than the interests of his company alone. He simply cannot be complicit in any misrepresentation or fraud, which may result in the defrauding of third parties such as investors and lenders.

In Real Life This scenario is based on a similar case in real life, in which the internal auditor went along with the CFO's policy and did nothing about it. The external auditors discovered the problem in their next audit engagement. When they raised the problem with the CFO, they were dismissed. At the same time, the President and CFO began to arrange for the sale of the company—presumably in order to pocket some handsome profits while abandoning a sinking ship. But they were thwarted in this. The prospective buyers hired an audit firm to evaluate the accounts receivable balance. The auditors promptly determined that the company's stated balance was unreliable. Since they now had reason to suspect the integrity of the company's management, they concluded that they could not rely on anything else about the company, and the deal was off.

The lenders for the company eventually learned of the problem as well. In response, they closed the company and liquidated it (at a bargain rate) in order to minimize losses. To recover the balance between what they had lent the company and the sale price under liquidation, they initiated claims against the Director and Officer coverage of the company's officers.

As for the internal auditor—he spent the better part of the next several years of his life giving depositions and in court, and during that time he was unable to find work.

SCENARIO 6

Suggested Resolution We consider that the second possibility—that Judson should do nothing—is excluded, on the grounds that his primary duty as an internal auditor is the protection of the assets of the bank, and that, however he came upon information that might impugn the objectivity of the senior loan officer in relation to a borrower, the intimate nature of that relationship requires that there be a review of whether the bank's loan policy was adhered to in this case.

We think the fourth option—that Judson approach the loan officer directly—is also excluded, on the grounds that the embarrassment and extreme emotions that such an encounter would likely arouse would make any reasonable outcome very problematic if not impossible.

This seems to be one of those cases in which an internal auditor is effectively required to act in such a way that he has to be prepared to lose his job. To the extent that he believes in the credibility of the rumors about a relationship between the president and this same officer, he should presumably go to the chairman of the board (Option 2). Otherwise, he should approach the bank president about the problem (Option 1). He might even combine these options by first meeting with the chairman, telling him of his plan to tell the bank president, but also sharing with the chairman his concerns that his job might be threatened.

Reasoning The profession of accounting is inherently altruistic, in the sense that an accountant, as a professional, has to be prepared to sacrifice his well-being, for the sake of the interests of those who rely, directly or indirectly, on his or her work as an accountant. In this case, since Judson is employed by a bank, he has to be prepared to sacrifice his job, for the sake of protecting the assets of the bank and its clients.

Judson probably did go "over the top" when he decided to hide out in the parking lot and observe his colleague's inappropriate behavior. At the same time, he did this simply to confirm what he already had reason to suspect very strongly. In any case, there is no "exclusionary rule" that would apply to what he saw. Even if he gained this information in a dubious way, once he knows about the senior loan officer's conflict of interest, he is obliged to act on this information.

In Real Life In the actual case on which this scenario is based, the head of internal auditing decided to do nothing.

A few months later, the borrower/developer defaulted on his loans and sought to renegotiate. An independent forensic accountant was brought in to review the circumstance and discovered that the borrower had an insatiable appetite for investing in exchange-traded options with less than a week to expiration. Over the course of the two previous years, he had lost more than 10 million dollars in doing so, most of which came from the loan advances made by the bank's senior loan officer in question. Since he had squandered so much money in this way, his development projects suffered from a complete failure of quality control. This led ultimately to a bank foreclosure and millions in additional loans being outlaid, in order to bring the construction projects up to acceptable level of quality.

The borrower/developer had deliberately seduced the senior loan officer, precisely to get additional loans from the bank. In fact he had made an assessment, from earlier meetings with her, that she bordered on being an alcoholic, and that, if he could ply her with enough alcohol, he could easily seduce her—which he succeeded in doing.

The loan officer lost her job, and the borrower/developer was prosecuted criminally. The head of internal audit lived for months in fear that his knowledge of the compromised relationship would be discovered. Eventually it was discovered, and he lost his job. He spent an interminable amount of time in the months that followed giving depositions and testifying in court.

SCENARIO 7

Suggested Resolution We consider that York's first option is excluded, as it is not permissible for her to sign off on work papers that she has not examined. This would be "subordination of judgment." Option 3 is practically excluded, because it is unlikely that other partners would have sufficient knowledge of the business to carry out the evaluation of Medicare reimbursements—which York has standardly reserved for herself precisely because it is so crucial to the audit. Option 4 is also excluded, on the grounds that calling the creditor would be inappropriate for an independent auditor; and, besides, such a call could raise concerns in the minds of the creditor. The only option open to York would be to call her friend and, regardless of any embarrassment she might feel, say that she is unable to complete the review in the time remaining.

Reasoning In the rush of demands and commitments of daily life, York is at risk of overlooking all kinds of red flags associated with the audit of Health Plus. Because she has been so busy, and Health Plus is her only client in the health care business that relies heavily on Medicare reimbursements, York had not kept up to date about what was happening in that industry, specifically, that recently Medicare had changed dramatically its criteria for reimbursement for mental health expenditures—which, if she knew about this, would raise in her mind serious concerns as to whether Health Plus's business was suffering as a result. That the work papers supporting the financial assertions were delivered to her so much later than usual would only add to this suspicion. And then, in this context, Eliot's frequent phone calls and insistence on her "friendly commitment" would begin to take on the appearance of his applying pressure on York to get the report done on time and without much review.

The skepticism that these considerations should naturally raise in her mind ought to lead York to take even more time than usual in evaluating the important Medicare client papers. Since it was not York's fault that she received the papers so late, we think she should leave it to the client to try to smooth out any difficulties this might create with the client's creditor.

In Real Life In the real life case on which this scenario is based, the partner chose to sign off on the papers without reviewing them. This proved to be a disastrous mistake, since Medicare reimbursement changes that year were devastating to mental health systems and necessitated a complete change in how such systems did their work. The audited health care system had not made appropriate changes. In fact, the president of this health care system did not even want to deal with the reality of what the new legislative requirements meant. His avoidance of reality was manifested especially in those work papers, particularly in the recording of receivables and revenue recognition.

The audit firm began the next years' audit but never completed it. The financial difficulties and cash deterioration were at that point so painfully obvious, that the firm asked for a retainer for the expected full cost of the audit, which was not given, since there was no cash to give. They therefore pulled out of the audit. Shortly thereafter the health system was put into receivership. The audit firm approached the receiver about completing the audit, which the firm would do only if they had a liability waiver. (They were looking for a liability waiver, in fact, to cover the deficiencies in their earlier work.) The receiver refused, after which another audit firm was brought in to do the audit.

The original audit firm had a significant liability exposure because of their failure to complete correctly the last full audit of the health system. The receiver eventually filed suit against the firm, asserting that the firm failed to file a going-concern opinion. (Because the firm had not done the crucial work, it did not even know that it should have filed a going-concern opinion.) In discovery in the course of this suit, the audit firm's failure was uncovered, and as a result it had to settle with the receiver for a very large amount.

SCENARIO 8

Suggested Resolution We consider that Option 1 is excluded. The other three are potentially valid approaches: which one would be best would depend upon facts and circumstances.

Reasoning A business valuation specialist, like an auditor, provides the conditions of trust on which certain marketplaces depend. As may perhaps not be fully appreciated by a fledgling business valuator, such a specialist is not merely an advocate but also a professional with an attest-like responsibility, which implies a level of objectivity and independence. He may promote the interests of his client, then, only insofar as that is consistent with his professional judgment as to the actual, objective value of the business, and never in such a way as to subordinate his judgment or abandon objectivity. Moreover, that Currie is a CPA carries with it its own ethical requirements, namely, all of the demands of professionalism that follow upon being a CPA.

We think that Currie has to use her common sense in light of these considerations. It is acceptable, of course, for a client to plump for his own, honest interests. Yet it is not acceptable for a client to seek fraudulent results, or to threaten or attempt to coerce a practitioner. Thus, if Lawson is simply "whining," Options 2 or 3 will be most appropriate, depending upon their relationship, since he will get over it and in due time will come to see things her way. Of course, to the extent that he advances good arguments, to that extent she should adjust her report in the direction that he favors.

If, however, Lawson crosses the line and either suggests that Currie do something fraudulent, or attempts to coerce her to produce a result the he desires, then we consider that Currie should follow Option 4.

In Real Life In the real-life case on which this scenario is based, the business valuation specialist followed Option 1, that is, she lowered inputs and values in a way that could not be supported by her professional judgment. About a year and a half later, Federal agents showed up at her door and handed her a warrant to examine her business valuation records and work papers. (In such cases, Federal authorities can become involved in various ways, such as that the appraisal was sent through the mails; or the valuation had tax ramifications; and so on.) The specialist called her lawyers, who inquired and learned that the agents were investigating the valuation she had done for her friend.

She eventually learned through her lawyers that her friend had no intention of using the valuation for estate planning but, rather, he had used it to purchase his minority interest owner's shares. The valuation supported him in paying $10 million for those shares, instead of the $12.5 million they were actually worth. (It turned out that the minority partner was having an affair with the majority owner's wife, and it was she who alerted him to her husband's fraud against him—another instance of a strange, accidental fact on which these kinds of cases often turn.)

The business valuation specialist's records contained what appeared to be clear evidence of fraud: (i) a change in valuation methodology; (ii) the consistent use of the lowest end of the range; and (iii) a production of one valuation and then a production of a much lower valuation. There are even scribbled notes in the work papers remarks such as: "N. wants the lowest valuation …."

About 6 months after the documents were taken by the Federal authorities, the specialist was indicted for criminal conspiracy to defraud. Ultimately, she was acquitted by a jury—but only after three years of litigation and close to a million dollars in legal fees, which were only partly covered by insurance. (Note: In such circumstances, prosecuting attorneys are able to represent the senior manager's work papers as far worse than they are, as constituting a criminal rather than merely a civil offense. In that case it becomes the senior manager's interest to throw his boss under the bus to preserve his own standing in the community. He has an interest in plea-bargaining for a reduced sentence and turning witness against his boss—making his boss's innocence even more difficult to sustain in court.)

SCENARIO 9

Suggested Resolution We consider that Option 4 is excluded, because the risk factors in the circumstances are too high. These circumstances include: his firm's going-concern opinion; EZ Duzzit's request for a second reduction of scope of audit, which makes little sense; and the bank's agreement on this reduction for a company that is "on watch," which also makes little sense.

Which of the other options would be best would depend upon the facts and circumstances.

Reasoning An attest professional can sometimes indicate something by what he does not do, as much as by what he does. Given that Lang's firm had audited the company for many years, there is the potential, if Lang's firm does only a compilation, for the public to be misled into thinking either that the scope of the engagement is similar, or that Lang's firm agreed that a lesser level of scrutiny would be acceptable.

Yet Lang's firm is in no position to make this latter judgment, and, given the circumstances mentioned, due diligence would apparently require that it investigate before reaching such a decision. But such an investigation would amount to an audit. That is, the requirement of due diligence suggests that Lang's firm would need to audit EZ Duzzit in order to be able to conclude responsibly that an audit was unnecessary!

Furthermore, Lang's firm had given EZ Duzzit a going-concern opinion. This serves as the "baseline" for any of the firm's future judgments and actions. In the context of a going-concern opinion, it would be strange and suspicious that EZ Duzzit should look for a cost-saving measure which happens to involve the omission of an audit.

Finally, good judgment would hold that more work than a review should be done, even if technically GAAS says nothing about such a situation. An accounting professional should not engage to examine a company at a lower level of scrutiny, if in his professional judgment a higher level would be needed for third parties not to be misled. Since he is a professional, he is not a financial "hired gun" prepared to do whatever his client enjoins. Rather, his professional judgment extends also to the question of what level of service his client should properly seek.

In Real Life In the real life case on which this scenario is based, the audit partner agreed to his client's request for a compilation. Within three months after the compilation was completed, the owner had shut down the plant and let everyone go—the business was bankrupt.

What had happened was this. When in the first year the review was completed, the owner took this review and pasted onto it the audit page from the previous year's audit. He passed this off as an audit, which he used to get a new line of credit of $10 million. Most of this money he used for his own purposes, to pay off personal debt or for sham payments to buy materials from front companies that he had established.

The next year, the auditor expected to do an audit and sent an engagement letter to that effect. The owner sent a signed copy of this engagement letter to the financial institution, as evidence that an audit was taking place. But the owner sent an unsigned copy back to the partner and verbally asked instead for a compilation. When he got the compilation, he once again pasted a copy of a previous audit certificate on the front and tried to pass it off as an audit, seeking additional credit.

By this time, however, the financial institution had begun to suspect that sales and inventories were overstated. It sent inspectors to the plant, who found serious concerns about capacity, production, and other matters, as a result of which it called the loan. This quickly led to the company's insolvency.

When these matters were placed in the hands of a bankruptcy trustee, he brought in criminal authorities to pursue charges of fraud against the audit firm. He also undertook on his own authority to recover funds for creditors—and naturally the audit firm was one of the best sources of recovery.

SCENARIO 10

Suggested Resolution We consider that Option 1 is perhaps the most common response to this kind of circumstance but should be excluded. The other options are all acceptable, but 2 seems the best, 4 second best, and 3 least best.

Reasoning Practically speaking, when an auditor or audit firm has a client for a long period of time, engagements can become rote. It becomes difficult to rethink them, or to view them afresh. This then exposes an auditor to the possibility of overlooking new and relevant data. His situation can be like that of the proverbial frog that gets boiled because the water is heated up very slowly, and the change goes unnoticed.

In the case described, the auditor is obliged to look at the audit afresh, because of the charges of fraud that have been publicly raised against the president of Starburgh. This presents him with a new situation. Thus, once the senior manager raises the question about an independent valuation, this question has to be put to rest in some way. It is not permissible to return to the status quo ante. (Consider: How would the auditor have evaluated the charges of fraud if this were the firm's very first audit of Starburgh?) That is why we think Option 1 must be excluded. In sum, this option is incompatible with due diligence.

Thus, concerns arising out of the public charges of fraud have to be taken into account. The only question is: How much weight should be given to the possibility that the president of Starburgh is dishonest, and that Starburgh has provided an inflated valuation of the investments in Mortgage Equity? To answer this, one should consider: Who is relying on the auditor? What do they expect the auditor to do?

Ultimately, it is the union workers who are relying on the auditor. These are the real "customers" or "users" of his professional services. And they are relying on the auditor to make sure that the market value of the fund is properly represented, in the determination of their yearly dues. The union workers are also relying on the auditor to insure that, if the funds sustain losses, then these losses are properly represented, so that the workers can make the appropriate decisions about mitigating these losses, and about who should serve on the union fund investment committees.

Seen in this light, it seems appropriate and even necessary for the audit firm to seek an independent valuation of the private mortgage securities. (In contrast, if the question is looked at only from unsatisfactory perspective that the auditor's job is to confirm what the investment committee expects, and to put a stamp of confirmation on this, then seeking an independent valuation looks like an unnecessary over-reaction.) This is so much the case, that the firm should be willing to withdraw from the engagement, if Starburgh or the union investment committees do not agree to this. Hence Option 2 above would be the best.

Option 4 would be less preferable, but acceptable, because reference to GAAS has authority even if it is not decisive in considering whether an independent valuation should be sought. In this regard there are two questions still in play: Has GAAS changed or evolved such that such a valuation is required?, and also, Once the public charges raised against the president of Starburgh are given sufficient weight (as explained above), then does GAAS, even if it has not changed or evolved with respect to obtaining a valuation, require an independent valuation? And a consultation with the other audit firms would help Danvers attain clarity about these questions. (Note that even if the other firms are not requiring a valuation, this will not alleviate Danvers of the responsibility of making their own assessment of the situation.)

Option 3 seems acceptable but least preferable because it bypasses the responsible authorities at the funds. It may also violate the terms of the engagement letter with regard to incurring potentially unnecessary expenses.

In Real Life In the real case on which this scenario was based, the audit firm did nothing differently. It failed to obtain an independent valuation. A few months later, newspapers reported that the president of the investment advisory firm had been acting in an unethical way, providing favors and kick-backs to some of the union fund directors (trips and vacations, donations, hiring them for consulting services—any way he could find to put money in their pockets).

It did not take reporters long to discover that four out of the twenty or so particular investments that constituted the private mortgage investment, accounting for about 40% of the value of that investment, were in default. The valuation which the investment advisory firm had provided covered up this loss. The loss implied on average a 10% annual loss in the union funds under management by the investment advisory firm.

When this loss was correctly accounted for, the union had to triple the yearly dues of its members, to make up the difference. The union fund directors were fired. Those directors, the investment advisory firm, and the audit firm were caught up in a scandal that was the subject of newspaper coverage for months to come. The U.S. Attorney and the state Attorney General brought criminal charges against everyone involved. At that point, the question of why the firm did not obtain an independent valuation was looked at very carefully, with all of the clarity that comes with hindsight. What had once looked like a theoretical question to the firm (Does GAAS require this?) now became the very real question: How could the firm have been so incompetent as to overlook this? The best legal defense available to the firm was to argue that, in its failure to seek such a valuation, it was not as incompetent as it might seem to be! The financial end result was that the firm—which had not been the object of a single claim in its 60 years of practice—had to accept a full policy limit claim settlement for malpractice.

Recommended additional reading:

Mintz, S.M.: 1995, "Virtue Ethics and Accounting Education," *Issues in Accounting Education* 10(2), 247-267.

Mintz, S.M.: 1996, "The Role of Virtue in Accounting Education," *Accounting Education: A Journal of Theory, Practice and Research* 1, 67-91.

Mintz, S.M.: 2006, "Accounting ethics education: Integrating reflective learning and virtue ethics," *Journal of Accounting Education* 24 (2/3), 97.

What Can Be Done?

15

"Our goal is not to say what virtue is, but actually to become good."—Aristotle

WE HAVE ARGUED AT LENGTH and in great detail that the study of ethics belongs essentially to what it is to be an accountant. Yet, there remains a substantial and, as yet, unsolved problem, namely: Can Ethics Be Taught? It has often been claimed that it cannot. Those who claim this put forward well-crafted and often very convincing arguments—which leaves us with a problem, since the purpose of this text is to teach ethics to those who are studying it. Obviously, if ethics cannot be taught, then this book is futile.

Ethics, even ethics as applied to accounting, is properly a branch of philosophy. However, the correct method in philosophy involves not simply showing why the right view is true, but also showing why incorrect views, although often plausible and well-motivated, are false. A philosophical difficulty always needs to be *dissolved* as well as *solved*. Our method, then, will be to present the arguments for the other side in their fullest and strongest form, stating ten reasons why someone might think that ethics cannot be taught. Then, in reply, we will show how each of them is wrong and why.

Our first step will be to begin with the proper context. The classical philosophers were the first to pose, and answer, this question of whether ethics can be taught. It turns out, then, that the best entry into the subject is to consider how classical philosophers approached the question—to which we now turn.

After we have resolved that initial question, we then turn to some practical suggestions, expedients, and possible reforms.

An Ancient Problem

"It's possible to teach *about* ethics, to be sure, but can we teach *ethics*? We can teach *what ethical accounting is*, but can we teach accountants *to be ethical*?" These questions are variations of concerns that date back to Socrates, Plato, and Aristotle.

Socrates (469-399 B.C.) lived in Athens and devoted his life to exhorting his fellow citizens to live virtuously. He was eventually put on trial, on charges of putatively "corrupting young people and denying the religion of the state," but probably because in fact his incessant questioning humiliated and angered many prominent Athenians. Socrates explained his understanding of his own life and mission in the following way during his trial:

> If you say to me, "Socrates, this time we … will let you off, but on one condition only—that you stop inquiring and speculating in this way, and that, if you were to be caught doing this again, you would be put to death." If this were the condition on which you were to let me go, I should reply: "Men of Athens, I honor and love you. But I shall obey God rather than you. And while I have life and strength I shall never cease practicing and teaching philosophy, exhorting in my usual manner anyone whom I meet, and persuading him, saying: 'O my friend, why do you—a citizen of the great and mighty and wise city of Athens—care so much about accumulating the greatest amount of money and honor and reputation, and so little about wisdom and truth and the greatest improvement of the soul, which you never pay any attention to at all? Are you not ashamed of this?' And if the person I engage in this way says: 'But I do care about these things!,' I don't walk away, and I don't let him leave. Rather, I interrogate him, and I examine and cross-examine him. And if I think that he lacks virtue-that he is only claiming that he has virtue—I reproach him with undervaluing the greater, and overvaluing the less" (Plato's *Apology*).

He reproaches his fellow citizens with valuing only "instrumental" or "market" goods, as we have called them, and not those goods that, we saw, are and should be regarded as incommensurably higher. It was a noble defense speech, but not calculated to be effective with the jury. The majority of the jury apparently took Socrates to be obnoxiously arrogant and sentenced him to death.

Socrates' gifted follower, Plato, was watching on as his teacher was arrested, put on trial, and put to death. He saw Socrates devote all his energies to encouraging his fellow Athenians to be virtuous, but the end result was that Socrates was crushed, and unprincipled people had apparently triumphed. Naturally enough, Plato called into question the basic premise of Socrates' life. Was it all futile? Was Socrates perhaps mistaken in presuming, as he apparently did, that virtue can be taught?

This is the question with which Plato begins his famous dialogue, the *Meno*, when the chief character, Meno, asks the fictional Socrates the following question:

> Can you tell me, Socrates, whether virtue is acquired by teaching or by practice; or if neither by teaching nor practice, then whether it comes to man by nature, or in what other way?

Plato's tentative answer, later in the dialogue, consists of a hypothetical: if virtue is a kind of knowledge, then it can be taught—because knowledge is the sort of thing that can be imparted to others.

But is virtue actually a kind of knowledge? Plato had his doubts. He pointed out that there are no recognized experts of virtue in society, yet there are recognized experts in various sorts of knowledge. There is medical knowledge, and physicians are recognized experts in that sort of knowledge. There is knowledge of construction, and builders are recognized experts in that. But if there were some sort of knowledge involved in being a good human being, then there ought to be recognized experts in human goodness. But, Plato thought, there do not seem to be such experts.

Plato also pointed out that the leaders of Athens who were generally regarded as extremely virtuous—men such as Themistocles and Pericles—typically had children who were not virtuous. It was striking that the children of these men did learn horse riding and military skill and musical skill from their fathers, but they did not learn how to be virtuous. However, Plato argued, surely a father would be more concerned about imparting this to his child than those other skills. The fact that fathers did not, after all, succeed in imparting virtue to their children, then, was a sign that virtue could not be thus imparted—that it was not some kind of expertise or knowledge.

Aristotle, who was Plato's student, did not share his teacher's same worries. For Aristotle, our practices of praise and blame, exhorting and discouraging, commanding and prohibiting, would make no sense if virtue could not be taught or at least encouraged. Furthermore, the entire project of making laws and attaching rewards and punishments to laws would also be senseless if virtue could not be taught. Aristotle believed that all of the factors mentioned by Plato—teaching, practice, nature—were relevant to the imparting of virtue. In Aristotle's view, the reason we think that virtue is not teachable is that we make the mistake of identifying virtue with only what we have called "intellectual virtue."

Our approach to accounting ethics has so far been broadly Aristotelian in spirit. We maintain, with Aristotle, that accounting ethics can and should be promoted in all of the above ways, and that teaching is only one component in the imparting of virtue. In essence, the question, "Can ethics be taught?" is a complex question. Everything depends on what one means by "ethics," and what one means by "teaching." When one draws the correct distinctions, then it becomes clear that ethics (in the appropriate sense) can indeed be taught (in the appropriate sense), and this result applies to accounting ethics as well as to ethics generally.

Ten Reasons Why Ethics (It Seems) Cannot Be Taught

Let us try to get clear about why people suspect that ethics cannot be taught. Here are ten reasons why.

(1) "If ethics can be taught, then it can be taught in a classroom. But no one could become ethical simply by taking classes." —If classroom instruction could impart ethics, then the effect would seem much greater than the supposed cause. How could something so mundane and ordinary as taking a class lead to something as distinctive as high ethical behavior? Also, the supposed effect seems different in kind from the supposed cause: being ethical is a matter of acting correctly; but being good at classwork is a matter of thinking, speaking, and writing correctly. No one could learn to be a good athlete, a good musician, or a good actor merely by sitting in a classroom. So how could someone learn to be a good human being in that way?

(2) "Being smart and being good are different. Teaching can help someone become smart but not to be good." —Being smart, intelligent, clever, and being good, virtuous, ethical, are clearly two sorts of things. Some people are intelligent without being particularly good; other people are good without being particularly intelligent. But only intelligence can be taught (partially so). So teaching has no effect on goodness. (And aren't there many examples of very clever accountants, who received excellent grades in courses in "professional ethics" at the best business schools, who nonetheless went on in their professional life to commit egregious fraud?)

(3) "Our upbringing determines our character. By the time anyone might attempt to teach us about ethics, it's too late to learn—our character is already fixed." —Whether someone is ethical or not depends on his character. But people acquire the character that they have when they are growing up. They become honest or not, trustworthy or not, truthful or not, depending upon how they associate with their childhood friends, and depending upon how vigilant their parents are in raising them and in insuring that they spend time with the right sorts of friends. By the time someone attends (say) high school, his or her character is largely fixed.

(4) "There really is freedom of action. In the same circumstance, and given the same upbringing and background, one person will act well and another person will not. Thus, teaching cannot reliably produce ethical behavior." —To say that something can be taught is to say that teaching reliably produces it. For instance, piano playing can be taught, because taking piano lessons reliably produces skilled piano playing for the most part (not in every case, and not in the same degree, but nonetheless there is a reliable connection). But teaching cannot reliably produce ethical action, because nothing reliably produces ethical action. Nothing does this, because our actions are essentially free. One can see this from how people react to a tragedy or disaster, say, the sinking of the Titanic: some men courageously allowed women and children to get into the boats first; others groped and clawed desperately for their lives, not giving any thought to others. In the end, our actions are inherently and essentially free. Thus, nothing determines them, and thus, in particular, teaching does not do so.

(5) "People often do what they know they should not do. But classes only teach us what we should do; they can't make us actually do this." —The difficult thing about ethics is usually not knowing what we should do, but rather doing what we know we should do. It is very common for people to realize clearly what they should do, but act otherwise. It is even more common, perhaps, for people to know what they should do "deep down," but to act against this. Dishonest and unethical behavior is not caused, then, by ignorance about what we should do, but by a kind of turning away from, or obscuring, of what we in some sense already realize is the right thing—a "dulling" or "darkening" of conscience, as it were. So the solution to unethical behavior does not lie in teaching and, in that sense, ethics cannot be taught.

(6) "Whether we act well or not depends upon likes, dislikes, preferences, and incentives, which don't have much to do with teaching." —In the end, we do what we most want to do, and we most want to do what we like, prefer, or are pleased in doing. One person is honest-because he would not have liked acting dishonestly. Another person is dishonest—because that's what appealed the most to him. Thus, our likes and dislikes, our preferences and the incentives attached to our actions, ultimately steer us to act in one way or another. Teaching does not change these things.

(7) "What is called 'teaching ethics' is giving explicit reasons for what we already implicitly accept and follow. Hence if we do not already have implicit reasons to act ethically, then teaching ethics cannot be of any help." —As explained above, some hold that to teach ethics is usually to teach a theory of ethics. But a theory of ethics, properly understood, is the explicit systemization of what we already in some sense

accept, implicitly so. Thus, if someone is not already ethical, ethical theory will have nothing to work with. Thus, ethics can be taught only to someone who is ethical already.

(8) "At the deepest level, everyone is selfish. Each person aims at his own self interest. So the best we can do is to arrange rewards and punishments in such a way that a person's pursuit of his own self-interest is in alignment with the 'ethical' behavior that society expects. But there is no possibility of 'teaching' someone to be 'ethical' beyond this." —We regard ethical behavior as valuable only because of what others would think, or because of punishments we would receive if caught.

(9) "If virtue could be taught, there would be recognized teachers and experts of ethics." As we saw, this objection was first stated by Plato. The form this objection might typically take today would be the claim that there are no objective, universally shared values. "Whose standards should we use?" someone might say, "Which values should we adopt? In fact, there are a variety of equally plausible ways of looking at behavior-none of these is privileged over any others."

(10) "If virtue could be taught, virtuous people would succeed in conveying it to their children—but they don't." —This is another objection first offered by Plato, as we saw. We might apply the objection to make it an argument against the possibility of professional ethics: if high standards of ethical behavior in accounting could be taught, then it would in fact be successfully conveyed by founders of accounting firms (such as Arthur Andersen) to successive generations of employees, just as technical accounting skill gets transmitted within firms. And yet firms have failed to transmit ethical standards: to wit, Andersen.

It All Depends on What You Mean by "Ethics" and "Teaching"

And yet, even given all of these apparent problems, it would be strange if ethics could not be taught.

This is so for various general reasons. For instance, we said that for someone to be good is for him to have the traits that enable him to carry out his distinctive task well. To be good is to be good at carrying out one's distinctive task. But in every other case of someone's having some distinctive task to carry out, it is possible to teach someone to be good at this: for instance, we can teach someone to be a good carpenter, a good physician, a good outfielder in baseball, or a good engineer. But then, by the same token, it should be possible to teach someone to be a good professional, such as an accountant. A good accountant, as we saw, is someone who carries out well the distinctive task of an accountant—which would mean fostering trust and truthfulness in financial reporting. That is, it would mean being an ethical accountant. (As we saw, it is misguided to draw a distinction between being a good professional and doing that professional work ethically.)

Again, if to be good at X is simply to do X well, and if doing X can be taught, then it would seem that doing X well can be taught. How could it be possible to teach some task, but not possible to teach doing that task well? Being ethical at some work or in some task is simply a way of doing it, and if the doing of it can be taught, then that particular way of doing it can be taught.

Again, what would be the point of laws, or recommendations, or commands, or rewards and punishments, if what we say has no effect on how others act? But if what we say does have an effect, then ethics can be taught—in the minimal sense, at least, that what we say makes it easier (or more difficult) for others to be ethical. (The same holds for the example we set or fail to set.)

But the question of whether accounting ethics in particular can be taught hinges on what we mean by accounting ethics. As Plato pointed out similarly in the *Meno*, the question of whether virtue can be taught depends upon our answer to the question, "What is virtue?":

> I am certain that if you were to ask any Athenian whether being virtuous was something inborn or acquired, he would laugh in your face, and say: "Stranger, you have far too good an opinion of me, if you think that I can answer your question. For I literally do not know what virtue is, and much less whether it is acquired by teaching or not." And I myself, Meno, living as I do in this region of poverty, am as poor as the rest of the world; and I confess with shame that I know literally nothing about virtue; and when I do not know the "what" of anything, how can I know the "what sort"? How, if I knew nothing at all of Meno, could I tell if he was handsome, or the opposite of handsome; rich and noble, or the reverse of rich and noble? Do you think that I could?

From what has been set down in previous chapters, it may be seen that, by way of summarizing, ethics in accounting involves basically four components:

1. *Understanding.* A familiarity with, and understanding of, the principles of accounting and the rules which are meant to express and safeguard these principles—in particular, an understanding of how the rules depend upon the principles.

2. *Idealism.* The aim or resolve, which consists in placing the ideals of the profession of accounting over one's own interests (which may be identified, roughly, with "integrity").

Moreover, the ability actually to carry out consistently this aim or resolve, which includes:

3. *Character*, that is, having the virtues, and

4. *Culture*, that is, a workplace in which it is easy to do what is ethical.

So the question of whether accounting ethics can be taught resolves into the question of whether any or all of these components can be "taught" and, if so, how they can be "taught."

But it is clear that they can be taught. Understanding of the principles of accounting can be taught precisely through classwork and study of the right sort. As we saw in Chapter 6, the right sort of understanding is acquired through seeing how accounting rules express and safeguard accounting principles, so that a practitioner comes to see rules as in the service of principles, not rules as trumping principles. And that sort of understanding, we have argued, is acquired best if a practitioner is led in turn to see how the principles of accounting are grounded in the nature and distinctive work of an accountant. Thus, classwork, and a study of the fundamentals of accounting ethics—in the manner presented in this text—is capable of imparting the requisite understanding.

Idealism of some sort is present in nearly everyone, except for extremely sociopathic personalities. "Hypocrisy is the tribute that vice pays to virtue," as La Rochefoucauld correctly remarked—but this implies that even a hypocrite has some sort of latent idealism, because otherwise how could he possibly know what others take ethical behavior to be?

But what one needs to do, however, is to appeal to a practitioner's idealism and "sense of honor"—or "magnanimity," as we called it—and this would be to "teach" this component of ethics. Idealism becomes livelier, the more we express our admiration for ideals and act upon them; it becomes diminished and weakened, the less we express our admiration for them and act upon them. Accounting firms can express their admiration for idealism by reviving the corporate "lore" that involves their exemplary founders—stories from the lives of exemplary practitioners, such as Arthur Andersen and George Oliver May. And any practitioner can give examples from his or her own experience of how it turned out that "honesty is the best policy." Indeed, a firm might solicit examples of these and publish them in a newsletter, or incorporate into company workshops discussion sessions in which practitioners exchanged stories that brought home this point. Idealism in ethics especially tends to be fostered by our natural desire to imitate: we see an example in another of some behavior that we admire very much, and then we keep this in mind as we act, aiming to imitate it in the manner that we can. That is why morality can be taught and encouraged through stories, anecdotes, lessons, and exemplary lives. Generally the profession of accounting needs to recover its humanistic dimension—accountants cannot be narrow professionals, but rather should be liberally educated men and women with specific professional skill.

But this is not to deny that the profession should take steps to test the motivation of those who aspire to be accountants and positively exclude those whose motives appear doubtful. One might think, for instance, that any instances of dishonesty and misrepresentation as displayed in student life (e.g. cheating, plagiarism) should disqualify permanently a student from a career in accounting, just as breaking the law excludes a student from a future profession in law.

Character, as we saw, is formed by and tested in small things and first things. This component of ethical accounting can be "taught," then, by any efforts to insure that a practitioner's work in these respects is exemplary. For instance, in small things: there should be a complete intolerance of dishonesty, misrepresentation, or action under conflict of interest in a firm, as regards what a practitioner does even outside of an engagement—in such "small matters" as the use of expense accounts; claiming of tax exemptions and deductions; and practices of billing. An accountant in how he or she lives all round, and not simply as a "job," should represent probity in financial matters, just as a physician is generally an advocate for good health. The right approach to "first things" would involve such things as: counting as an argument against a certain kind of accounting treatment that one could easily be tempted to abuse it in future instances; an initial conservativism in decisions, and the recommended attitude of skepticism, as regards a new engagement; a sharp and uncompromising attitude when encountering the first instance of fraud in management, no matter how small or apparently insignificant; and so on.

Culture in a firm is determined above all by the "tone at the top"—the example set by management of moderation and integrity. But it is fostered of course by practices which draw attention to and reward action in which practitioners apparently sacrifice personal advantage for the sake of principle and probity.

And so, in the end, the answer to the question, "Can accounting ethics be taught?" is straightforward. There is no difficulty in principle in teaching it; in fact, the means for imparting ethics in accounting are all familiar. The real question is: Do we really want to teach it? And here one might be reminded of the famous prayer of Augustine of Hippo: "Lord, give me chastity—but not just yet."

But Why the Difficulty?

As Aristotle remarks in his *Ethics*, in order to see clearly that a view is true, it is necessary not only to argue for it directly, but also to explain why the false positions seemed to be true. Why does it seem that ethics cannot be taught?

Some of the difficulties stated above came from a confusion between Understanding (a matter of "intellectual virtue," as we called it) and Idealism and Character (which involve motivation). Some components of ethics can be taught in the classroom: to learn these well is generally a necessary part of being ethical, but not sufficient. "If ethics can be taught"—went the first objection— "then it can be taught in a classroom." Obviously, anything teachable in a classroom setting would involve intellectual virtue only. Virtue of character, which involves motivation, is instead inculcated through example; mentoring; friendly advice; exhortation; rules and laws; and rewards and punishments. It is a matter of "practice," in Plato's sense.

Again, it was claimed that "Being smart and being good are different," and that the former but not the latter can be taught. —However, there are two senses of "being smart." In one sense, this means mere technical proficiency or cleverness-how to get effectively what you want. For instance, "aggressive" yet non-transparent accounting is like that, or accounting that observes the "rules" but only to get what is in the practitioner's or the client's interests (and does not serve the public interest). In another sense, "being smart" means sagacity, good judgment, prudence, real insight and understanding—the sort of practical intelligence that we admire as being itself remarkable. This sort of "being smart" is inseparable from being good.

The argument that "our upbringing determines our character" is to some extent true. Character is fairly settled by the time someone begins a professional career, or even by the time one begins professional studies. But, although settled, it can change—certainly it can become worse (think of the example of a young idealistic practitioner being instructed for the first time in the practical work of the profession by a cynical and not entirely upright older associate). Moreover, because of the importance of little things and first things, the initial experiences of a new practitioner in a firm, and the expectations of the firm, are crucial in settling that practitioner's "professional character"—his or her "standards" as a professional.

"There is freedom of action." Yes, but not unpredictability, if someone has the relevant virtues. For instance, consider trustworthiness. A good person is trustworthy. If you are a mountaineer, you can really trust a good fellow climber, who is both technically skilled and loyal. The actions of such a person are not at all unpredictable. You could say exactly how such a person would act—and you would stake your life on it. (Being a partner in a firm is remarkably similar: one stakes one's life and reputation on the predictability of his or her fellow partners.) Or, again, consider integrity: true integrity is unswerving and exceptionless. It is impossible to have integrity most of the time—to waver, vacillate, to be open to bribery or monetary inducements, is *ipso facto* to lack integrity.

"People often do what they know they should not do. Classes can teach us what we should do; they can't make us actually carry that out." —But this is another objection based on a conflation of intellectual virtue with the whole of virtue. To know what a person should do (which, by the way, is in some cases a great achievement) is what intellectual virtue achieves; but actually to carry it out is the work of other sorts of virtue-and these are acquired through "practice" in the broad sense, not through class instruction.

"Whether we act well or not depends on our likes or dislikes"—yes, but these are malleable. A person who hates getting up early but sets her alarm for 5:30 a.m. and gets out of bed nonetheless, whether tired or not, will (in most cases) eventually turn into a "morning person" who loves being up at sunrise. When a person first begins athletic training, he hates to run or lift weights; but after months on a training regimen, he hates not running or lifting weights. That is why one might say that the task of imparting accounting ethics is to bring a practitioner to the state where he or she dislikes anything that has the appearance of dishonesty, lack of independence, lack of objectivity, or lack of integrity.

"To teach ethics is to give explicit reasons for implicit practices, so we cannot teach someone to be good who isn't implicitly good already." But most people act correctly in most of what they do. Even a malicious murderer will for much of his time be doing the right thing—paying bills, observing traffic laws, not attacking or harming others. It is fair to say that most of us in most of what we do are committed implicitly to the right principles.

"Everyone is self-interested at the deepest level." Yet not everyone would act dishonestly if he could do so without getting caught. People can and do sacrifice their self-interest for the sake of a higher ideal: that's clear from observation. So it is false that all of us must always be "self-interested"—that is, if by "self-interested" one means "selfish."

"If virtue could be taught, there would be recognized teachers and experts." But there are. Everyone is potentially a good "teacher" of ethics, because everyone (or nearly everyone) can recognize bad behavior well enough in others. (The trick is to recognize it also in oneself.) Typically the wisdom embodied in the laws of a society is a "teacher" of ethics. And then anyone whose life is in some respects at least held up as an example (Mother Teresa, Martin Luther King), or whose writings are truly edifying or challenging (Thomas à Kempis, Marcus Aurelius), is also a recognized teacher of ethics.

"If virtue could be taught, then the children of virtuous parents would be virtuous." But the objection presupposes that anyone who has virtue is able to teach it. It takes "virtue can be taught" to be equivalent to "every virtuous person can teach virtue" (and perhaps also "only virtuous persons can teach virtue"). But why should one accept these further claims?

An Analogy

We should replace the question, "Can ethics be taught?" with "Can we take effective steps to make it so that practitioners are less disposed to act unethically?" And then clearly the answer is "yes."

It helps to consider an analogy: consider the campaign against drunk driving. When twenty years ago various groups such as Mothers Against Drunk Driving (MADD) initiated a campaign in the United States against drunk driving, it would have been ridiculous for someone to argue: "There's no point in attempting that. Ethics can't be taught. Nothing can be done to make people less disposed to drink and drive." Rather, everyone recognized what steps should be taken, if in fact we had the "will" to get tough on drunk driving. Our society adopted a many-dimensional approach. Increase legal penalties. Be more vigorous in arrest and prosecution. Institute classes in Driver's Ed courses. Buy time on major networks for advertising. Create a culture that "frowns" on driving while drinking. Invent the new cultural role of "designated driver" (which has since become part of ordinary language). Make people aware that drinking affects above all one's ability to recognize the effects of drinking on one's own judgment. Hold up European cultures as a model for us, which were more ethical in these regards. Similarly, a multi-faceted approach to reforming the accounting profession is possible, which would begin from principles-based education, and move from there to changes in the culture of firms, and a more exacting prosecution in law.

But here too perhaps the most basic question is not whether the profession can be reformed, but whether we want to reform it enough, so that we actually do so. "Can ethics be taught, that is to say, promoted?" Yes, certainly. "Are we concerned enough with the profession, in order to preserve and promote its ethical foundation in all of our efforts and actions as practitioners?" But this is something up to us. We do our part in upholding the high ideals of the profession, by how we approach our own professional work and responsibilities. Beginning here and now, we can make definite resolutions, and take concrete steps, to promote unswervingly and with high integrity, principles-based accounting, true professionalism, and an honorable pride.

But what are some specific ways in which one may grow and make progress in the ethical practice of accounting? Below we give concrete suggestions as to how precisely this may be achieved. After discussing some background considerations, and drawing some useful distinctions, our discussion will have two main parts: (I) "Personal Growth," that is, how a practitioner through his own individual effort may maintain and grow in his or her commitment to the highest professional standards of accounting, and (II) "Corporate Culture," that is, how practitioners through their common efforts in a firm, or management through setting a proper "tone at the top," may help to create those conditions which maintain and foster accountants' commitment to the highest professional standards. In each part we offer a series of practical suggestions, since this chapter is basically a "how to" guide for accounting professionalism.

Background Considerations

Recall that we said that virtue is a kind of excellence. But we know from experience that growth in any sort of excellence requires regular effort and perseverance. This is true of excellence in sports, music, crafts, and art. But it is also true in a profession. Recall too that a profession is inherently ethical. The ethical nature of a profession such as accounting is akin to an aspect or quality of the technical skill of the practitioner. Consider the following analogy from music. A trumpet player might be able to hit all the notes—that is, he has a mere technical skill—but his playing might nonetheless lack musicianship, which is a quality or aspect of his skillful playing. Just as he has to practice note-playing to have the technical skill, so he has to practice *musical* note playing, if he is to become truly excellent as a trumpet player and have musicianship. When it comes to excellence at the trumpet, it is not really possible to distinguish sharply between technical skill and musicianship. Musicianship is not some kind of add-on, or a superfluous thing, or a luxury. To be an excellent trumpet player simply is a matter of musicianship blended together with skill. In the same way, observing ethical standards in a profession is not something superfluous in relation to technical expertise, a "luxury" that one might not be able to "afford." To work at becoming a good professional just is, at the same time, to work to exemplify the highest ethical standards of the profession in the course of achieving something with technical skill.

The regular effort required to develop any exercise must be matched to time periods. Corresponding to each natural division of time—day, week, month, year—there is something matched to that time, which needs to be done in order to grow in excellence. Each day, someone who wants to become an excellent trumpet player must practice his scales and exercises. Each week, he should have a trumpet lesson with a skilled teacher. Every month or so he should aim to perform something for others. Again, each year he should give a formal recital and perhaps attend a music camp, master class, or equivalent. The same principle holds for other forms of excellence, including growth in accounting professionalism. There is something to be done for each period of time. For example, an aspiring practitioner might form a specific resolution for each day; he might engage in discussions with a colleague on some matter of professional ethics every week or so; he could attend a workshop or the equivalent roughly once a month; and every year or so he might participate in a study group or course.

Anything that we seek, we can seek either through our own efforts (individual effort) or through coordinated effort with others (common effort). Anyone who wishes to be excellent at something, will need of course to do many things just on his own. A basketball player who wants to be excellent at shooting jump shots needs to spend many lonely hours on the court practicing his jump shots. However, no one ever became excellent at anything by working just on his own. We all need help from others, inevitably so, because we are social beings. That same basketball player, if he is to become truly excellent in basketball, needs an athletic trainer and an instructor in basketball technique. He needs to play the sport regularly with good players—with players who are even better than he is, if possible, because he needs the improvement that comes only from competition. He needs the perseverance that comes only from having the support of others and sharing together with them in the same difficulties and trials. He needs to be part of an association or group of friends in which everyone shares the same goal of wanting to be good in basketball.

The same holds true with excellence in a profession, not merely as regards technical skill, but also as regards its ethical standards and professionalism. A practitioner will of course need to do lots of things on his own to maintain and grow in professionalism; for example, he needs to spend time on his own studying, and only he can do his own actions! However, he cannot do even his own actions solely by his own efforts, because it is practically speaking impossible for someone to maintain high standards of professionalism over the long haul if he is trying to do so solely on his own. He needs the advice and direction of a mentor; the support of like-minded colleagues to do the right thing when that is difficult; and above all a culture which inculcates habits of thought and action, that is, habits which simply exclude automatically, as "unthinkable" and repugnant, any impropriety or even appearance of impropriety.

I. Personal Growth

The task of growing in commitment to the highest standards of professionalism is different depending upon whether one is a student, a beginning practitioner, or a seasoned practitioner. We therefore offer different sets of practical suggestions, directed at persons in these different stages of their career.

Suggestions for students

1. Seek a broad, liberal education in your undergraduate years.

Avoid an overly narrow or overly specialized education, and especially do not view your education in a purely utilitarian way, that is, as no more than pre-professional training. If one has started out following a specialized curriculum, seek ways to broaden it.

This may at first seem a strange and even an irrelevant recommendation. What could possibly be the connection between a broad and liberal education, and professionalism in accounting? Yet it is noteworthy that the great founders of modern accounting, such as Charles Waldo Haskins, Robert Montgomery, and George May, were extremely well-educated and cultured men, while being consummate professionals and articulate exponents of professionalism. Was this a mere accident?

There are a variety of reasons why a broad and liberal education contributes to sound professionalism. Consider, first, *breadth*. Someone with a broad education more easily sees the "big picture," yet accounting failure often results from a practitioner's looking at things in a partial and restricted way, for instance, by focusing solely on what *this* manager is demanding right *now*; what numbers need to be met for *this* quarter; or what accidental technicality can be invoked to attain a desired result, regardless of the substance of the transaction. Moreover, a broad education is needed for seeking and declaring truth, which was shown above to be at the basis of an accountant's distinctive task:

> The man of affairs has need for as much intelligence, as much force of mind, as much character, as much judgment as he who follows another profession.[64]

> Accountancy in the later professional sense includes not only a detailed and scientific knowledge of accounting and of books of account, and their relationship to one another, and to any form of business, but also the oversight and scrutiny of honesty, order, facility, and clearness of comprehension. It includes, moreover, a comprehensive mental and mathematical grasp of a business enterprise in its totality and in all the inter-related details of its organization and conduct, for purposes of diagnosis, consultation, and suggestion.[65]

---

[64] From "Business Training", in Haskins, C. W.: 1904, *Business Education and Accountancy* (Harper & Brothers Publishers, New York and London), p. 28.

[65] From "History of Accountancy: Introductory" (Delivered at the opening of the School of Commerce, Accounts, and Finance, of New York University, October 2, 1900. Reprinted

Consider next what hinges on whether a student seeks a "liberal" education. Let us define terms. A course of education is called "liberal" if it is "free" (the Latin word for freedom is *libertas*, whence the term "liberal" is derived); and it is "free" if it is not constrained by or directed solely by something external to it, viz. if it is sought for its own sake. Thus, by definition, a pre-professional education is not a liberal education. A liberal education is not pursued solely because of something external to it; but a pre-professional education is pursued for precisely such reasons.

Why should it matter whether an accountant has a liberal education? A liberal education by definition is sought for its own sake. This means that it is sought for the contribution that it makes to the person who acquires it. A liberal education is desirable because it makes the person who acquires it a better human being: it improves *who he is*, not *what he can do*. How does such an education improve who someone is? By improving his mind, so that he can think more clearly, comprehensively, and broadly; and understand things more deeply; and express the truth about things more effectively and artfully.

Now consider these goods that a liberal education seeks. These not commensurable with elements in the broad class of commercial goods but are "honorable" goods. A liberal education is essentially directed at honorable goods; whereas an education that seeks to prepare someone for employment is sought in the manner of a market or instrumental good. The very project of seeking a liberal education, then, is an extended exercise in the preferring of honorable over markert or instrumental goods. An accounting student who affirms that priority, by devoting at least some of his time to liberal education, is to that extent affirming the priority of honorable over instrumental goods. But, as we saw, this is exactly the ordering of preferences that is required for sound professionalism, because a professional needs to prefer the honorable good aimed at by his profession over any profit or advantages that might come to him by acting otherwise.[66]

Lack of breadth in education, and lack of liberality in education, tend to go together. A broad education contributes best to making someone better as regards who he is; similarly, perhaps the main reason for making education narrow and specialized is that it equips the person who receives that sort of education to be better at what he can do.

---

from the publications of the American Academy of Political and Social Science, Philadelphia), from Haskins, Ibid., p. 157

[66] For a compelling treatment of this and related themes, see Pieper, J.: 1998, *Leisure the Basis of Culture* (St. Augustine's Press, Notre Dame, IN). Also helpful is Lewis, C.S.: 1943, *Abolition of Man* (Oxford University Press, London).

To be clear: we are not maintaining that there is something misguided with wanting to achieve or do something with what one has learned. Our point is simply that, in education as in professionalism, the priority of honorable over useful goods should be acknowledged and preserved, and this is honored and preserved best in a liberal education. Nor are we arguing that a liberal undergraduate education cannot have a pre-professional component, such as a sequence of courses leading to a BBA in accounting. Rather, we are maintaining that it is best if such a sequence is embedded in a framework of a truly liberal education and is viewed in that way.

2. Practice habits of integrity and truthfulness in all areas of your life, especially in seemingly small matters.

Recall from earlier chapters that an orientation toward truth, and a commitment to seek and declare the truth, are essential to accounting: "it belongs to the spirit of professional Accountancy to seek out and reveal to them the truth" (Charles Waldo Haskins). But this attitude of truthfulness is easily cultivated during an accounting student's undergraduate education by a scrupulous adherence to standards of intellectual honesty and integrity. The point is stated quite well in the Code of Conduct of one of the nation's leading accounting programs:

> It is in all students' interest to avoid committing acts of scholastic dishonesty and to discourage others from committing such acts. Each dishonest act can harm the quality and reputation of the Bachelor of Business Administration (BBA) degree and thereby lower the value of the honest work of all other students. In a culture of dishonesty, it is impossible to know whether achievements were honestly earned or accomplished through unethical means. In such a culture, grades are not a valid indicator of achievement, and the final degree is not a valid indicator of a minimum level of knowledge. Were the Business School to acquire a reputation for tolerating dishonesty, it would devalue the degrees of all present and future alumni.
>
> Maintaining the quality and integrity of the undergraduate business programs at UT is not the only reason why it is important to emphasize ethical conduct. The curriculum within the Business School prepares students for a profession in which honesty and ethical behavior are essential characteristics. It is important for students to develop a strong sense of ethics while still in school and to carry it with them into the workplace. Students who have completed their education in a culture of

ethical behavior should easily make the transition to a culture of ethical behavior as employees.[67]

Of course it would be artificial to hold that a student's commitment to "honesty and ethical behavior" should extend only to academic work. As we saw above, to be a professional implies a commitment to a certain way of life, and it does and should affect and be influenced by one's entire life. Honesty and ethical behavior therefore needs to be a distinctive "note" or "mark" of the entire life of someone who is set apart for service to others as an accounting professional.

3. Be attentive to signs of greed; resist it, and avoid occasions of feeling it.

Greed involves loving wealth in an unrestricted way (as Aristotle says, in an "infinite" way), as if it were the best thing, when it is not: "wealth ought not to be the one end of life, nor even its chief end—only the means to be employed towards an end" (Charles Waldo Haskins). Now the best way to resist some tendency or temptation to do something bad is to do an opposing good thing. Thus, the best way of cultivating a resistance to greed is to cultivate the attitude of treating wealth as a limited good which is instrumental to something else. There are various ways to do this.

One way to achieve this is to live "two notches below" what you can afford. Suppose Smith could buy the very best MP3 player if he stretched his budget and charged the sum on his credit card, but if he bought a model which was perfectly adequate for his needs, without however being the latest, most desirable model, he could afford to buy it with cash and have something left besides. If he adopted the latter course most of the time (no one is claiming that one need do that always), then he would clearly be the sort of person who is used to viewing wealth and material goods as instruments. In his very actions, Smith would be drawing a distinction between "needs" and "wants" and viewing money as directed principally to the former.

Again, the ancient practice of tithing, where one gives away some definite amount away to a charity or one's church, has long been recognized as a check against greed. For suppose someone gives away a certain percentage of his wealth on a consistent basis. Such a person is declaring, in effect, "I am not the sort of person who is yearning for ever more money than I have" (because he is making do with less) and also "Money is valuable to me only as an instrument" (because he is

---

[67] Code of Conduct for the McCombs School of Business, Undergraduate Programs, University of Texas at Austin.

acknowledging, in his actions, that the money he gives away is more useful to someone else—e.g. the poor—than it is to himself).

4. Seek out those accounting professors who in your view exemplify the highest ethical ideals: get to know them and "mentor yourself" to them.

The example set by those we admire is extremely important for growth in virtue, because when we admire someone, we want to become like that person (hence "imitation is the sincerest form of flattery"). Because virtue involves the whole person and develops over time, we acquire it best when someone we admire also at the same time stands over us in a relationship of guidance and mentoring, for then that other person will have a lively concern for our all-round and long-range good.

In the modern university, such "mentoring" relationships hardly ever form by accident. True enough, sometimes a professor will seek out a student he regards as especially promising and invite the student, for example, to help with his research. But more typically the initiative needs to be taken by the student, through being persistent in going to office hours and arranging opportunities to know the professor better and to work under his or her guidance.

It is especially important to have many unplanned and spontaneous conversations with a mentor, because often it is in offhand comments that someone's personality and outlook are best revealed. In fact, sometimes a mentor will have a huge effect on a student even without saying a word—a look of astonishment on a professor's face when someone mentions to him an act of fraud or dishonesty can speak volumes.[68]

5. View your professional training as part of a unified life marked by integrity.

We have noted several times above that, because a professional is dedicated to providing an honorable good, his or her work has the character of a *way of life*; there is a distinctive way of life associated with the profession that he or she practices. Thus, a physician should in every realm of his or her life be someone who fosters health and protects human life. A lawyer is expected to be upstanding and lawful throughout his or her life, not simply when practicing law: hence, the conviction of a felony typically disqualifies someone from admission to the bar and will usually keep an applicant from getting admitted to law school.

---

[68] The word 'mentor' derives from Homer's *Odyssey*. Mentor was Odysseus' trusted counselor, whom Odysseus put in charge of his son, Telemachus, when he went away to fight in the Trojan War. When Odysseus after his wanderings returned home, the goddess Athena appeared to him disguised as Mentor to assist him.

Since a profession has this kind of importance in the life of a practitioner, then a student who is studying with a view to joining a profession should approach his or her training not simply as a matter of acquiring technical expertise, nor of becoming "socialized" and "acculturated" into the norms and customs of the profession, but also as a matter of embodying the ideals distinctive of that profession. This way of looking at one's professional life is sometimes referred to as displaying a "unity of life." It should not be possible for an accountant to check at the door, when he is leaving the office, his concern for honesty and truth. It was a conviction of the "unity of life" of an accountant that led the founders of modern accounting to say such things as: "Aside from all personal interest in Accountancy, I hold our common calling, gentlemen, in the highest honor and admiration—not only for its worthy record of achievements already past, but for the stupendous possibilities within its grasp as one of the moral and educational forces of the modern world,"[69] or "There is no more vivid reality for any human being than his relations with other people. When 'professional ethics' is seen in its proper light, as a guide to behavior which will lead to pleasant and rewarding relations with other people, it will become an even more popular subject for study."[70]

Some practical ways to foster this holistic approach to professionalism in one's life might include: (a) reading informative newspapers and business magazines, with a view to practicing the application of professional skill and insight to social and political problems; (b) helping those who need help with elementary bookkeeping tasks; (c) volunteering to help non-profit organizations with elementary bookkeeping or business organization type tasks.[71]

Suggestions for newly-licensed CPAs

Our suggestions in this section are largely guided by the maxim, "first things, small things, similar things."

---

[69] Charles Waldo Haskins, "The Possibilities of the Profession of Accountancy as a Moral and Education Force" (Address to the New York State Society of Certified Public Accountants, June 11, 1900), in Haskins, ibid. p.93.

[70] Carey, John L.: 1956, *Professional Ethics of Certified Public Accountants* (American Institute of Accountants, New York, N.Y.), p. 212.

[71] We of course do not wish to suggest that a student of accounting should in any way act so as to give the impression that he is licensed or qualified to 'hold himself out' as an accountant.

1. *Be especially careful in one's first engagements to uphold the highest and most strict standard of professionalism.*

This point is well-illustrated with a story told by George O. May, which it is worthwhile recounting in full:

> A good many years ago—as a matter of fact, in 1899—owing to the death of one of the senior partners, I was called upon to settle with an important New York banker the form of a certificate for use in connection with a prospectus. As the issue was to be made on both sides of the Atlantic, it was planned to print the accountants' certificate in the prospectus as was and is customary in England.
>
> The profits of the company showed a fairly steady decline over a period of ten years except that in 1898, owing to the Spanish-American War, they rose considerably to a point higher than the average of the ten years. The banker desired the certificate to show only the average for the ten years and the profits for the last year. I demurred to this suggestion on two grounds: first, that it was contrary to the practice of my firm to show only averages where the profits for separate years were readily ascertainable; and, secondly, that the information proposed to be given would create a natural but erroneous impression as to the trend of profits.
>
> The discussion became difficult, and it was indicated that if we adhered to the position I had taken there would be no possibility of any similar differences with that particular banker in the future. However, I refused to modify the stand I had taken and was supported by the senior partner, with the result that no certificate was printed in the prospectus, but a statement was made by the banker on his own responsibility. I felt that I was right, but I could not fail to be conscious of the fact that my first important interview with a banker had not been a success and promised to result in the loss of an important client.
>
> There was, however, a sequel. Some six months later, the same banker was contemplating the purchase of a business and desired a full and reliable report on its operations. His lawyers approached the firm saying that while he still thought we were entirely wrong in the stand we had taken six months earlier, he believed that we had taken it in perfect good faith and that the incident should not, therefore, be a bar to friendly relations between us. They thereupon gave us instructions to make the investigation, and further intimated that the banker desired that I should personally take charge of it; and I may add that the banker is today a valued client of the firm.

> This sequel made the whole incident one of the most helpful of my experiences, and I hope it may also be of service in encouraging those of you who may be about to start practice, or are in the early days of practice, to take a firm stand for sound ethical principles, which I am sure will ultimately tend to bring you professional success as well as a consciousness of professional integrity.[72]

May observes that "[t]he young accountant may find it hard to take the first stand for the principles that have been suggested for his observance, but he will find this is essentially a case in which 'it is the first step that costs'."

2. Be scrupulous in honesty about unseen things, unchecked things, and small things.

Laxness in these matters affects the entire tone of one's work and easily spreads into larger and more important matters, and matters which will inevitably come to light. Always act as though each thing you do as a professional will be scrutinized the next day on the front page of the *New York Times*.

The reason that "magnitude" is, in an important sense, irrelevant when it comes to dishonesty and fraud, may be traced to the incommensurably higher status of integrity over instrumental goods. Someone who fails to recognize integrity as incommensurably higher in slight circumstances has in effect declared his preparedness to disregard its status in more demanding circumstances.

This principle is acknowledged indirectly in professional standards governing investigation of fraud. Fraud is always regarded as potentially expansive; it is only "accidentally" limited, by lack of opportunity. For instance, suppose an auditor discovers inconsistencies which seem to indicate fraud in a small matter such as the use of a petty cash fund. He would be justified in concluding that the matter is unimportant (not material) only because of reasons that are extrinsic to the fraud, and accidental to it—something *besides* the fraud that places limits on the harm that could have been done by it. Moreover, the auditor should investigate whether that same impulse to fraud might have led to defalcation elsewhere:

> If the auditor believes that misstatements are or may be the result of fraud, but the effect of the misstatements is not material to the financial statements, the auditor nevertheless should evaluate the implications, especially those dealing with the organizational position of the person(s)

---

[72] "The Accountant and the Investor" in May, G.O.: 1971, *Twenty-Five Years of Accounting Responsibility 1911-1936: Essays and Discussions*, Hunt, B.C. (ed.) (Scholar Books Co., Texas).

involved. For example, fraud involving misappropriations of cash from a small petty cash fund normally would be of little significance to the auditor in assessing the risk of material misstatement due to fraud, because both the manner of operating the fund and its size would tend to establish a limit on the amount of potential loss, and the custodianship of such funds normally is entrusted to a non-management employee (SAS 99, n. 76).

Whenever the auditor has determined that there is evidence that fraud may exist, that matter should be brought to the attention of an appropriate level of management. This is appropriate even if the matter might be considered inconsequential, such as a minor defalcation by an employee at a low level in the entity's organization (SAS 99, n. 78).

On the same principle, a fraud involving very small sums among high-level management is *ipso facto* "material," because high-level management will presumably have had the opportunity to act fraudulently in matters involving large sums:

Conversely, if the matter involves higher-level management, even though the amount itself is not material to the financial statements, it may be indicative of a more pervasive problem, for example, implications about the integrity of management (SAS 99, n. 76).

3. Identify senior accountants and partners in your firm whose commitment to professional standards you admire and seek them out as mentors.

As mentioned above, it is important to have a mentor because accounting professionalism is a matter of virtue, and as a rule we grow in virtue through admiring others, wanting to imitate them, and being supported and encouraged by them.

Much of ethics involves being led to see first *that* something is so, and only later coming to appreciate the reasons *why* it is so. Only a mentor can play this role, someone who has gone along the path ahead of you and can "see" and tell you about what you do not yet see.

4. Find fellow practitioners at roughly your same level in the firm whose commitment to professional standards you admire and befriend them.

In just the same way that we need mentors who are above us in authority, and have "gone before us" along the way, we similarly need friends who are on the same level with us in authority, and who are "going along with us," side-by-side, and are committed to the same things. As Aristotle pointed out, association with good friends makes us better, whereas association with bad persons makes us worse:

> And whatever existence means for each class of men, whatever it is for whose sake they value life, in that they wish to occupy themselves with their friends; and so some drink together, others dice together, others join in athletic exercises and hunting, or in the study of philosophy, each class spending their days together in whatever they love most in life. Since they wish to live life with their friends, they do and share in those things which give them the sense of living life together. Hence friendship between bad men turns out to be a bad thing (for because of their instability they unite in bad pursuits, and besides they become bad by becoming like each other), while the friendship of good men is good, as their goodness is augmented by their companionship. It seems they become better too by their activities and by improving each other; for from each other they take the mold of the characteristics they approve—whence the saying "noble deeds from noble men" (Aristotle, *Nicomachean Ethics*, IX.12).

Friendships that build us up and support us in this way rarely form by accident, especially among very busy professionals. Friendships require time to form. Thus, you will need to give the matter some thought. Identify those you would like to befriend and seek out opportunities to spend time together. Try to do thoughtful things for one another, and look for opportunities outside the workplace to spend time together (entertainment on weekends, golf, etc.).

It not infrequently happens that someone who gives in to pressure or temptation to do something bad would have been able to resist and do the right thing if he had just one friend who supported him in this. Two friends can together create a "worldview" which preserves clearly for them the perception of what the right course of action is, even if it seems as if everyone else is opposed.

5. As part of your professional development, draw up a good list of books on ethics and "the meaning of life" and make steady progress in reading them.

It has been pointed out how growth in professionalism is a constant, lifelong project, and also that ethical conduct and high standards of professionalism are inseparable from excellence in a profession. It follows that just as any professional needs to continue growing in professional expertise, so he or she needs to keep growing in ethical insight and understanding. It is in view of this that the majority of states now require regular CPE courses in ethics and professional education for CPAs. However, it is essential that a practitioner not view the ethics requirement as a nominal legalism, to be satisfied and dispensed with as soon as possible. In order to select the most helpful CPE courses, and profit from them, these exercises in continuing education should be only one element in a plan of professional improvement, which a practitioner is following on his own. Here is a brief list of books to get started in that direction:

> Augustine of Hippo, *Confessions*
> Marcus Aurelius, *Meditations*
> Martin Buber, *I and Thou*
> G.K. Chesterton, *What's Wrong with the World*
> *The Bible*
> Cicero, *On Duties*
> Fyodor Dostoevsky, *Brothers Karamazov; Crime and Punishment*
> Viktor Frankl, *Man's Search for Meaning*
> C.S. Lewis, *The Abolition of Man*
> Plato, *Republic*
> Leo Tolstoy, *Anna Karenina; War and Peace*

Also highly recommended are biographies of great men and women, and good histories.

6. Cherish a high opinion of your calling and communicate that to others in speech and through actions.

Just as the profession of accounting for a practitioner should be embedded in a life which displays what we have called "unity of life," so an individual practitioner should strive to live out his or her professional commitments in a way that extends to his neighborhood, community, and city or town. As time allows, join civic associations, join clubs, volunteer for worthy charities, and develop a network of friends and associates. These relationships will enable you to place your accounting work in a context of contributing generally to the good of others.

Essential to living "unity of life" in the way described is commitment to the profession and a desire to have one's actions and life contribute to the standing of the accounting profession as a whole:

> The well-being of the Accountancy of tomorrow is, in very large measure, dependent upon the faithfulness and magnanimity of the mere handful of accountants who comprise our young profession of to-day. Oneness of method and of professional aspirations, enlarged and exalted views of the worth and dignity of our calling, and a steady, studious, and conscientious aim to discharge well our obligations to the business world will insure to

us as a brotherhood that universal and permanent recognition and appreciation upon which hang the hopes of higher Accountancy.[73]

Suggestions for seasoned practitioners

Our suggestions in this section are similar to those for newly-minted CPAs, because in matters of ethics and professionalism, there is no such thing as "standing still." One is either improving, or falling backward. Thus, to continue to maintain high standards implies to continue to grow and improve. No practitioner has ever "made it" and in a position to cease the practices of reflection, self-examination, self-criticism, and specific resolutions for positive change that must mark also the outlook of a young practitioner.

1. Seek out CPE courses in ethics and professional conduct that are truly valuable, not simply those that satisfy the requirement as easily as possible.

A seasoned practitioner needs to be concerned about the ethics CPE requirement becoming a matter of routine. It should be an occasion for a full and thorough re-examination of his or her career in relation to standards of ethics and ideals of professionalism. The CPE requirement in principle should reinvigorate and re-inspire. It should be something of an antidote to an outlook of "weariness" or cynicism which can set in over time.

2. Convene formal and informal discussion groups among those of your colleagues who are similarly enthusiastic about promoting high-ethical standards.

As a practitioner grows in standing in a firm, his or her efforts to befriend others might usefully go beyond individual friendships and begin to acquire some kind of a structured manifestation in a firm, such as regular lunch meetings (an "ethics table") or study groups.

3. Seek to mentor younger members just as you were mentored.

This is simply the necessary flip-side of the maxim to seek out mentors. Note that the person who mentors another is always assisted by that relationship as well,

---

[73] "The Growing Need for Higher Accountancy" (An address delivered at the annual dinner of the Pennsylvania Institute of Certified Public Accountants, Philadelphia, April 15, 1901), in Haskins, C. W: 1904, *Business Education and Accountancy* (Harper & Brothers Publishers, New York and London), p. 11.

because we naturally acquire a stronger sense of responsibility and accountability when we are aware that we are serving as a model for others.

4. Take steps to contribute to the community at large.

As an established professional, cultivate a presence in worthy community associations, and aim to use your insight into business and the economy for the benefit of society at large.

II. Efforts within the Firm

In this section we give suggestions for how practitioners through joint efforts in a firm can foster ethics and professionalism. We arrange these suggestions under four headings:

1. "Good corporate culture": cultivate a culture supportive of ethics and professionalism
2. "Tone at the Top": encourage those at the top to act in such a way as to be imitated
3. "Accountability"
4. "Reward ethics and professionalism"

"Good Corporate Culture"

1. Know the firm.

The first step is simply to know the firm and especially the perceptions of employees. This may be accomplished by well-designed surveys and suggestion boxes, and supplemented by informal conversations. Try to determine if there are any of the following signs of a poor workplace environment, which have been shown to be correlated with ethical lapses and misconduct:

- Management seems not to care about or reward appropriate behavior
- Lack of recognition for job performance
- Perceived inequalities in the organization
- Autocratic management style
- Low loyalty and sense of ownership
- Relatively poor compensation
- Poor training
- Poor opportunities for advancement
- Unclear assignment of responsibilities

- Poor communication within the firm

2. Have a clear and recognized code of ethics for the firm, which lets employees clearly know what is expected of him, and which is scrupulously observed and vigorously enforced by senior management.

The Foreign Corrupt Practices Act (FCPA) of 1977 mandated reporting by a parent company or issuer of its internal controls and those of its subsidiaries, marking, really, the beginning of the modern and praiseworthy emphasis on internal controls. This mandate although ineffectual because of a lack of a corresponding requirement that internal control reporting be audited, nonetheless, was strengthened in various ways over the following three decades, in part, largely, to accounting scandals. One of the important effects of this trend has been widespread recognition of the importance of a code of ethics for a firm, and for someone in senior management to occupy the role of "Compliance and Ethics Officer," to see that a code of ethics really does reflect and inspire a culture in the firm, and is not simply symbolic or a laudable but irrelevant expression of the mere ethical aspiration. Accounting firms, as firms, not as associations of accounting professionals in particular, have followed suit and devised and implemented their own internal codes of ethics, and now have Compliance and Ethics Officers. So, ironically, accounting scandals have led to a movement of reform in the corporate world which indirectly has an effect on accounting firms as well.

The reader of this book, in order to see examples of this kind of thing, is encouraged to go to the websites of each of the big four firms and examine their codes of ethics. One will find that these codes are clear, intelligently written, and provide helpful guidance. Most of the codes provide a good list of rule of thumb criteria for judging whether a proposed course of action is ethically doubtful, such as the following from the Deloitte Code of Ethics:

- Are my actions illegal or unethical?
- Am I being fair and honest?
- Would I be unwilling or embarrassed to tell my family, friends, or co-workers?
- Would the reputation of a Deloitte U.S. Firm be harmed if the action were revealed in the newspapers?
- Am I personally uncomfortable about the course of action?
- Could someone's life, health, safety, or reputation be endangered by my action?
- Could the intended action appear inappropriate to a third party?

The KPMG Code is noteworthy for giving vivid, concrete indications of how practitioners might swerve from ethical conduct in a helpful "be alert to" section found after each of the major points covered in the code. For example, after the point concerning "Accurate Books and Records," the code lists the following flags:

- Pressure to refrain from charging all time spent working on client projects, to charge any client-related time to administrative codes, or to charge a client engagement code for work not performed or done for a different client or administrative activity
- Improper engagement charges either due to miscoding or that are outside the terms of the engagement letter
- Accounting methods that appear to favor form over substance
- Transactions that may suggest a third party is attempting to use its relationship with KPMG for an unlawful purpose. Transactions that should be evaluated carefully include:
  - Complex business arrangements not well understood and appearing to serve little practical purpose
  - Transaction structures that are unnecessarily complex, lack a legitimate business purpose, or benefit from unusually favorable payment terms
  - Attempts by third parties to make payments in cash, or the use of suspicious financial instruments
  - Large last-minute transactions that result in significant revenues at the close of a financial reporting cycle

These flags represent, at the same time, warnings about practices that are likely to receive scrutiny from one's peers and from the Office of Compliance and Ethics, and also "things to be on the lookout for" by employees in a firm whose culture is marked by a correct balance of trust and circumspection.

These codes of ethics, if implemented through serious and sincere mentoring, and supported by a sound system of incentives, are likely to make a significant contribution to professional ethics and conduct in an accounting firm. The chief drawback of such codes is that they tend to be generic, covering points which are involved in upright business practice generally, and are not specifically matched to the inherently ethical demands of a "learned profession," or the distinctive vocation and tasks of the profession of accountancy. However, as the KMPG Code illustrates, it is possible to go a fair way toward adapting an originally generic code of conduct for a firm to the particular tasks and challenges of the accounting profession.

3. Create an ethics training program.

Such a program should be engaging and emphasize "commitment" over "compliance," as befits a subject which, as we have seen, cannot be fully captured in rules. It should be direct, personal, and part of an ongoing commitment. It should also make ample use of case studies, for three reasons: (i) to illustrate important ethical principles; (ii) to give practitioners experience with cases that involve genuine perplexity; and (iii) to give guidance as to how such cases may nonetheless be dealt with while steering well clear of any wrongdoing or suspicion of wrongdoing.

4. Encourage an atmosphere that is open and supportive of ethical conduct.

Appoint someone to be the firm's "historian," and interview retired firm members, to accumulate stories of heroism in accounting, which could be circulated around the company as appropriate, or used as the basis of case studies for common discussion. Create discussion groups and newsletters to discuss new developments, and any ethical ramifications of new standards or legislation. Institute a "question box" for anonymous questions, or have an anonymous hotline which employees can call for "no questions asked" advice about ethical quandaries.

Acknowledge openly in the firm the common truth that acting ethically is sometimes extremely inconvenient and often has the appearance of being "harmful" to others. But also acknowledge and draw attention to the fact that people are generally able to recognize what is truly right and fair, even when this is not to their advantage. A story from Harold Tinkler, a Chief Ethics and Compliance Officer at one of the Big Four illustrates this very well:

> I remember one occasion very clearly when my values were put to the test. I had already graduated college and was a CPA when I was drafted into the US Army. After basic training, I went to finance school and was sent to a military base in Germany. It was a terrific job, with a lot of responsibility. I was handling the payroll for most of the US officers in central Germany. The year was 1969.
>
> One day I was going through some pay records when I noticed some entries had been deleted. Someone had erased them to make it appear as if certain people had not yet taken their military leave, and I knew they had. By making the changes, these people would get reimbursed for unpaid leave when they were discharged. I remember my disappointment when I figured out who was doing it. He was a buddy of mine.
>
> I remember agonizing over what to do. It's not easy when you're in that spot. I know it. Finally I decided to confront him privately in the

office. His reaction was: "Don't worry, I've got it covered. And besides, these soldiers deserve the extra pay." He had totally justified to himself that there was nothing wrong with his actions.

So I decided to speak up and correct the situation. He wasn't too happy about it, especially since it ended up costing him a loss of rank. Neither were the other soldiers in the unit, when they found out. I guess you could say I wasn't the most popular guy in the barracks. Some months later, when I was being discharged, on my last day with the unit, several of these same soldiers came up to me and said they appreciated what I'd done. They realized that despite their friendship with the soldier, what he was doing was wrong.

So what did I learn from this episode? I learned that everyone knew all along the difference between right and wrong. The problem is not that people don't know. In fact, many studies have shown that people involved in unethical behavior know full well they're doing something wrong— they simply don't have the personal fortitude and courage to make the right choice.[74]

5. Encourage "unity of life" in the firm's practitioners.

Encourage and give recognition to practitioners' involvement in community and civic associations. Make it clear that the firm values and even expects this. Do not ask or expect practitioners to "sacrifice" such things to the firm.

This point is simply the complement to the suggestion that practitioners in their own efforts aim to foster unity of life. Each individual needs to foster this in his own life, but he cannot easily succeed at this if he lacks the consistent support of his firm.

"Tone at the Top"

The keys to a proper "tone at the top" are: *involvement of senior management*, and *setting an example*. It is essential that senior management not make themselves an exception, or appear to be in any way "above" the ethical standards that others must observe. What holds for others must hold for them also. Involvement implies leadership, presence, and public expression. Example implies unimpeachable adherence to standards, especially where the stakes are large when it comes to financial gain or loss.

---

[74] Tinkler, H: 2005, "Ethics in Business: The Heart of the Matter", *Executive Speeches*, 19 (5), 14-18.

6. The firm's leadership should be actively involved in the firm's ethical training program and initiatives for professionalism.

There cannot be a double standard, such as management's zealous involvement in matters that carry an immediate financial advantage, but apathy about ethics initiatives. This sends an implicit message that ethics is less, rather than more, important. The firm's leaders should either lead or play a large role in the ethical training program. Their involvement should be personal if possible, for instance, telling personal stories of how ethics has been important in their career, and challenging "doubters" with concrete examples. Also, the senior partners of the firm will be able to provide the best insights in steering through difficult cases which seem to have lots of "gray areas."

In many informal settings, the firm's leadership should talk with employees and convey (both in *what* they say and in *the way* they say it) the importance of ethics and professionalism in the firm. Regularly talk with employees privately while "wandering around" the office. Always make it clear to them, when they ask questions or raise issues, that what is most important is what is morally right and that, most often, the morally right course of action also turns out to be the financially lucrative course of action. Give occasional talks to the whole company encouraging ethical conduct and discussing any new problems that may have come up.

7. The firm's leadership must not only act in a way that is above reproach, but also always give the appearance of doing so.

Those at "the top" should always act with the greatest refinement, as though someone were always watching, because someone probably is. Employees will notice the habits, attitudes, and actions of those at the top and think, "If they can do that, so can I."

Senior management must act ethically especially where there would be large financial benefits from dishonest behavior. When employees see that management is willing to give up a large client rather than act unethically, that will have a tremendous effect on their belief that the company takes its "code of ethics" seriously.

> "At _____, we tried to reinforce our shared beliefs through a series of case studies, but the real changes were made when they saw leaders 'walking the talk'; when they saw compensation, evaluation, and promotion affected by our shared beliefs. Performance cannot trump values. ... Our colleagues also saw us walk away from unethical clients. I

remember three we walked away from in the midst of a recession. That was tough, it cost us jobs. But it convinced our people that we were truly committed to our values."[75]

"Accountability"

8. Make it clear within the firm that each practitioner has genuine authority and bears responsibility for his or her own decisions.

Set up standards that make each person bear the brunt of his own actions. Discourage (with actual punishment if necessary) "passing the buck" to superiors. Give employees the authority to use discretion in a broad domain, depending of course on their training and ability, but then hold them responsible for their use of that discretion. The best way to encourage that sort of accountability is to follow the so-called "principle of subsidiarity," which is that in a large, complex association, with many levels of authority, decisions should be made by the lowest level which is competent to make them, and higher levels should intervene only as a matter of review and to correct abuses, never in such a way as to micro-manage or negate the genuine authority of the lower level. Accountability must be matched with high expectations, whereas lack of accountability usually goes along with low expectations, because low expectations are a self-fulfilling prophecy.

9. Publish widely the firm's code of ethics, to create expectations among clients and the public, and therefore a corresponding sense of accountability to them.

Publish your code of ethics widely (brochures, inserts, on the web), and insist that your work be judged by that standard, not by the standard of mere legality.

"Reward ethics and professionalism"

10. Use stringent ethical criteria in hiring.

Insist on several, detailed letters of recommendations from trustworthy referees who are in a position to know the character of the candidate. Pose questions about ethics in job interviews to see how the candidate responds to them and the criteria that are appealed to. Be very clear to job applicants about the quick and unhappy consequences for continued employment that follow upon poor conduct.

11. Reward employees in concrete ways when they show good professional judgment under difficult circumstances.

---

[75] Copeland Jr., J.E.: 2004, "Whence Ethics?", *Consulting to Management* 15(3), 24-26.

Be sure to reward them especially when it seemed to them that, in honoring high ethical standards, they were deciding against the financial advantage of the firm.

12. Make it clear that unethical conduct serves as automatic grounds for punishment, and that serious unethical conduct should be automatically punished with dismissal.

It is crucial that this policy be followed consistently. "Will you discipline a top performer for violation of your ethics standards? One of our very best consulting partners had a problem with gender-related issues. We asked him to leave. That decision went through the organization like wildfire. It communicated more about our seriousness concerning our ethical expectations than all the case studies in the world."[76]

Conclusion

We present no *policy* recommendations based on the considerations of this text, as our argument is directed at individuals in the profession—students and practitioners. But the book raises questions that need to be addressed through policies. For example, a repeated theme of the book has been that the internal accountant, not the external auditor, is the "first line of defense" for the shareholder or interested third party investor in a business. The internal accountant is the most important "public watchdog." Hence it would be possible to raise and debate institutions or regulations aimed at strengthening the professionalism and integrity of the internal accountant.

For instance, a wise policy might require that anyone involved in accounting type work in a public company (translating, recording, explaining, estimating, or valuing economic activities) both be a CPA and possess a certificate of having passed a course of study. In the course they would be made aware of their disclosure and public interest responsibilities and the historic responsibilities of the accounting profession. Moreover, they would study the "public watchdog" function of internal accountants and be led to recognize with clarity that, as CPAs, they have a truth-telling role which implies that their loyalties do not lie solely with those of the company which employs them. One might imagine that for public companies of a sufficient size, internal accountants would be required to form an association for that company, perhaps under the auspices and guidance of the state board of accounting of the state where the company is headquartered.

---

[76] Copeland Jr., J.E.: 2004, "Whence Ethics?", *Consulting to Management* 15(3), 24-26.

This book raises such policy questions, but it is beyond its scope to attempt to settle them. We end appropriately with Robert H. Montgomery's closing remarks from his 1937 Presidential Address to the AIA:

> "We cannot hope to make progress unless we *fight* for the ideals and standards which have come to us from the founders of the profession. There are a thousand obstacles to the attainment of any worth-while good.
>
> Let's *fight* to maintain all that has come to us which is good and to eliminate everything inimical to progress.
>
> Let's *fight* to raise the standards of the Institute in every way. Let's fight to suspend or expel any member who is guilty of conduct unworthy of a member...
>
> Let's *fight* for sound business practices. Don't let's wait until unsound practices creep in, are reflected in balance-sheets and embarrass the accountants who are asked to certify to them...
>
> Let's *fight* for honest accounting, clear financial statements and full disclosure of all essential facts.
>
> Let's *fight* anyone who seeks the assistance of a certified public accountant in the issuance of any kind of misleading statement.
>
> Let's *fight* anyone who thinks that one certified public accountant will supplant another who has done a good job.
>
> Let's *fight* for easily understood accounting terms. Let's fight weasel words.
>
> Let's *fight* bunk whenever and wherever it appears."[77]

---

[77] "Report of the President: What Have We Done, and How?" (American Institute of Accountants, Year 1937), Montgomery, Robert H.: 1939, Fifty Years of Accountancy (The Ronald Press Company).

About the Authors

MICHAEL PAKALUK, educated at Harvard (A.B., Ph.D.) and, as a Marshall Scholar, at the University of Edinburgh (M.Litt.), is currently Professor of Philosophy and Chairman of the philosophy department at Ave Maria University in Naples, Florida. Formerly at the Institute for the Psychological Sciences and Clark University, where he had a long and distinguished tenure as Director of the Boston Area Colloquium in Ancient Philosophy, Dr. Pakaluk has been a visiting scholar or visiting professor at Brown, Cambridge, Catholic University, Harvard, St. Andrews (Scotland) and Santa Croce (Rome). Currently he serves as Dean of the Faculty at the Neuwaldegg Institute in Vienna, Austria and on the faculty of the Korcula Institute in Croatia. Widely published in academic journals on a wide range of topics in ethics, political philosophy, and the history of philosophy, his books include *Other Selves: Philosophers on Friendship* (Hackett Publishers, 1991); *Nicomachean Ethics, Books VIII and IX, Translation with Commentary* (Oxford University Press, 1998); *Aristotle's Nicomachean Ethics, An Introduction* (Cambridge University Press, 2005); and *Moral Psychology and Human Action in Aristotle* (Oxford University Press, 2011). Dr. Pakaluk's expertise in accounting ethics, in conjunction with his position as Senior Research Analyst and Public Policy Consultant with the Ives Group, Inc., led to an invitation to present a seminar on the accounting professionalism and IFRS convergence for the Financial Accounting Standards Board (FASB) in 2009. He is a regular lecturer on accounting ethics in the Boston Tax Institute.

MARK CHEFFERS is the Founder and CEO of Ives Group, Inc., an independent research provider focused on developing web based due diligence and market intelligence tools that allow analysts to better assess risks being presented by public company audit, internal control, and legal exposures. Ives' flagship service is Audit Analytics. Ives counts among its clients many of the largest professional service, academic research, regulatory, and financial services organizations in the world. In addition to work at Ives, Mr. Cheffers holds a current CPA license and has worked extensively as a researcher, author, and litigation consulting specialist. He has delivered numerous seminars and written extensively on accounting malpractice, ethics and financial reporting matters. Prior to founding Ives Group in 2000, Mr. Cheffers spent 13 years operating a successful litigation consulting firm, specializing in fraud investigations and litigation consulting on large and complex fraud, D&O and professional liability cases. Mr. Cheffers began his career at KPMG in Boston and later joined PricewaterhouseCoopers in Sydney, Australia, where he was promoted to Manager. Later he spent time as an acting public company CFO before leaving that assignment to attend graduate school. He is a member of the American Institute of Certified Public Accountants (AICPA) and has achieved its Accredited Business Valuation (ABV) professional designation. Mr. Cheffers has a BSBA, magna cum laude, in accounting and finance from Boston University (1982) and an MBA from the Harvard Business School (1990).

Index of
Proper Names